Nation of Outlaws, State of Violence

NEW AFRICAN HISTORIES

SERIES EDITORS: JEAN ALLMAN AND ALLEN ISAACMAN

Books in this series are published with support from the Ohio University National Resource Center for African Studies.

David William Cohen and E. S. Atieno Odhiambo, *The Risks of Knowledge: Investigations into the Death of the Hon. Minister John Robert Ouko in Kenya*, 1990

Belinda Bozzoli, *Theatres of Struggle and the End of Apartheid*

Gary Kynoch, *We Are Fighting the World: A History of Marashea Gangs in South Africa, 1947–1999*

Stephanie Newell, *The Forger's Tale: The Search for Odeziaku*

Jacob A. Tropp, *Natures of Colonial Change: Environmental Relations in the Making of the Transkei*

Jan Bender Shetler, *Imagining Serengeti: A History of Landscape Memory in Tanzania from Earliest Times to the Present*

Cheikh Anta Babou, *Fighting the Greater Jihad: Amadu Bamba and the Founding of the Muridiyya in Senegal, 1853–1913*

Marc Epprecht, *Heterosexual Africa? The History of an Idea from the Age of Exploration to the Age of AIDS*

Marissa J. Moorman, *Intonations: A Social History of Music and Nation in Luanda, Angola, from 1945 to Recent Times*

Karen E. Flint, *Healing Traditions: African Medicine, Cultural Exchange, and Competition in South Africa, 1820–1948*

Derek R. Peterson and Giacomo Macola, editors, *Recasting the Past: History Writing and Political Work in Modern Africa*

Moses Ochonu, *Colonial Meltdown: Northern Nigeria in the Great Depression*

Emily Burrill, Richard Roberts, and Elizabeth Thornberry, editors, *Domestic Violence and the Law in Colonial and Postcolonial Africa*

Daniel R. Magaziner, *The Law and the Prophets: Black Consciousness in South Africa, 1968–1977*

Emily Lynn Osborn, *Our New Husbands Are Here: Households, Gender, and Politics in a West African State from the Slave Trade to Colonial Rule*

Robert Trent Vinson, *The Americans Are Coming! Dreams of African American Liberation in Segregationist South Africa*

James R. Brennan, *Taifa: Making Nation and Race in Urban Tanzania*

Benjamin N. Lawrance and Richard L. Roberts, editors, *Trafficking in Slavery's Wake: Law and the Experience of Women and Children*

David M. Gordon, *Invisible Agents: Spirits in a Central African History*

Allen Isaacman and Barbara Isaacman, *Dams, Displacement, and the Delusion of Development: Cahora Bassa and Its Legacies in Mozambique, 1965–2007*

Gibril R. Cole, *The Krio of West Africa: Islam, Culture, Creolization, and Colonialism in the Nineteenth Century*

Matthew M. Heaton, *Black Skin, White Coats: Nigerian Psychiatrists, Decolonization, and the Globalization of Psychiatry*

Stephanie Newell, *The Power to Name: A History of Anonymity in Colonial West Africa*

Meredith Terretta, *Nation of Outlaws, State of Violence: Nationalism, Grassfields Tradition, and State Building in Cameroon*

Nation of Outlaws, State of Violence

Nationalism, Grassfields Tradition, and State Building in Cameroon

Meredith Terretta

OHIO UNIVERSITY PRESS ᵚ ATHENS, OHIO

Ohio University Press, Athens, Ohio 45701
ohioswallow.com
© 2014 by Ohio University Press
All rights reserved

To obtain permission to quote, reprint, or otherwise reproduce or distribute material from
Ohio University Press publications, please contact our rights and permissions department at
(740) 593-1154 or (740) 593-4536 (fax).

Printed in the United States of America
Ohio University Press books are printed on acid-free paper ∞ ™

24 23 22 21 20 19 18 17 16 15 14   5 4 3 2 1

Library of Congress Cataloging-in-Publication Data
Terretta, Meredith, author.
 Nation of outlaws, state of violence : nationalism, Grassfields tradition, and state building in Cameroon / Meredith Terretta.
  pages cm — (New African histories)
 Includes bibliographical references and index.
 ISBN 978-0-8214-2069-0 (pb : alk. paper) — ISBN 978-0-8214-4472-6 (electronic)
 1. Cameroon—History—Autonomy and independence movements. 2. Cameroon—History—To 1960. 3. Cameroon—History—1960–1982. 4. Union des populations du Cameroun—History. 5. Bamileke (African people)—History—20th century. 6. Nationalism—Cameroon—History—20th century. I. Title. II. Series: New African histories.
 DT574.T47 2013
 967.1103—dc23
                            2013030968

TO ELI AND ALI-YOUN

Contents

Acknowledgments ix
Abbreviations xiii

Introduction Layering Nationalism from Local to Global 1

PART ONE   GRASSFIELDS POLITICAL TRADITION AND
           BAMILEKE IDENTITY

Chapter 1 God, Land, Justice, and Political Sovereignty in
             Grassfields Governance 29

Chapter 2 "Bamileke Strangers" Make the Mungo
             River Valley Their Home 61

PART TWO   BAMILEKE NATIONALISTS CLAIM INDEPENDENCE
           (*LEPUE*) FOR THE NATION (*GUNG*)

Chapter 3 Troublesome, Rebellious, Outlawed
             *International Politics and UPC Nationalism
             in the Bamileke and Mungo Regions* 97

Chapter 4 Nationalists or Traitors?
             *Bamileke Chiefs and Electoral Politics
             in the Year of Loi-Cadre* 134

PART THREE UPC NATIONALISTS GO GLOBAL

Chapter 5 The Maquis at Home, Exile Abroad
             *Grassfields Warfare Meets Revolutionary
             Pan-Africanism* 177

Chapter 6 "Here, God Does Not Exist"
             Emergency Law and the Violence of State Building 217

Conclusion	"After the War, We Stop Counting the Dead" *Reconciliation and Public Confession*	250
Notes		265
Glossary		337
Bibliography		341
Index		359

Acknowledgments

The conception, research, and writing of this book would not have been possible without the support of a wide and varied network of mentors, friends, colleagues, and family.

I am grateful to the teachers who first recognized my interest in African history, developed my research and writing abilities, and advanced my conceptual thinking: while an undergraduate at the University of Tennessee–Chattanooga, Larry Ingle and Martin W. Daly; and while a graduate student at the University of Wisconsin–Madison, Florence Bernault, Tom Spear, Michael Schatzberg, and Stanlie James. Florence Bernault is deserving of gratitude not only for relentlessly directing my doctoral studies but also for generously recommending me to her colleagues in France and Cameroon. These included Marc Michel and Odile Chatap-Ekindi, who provided invaluable orientation to the archives in Aix-en-Provence, Yaoundé, and Nkongsamba. I owe a special thanks to fellow students at Wisconsin—Mukoma Wa Ngugi, Dior Konate, Ousman Kobo, Cheryl Sterling, Ryan Ronnenberg, and Penelope Pack—whose friendship made getting through graduate school much shorter and sweeter.

I began this book in upstate New York, at Le Moyne College, and could not have completed it without the support of my colleagues and department there and at subsequent institutions: at Le Moyne, Doug Egerton, Keith Watenpaugh, Pat Keane, Charles Onyango Oduke, Donna Marcano, and especially Linda LeMura, then Dean of the Arts and Sciences, who motivated me to remain committed to my scholarship while in the teaching college environment; while on postdoctoral fellowship at Cornell University, Sandra Greene, the late Martin Bernal, Judith Van Allen, Wilson Chacko Jacob, Edward Baptist, and Carina Ray, all of whom offered critical feedback to various portions of this book, and to the Fellows in the Society for the Humanities for stimulating discussions and exchanges; and at the University of Ottawa, my current institutional home, Naomi Davidson, Corinne Gaudin, Jeffrey Keshen, Paul Lovejoy, and Antoni Lewkowicz. Elizabeth Schmidt has graciously served as a critically encouraging reader of this and other work over the years.

Many excellent people outside of academia provided nurturing support throughout years of scholarship, research, travel, and writing. In Madison, Emilie Ngo Nguidjol and Aliko Songolo opened their home and allowed me to share many of life's sweeter moments with them and their wonderful children, Tosha, Ngijol, and Koko. In Nkongsamba, Jean-Bernard Pogo, a member of the Elite Association of Baham, and his wife, Mercedes Yougaing, accepted me as part of their family. The Pogos and their children, particularly Eric, Elisabeth, and Clemence, patiently assisted me throughout my time in Cameroon. They answered my questions and imbued me with an immeasurable quantity of knowledge of what it meant and means to be Bamileke in the Mungo region, then and now; the research for this book would have been far sparser were it not for the generous foundation they provided.

In Cameroon, on various occasions from 1999 to the present, a number of people routinely ensured that I was well, cared for, and had access to the documents and persons necessary to my research there; they include Maurice Takam, Dieudonné Pouhe Pouhe, Odile Chatap-Ekindi, Marcelline Betene, Monita Baba Djara, Perry Burtch, the late Ignace Djoko Néguin, David Benson, Chantal Ndami, and Brigitte Wami, as well as Joseph Kiegaing, Djoko Domguia, and André Gabiapsi, who assisted me in gathering oral data in Baham, particularly from 2001 to 2003, and Chaïbou and Eitel Mambingo, who helped me gain access to the prefectural archives in Nkongsamba and Dschang. I remain especially grateful for the hospitality and assistance of the late Abbé Jean-Noël Potago of Melong II, at whose presbytery I was a regular visitor. I appreciate my parents, Roy and Zeleny Terretta, for instilling in me a love of learning, reading, and travel from an early age, and for visiting me during periods of field research in Cameroon.

This work could not have come to fruition without the generous financial and institutional support of the Fulbright Institute of International Education, the Jacob K. Javits Fellowship Program, the Mellon Postdoctoral Fellowship Program and the Society for the Humanities at Cornell University, the Le Moyne College Research and Development Program, the University of Ottawa Research Development Program, and the American Council of Learned Societies.

For their role in the various logistics of the book's publication, I owe an additional thanks to Jean Allman and Allen Isaacman, series editors; Nancy Basmajian, managing editor at Ohio University Press; Jane McWhinney, my editor; Brian Balsley, cartographer; and Beth Pratt, cover designer; as well as to the anonymous readers who provided helpful feedback. Perhaps most memorably, I am grateful to Gillian Berchowitz, who, to accommodate Eli Terretta Gueye's gestation and arrival into this world, was very flexible with deadlines for final revisions and the like.

I am indebted to Abdoulaye Gueye for lighting a spark in my mind and spirit that ultimately led to the book's completion.

Abbreviations

AB	Africa Bureau
AAPC	All-African Peoples' Conference
ALCAM	Assemblée législative du Cameroun
ALNK	Armée de libération nationale du Kamerun
ANY	Archives nationales de Yaoundé
APD	Archives préfectorales de Dschang
APN	Archives préfectorales de Nkongsamba
ATCAM	Assemblée territoriale du Cameroun
BDC	Bloc démocratique camerounais
BEDOC	Bureau de documentation du haut commissariat
BMM	Brigade mixte mobile de recherche et d'exploitation opérationnelles
BTC	Battalion of the Tirailleurs of Cameroon
CAOM	Centre des archives d'outre-mer
CGT	Confédération générale du travail
CHAN	Centre historique des archives nationales
CHETOM	Centre d'histoire et d'études des troupes d'outre-mer
CIDEO	Comité international de la défense d'Ernest Ouandié
CNO	Comité national d'organisation
ESOCAM	Évolution sociale camerounaise
FCFA	francs issued by the Communauté financière africaine
FLN	Front de libération nationale
FO	Foreign Office
FOPROJEUBA	Foyer de progrès de la jeunesse de Bayangam
FPUP	Front populaire pour l'unité et la paix
GPRA	Gouvernement provisoire de la République algérienne
IISH	Institute of International Social History
ILRM	International League of the Rights of Man

INDECAM	Coordination des indépendants camerounais
JDC	Jeunesse démocratique du Cameroun
JEUCAFRA	Jeunesse camerounaise française
MACNA	Mouvement d'action national
MAE	Ministère des affaires étrangères
MTLD	Mouvement pour la triomphe des libertés démocratiques
NA	National Archives
NYPL	New York Public Library
PCF	Parti communiste français
PDG	Parti démocratique guinéen
PMC	Permanent Mandates Commission
RDA	Rassemblement démocratique africain
RPC	Rassemblement du peuple camerounais
SDNK	Sinistre de la défense nationale du Kamerun
SDECE	Service de documentation extérieure et de contre-espionnage
SEDOC	Service des études de la documentation
SMEP	Société des missions évangéliques de Paris
UC	Union camerounaise
UCU	Usambara Citizens' Union
UDEFEC	Union démocratique des femmes camerounaises
UDHR	Universal Declaration of Human Rights
UDN	Union démocratique nigérienne
UDS	Union démocratique sénégalaise
UFC	Union des femmes camerounaises
UNC	Union nationale camerounaise
UNGA	United Nations General Assembly
UNTC	United Nations Trusteeship Council
UPC	Union des populations du Cameroun
USCC	Union des syndicats confédérés du Cameroun
WFDY	World Federation of Democratic Youth
WFTU	World Federation of Trade Unions
WIDF	Women's International Democratic Federation
ZANLA	Zimbabwe African National Liberation Army
ZANU–PF	Zimbabwe African National Union–Patriotic Front
ZOPAC	Zone de pacification

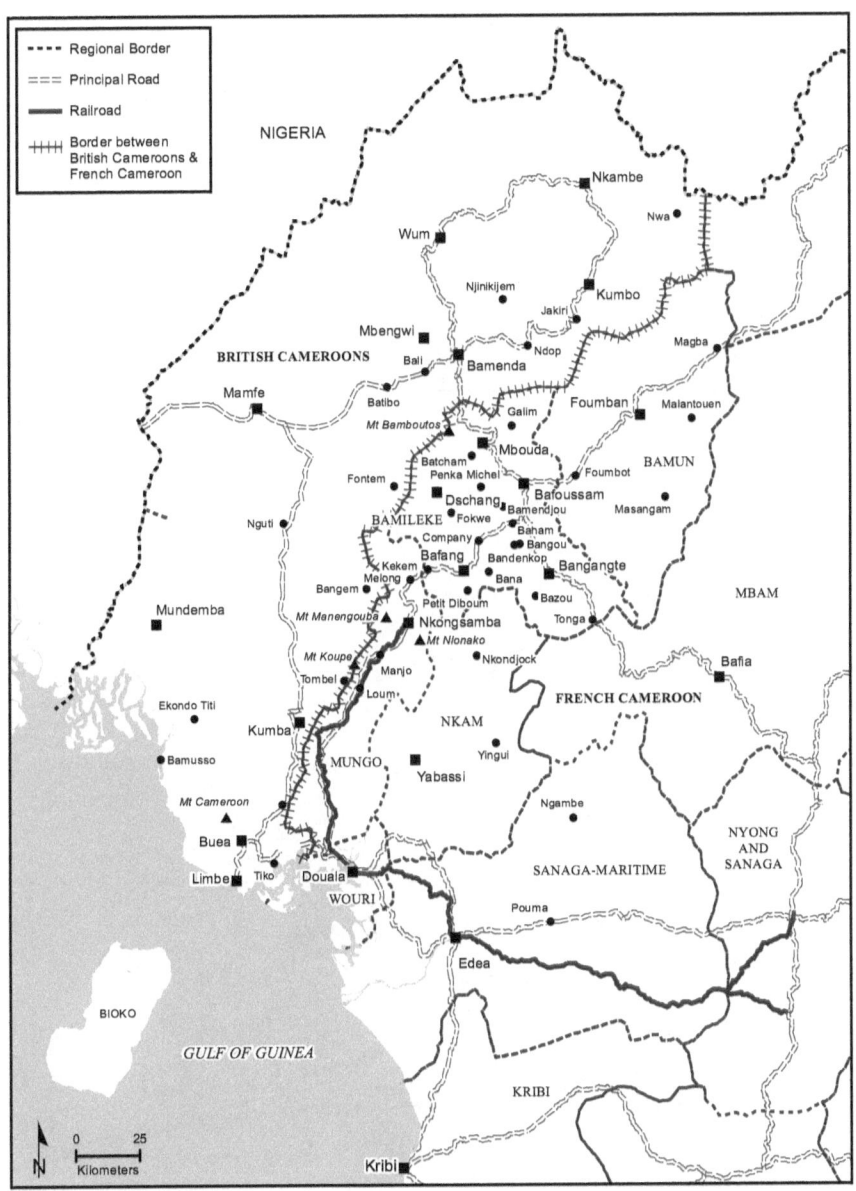

British Cameroons and western French Cameroon, 1950s. *Map by Brian Edward Balsley, GISP.*

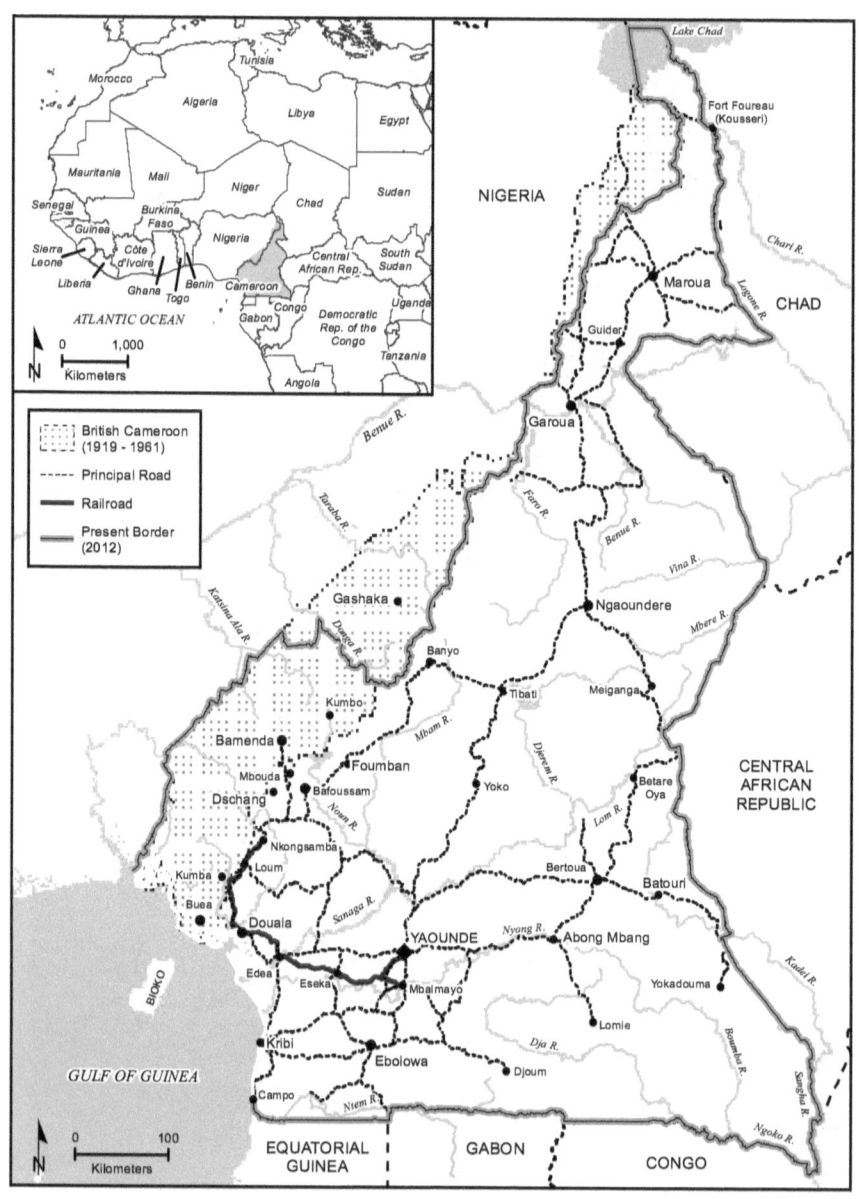

Cameroon. *Map by Brian Edward Balsley, GISP.*

INTRODUCTION

Layering Nationalism from Local to Global

IN DOUALA in 2003, I was speaking in French with a Cameroonian woman in her sixties about George W. Bush's decision to go to war against Iraq. She was from the West Province, or the Bamileke Region, the portion of the Grassfields that fell under French administration from 1919 to 1960.[1] She was unschooled but spoke fluent French, pidgin English, and her mother tongue, Medumba. She was against the US invasion and, referring to the United Nations Security Council's vote against military intervention in Iraq, she said, "But all the other villages did not want to go to war." Her grandchildren laughed at her use of the term *village*, but her word choice and the youngsters' reaction to it revealed a generational, linguistic memory gap.

She had lived through "the time of troubles," as Bamileke survivors describe the conflict that, at its beginning, in late 1956, resembled a nationalist war for independence from European rule; in its middle, the early 1960s, a civil war; and by its end, the late 1960s, seemed to have unraveled into random, unpredictable violence, looting, and revenge. In 1964 the British embassy in Cameroon[2] reported that between 61,300 and 76,300 civilians had lost their lives as a result of independence-era violence, from December 1956 to June 1964, and that nearly 80 percent of these casualties had occurred in the Bamileke region.[3] Inhabitants of the region had plenty of reason during those years to think about the meanings of nation and independence. Since the French and British Cameroons were UN trust territories rather than colonies, Cameroonians who lived through "the time of troubles" also became familiar with the UN and its

1

legal role in the politics of decolonization. In 2003 the grandmother's words carried a memory of a time when Cameroonian nationalists from the Bamileke region used *gung*, the indigenous word for chieftaincy, which French administrators had translated and codified as "village," to define the nation they envisioned. Her words also carried the faint echo of a time when many Cameroonians overestimated the ability of the UN to serve as a forum for international consensus and as an arbitrator and protector in world affairs.

This book recounts the history of the practice and discourse of Cameroonian nationalism, spearheaded by the Union des populations du Cameroun (UPC), as it unfolded in intersecting local, territorial, and global political arenas in the 1950s and 1960s. I have found this multidimensional perspective most effective for explaining why the UPC attracted the largest number of members and sympathizers of any political party in French Cameroon, becoming the most popular nationalist movement in the territory. Only by examining the ways in which UPC nationalists engaged shifting local, territorial, and international political currents can we approach a full understanding of why, despite the movement's grassroots popularity, its support throughout Africa and beyond, and its decade-long armed struggle, *upécistes* (as UPC members called themselves) failed to achieve political power in the postcolonial state government when official independence was declared on January 1, 1960.

The UPC nationalist party and its affiliated women's, youth, and trade unionist wings, initially launched to reunify the territories of the French and British Cameroons (administered together as Kamerun during the German colonial period, which lasted from 1884 to 1916) and to gain their independence, soon evolved into an "extrametropolitan" movement that deliberately bypassed inclusion in or collaboration with metropolitan political institutions.[4] To escape the constraints of European rule, Cameroonian nationalists grounded their political ideology in particular locales within the territory, recycling and, in many cases, rediscovering elements of local political culture that they tailored to their contemporary objectives—independence from European rule, the reunification of the French and British Cameroons, and the establishment of a sovereign nation-state. They also traveled—imaginatively and literally—beyond territorial boundaries, attributing symbolic and political importance to the United Nations, Pan-Africanism, Afro-Asian solidarity, other anticolonial struggles, antinuclear pacifism,[5] and the burgeoning notion of universal human rights.⁶ In so doing, Cameroonian nationalists sought to supersede the metropole-colony paradigm that seemingly underwrote political processes in late-colonial Africa.

Charting the particularly local and expansively global trajectories of UPC nationalists requires a revision of existing historical accounts of Cameroonian nationalism⁷ and leads us to question the extent to which independence-era politics were guided by affiliations with (or resistance to) metropolitan governments. Historian Frederick Cooper has stressed the need for a greater appreciation of the "political alternatives" imagined by African political actors on the eve of independence, in order better to understand how and why political possibilities expanded and narrowed in colonial territories.⁸ But to truly comprehend the political alternatives envisioned by nationalists, we must look beyond the metropole-colony boundaries that have so often guided our research, scholarship, and assumptions. This means retrieving the local spiritual, political, and cultural content of nationalist movements like the UPC, and then following the connections that nationalists created with political actors beyond their territorial borders, even (or especially) when these routes do not lead to Paris, London, or Brussels.

In following the paths of Cameroonian nationalists where they actually lead, rather than limiting their range to French territory, this study does a number of things that no previously published histories of Cameroon's decolonization have done. Rather than focus exclusively on French, UN, and Cameroonian documents,⁹ it draws on a breadth of sources from the UN, France, Great Britain, Ghana, and both provincial and national archives in Cameroon, as well as oral material collected throughout Cameroon and in Ghana. This history includes previously unknown actors—traditional chiefs, local politicians, ordinary farmers and workers, and women—in the story of Cameroonian nationalism. The inclusion of subaltern actors is crucial since, by 1957, most of the nationalist party leaders had been deported, and in 1958, the movement's fountainhead, Secretary-General Ruben Um Nyobé (1913–58), was gunned down by a French military patrol in the forest of the Sanaga-Maritime.¹⁰ And yet, in the absence of central coordination and leadership, the movement only spread, intensified, and increasingly drew on sources of local inspiration.¹¹

Finally, this work is the first published scholarly study of Cameroonian nationalism to examine the nationalist vision that persisted, albeit fragmented and factionalized, for nearly a decade after Cameroon's official achievement of independence. The primary task of President Ahmadou Ahidjo's regime during the first postcolonial decade was to eradicate and suppress the ongoing UPC rebellion. The elements of Cameroon's state building in the early years after independence, many of which were inherited from the French administration in the late trusteeship period, consisted mostly of heavy-handed violence, interrogations, imprisonment, "disappearings," resettlement and concentration camps, public beatings, intrusive intelligence gathering, and propaganda campaigns designed to instill fear of the state and its agents.[12] While the history of the UPC is a story that ends with the party's failure to gain access to the seat of power with the dawn of independence, it is also a story of the state's failure to become a nation.

BLENDING LOCAL AND GLOBAL POLITICS

In the late 1940s and early 1950s, UPC nationalism synchretized local, regional, and international political processes. Some of these, including the legitimacy of traditional chiefs, inheritance laws, spiritual technologies, and the translation of nationalist ideas into indigenous languages, derived from remembered political, cultural, and spiritual traditions that predated European rule. Others, such as labor unions, planters' cooperatives, political parties, and elections, emerged under foreign rule. Nationalists' awareness of current international politics stemmed from the status of the French and British Cameroons as UN trust territories. From the UPC's inception, in 1948, leaders quoted from both the UN Charter, which promised autonomy to trust territories, and from the Universal Declaration of Human Rights (UDHR). The party's global perspective was reinforced through the alliances that upécistes forged with Nkrumah-style Pan-Africanists beginning in 1957.[13] UPC nationalist leaders mediated the links between global and local more adeptly than other territorial politicians, and in this mediation lay the source of the movement's strength and tenacity, and of ordinary Cameroonians' awareness of the UN, human rights, and anticolonial struggles beyond the territory's borders.

While the "glocal"[14] political articulation first formed in the minds of a handful of nationalist leaders in the late 1940s, it became stronger as the movement spread from cities and towns to the countryside until, by 1955, a global-local connection guided nationalists' practice, discourse, and mobility throughout French Cameroon and beyond. Beginning with Um Nyobé and Abel Kingue's first trip to the United

States, in 1952, nationalist leaders traveled internationally with great regularity: to New York to speak before the UN General Assembly, and to Vienna, Stockholm, Budapest, Bucharest, Moscow, and Prague to attend congresses organized by NGOs such as the Women's International Democratic Federation, the World Federation of Trade Unions, and the World Federation of Democratic Youth. By the late 1950s, Cameroonian nationalists had arrived in Khartoum, Rabat, Accra, Conakry, and Cairo, where they consistently took part in All-African Peoples' and Afro-Asian Solidarity conferences.[15]

There is nothing surprising about an internationally mobile African party leadership. If by the nineteenth century a "black transnationalist imaginary" was already well formed,[16] black internationalism only increased throughout the first half of the twentieth century.[17] The 1950s marked the heyday of traveling anticolonial and nationalist delegations, political leaders, and intellectuals; and scholars have begun to explore the implications of these Third World transregional networks.[18] But the political cosmopolitanism that swept French Cameroon and, later, the British Cameroons belonged not just to a jet-setting elite. Thousands of Cameroonian nationalists gathered en masse or in local committee meetings to listen to traveling leaders' accounts of their ventures abroad. And thousands of upécistes—regardless of their degree of education, their gender, their age, or whether they lived in cities or villages—laid claim, through the act of petitioning, to the UN, where decisions were made about trusteeship inhabitants' right to autonomy, human rights, economic independence, and an end to racial discrimination.[19]

Although these petitions were addressed to the UN General Assembly and Trusteeship Council in New York, other countries—such as Vietnam, Algeria, Indochina, and Madagascar—figured in petitions protesting the violent repression that upécistes faced at the hands of French administrators. But if petitions to the UN indicated an awareness of anti-imperial global trends and the meaning of trust territory, their content bespoke the local elements of UPC nationalism. For example, petitions often decried the French administration's "unjust" or "unlawful" deposition of chiefs, describing the violence and humiliation unleashed by a crisis in traditional governance.[20] Women who belonged to the Union démocratique des femmes camerounaises (UDEFEC), the women's wing of the UPC, demonstrated their mistrust of French medical facilities and health care. In early 1957, Mrs. Passa Tchaffi and Mrs. Agathé Matene wrote, "The French . . . have prepared injections and put schoolchildren into a hut, where they gave them these shots to weaken their minds."[21] Chrestine Emachoua believed that "when a woman gives birth at the dispensary, they give the baby an injection to kill it," and ended her petition with "Long live the United Nations! Long live a unified and independent Cameroon!"[22] Other petitioners protested the expropriation of land. In a letter to the French high commissioner, a copy of which she included in her petition to the UN Trusteeship Council, Mrs. Lydia Dopo wrote:

> On 12 February 1954, a European Official of the Water and Forestry Service asked me to . . . show him the boundaries of my plantation. . . . He refused to accept the boundaries I showed him, and . . . he cut off a large part of my plantation, which was under cultivation, for classification in the private domain. From time to time this European Official . . . tells me that he will send me to prison . . . if I persist in claiming my rights.[23]

The thousands of petitioners who cited matters of chieftaincy, land ownership and usufruct, fears of biomedicine, or unjust taxation demanded to be heard on their own terms on issues of local concern, but within the global forum of the UN.[24] The act of petitioning and the problems discussed in these missives engendered a new political repertoire within which people—whether literate or not, whether benefiting from French administrative support or on the run to escape arrest, whether urban or rural dwellers—expressed their concerns and aspirations in a changing political landscape.[25] The new political repertoire was central to the vernacularization[26] of the international political discourses that nationalists found most useful. Through these new ways of speaking, and new channels for expressing their ideas about independence and nation, Cameroonian nationalists constructed a politics of nationalism.[27] Speech and writing became one avenue through which Cameroonian nationalists forged the articulation between local political cultures and international politics.

Familiarity with the international politics of decolonization and human rights formed a significant part of UPC ideology even before the nationalist parties' official proscription—first by the French administration, in July 1955, then by the British, in June 1957. These bans had the effect of strengthening the link between global and local in the minds of UPC nationalists—particularly the movement's architects—for whom it now became even more pressing to solicit the understanding and support of international allies, whether at the UN or in the human rights NGO affiliated with it, the International League of the Rights of Man (ILRM), on which they relied for support, in newly independent African states, or among the various political sympathizers throughout the West (France, the UK, and the US) and the Eastern Bloc.[28] Once the proscriptions rendered the movement illegal, excluding it from the legal, territorial, political landscape, Cameroonian nationalists who were familiar with the international political sphere interwove indigenous political traditions and global revolutionary currents even more deliberately—in practice as well as in discourse. It was as if the official proscriptions allowed the movement to evolve into an explicitly extrametropolitan nationalism.

The articulation between international and local political orders after the movement's official proscription surfaced, not just in the petitions on record at the Trusteeship Council, but also in the formation and practice of the UPC's underground militias. UPC soldiers were either former exiles trained abroad or fighters recruited locally. When the British proscribed the UPC, they deported the leaders of the directors' bureau, who had left French territory in 1955 and taken refuge in the British Cameroons. From the late 1950s through the 1960s, a majority of UPC, Jeunesse démocratique camerounaise (JDC), and UDEFEC leaders, headquartered in turn in Khartoum, Cairo, Rabat, Accra, Conakry, Algiers, and Brazzaville from 1957 to 1968, worked to change the movement into what Matthew Connelly, referring to the Algerian War of Independence, calls a "diplomatic revolution."[29] Others remained within the Cameroon territories but, like Ruben Um Nyobé, the secretary-general, they took to the forests and mountains in their regions of origin, or settled in underadministered zones along the Anglo-French border in the Mungo River valley and the Grassfields.[30] Nationalists in exile remained connected to the internal underground resistance—the *maquis*[31]—that formed in the Sanaga-Maritime in late 1956 and spread into several regions throughout the southern French and British Cameroons. Later, as exiles returned to make up the ranks of the UPC militia groups fighting for independence from foreign rule, the names of maquis camps—Accraville or ONU—and fighters' noms de guerre—Fidel or Karl Marx—bore witness to the importance of the international in the nationalist imaginary. UPC military strategies paralleled the local-to-global range of the party. Fighters trained abroad used guerrilla tactics of sabotage and terrorism modeled on principles outlined in Mao Tse-tung's *Little Red Book* and learned in China and in Front de libération nationale (FLN) training camps in Algeria and Tunisia. Those who had never been abroad relied on local, culturally specific strategies of warfare—magical technologies, the protection of sacred forests, intimate knowledge of the terrain, and hunters' skills.[32]

A deliberate rejection of metropolitan connections can also be seen in the upécistes' decision, after the official bans rendered them outlaws, to begin spelling the nation's name with a K—Kamerun. The German spelling denoted not only the movement's leaders' desire to be free of British and French administration and influence but also their goal of reunification of the territories. The letter *k* became a ubiquitous symbol of UPC nationalism beginning in mid-1957, appearing not only in the nation's name, but also in nationalists' spelling of other words such as *kolos* (*colons*, or colonialists) or *loi-kadre* (*loi-cadre*).

With such a broadly global and deeply local scope, it is no wonder the collective political imaginary of independence-era Cameroon spanned the village, the nation, and the world beyond. Seemingly disparate political practices and discourses converged and overlapped in ways that UN representatives or European administrators may have found surprising. But UPC nationalists gradually fitted these different ways of speaking and practicing politics together over the years, discovering that indigenous political traditions had something in common with the new Third World politics: an optimistic belief in the UN, Afro-Asian solidarity, human rights, nonalignment, and the possibility of political, cultural, and economic rupture with colonial powers.[33] Both were conceived and sustained beyond the governing metropolitan centers that administered the territories of colonial Africa.

CAMEROON: AN EXCEPTIONAL COLONIAL HISTORY?

Cameroonian nationalism lends itself especially well to an extrametropolitan historical analysis. In Cameroon, as elsewhere along Africa's western coast, European powers came and went throughout the era of the transatlantic trade, and pidgin English spread and took root as a lingua franca among the populations involved in translocal commerce.[34] But even after the Berlin Conference allotted Kamerun to Germany in 1885, the revolving door admitting European powers seemed to continue spinning, making the territory's affiliation with any particular metropolitan power relatively tenuous. Not until 1910 did

Germans "pacify" areas in the hinterland, such as the densely populated Grassfields region, which comprised over a hundred hierarchically organized and mostly autonomous chieftaincies. Just a few years later, Britain and France took over the German colony in a joint military operation during the First World War, and divided the spoils at Versailles in 1919 with the delineation of the Anglo-French boundary.[35]

The new international frontier separated several communities, societies, and polities from north to south, including the western portion of the Grassfields around Bamenda, which now fell under British control, from the eastern Bamileke Region, under French administration. In both territories, the British and French were merely administering authorities under the supervision of the League of Nations and then, after the Second World War, the UN.[36] In the Grassfields region, as in the northern, Islamized regions, the British and French, who had hastily cobbled together stopgap administrations after the war, relied on African rulers to govern. From the point of view of local populations in regions such as the Grassfields, where rulers had wielded significant power and authority before European occupation, traditional chiefs represented the most consistent form of governance throughout the colonial period, as European administrations seemed to come and go, and political borders shifted.

Despite the territories' particular status as UN Trust Territories after the Second World War and the relatively brief period of European rule in regions such as the Grassfields, decolonization progressed in much the same way in the Cameroon territories as in other British and French colonies. After the war, the French administration organized elections at the same time as they were held in the rest of France's territories, while the British permitted the formation of political parties in the Cameroons. In 1956, France held loi-cadre elections to establish parliamentary assemblies to govern internal affairs in French Cameroon, as it did in its other overseas territories. For many of France's African colonies, loi-cadre meant increased political representation and greater political autonomy, and it was widely viewed as a necessary transitional stage en route to decolonization.[37] In French Cameroon, as elsewhere in French Africa, administrators groomed African politicians to eventually take their places in political bodies and institutions that resembled France's own. The political parties that benefited from French support, including the Évolution sociale camerounaise (ESOCAM) and the Bloc démocratique camerounais (BDC), failed, however, to attract mass followings or to build up a popular base.[38]

If administrators and pro-French politicians missed noting the significant differences in the legal status and colonial histories of the Cameroon territories, Cameroonian anticolonial nationalists certainly did not. From the party's inception, in 1948, UPC leaders consciously dismissed the territorial, political, and historical markers that guided French and British decolonization processes in the Cameroon territories and instead built a nationalist movement on a blend of anti-imperial global trends and local political practices. When, after the UPC's ban, in 1955, the French administration organized the first territorial elections in which universal suffrage was applied, upécistes sent some forty-five thousand petitions to the UN in lieu of votes, claiming their right, as inhabitants of a UN trust territory, to participate in political processes even if French administrators denied their access to elections.[39] As French administrators worked with Cameroonian collaborators to make French Cameroon part of a "greater France" through an interterritorial application of loi-cadre, UPC nationalists invoked the UN Charter to argue that implementation of loi-cadre was illegal in a UN trust territory and that Article 76 had in 1946 already granted the right of self-government to territories under European rule. As French administrators sought to do away with traditional chiefs, UPC nationalists protested their deposition throughout the Bamileke Region.[40] And as French administrators pushed Cameroon toward interterritorial federation with other French colonial territories in 1958, upécistes in exile signed on to Kwame Nkrumah's plan for a United States of Africa.

Most tellingly, as French administrators sought to standardize political discourse throughout French Africa on the eve of independence, upécistes were primarily concerned with how to translate nationalist terms into indigenous languages. The translation needed to be cultural as well as linguistic, as made clear in the petition that Marthe Penda sent to the UN Trusteeship Council in December 1954, discussing the primary-school curriculum: "The children learn nothing but passages from plays written centuries ago by Molière and no teaching is given on indigenous history, or customary and traditional dancing; the children only learn the history of distant countries so that a child who can recite details of the map of France does not know the name of a river flowing through his own village."[41]

Upécistes' quest for independence from foreign rule amounted to a struggle to define, on their own terms, what constituted legitimate political practice for a soon-to-be-independent African nation. The UPC definition included a rejection of a metropolitan political modality—based on allegiance to a greater France, electoral politics and *évolué* elitism—and its replacement with something else. The something else, a blend of contemporary global and neotraditional[42] local political culture, formed the stuff of Cameroonian nationalism. Although at first glance the blend of international and local elements in UPC nationalism seems exceptional, it is more likely that the articulation between local political culture and global political trends in African nationalisms could be argued to constitute the norm, not the exception. Historians such as Joey Power and Elizabeth Schmidt have shown the ways in which grassroots political activists referenced and reframed transregional political discussions in colonial territories.[43] The works of Steven Feierman, Carol Anderson, and others have demonstrated the importance for activists in UN trust territories of petitioning the UN and engaging in human rights talk.[44] Additional close-up histories of grassroots nationalisms and transnational connections are needed, to shed light on the immediate and residual importance of the independence-era marriage of local and international political processes during Africa's decolonization.

SETTING THE STAGES: THE FOCAL POINTS

Three geographical focal points anchor this three-tiered history of Cameroonian nationalism: Baham, a strong chieftaincy situated in the densely populated, mostly rural Bamileke Region; Nkongsamba, the capital of the Mungo Region, French Cameroon's fertile plantation zone; and Accra, Ghana, where the Kwame Nkrumah government that came into power at independence, in 1957, founded the Bureau of African Affairs to support and assist anti-colonial liberation movements in territories still under European rule.[45] Nationalist activity radiated outward from these three points, creating regional epicenters with overlapping peripheries. Although the present analysis ranges beyond these three centers, each one is symbolic of the local, territorial, and transregional layers of Cameroonian nationalism. The book is structured in three parts of two chapters each, and progresses chronologically against the backdrop of these interconnected locations.

Grassfields Political Tradition and the Creation of a Bamileke Identity

Part One historicizes the political practice of Grassfielders before European rule, and evaluates the formation of a "Bamileke identity" in the Mungo Region under French administration during the interwar period. The Bamileke Region, as the French called the portion of the Grassfields that fell under their administration with the delineation of the Anglo-French boundary in 1919, was the most densely populated region in French Cameroon. Some three hundred fifty thousand to half a million people lived in the region itself, which remained mostly rural and agricultural, although Dschang, Bafoussam, and Bangangte developed over the decades into administrative centers and market towns. The rest of the region consisted of a mosaic of chieftaincies (gung), each governed by a chief and a network of notables, associations, and spiritualists.

Before colonization, the Grassfields region was composed of approximately one hundred chieftaincies, some autonomous and regionally dominant, others in a state of subordination to more powerful neighbors.[46] Alliances between chieftaincies were made and sometimes broken, and boundaries between polities shifted as a result of interchieftaincy battles, diplomatic negotiations, and intrachieftaincy independence movements.[47] Although by the nineteenth century Grassfields chieftaincies together made up a coherent cultural system distinct from neighboring regions, Grassfielders had no "shared consciousness of belonging to a named group."[48] On the eve of colonial rule, Grassfields polities had certain political and spiritual practices in common and manifested these in similar material cultures. Yet linguistic diversity[49] and the chieftaincy-specific content of political histories (narrating each polity's foundation and diplomacy), spiritual technologies (particular sacred sites and commemoration of lineage ancestors), and material culture (masquerade performances, architectural style) meant that the identification of Grassfields inhabitants with a particular chieftaincy of origin was far stronger than their sense of belonging to a "Grassfields" collectivity.

Even after the French had labeled the administrative region "Bamileke"—the word a combination of erroneous translation and a mispronunciation first uttered by a German soldier around 1905[50]—inhabitants continued to identify themselves by chieftaincy of origin. Only as they emigrated from their chieftaincies and settled in towns such as Nkongsamba or Douala (the port city) in the territory's other regions did they begin to apply the term Bamileke to themselves. During the interwar period, a Bamileke identity began to coalesce in places such as the Mungo Region, where host populations and European administrators viewed Bamileke migrants as "strangers." In the 1950s the meaning of "being Bamileke" continued to evolve concurrently with Cameroonian nationalism as it spread both through emigrant Bamileke communities and through home chieftaincies.

To help understand the engagement of Bamileke actors with UPC nationalism, this book situates the region's (de)colonization in a Grassfields' "long time-span"[51] and plumbs the ways in which upécistes engaged Grassfields political tradition to express and define the UPC platform for Bamileke communities.[52] Chapter 1 focuses on the nineteenth-century traits of Grassfields governance and spirituality that nationalists recycled in the 1950s to "translate the message" of UPC nationalism.[53] Bamileke nationalists accented two political concepts indigenous to the Grassfields region—*lepue* and *gung*—as the terms used to translate "independence" and "nation," respectively. In the 1950s, Bamileke nationalists redefined the meanings of these terms through the UPC, in order to restore autonomy and legitimacy to chiefs, and to separate "traitors" (*mfingung*) from "patriots" (*mpouogung*). Chapter 1 also presents Grassfields political power and spirituality as inscribed in the communal and familial sacred sites (*chuep'si*) of each chieftaincy. These sacred sites dotting the landscape were the geographical locus of a spiritual alliance between an invisible, metaphysical world governed by a supreme being, *Si*, and the visible, material world inhabited by human beings. Throughout the region, this spiritual alliance shaped Grassfields governance and constituted an essential part of the political culture, underwriting power, land distribution and usufruct, and justice within each chieftaincy. During the war for independence, Bamileke nationalists reified the politicospiritual importance of these sites when they risked arrest to travel from the maquis to make sacrifices to deities inhabiting lineage or community chuep'si.[54]

Through the nationalist movement, and the cultural and linguistic translation it necessitated, Bamileke upécistes reshaped understandings of their past.[55] In this, they were doing nothing new. As elsewhere in equatorial Africa,[56] in Bamileke communities, identity and political tradition have been "constantly reworked."[57] But independence-era constructions of Bamileke identity and reconstructions of political tradition were "nonetheless 'fixed' in narratives of the past."[58] My intention is to show how "narratives of the past" underwrote the politics of anticolonial nationalism in Bamileke communities. But, as Grassfields political culture shaped nationalism, so, too, territorial political processes reframed the views of Bamileke populations on the political legitimacy of their chiefs, the sovereignty of their chieftaincies, and the political and cultural importance of Grassfields spiritual practice. The Mungo Region and its capital, Nkongsamba, became the channel through which reciprocal influences flowed between Grassfields political culture and territorial politics.

Chapter 2 recounts the ways in which Bamileke migrants kept Mungo towns connected to their chieftaincies of origin in the Bamileke Region and to the city of Douala. By the 1950s, the fertile Mungo River valley, site of European-owned plantations and a flourishing cash-crop economy, had become home to tens of thousands of migrants from other parts of the Cameroon territories.[59] Drawn by opportunities offered by waged labor and commercial agriculture during the interwar period, migrants from throughout French Cameroon transformed the Mungo River valley into the most ethnically and culturally heterogeneous region in the territory. The majority of immigrants hailed from the adjacent Bamileke Region, located just to the northeast. By the late trusteeship period, Bamileke immigrants made up a significant portion of the Mungo Region's population, as high as 80 percent in some towns, including Nkongsamba, the regional capital, the third-largest town in French Cameroon and the northern terminus of the railroad from Douala. Situated as it was along the Anglo-French boundary, the Mungo Region became a microcosm of the political, economic, and social tensions that emerged in the Cameroon territories under foreign rule.

Conflicts over land ownership in the Mungo Region encouraged African planters to become familiar with laws, the processes of obtaining titles and deeds, petitioning, and filing grievances and appeals. The relatively high percentage of waged laborers working on the railroad and in plantations ensured that French Communist organizers prioritized the Mungo Region as they organized Marxist study circles and trade unions after the Second World War. The white settler population, the Cameroons' highest outside Douala, made constant demands on administrators and formed their own defensive political lobbies. In short, the Mungo Region provided fertile ground for UPC nationalism, and Bamileke populations served as conduits for political ideas flowing back and forth from home chieftaincies, via the Mungo River valley, to the largest city, Douala.

Independence (Lepue) and Nation (Gung): Contested Meanings

Part Two shows how the UPC, which formed as a political party in 1948, evolved into a nationalist movement, and examines the ways in which local and territorial politics became articulated in the Mungo and Bamileke Regions. Chapter 3 explains how party leaders "translated" the UPC's international message throughout the Mungo, Bamileke, and other regions with such success that, by early 1955, upécistes numbered close to 100,000 out of a total electorate of 747,000. French administrators, alarmed by its popularity, remarked that the UPC's influence was "large relative to [that of] other political movements in the territory,"[60] and officially banned the UPC and its affiliate youth, women's, and trade unionist wings on 13 July 1955.

In 1956, just after the UPC's proscription in French Cameroon, French administrators deposed, imprisoned, and sometimes forced a number of young Bamileke chiefs who had recently inherited power to flee into exile. As chapter 4 recounts, this younger generation of chiefs became spokespersons for UPC nationalism throughout the Bamileke Region and in their emigrant communities. The first one to be deposed, the chief of Baham, Pierre Kamdem Ninyim, was preparing to run for a seat in the territorial assembly in the December 1956 elections. After the young chiefs' respective depositions, the French replaced them with chiefs less likely to support the UPC and more likely to support the administration's efforts to eradicate UPC influence in Bamileke communities. In the December elections, five such Bamileke chiefs were elected to French Cameroon's territorial assembly to serve as deputies in the new loi-cadre administration. After the depositions and the elections, chieftaincy became an idiom through which Bamileke populations, whether residing in their home chieftaincies or in emigrant communities beyond, discussed the politics of decolonization.

In many ways, by outlawing the UPC and its affiliated parties and by selectively deposing traditional chiefs in the Bamileke Region, French administrators shaped electoral processes on the ground in 1956, forcing people to choose one side or the other. The result was a political landscape flattened into two opposing and confrontational sides, and this enabled UPC leaders to simplify their message accordingly, effectively painting anyone who supported the territory's integration into the French Union rather than the UPC's envisioned rupture with France as a "traitor" (*fingung*) while portraying pro-UPC chiefs, notables, and civil servants as mpouogung—patriots or (lit., children of the nation).[61] Bamileke chiefs who chose to ally with the Franco-Cameroonian administration in power as of late 1956 had been in power longer and relied on the French administration as the main source of their legitimacy within the chieftaincy. On the other hand, most of the chiefs who joined the nationalist movement had more recently inherited the stool of power.[62] They were young and schooled, and sought to establish their legitimacy both through new political developments and through "traditional" culture as they understood it. They enjoyed the support of significant portions of their emigrant populations in Cameroon's cities—Nkongsamba, Douala, and Yaoundé.

Differences over the role of Bamileke chiefs in territorial politics can be read as the continuation of a long-standing political debate over the meaning of lepue and whether it might best be achieved through diplomatic negotiation or through direct, even violent, confrontation.[63] For Bamileke nationalists in the late 1950s, lepue meant reclaiming the chieftaincy as a sovereign space and the chief as the people's representative, and it was the more dramatic form of lepue—a refusal to submit to foreign rule at all costs—that held the greater popular appeal in late 1956 and 1957. This form of lepue implied a complete political, economic, and cultural break with former colonial powers and facilitated the interweaving of Grassfields political culture with an international Spirit of Bandung, the African cornerstone of which was situated in Accra from 1957 to 1966.[64]

UPC Nationalists Go Global

Part Three considers the importance of the UPC's international influences and transregional support by focusing on the strategies that upécistes employed after the movement's proscription in the Cameroon territories—transnational exile, Pan-African connections, and violence. It charts the progression of violence in the Mungo and Bamileke Regions before and after independence, and documents the lasting effects of the Cameroonian state's eradication of the movement from the postcolonial political landscape.

In 1957, Ghana opened its borders to political activists deemed radical by their respective colonial administrations. Under the direction of

Kwame Nkrumah and Pan-African cabinet members, including Ras T. Makonnen and George Padmore (who helped create the Bureau of African Affairs), Accra became the site of an African Affairs Centre, which from 1957 to 1966 hosted anticolonial activists and exiles from Egypt, Kenya, Uganda, Malawi, the Belgian Congo, Angola, Lesotho, Zambia, and Cameroon.[65] For upécistes, this Pan-African political support proved essential and came not a moment too soon. Nkrumah declared his intent to fight for Africa's liberation and in March 1957, just a few months after UPC party leaders had decided to organize an armed offensive within the territory and only three months before the party's proscription in British territory, described anticolonial freedom fighters as "the gem of the revolution." Facing arrest within their own territories, upécistes needed a place to go. To sustain the maquis within the Cameroon territories, they required funds, access to weapons, and military training. It was in Accra and Conakry that UPC directors found the diplomatic, financial, and military support necessary for the movement at the moment of its revolutionary turn.

In November 1958, Ahmed Sékou Touré of Guinea and Kwame Nkrumah of Ghana officially declared their two states to constitute "the nucleus of a Union of West African States" on which a United States of Africa would build. A month later, Nkrumah hosted the first All-African Peoples' Conference (AAPC), in Accra. At the assembly of anticolonial political activists and intellectuals, which included Tom Mboya of Kenya, Holden Roberto of Angola, Patrice Lumumba of Congo, and UPC president Félix Moumié, Frantz Fanon declared that violence was the only path to economic, psychological, cultural, and political decolonization.[66] His legitimization of revolutionary violence and the Pan-African foothold gave Moumié sufficient confidence to proclaim at a press conference on 12 December 1958, less than three months after FLN leaders announced the establishment of the Republic of Algeria's provisional government (Gouvernement provisoire de la République algérienne — GPRA), that the party's exiled directors' bureau constituted the legitimate Cameroonian government.[67]

By late 1958, the UPC fit Frantz Fanon's recipe for anticolonial revolution, itself modeled on the Algerian case, as if it had been made to order. Bourgeois intellectuals, members of a lumpenproletariat, and significant numbers of the "peasantry" had all signed on to the movement. It had spread through cities, towns, and rural areas. UPC militia camps had been put in place throughout southern French Cameroon and near

Tombel, in British territory. Exiled upécistes sought out the ideological circuits of Pan-Africanism, socialism, and Afro-Asian solidarity, ensuring that Cameroonian nationalism would not stop with national liberation but would be a part of a transnational, perhaps eventually global, revolution defining "a new humanism both for itself and for others."[68] Faced with the movement's exclusion from territorial political processes and the UN's unwillingness to intervene to restore the movement to legality, upécistes turned to violence as the only path to liberation from foreign rule. Although upécistes continued to petition the UN to have the proscription lifted, to offer amnesty to political prisoners, and to organize elections under its supervision, from 1957 forward, violence became the new channel linking the UPC to international political currents.

Chapter 5 historicizes the formation, organization, and operation of internal maquis camps in the Bamileke and Mungo Regions and shows how, in its early stages, violence within the maquis worked in tandem with the activities of the UPC in exile. The UPC's use of violence in the postproscription phase coincided with the period in which increasing numbers of upécistes left their homes and began long years of peripatetic exile or hiding out in the hills and forests of the internal maquis. Through the mobility of exiled upécistes, UPC militia camps located along the Anglo-French boundary and in the Sanaga-Maritime, the Bamileke, the Mungo, the Mbam, the Nkam Provinces, and the Dja-et-Lobo Department became connected to Accra, Conakry, and Algiers, and to military training camps in China and Morocco. Ernest Ouandié, who had left the British Cameroons in 1957 as UPC vice president and returned in 1962 as commander in chief of the UPC paramilitary, the Armée de libération nationale du Kamerun (ALNK), after years spent in Khartoum and Accra, sought to organize troops, training, and the location of maquis camps. The connection between the internal maquis and the international sites of revolution thrived in the nationalist imaginary and in the leaders' planned military strategies. It lived in the exiles who returned to replenish the troops of the UPC army, the and in the couriers such as Emmanuel Fankem, alias Fermeté (Steadiness), who crisscrossed international boundaries to keep upécistes in contact.[69] Exiles were the go-betweens who brought the international to life in the minds of freedom fighters and translated the local fight into global, revolutionary terms.

The disintegration of the movement and its armed resistance, the rising then falling degree of complicity of civilian populations, and the

French, British, and Cameroonian administrations' methods of eradicating the UPC rebellion are evaluated in chapter 6. As the war raged on after Cameroon's independence, transregional support dwindled, the connection between the internal and external UPC became more difficult to maintain, militia camps became isolated and cut off from each other, and the UPC was irreversibly factionalized. Ideological, political, and strategic differences wedged their way into the ranks of freedom fighters, separating those trained abroad from those who had never left, or fighters in one maquis camp from those in a different region. After 1960, the gendarmes, military, and police maintaining order on behalf of the Ahidjo government clashed daily with *maquisards* in a several provinces. For fighters on both sides, the structured, organized violence of war unraveled into random violence as a way toward revenge, elimination of personal enemies, looting, and financial profit. Caught in the crossfire, ordinary Cameroonians collectively adopted a strategy of silence as a means of survival, while a distrust of the political seemed all pervasive. The book concludes with a discussion of the residual political and social effects of the postcolonial state's heavy-handed repression of the nationalist movement, and its punishment of upécistes and their suspected sympathizers.

A HISTORY OF UPC NATIONALISM — NEW PERSPECTIVES, NEW CHRONOLOGIES

Today, Cameroon's president, Paul Biya, who served as Ahidjo's prime minister before being selected to be his successor in 1982, cannot spin UPC history as the nation-state's patriotic narrative as Zimbabwe's president, Robert Mugabe, has the history of the Zimbabwe African National Union–Patriotic Front.[70] Biya inherited power from the regime the French put in place upon their departure, a regime that made the repression of the UPC its primary goal in the early postcolonial period. *Nation of Outlaws, State of Violence* is neither a nationalist history nor a patriotic one, but rather a history of a nationalist movement that could not achieve its political goals. In a retrospective article on Zimbabwe's history, historian Terence Ranger writes that there are "two circumstances under which historical scholarship was crucially important." First, "when people had been denied a history," and second, "when a single, narrow historical narrative gained a monopoly and was endlessly repeated" as in the patriotic history of Mugabe's Zimbabwe, today.[71] In the first instance, history must fill a void, and in the second, it must serve to "complicate over-simplifications" and "to offer a plural history."⁷² Ranger's discussion of the differences between the history of nationalism, nationalist history, and patriotic history and the purpose of each helps to situate this study of the UPC.

In Cameroon, people were denied a history of the UPC for over three decades after official independence. Until 1991, writing the history of UPC nationalism could result in the author's exile, while books recounting UPC history were banned.⁷³ Since the so-called democratic opening of the early 1990s and the legalization of political parties other than the one in power, scholarly and popular histories of the UPC have proliferated as though to fill a vacuum. And yet they are "too much" in a different way than the official history of ZANU–PF in Zimbabwe: they are so plural and fragmented that they remain at the periphery of Cameroon's national history.

The history of UPC nationalism is crucial in part because its study was forbidden within Cameroon for so long.⁷⁴ It is crucial beyond Cameroon's borders because it illustrates the interlinking of local political cultures with an extraordinarily internationalized political agenda and is thus a part of a larger history of Third World revolution. Finally, because the UPC movement continued past the date of Cameroon's official independence, its history offers a new chronology for African anticolonial nationalisms by elucidating the lasting political repercussions of a popular nationalist movement's failure to achieve political power.

The Vernacularization of an International Political Platform

As Achille Mbembe has shown for Cameroon and as other revisionist historians have demonstrated elsewhere, popular African nationalisms were constructed in large part on a retrieval and revalorization of indigenous political culture.⁷⁵ But, as *Nation of Outlaws* demonstrates, grassroots nationalisms required more than a cultural renaissance and a refashioning of local political tradition. Emerging as a current of anti-imperialism swept much of the globe, grassroots nationalisms had to undergo a two-way translation in order to achieve meaning in both local contexts and in a larger geopolitical arena. UPC nationalists found ways to express formal political discourse of party platforms in local vernaculars. They also integrated elements of a symbolic cultural reservoir into political practice on a territorial scale. This book examines the mutual influences connecting the political cultures of particular locales to territorial and transregional political currents by considering the local, territorial, and global politics of the 1950s and 1960s in the same analytical plane. In so doing, it builds on—but goes beyond—the rich revisionist histories of African nationalisms that have emphasized culturally specific political practices without exploring the ways in which local politics of decolonization became articulated with international political trends. The case of the UPC shows the ways in which African nationalists and anticolonialists actively sought to link their local liberation struggles with larger global trends and to appropriate, on their own terms, international connections and discourses as alternatives to their continued interdependency with metropolitan centers.[76]

UPC Nationalism and Postcolonial Politics: A New Chronology

In continuing past the date of Cameroon's official independence, this book questions the historical usefulness of choosing official independence as a temporal marker in histories of Africa's decolonization. By emphasizing the beginnings of transitions, and by selecting the date of official independence as a chronological endpoint, all but ignoring their aftermaths, many works on African decolonization fail to assess the effects of preindependence political processes on postindependence nation building.[77] Yet the aftermaths are crucial to understanding what kind of states colonial territories became. This study of UPC nationalism details the ways in which French and British administrators barred Cameroonian nationalists from participation in territorial politics and, as a result, limited their access to the postcolonial political terrain.

The policies of the Ahidjo regime, after 1960, undergirded by a strong French military presence, continued the political tactics established during Cameroon's transition to independence—cordons and searches, interrogations, the imprisonment of political oppositionists, public executions, population resettlements, and curfews. In 1966, Ahidjo reinforced the political tradition of proscription inherited from European administrators when he declared all political parties save his own, the Union nationale camerounaise (UNC), to be illegal.[78] By that time, a host of Cameroonian political "exiles," whether excluded from political processes within territorial boundaries or on the move abroad, recognized that the state that had come into formation was no longer theirs to mold or to govern. In many cases, as in the case of Cameroon, political exclusions enacted during and after the transition to independence restricted political possibilities, shaped political communities, birthed a culture of violence, and dictated a limited vision of what postcolonial states could become.

SOURCES AND METHODOLOGY

Research for this book began with the thousands of petitions sent from the Cameroon territories to the UN Trusteeship Council from 1948 through 1960. These petitions, the vast majority of which were sent by men and women who supported the nationalist movement, provide a catalogue of names of nationalists, party chronology, locales where the movement took root, and issues that upécistes found most important at various times and places. As the act of petitioning became more widespread, petitioners, whether literate or relying on scribes, wrote to the UN from towns across the southern Cameroons, including many of the Bamileke chieftaincies, the Mungo Region, and British territory. In the preliminary stages of my research, the petitions served to highlight which concerns and goals of upécistes had not been previously addressed in the scholarship.

The fresh perspective the petitions provided led me to base my research in Nkongsamba, the capital of the Mungo Region, and to consider the region's connections with the British and French Grassfields. In Nkongsamba, I resided for two years in the home of a Baham notable, Jean-Bernard Pogo *dit* Defotimsa, who had settled there in 1957. From 2001 to 2003, and again in 2005 and 2008, I carried out oral interviews in the Mungo, the Bamileke, and, to a lesser extent, the Bamenda regions. The bulk of the interviews took place in Baham and surrounding chieftaincies in 2002 and 2003 and were carried out with the assistance of Joseph Kiegaing of Baham, a doctoral student in sociology at the University of Yaoundé I. Mr. Kiegaing accompanied me on foot throughout chieftaincies of Baham, Bandenkop, Bamendjou, and Bafoussam and served as interpreter for the Ghomala' language. I selected a number of interviewees with the assistance of Mr. Kiegaing and Mr. Pogo of Nkongsamba who were familiar with my topic of research. Present-day upécistes as well as state officials (most of whom requested anonymity) pointed me toward additional possible interviewees. I also found interviewees as a result of the information I had gleaned from archival records, whether the UN petitions, French sources, or the prefectoral archives of the Mungo Region. While in Cameroon from 2001 to 2003, I was able to make three back-and-forth journeys to France, which enabled me to read colonial sources against oral interviews and vice versa, thus facilitating corroboration and cross-referencing. As a result, the information I gathered from oral sources continually built on the archival material I collected, which in turn led me to new interviewees and to rephrase old questions as I progressed in my research.

The oral interviews largely shaped my understanding of the nationalist-era events in Baham and surrounding chieftaincies. Many of the people I spoke with included fragments of songs in their accounts of the nationalist period. Eventually I began to collect these songs and they proved to be an invaluable historical source. André Gabiapsi, an academically trained linguist from Baham, assisted me with their analysis and transcription, but I also interviewed people for contextual etymological information pertaining to political tradition and history contained in the songs. From 2001 to 2003 I did not stay in one place, with the exception of Nkongsamba, for longer than three weeks at a time. Instead, I came and went, thus returning to the same places and people again and again, which permitted further inquiry based on new levels of mutual familiarity.

I learned not to present my inquiries as political lest I alienate my informants (with the exception of those who had been the most active in UPC politics during the 1950s and, accordingly, are invested in the narration of the movement's history). Interviewees' reluctance to "talk politics" or describe their actions as political ultimately strengthened my approach since it encouraged me to leave behind the arena of formal politics and delve into the roots of Grassfields political culture and tradition in my quest to better understand the popularity of UPC nationalism in the Bamileke and Mungo Regions. I had to learn the ways in which survivors of the independence era could comfortably talk about the "troubles" of the independence era in ways that they did not find threatening. These conversations pushed me to reformulate my own understanding of nation and what constitutes the political, to whom, and why.[79]

Written archives can be as elusive and difficult to access as oral ones, and those serving as the foundation of this historical work are no exception. Archival research in both France and Cameroon proved difficult, although for different reasons. I knew of the archival collection in the Nkongsamba prefect through word of mouth, but was denied access to it for four months after my arrival in town (during which time I was told that there were no documents). Chantal Ndami, a friend who was pursuing a PhD in history in France, placed an international phone call to one of her former classmates who was a judge in the Court of Appeals of Nkongsamba. He introduced me to the prefect's first assistant, who provided me with a key to the archival room. Thereafter, I came and went as I pleased, but the documents were stacked, unfiled, on the floor. Similar arrangements were made, via the prefect's first assistant in the Mungo Region, to allow me access to the prefectoral archives housed at Dschang, where I found the documents piled in similar haphazard fashion in a small building with no cement floor or finished ceiling.

The National Archives, in Yaoundé, no longer contain much on the UPC, particularly as documents are rarely refiled after consultation. Even more problematic for researchers of Cameroon's independence-era politics is the unavailability of the collection of UPC documents formerly in the possession of the late Professor Owona. Although these documents were to have been made accessible through the Department of History, University of Yaoundé I, they are, as yet, unavailable to the public. Researchers and students of UPC nationalism can only hope that they are in safekeeping and will one day be made accessible. The archives of the Nkongsamba Diocese, although well catalogued and classified, are kept under lock and key, available only to clergy of the diocese.

In France, a number of documents, particularly those pertaining to postindependence political processes, are kept under lock and key as well through the special dispensation (*dérogation*) system legalized in 1976. Although I was able to obtain permission, after waiting nearly a year for approval from Elysée after sending my official request, to see some papers from the collection of Jacques Foccart housed at the Centre historique des Archives nationales (CHAN) in Paris, I was denied access to documents relating to the assassination, by poisoning, of UPC president Félix Moumié in Geneva, in 1960, or those relating to the trial of Archbishop Ndongmo and ALNK commander in chief Ernest Ouandié, in 1970. According to current French law, the latter will be made available to researchers only after 2030. Documents pertaining to independence era politics in other archives in France were still under the dérogation system when I carried out the bulk of my research, including those in the Centre des Archives d'outre-mer (CAOM), in Aix-en-Provence, and the Centre d'histoire et d'études des troupes d'outre-mer (CHETOM), in Fréjus. I was eventually granted access to the documents in these centers, although the waiting period varied in length from one to three months. In contrast, records pertaining to Cameroon's postcolonial period housed at the National Archives in the Royal Botanic Gardens, in Kew, United Kingdom, which I visited in 2005, proved easily accessible and a valuable source of information.

Official French and British sources—as well as those generated by the postcolonial Cameroonian state—are problematic for their overt bias against the UPC, which they depicted as a Communist Party satellite sponsored by Moscow or Beijing, and later as a terrorist organization that employed guerilla warfare to overtake large portions of the Sanaga-Maritime, Mungo, and Bamileke Regions. Reading along the archival grain for clues to the social epistemologies that informed the administrative production of records about the Cameroonian nationalist movement in the 1950s and 1960s permits the researcher to keep in mind that these sources do not so much describe the political nature of the UPC movement or narrate its activity as much as they provide records of governance against the backdrop of Africa's decolonization and postcolonial state building in the context of the Cold War.[80] Although geographical, biographical, and chronological information can be gleaned from official state records, they provide a clearer window onto state policies than they do the collective political imaginary of Cameroonian nationalism. As far as possible I have tried to mitigate the problematic nature of official state sources through corroboration and cross-referencing other source material and reading against the grain as well as along it. Upécistes were meticulous record keepers in their own right, an institutional characteristic visible in the petitions sent to the UN that unfailingly recorded names, dates, locations, and occupations of petitioners. Accordingly, the UPC, UDEFEC, and JDC's primary documents, where available, contained information about party activity, membership, and chronology that was often more reliable and accurate than that contained in state sources.[81] In many cases, particularly after official independence, state forces captured upécistes or ALNK fighters who were carrying UPC documents that ended up in the official archival record.

There are a number of avenues left to explore in the study of UPC nationalism. A close-up analysis of other Grassfields chieftaincies, particularly around the Bamileke Region towns of Mbouda, Dschang, and Bangangte, would continue to fill in the gaps in the historiography. A number of graduate students in Cameroon are producing monograph studies of this type, and a few local scholars have recently published regional chronologies of UPC and counterrevolutionary activity.[82] Few, if any, studies exist of the UPC and its successor, One Kamerun, in the former British Cameroons. The town of Tombel, located in the Mungo River valley, just across the former Anglo-French boundary, undoubtedly has an enormously rich history dating to the nationalist period—but remains almost entirely unexplored. A number of crossroads regions, such as the Mbam, played an important role in the UPC's armed struggle, and there is evidence that regions as far away as the extreme northern and eastern provinces witnessed far more nationalistic activity than is reflected in the scholarship to date. Finally, the paths of exiled nationalists, as this book shows to some extent, were varied and far-flung. The influence of these exiles on the postindependence phase of UPC nationalism—or on political processes in the states that hosted them, including Ghana, Guinea, and Algeria—has yet to be analyzed in depth. The FLN's GPRA files may contain a wealth of information on the activities of UPC exiles and their Pan-African connections. Undoubtedly, fresh new leads will be opened up with the release of Britain's Foreign and Commonwealth Office and Predecessors Records of Former Colonial Administrations, also known as the Migrated Archives. The Cameroons' files, which unfortunately had not been released at the time of the completion of this book, have since been made available to the public.

PART ONE

Grassfields Political Tradition and Bamileke Identity

1 ∽ God, Land, Justice, and Political Sovereignty in Grassfields Governance

TWO WORDS and the history of their use encapsulate the genealogy of Cameroonian nationalism, as practiced and spoken of by Bamileke populations in the late-trusteeship period of the 1950s: *gung*, which translated as nation, and *lepue*, the word for independence. The word *gung*, in present-day Mifi, Menoua, Haut-Nkam, and Nde Departments of the West Province (formerly the Bamileke Region, under French rule), designates the entirety of a population or chieftaincy, its government (composed of a *fo*, or chief, and his notables), and the land they occupy.[1] *Gung* can be contrasted with *la'a*, which refers to a district[2] within a chieftaincy or to the family compound, the birthplace of one's forefathers. One might use a singular possessive pronoun to describe one's own home—as in *la'a tcha*, my home or compound—but in speaking of *gung*, only plural possessives are used, suggesting that this larger polity could only belong to a community, not to an individual. Since Cameroon's independence, these words together, *la'a gung* (lit., village-country), have been used to designate Grassfields chieftaincies such as Baham in order to differentiate them from gung, the nation-state. When referring to their native chieftaincy, Grassfielders have almost completely omitted *gung* from their common speech, effectively reducing their gung of origin to the lesser status of la'a, or village.

The discursive belittling of Grassfields chieftaincies began in the colonial period, when administrators referred to them as villages. But during the fight for independence, Grassfielders recalled the historical sovereignty of powerful chieftaincies through the words and events they selected to frame their nationalist narrative. The two key words recurred in independence songs from that era: *gung*, then commonly used as equivalent to nation, and *lepue*, which translated as independence in everyday Grassfields parlance. Historically, the ideal of lepue denoted the status of absolute autonomy acquired by the dominant chieftaincies in the Grassfields. During the nationalist period, the image of a politically independent, powerful chieftaincy grew in the collective imaginary and overlapped with concepts of self-determination and national sovereignty, only to fall away again under the postcolonial regime.

Using language as an archive, this chapter explores the semantic bedrock of Bamileke communal memory of political and spiritual practices that predated foreign rule, particularly the elements that later guided the diffusion of UPC nationalism. It provides the historical context for understanding what Bamileke nationalists hoped to regain through their involvement in the UPC, and what cultural and historical materials they worked with as they undertook the decolonization of the imaginary. In other words, this chapter is not a history of the Grassfields under European rule but rather seeks to provide a foundation for the interpretations of Grassfields political culture that anticolonial nationalists found most useful as they sought to popularize the movement to cast off the colonial yoke. Insofar as the anticolonial period entailed a reconfiguration of traditional power in the Bamileke Region, as discussed in chapter 4, it is necessary to understand the tenuous balance of power within and among chieftaincies, as well as the factors that could shift that balance of power within the boundaries of what political scientist Michael Schatzberg terms a "moral matrix of legitimate governance."[3] The present chapter's purpose is thus to provide the reader with a vantage point from which to perceive and understand the articulation between UPC nationalism and Grassfields political culture that became widespread throughout the Bamileke Region and among Bamileke emigrant communities throughout the Cameroons in the 1950s.

THE FORMATION OF GRASSFIELDS CHIEFTAINCIES

Orally transmitted myths of origin, emphasizing the role of the founder who often figures as a wandering hunter, abound throughout the Grassfields. The founding myths serve as centralizing narratives—the official version of the past as propagated by the chief's palace with the political intent of legitimating the chieftaincy.[4] These stories of origin reveal a great deal about the Grassfields political philosophy that emerged in the eighteenth and nineteenth centuries in tandem with the region's increasing centralization and settlement density.

The conventional scholarship has posited the settlement of the Grassfields into chieftaincies as coinciding with the growth of the region's involvement in international commerce as Atlantic and Sahelian trading networks infiltrated from the west and the north.[5] However, in an article published in 2012, anthropologist and specialist of the Grassfields region, Jean-Pierre Warnier—fleshing out his own previous argument about Grassfields settlement and chieftaincy formation—suggests the emergence of kingship lineages and chieftaincies much earlier, perhaps even one or two millennia ago, and stipulates that for at least twenty-five hundred years the region has been characterized by the incorporation of newcomers due to the mobility of regional and long-distance traders and exogenous marriage.[6] Regardless of when political centralization of the Grassfields chieftaincies began, the eighteenth century ushered in significant regional changes: Fulani traders north of the region began frequent slave raids throughout the area, while traders from the coast based at Old Calabar and Douala tapped the region for slaves. Because of its inland location, historians have little statistical data on the precise number of slaves originating from the Grassfields region; however, recent scholarship suggests that the combined figures for slaves exported per year at the peak of the trade, in the late eighteenth and early nineteenth centuries, may have reached as high as sixteen to eighteen thousand.[7] During the period of intensive slaving, the Grassfields served as a melting pot of populations and lineages from many different origins. The nineteenth century—within reach of remembered tradition and political history for Grassfielders—was characterized by skirmishes over territory and succession, wars over boundaries between polities, and shifting rivalries and alliances between chieftaincies.[8]

Against this backdrop of violence, massive displacements, and rampant insecurity, small, autonomous chieftaincies expanded and vied for positions of strength in the region. Internally, founders of new chieftaincies used centralizing narratives to construct a common identity for a diverse population.[9] Externally, Grassfields chieftaincies engaged in a complex diplomacy of shifting alliances and competition over territory. While oral founding myths bespeak each polity's assertion of an origin and history distinct from those of its neighbors, they also emphasize their interrelatedness. Baham's founding myth, for example, features a skilled hunter who left an established chieftaincy in the Grassfields region with his twin and their younger brother and each of their families.[10] They founded the chieftaincies Baham, Bahouan, and Bayangam, respectively, across the Noun River to the west of the Islamic kingdom of Bamum, and bordering the strong chieftaincy of Bandjoun.

Despite the importance to them of their political autonomy, the hundred or so Grassfields chieftaincies were linked by shared cultural, spiritual, and political practices, which appeared similar in content but contained particularities and historical references specific to each chieftaincy.[11] Nevertheless, Grassfields settlers identified themselves more with particular chieftaincies than with any named group with a common language or common ancestor. As such, Grassfielders demonstrated none of the usual criteria for defining an ethnic identity.[12] Self-differentiation from their neighboring chieftaincies was more important to them than differentiation from groups beyond the Grassfields who had different cultural practices. By the nineteenth century, the Grassfields connection to transregional trading networks was well established, and polities in the region exported kola, cloth, ironwork, and other artisanal goods in addition to slaves. This was the situation in the region that the Germans designated Bamileke as they began its occupation in the early twentieth century.[13]

Oral accounts of the founding of chieftaincies bespeak the prevalence of internal competition among founding patriarchs of equivalent social status. A young man with his sights set on power might, for instance, employ ruse, oratory skills, mystical technologies,[14] or wealth (particularly in the form of people, in other words, wives or dependents) to achieve social prominence. Several versions of Baham's origin story recount a years-long rivalry for the position of fo among the chieftaincy's founders. During this period, Zuguiebou, a contender for the chief's three-legged stool, was tricked into being trapped in a house without doors. He could escape only after relinquishing his copper bracelet, or *kwepe*, a symbol of a fo's right to reign, to Bussu, who thus became the first fo of Baham.[15] This account suggests that ruse and magic were important ways of negotiating power and social mobility. It also hints that, although oral tradition portrays the chief's power as central and absolute, rivals and competitors were never far away. Historically throughout the Grassfields, ruse, magic, oratory skills, or wealth—the wild-card variables that enable cunning competitors to acquire positions of nobility—surfaced in times of crisis when socially disenfranchised groups tried to reshape the chieftaincy's balance of power in their favor. While internal crises coincided with succession disputes or secessions, external factors such as the imposition of foreign rule, or wide-scale political transitions could also destabilize the status quo.

LEPUE AND GUNG: POLITICAL SOVEREIGNTY, AUTONOMY, AND INDEPENDENCE IN GRASSFIELDS CHIEFTAINCIES

Grassfields rulers achieved political centralization in the eighteenth and nineteenth centuries through wars designed to expand territory, create or dissolve alliances, and kidnap women or slaves. During the political reshaping of the Grassfields that accompanied the region's settlement and engagement in transregional trade, the concepts of gung and lepue became essential components of Grassfields political culture. *Lepue* meant to submit to no one or, as many Grassfielders put it today, to not *have to* submit to another.[16] Lepue could refer to the status of an individual, denoting a person's relative dependency or autonomy, or to the relative status of a polity such as gung. By the nineteenth century, lepue had become crucial to defining a chieftaincy's position and strength in a region plumbed for slaves and plagued by wars and migrations, where boundaries were in constant flux.

Lepue was a standing to be achieved and maintained at whatever cost—certainly it was worth fighting a war and spilling blood. Many of the smaller Grassfields chieftaincies preferred to pay tribute to Bamun or Bali and gain their protection, perhaps because, with such alliances they could maintain their autonomy vis-à-vis other Grassfields polities while paying tribute to a foreign king.[17] Submission to a Grassfields neighbor usually resulted in absorption into or annexation by the stronger chieftaincy. Smaller chieftaincies could try to achieve lepue status by waging war, first on smaller neighbors in order to expand their territory and increase their strength, and then by confronting other powerful chieftaincies in the region.[18]

The strongest autonomous chieftaincies were often the ones to resist German colonization. For example, only after German soldiers had set fire to the chief's palace during the rule of Kamdem III, in 1905 did Baham submit to German rule. After the fire Kamdem III, who had successfully extended the territory of Baham to the north, west, and south during his reign through three well-waged wars, paid a per capita tribute to the Germans and supplied them with laborers to build a road to the coast. Other Grassfields chieftaincies fought to preserve their lepue status in the face of foreign domination. Bafoussam, Baleng, Batie, Bamougoum, Fodjomekwet, and Batcha, chieftaincies that had refused to recognize German authority, were burned by the German military, while Bameka, Bansoa, and Bamougoum formed an unsuccessful alliance of resistance against the invaders.

It took some time for the Germans to completely occupy the Grassfields; not until 1910 did they penetrate to Bana in the present-day Nde Department, where they established a military post.[19] Yet not every chieftaincy resisted foreign rule. During the German occupation of the Grassfields, in the early twentieth century, some chieftaincies allied with the European invaders in a strategy to maintain or regain their dominance in the region. Baham's rival, Bandjoun, submitted willingly to German rule and became a supporter of European rule, reaping the benefits of allegiance to the state throughout the colonial period and beyond. Whether with the Fulani in the eighteenth century, Bamun and Bali in the nineteenth, the Germans in 1905, or the French and British in 1915, Grassfields chiefs were historically skilled at leveraging greater regional standing by either resisting or negotiating with powerful foreign invaders.

By the twentieth century and into the colonial period, dealing with external challenges to political autonomy was part and parcel of Grassfields politics. Certainly, the three or four decades of European rule in the Grassfields region were insufficient to erase the concept of lepue from the collective memory. There had been a long precedent of acquiring lepue status through violent conflict and great sacrifice. And so it is not surprising that this ideal figured in the slogans and songs of Bamileke nationalists in the era of the quest for independence from European administration. By this time, *gung* appeared in nationalist discourse in another form, *mfingung*, usually to denote traitors as "sellers of the country." While the meaning of *lepue* and *gung* had shifted by the 1950s to speak for contemporary political concerns and define the place of chieftaincy in the independent nation-to-be, remnant memories of nineteenth-century meanings conjured independence and nationhood in the imaginary of Grassfielders fighting for freedom from colonial rule.

That lepue survived as an ideal until the nationalist era shows that it remained important during the half century of European rule. A historical analysis of Grassfields political power and governance will help to contextualize the strategies devised by Bamileke chieftaincies to maintain as much autonomy as possible during the colonial, mandate, and trusteeship periods in Cameroon. Because this chapter examines traditional political power and practice for the purpose of understanding how UPC nationalists later vernacularized the movement's political platform, rendering it legible in terms of Grassfields political culture, the focus here remains on the structure, philosophy, and practice of governance itself, more than on the ways in which shifts in traditional power prompted by European rule acted on ordinary Grassfielders during the colonial, mandate, and trusteeship periods.

The fo was the figurehead of the Grassfields chieftaincy, but his power was more symbolic than absolute. Certainly, he made no decisions alone. The fo governed in concert and in consultation with ancestors: his "cabinet" of *wala* (Bamileke scholars today most often translate this term as ministers); his governing council (*kamveu*); secret regulatory associations, such as the powerful and dangerous *kungang*; and notables, district heads, and spiritualists. Although the figurehead, and thus the most visible representative of power in gung, the fo was not the most powerful component of chieftaincy governance. At the moment of a young fo's succession, the elder notables of gung shaped him into a respected and authoritative ruler.[20] Officeholders in his father's government were essential to the rite of succession and remained influential throughout his reign.

The balance of power at the highest echelons of government was revealed to a new fo during his period of initiation, during which he was secluded in a provisional shelter, the *la'akam*, for nine months.[21] During this period, members of the kamveu, the government council, offered extensive counsel to the neophyte, while members of the kungang secret society officiated over religious rites. During the la'akam, notables challenged the fo emotionally and physically, questioning his ability to rule, subjecting him to severe beatings, and threatening to kill him should he try to escape. In this transitional phase, the fo's strength, courage, and commitment to rule were tested. It is probable that the fo-to-be developed resentments toward the elders who stripped him of his subjectivity and sought to convince him that he was merely an instrument of their power. But surely one of the reasons for the ordeal was to teach the neophyte the self-control necessary to master his resentment and demonstrate deference and submission to elder, more powerful notables. Upon leaving the la'akam, the fo took up the challenge of establishing his authority—vis-à-vis that of his notables—as supreme governor of the polity. It was a task that took a lifetime, and certainly not every fo succeeded. The uneasy balance of power between notables and fo explains, in part, the tense political atmosphere surrounding a fo's succession, and the historical frequency with which districts of a given chieftaincy seceded or attempted to do so.

During his isolation in the la'akam, the fo learned that he depended on associations of his elders to rule. The most powerful were kamveu and kungang. Oral accounts describe the members of kamveu as descendants of the nine cofounders of the chieftaincy.[22] The reigning fo selected his successor with the help of the kamveu council, and upon the ruler's death, it was kamveu who placed the legitimate successor in the chief's palace. Although inhabitants knew who belonged to the kamveu council, the identities of the members of the kungang—the secret association of diviners, healers, and guardians of chieftaincy protocol—were concealed from everyone except the most powerful notables of the chieftaincy.[23] Kungang assisted in the installation of the fo in power by carrying out the initiation rites, ensuring his spiritual protection, and bestowing on him the mystical powers necessary to govern.

Governing institutions such as kamveu and kungang ensured the fo's dependence on his elders and minimized the likelihood that the figurehead would govern as a despot by counterbalancing the fo's power. They could accuse the fo or other notables of crimes or treachery, oppose the fo mystically or physically (leading to his displacement), and in the event of his death without a successor, select the new fo.[24] If kungang questioned a successor's legitimacy, they could simply omit essential parts of the secret rituals necessary to complete the initiation, leaving the new fo unprotected against unseen, mystical forces threatening to an imposter.[25] Without the support of kamveu and kungang—the powerful associations through which he was imbued with political and spiritual legitimacy—the successor could not be "made" a fo.

A fo succeeded his predecessor under the yoke of the chieftaincy's past history, since the power structure in place rested on the notables, each with his or her own title, rank, role, and particular relationship with the chief's palace. A fo had to be well versed in chieftaincy history in order to know which members of the nobility had remained loyal to the palace for generations and which might be prone to plotting its overthrow. Nobility positions were hereditary, but the number of nobility titles increased as each successive fo granted new titles during his reign. Titles were both earned and purchased; one had first to earn the title and then to express gratitude for the entitlement with a gift to the fo. The entitlement process was a primary source of revenue for the chief's palace, before, during, and after colonization.[26]

Spatially, Grassfields chieftaincies were made up of the core, which comprised the palace of the fo and its designated spaces, and the periphery, consisting of the roads dividing the polity into sections, the remaining districts, the sacred sites, and the border zones or no-man's-lands.[27] Nobility not directly associated with the core presided over the peripheral areas—the roads, the districts, and the sacred sites, but still had an important influence on chieftaincy politics.

The *wala* (sing., *mwala*), or, as Bamileke French-speakers say, *ministres*, in a chieftaincy made up the fo's cabinet. In local languages, a *mwala* was described as *ta djie*, or father of the road,[28] and like the roads radiating outward from the palace, their role in governance cut across all districts in the chieftaincy. The fo counted on the wala to uphold the legitimacy of his right to rule even in the face of plots to overthrow him. In the 1950s the Baham chieftaincy had four wala, each specialized in a particular area of governance—justice, diplomacy, commerce, and the maintenance of fertility and fecundity.

Notables who governed the districts of a chieftaincy, often called quarter-heads in colonial nomenclature (and hence, in much of the scholarly literature), were divided into two groups: the *wabo*,[29] who had been named by a past or current governing fo; and the *mfonte*, whose forefathers had in the past submitted to a conquering fo, relinquishing their lepue status and pledging loyalty upon the annexation of their territory.[30] A *mwabo*'s personal history with the fo distinguished him from a fonte, a distinction made more pronounced by the latter's placement in districts bordering the chieftaincy's most hostile enemies. The positions of wabo and mfonte recalled the chieftaincy's past as each district preserved the memory of pacts, alliances, or enmities between their governor and the fo. In the Ngougoua District of Baham, for example, elders still sing of a past fo's violation of his promise to exempt Ngougoua from paying tribute to the chief's palace in return for the wabo's peaceful surrender.[31] Stories and songs like this one indicate that lepue was as important to internal politics within a chieftaincy as to external relations with neighbors.

Almost any powerful notable within a Grassfields chieftaincy could, under certain circumstances, undermine the power of the fo: as a member of kamveu or kungang, he might omit the requisite rites at the fo's inauguration; as a mwala, fail to uphold the fo's claim to the throne; or as a fonte in a border region, lead a secessionist movement or pledge allegiance to another powerful fo. Transgressions of this nature were, broadly speaking, unthinkable and thus were not a part of "the moral matrix of legitimate governance,"[32] but they did occasionally occur, especially when the chieftaincy passed through the liminal phase of its fo's succession. Furthermore, while colonial administrators promoted the notion that they had pacified the Grassfields by imposing stability in a region once plagued by warfare and rivalries, the administration they implemented often exacerbated tensions among members of the nobility. Many notables viewed colonial rule as an opportunity to change their political standing in the chieftaincy, to break away from a fo's rule, or to gain power by forming an alliance with foreign administrators.

MAGIC AND MYSTICISM: THE SPIRITUAL TECHNOLOGIES OF GOVERNANCE

The undeniable political influence of the notables on the chief is often underestimated in the literature, as it was by European colonizers, including the French, who sought to make "traditional chiefs" their administrative auxiliaries. But the leadership of a Grassfields chief was also tempered in crucial ways by the forces of an unseen world—spirits, ancestors, and a mystical energy called *ké* (a term often glossed as magic or power).[33]

The fo depended on kungang for knowledge of the invisible, metaphysical world of spirits, ancestors, and people who shape-shifted into animals—the world of things ordinary people could only imagine, but a world nonetheless crucial to governance. The duty of kungang was to regulate and domesticate this invisible sphere and to harness it within the chief's field of power. It was a role that required constant vigilance and an intimate, sophisticated knowledge of both the chieftaincy and the mystical dangers beyond its boundaries. Members of kungang were responsible for protecting the chieftaincy from mystical attacks—whether from within or from without. Once they discovered the mystical causes of misfortunes affecting a chieftaincy or the communities within it, they took measures to repair the spiritual disequilibrium through purification rituals or sacrifices carried out at sacred sites.[34]

To perform these spiritual duties, members of kungang needed a knowledge of ké, the potent, vital force present in the transformation of one thing to another—ore into iron, seeds into plants, and people into animals.[35] Iron smelting depended on the proper management of ké by ironworkers, who had to refrain from violence of any kind, both during the smelting process and during wars with enemies. Because of the danger associated with metal, feuds within a given Grassfields polity or with its allies could not be fought using iron weapons.[36] Ké saturated the sacred sites and forests of the chieftaincy's landscape and was essential to reproductive and agricultural fertility, childbirthing, rainmaking, and spider divination.[37] Grassfielders believed this force or energy to be indigenous to the region, in other words, to have preceded the arrival of the founders and settlers of the chieftaincies. Chieftaincy founders had had to rely on spiritualists among their adversaries to make the land habitable and to protect the new settlers from the potentially harmful effects of ké. In many chieftaincies, this initial negotiation is memorialized in periodic masquerades to recognize ké, during which the descendants of the autochthonous populations dance before the fo and the notables.[38]

Grassfields political philosophy was and is bound up in a belief in ké. In 2002 the late fo Marcel Ngandjong Feze of Bandenkop explained the role of mysticism and magic in chieftaincy governance by saying, "It's not that I must be the greatest magician in the region. It's that people must *think* that I am the most powerful magician in the region."[39] In the instability and insecurity of the eighteenth and nineteenth centuries, early rulers had to remain vigilant against plotted rebellions from within or beyond chieftaincy bounds. The presence of an invisible, tenuously controlled energy in the land must have made the founders of Grassfields chieftaincies uneasy, and they took every possible measure to harness ké to their advantage. The management of ké was a primary purpose of Grassfields secret societies, and a significant part of Grassfields governance was devoted to its regulation for the health of the community. Notables and spiritualists did not have a monopoly on ké, however. Others both within and outside the chieftaincy could access ké and put it to malefic use. These unregulated uses of ké, beyond the control of the leaders and protectors of the chieftaincy, were the most threatening to collective and individual well-being.

GOD, LAND, AND SACRED SITES (CHUEP'SI): THE SPIRITUAL ALLIANCE

Given the continuous mobility and competition among Grassfielders and their often antagonistic relationship with the autochthonous dwellers as they settled the region, claiming the right to occupy lands and legitimizing the chieftaincy's presence constituted another essential part of Grassfields political philosophy. That Grassfielders believed the landscape hosted God is evidenced in the term *Si*, which means both god and land in the language groups Medumba, Fe-Fe, and Ghomala (spoken in the Nde, Haut-Nkam, and Mifi Departments, respectively).[40] The connection between land, religious practice, and Grassfields moral economy was physically embodied in sacred places (*chuep'si*) that served as sites of protection, justice, reconciliation, and familial or community identity. Grassfields sacred sites were the visible manifestations of a spiritual alliance between the living humans and the spirits, ancestors, and gods inhabiting the chieftaincy. The chuep'si also served as historical markers inscribed into the landscape of gung, designating the rightful occupants of a plot of land and legitimizing the presence of Grassfields settlers on the territory. As sites where justice was meted out by notables and chiefs, wills were read aloud before witnesses, and conflicts were resolved, chuep'si were places of mediation where people negotiated legal contracts and relationships with each other.

In each chieftaincy, these sacred sites marked the interstices between the material and the spiritual worlds. The Grassfields are situated in a volcanic, mountainous region that straddles the margin between forest and savannah, five degrees north of the equator. Massive rounded boulders are balanced on hilltops, resembling giant pebbles tossed about by a child at play. Grassfielders offered sacrifices to the gods at these sites embedded in the landscape of gung. Larger sacred sites that served the spiritual needs of the entire chieftaincy were situated at or near extraordinary natural phenomena in the landscape, such as rock formations or caves often adjacent to a source of water, such as a stream, a waterfall, or a spring. In Baham, the chieftaincy sacred site is called *feuveuck* and is located near Chiala, the chiefly district at the center of the polity.

At feuveuck in Baham, the flow of water appears to come from the face of the rock itself. As one walks down into its depths, entering the vast, cavelike crevices between the rocks, the air suddenly becomes cooler and more humid. Sounds echo off the rock, amplified by the acoustic space. The boulders form alcoves and partitions, and the spatial arrangement inside the site recalls a human dwelling; present-day inhabitants describe one area as the kitchen, another as the parlor of the gods. The stones inside feuveuck bear signs of sacrifice: orange remnants of palm oil splashed against the rock, white grains of salt collecting in crevices, scattered *djem djem* (pods full of seeds, associated with twins), and small chicks, strutting along the ground beneath the rocks as they peep.

Like other Grassfields community sacred sites, feuveuck marks the gathering place of the forefathers of Baham at the time of gung's foundation. At these sites, the founding fathers are said to have planned the settlement of the chieftaincy, selected its leader, and thanked the gods for their guidance and protection.[41] Whether for the site's history or its natural characteristics, the community believed that divine benedictions for the chieftaincy were first channeled through feuveuck. To ensure the continued benevolence of the gods, the living had to carry out sacrifices, which served too as a reminder of the presence of the divine in this sacred site and the need to adhere to the moral norms of justice upheld by the forefathers. Sacrificers, guardians of the site, and *kamsi* (lit., nobleman of God) officiated at community sacrifices to express gratitude to Si, to purify the chieftaincy of mystical attacks, to promote harmony among the residents, both living and dead, and to ensure reproductive and agricultural fertility. For inhabitants of Grassfields chieftaincies, acts of sacrifice at cheup'si carried collective identity and memory, and thanksgiving: they were acknowledgments of the spirits in their lives, who could bless or curse them.

Chuep'si also served as loci for the administration of justice at different levels. The administration of justice reflected the involvement of spirits and gods in the mediation of human conflict, crime, and punishment.[42] Major community sacred sites such as *feuveuck* were the locale for public confessions or truth-telling ceremonies undertaken after times of conflict or misfortune.[43] Public confessions or declarations of innocence occurred most often at district-level chuep'si, presided over by district chiefs (wabo or mfonte) and the site guardian, and attended by all inhabitants. On rare occasions, if truth-seeking or public confessions involved an entire chieftaincy and its inhabitants, they were held at the chieftaincy's communal sacred site. In 1967, after the long period of independence-era war and violence in Baham, a public confession meant to restore peace was held at the chieftaincy's central sacred site, or feuveuck.[44]

Serious matters of justice were brought before the fo, and smaller conflicts were dealt with at the district or compound level. The fo's jurisdiction included cases of criminal acts and transgressions of the chieftaincy laws, including murder, rape, flagrant adultery, theft of precious objects, insulting the fo, or repeat offenses. The fo also intervened in smaller cases when an agreement could not be reached. The fo's court resembled a trial and was carried out not on the sacred site but in the fo's palace. In serious matters brought before the fo, guilt or innocence could be a life or death matter. In the fo's court, the defendant, the accuser, the witnesses, and those presiding carried out the trial in an elaborate performance including investigation and witness testimony during which the accused and sometimes the accuser underwent various truth-telling trials.[45] The ultimate symbol of justice and honesty in the Grassfields was the tortoise. Only the fo could use the tortoise in rendering judgment, and the verdict could not be appealed.[46] While the accuser and the accused declared their respective version of events, a tortoise was released. If it crawled to the feet of the fo, the defendant was declared innocent. If it crawled toward the defendant, he was considered guilty. Depending on the gravity of the crime, the punishments entailed hanging, live burial, sale into slavery, banishment from the chieftaincy, or bodily mutilation, such as particular tattoos, or amputation of fingers or ears. Each bodily marking referred to a specific crime, thus warning the rest of the community of the wrongdoer's past behavior.

Truth telling and oathing were common features of justice in the fo's palace, just as they were at sacred sites. In both cases, individuals either declared their innocence aloud, by asking the gods to punish them promptly if they had committed a crime, or confessed their guilt and begged for leniency.[47] These declarations reminded participants of the presence of divine administrators of justice and established the credibility of those performing the truth-telling ceremonies. If the accusations were unfounded, the accuser faced severe spiritual repercussions.[48]

When truth-telling ceremonies did not require the fo's presence, they took place on sacred sites in the chieftaincy's districts and family compounds. Matters such as disputes between families over property boundaries, payment or reimbursement of bridewealth, divorce, thefts, vandalism, or difficult marriage arrangements were treated at the district level. Notables and any elders available to serve as counselors and mediators presided over the "trial." Matters judged at the district level were usually settled by reconciliation of the parties and fines or corporal punishment.

Family conflicts were resolved at the lineage chuep'si put in place at the time of each new compound's establishment. According to Grassfields oral histories, after a founding fo conquered or annexed autochthonous populations, he distributed large sections of the territory to the nine cofounders of the village (members of the kamveu council), his mwala, and the lesser mfonte, or the leaders of the la'a, or districts. These privileged notables distributed the land within their own districts, in the fo's name, dividing the land among lineage heads, who in turn redistributed it among wives (for cultivation) or sons (to establish their own compounds and become heads of dynasties).[49] The new occupant of a plot of land provided the fonte or the fo with gifts, both when making the initial request for a parcel of land (a goat and palm oil) and after having settled it (salt).[50]

After being granted the plot of land, the founder (or lineage head) of the compound arranged a ceremony to "plant" a small sacred site, *chuep'si mbem*, in the presence of witnesses from the surrounding compounds.[51] A ritual specialist planted a *yam* tree (*Ficus aganophila* Hutch.) and trees of peace, *pfeukang* (*Dracaena deistelina*), and placed a stone at their roots.[52] The yam marked a family's right to occupy and use the plot of land. The uprooting or destruction of the yam, especially by burning, desecrated the cheup'si and constituted an assault on the gods and on the fo's authority as land distributor. The deliberate destruction of a yam was a crime dealt with at the chief's palace, and a finding of guilt carried a sentence of forced labor in the service of the fo.[53] The creation of a chuep'si within a compound legitimized the founding patriarch as the lineage head—the site's primary sacrificer—and secured his offspring's right to reside on the land.

The spirit protectors (*mbem*) of a lineage dwelt in the site around the altar. The chuep'si mbem ensured everyday access to spirit guardians who protected a particular lineage and interceded between them and a more distant being. The chuep'si mbem in family compounds personalized Si and established a permanent contact with the sacred through the land. The site was a visual, inviolable symbol of a lineage's connection with the sacred. At the level of the lineage compound, the chuep'si was the place where family members settled their disputes.

In case of family conflict, the lineage head called a family gathering at the chuep'si, where each person involved had a chance to speak before the spirits of the site. This event represented a dramatic deviation from the daily norm, since each wife and her children usually led a semiautonomous existence centered around the maternal kitchen/hut.[54] Each family member made his or her declaration of truth at the chuep'si and asked for divine punishment in case of falsehood within seven to nine days—by death, accident, or insanity.[55] The sacred altar in the compound also served as a site for the reading of an elder lineage head's final will and testament in the presence of witnesses and descendants from the compound. Those presiding over these ceremonies poured raffia wine on the sacred ground to seal the alliance between those speaking their truths and the living human and the unseen witnesses present.

The French administration introduced radical changes in the justice system for Grassfielders, but only in matters the French sought to legislate (see below). Throughout the period of foreign administration, truth-telling practices and conflict resolution continued on the sacred sites in chieftaincies throughout the Bamileke region. The presence of unseen witnesses was crucial to the administration of justice, and in the 1950s, Bamileke upécistes employed truth-telling ceremonies and oathing practices on sacred sites to ensure the loyalty of their members.[56]

The chieftaincy government could not monopolize the spiritual powers dwelling in the chuep'si. Sacred sites were accessible to anyone, rich or poor, titled notable or commoner. Even individuals accompanied by a spiritualist authorized to officiate at a given site could approach the chuep'si to offer a sacrifice to Si, make a confession or supplication, ask for protection from harm, or declare his or her own innocence in personal matters that for some reason could not be brought before family or community authorities. One could also take a vow before the sacred altar, establishing an alliance with Si. The spiritual punishments for lying at a sacred site were so severe—infertility, illness, or death—as to ensure that only those who knew themselves to be innocent spoke before the gods at the sacred sites. To Grassfielders a just man was one who could stand and affirm his truth before a chuep'si, one who walked a straight path (*djie dandan*).[57]

No one addressing the gods at a chuep'si came empty handed, although the quality of the gift depended on the supplicant's material wealth. In the official chieftaincy ceremonies, officiates offered a domestic animal or fowl. People of lesser means brought palm oil, kola, salt, djem djem, or raffia wine—staples indigenous to the Grassfields region. Wild game or plants could not be offered, but only plants and animals dependent on humans for their care. Offerings were thus symbolic of the link between the world of the living cultivated and tamed by humans, and the wild, unregulated domain of nature, presided by spirits. These same elements—goats, hens, kola, raffia wine, and salt—also were used in legal and commercial transactions throughout the Grassfields, for any negotiated contract or alliance: pledges of loyalty to a fo, matters of trade, marriage, and justice.

In sum, the chuep'si symbolized a standard of justice, whether on an individual, family, or community level. They symbolized the community's historic juridical norms, resolved conflict, and protected the group spiritually.[58] They legitimized living settlers' occupancy of the land, signified chieftaincy law, and were the locus of the negotiation of legal contracts.

They also served external purposes. As the material and spiritual location of the continuity of gung, in times of political crisis or war, community sacred sites preserved and protected a chieftaincy without a fo. For example, Kamdem Guemdjo, the eighth fo of Baham (whose rule began around 1890), went into exile for nine years to escape a plot arranged by members of his own family who reproached him for not having produced an heir since his enthronement. During his absence, guardians of sacred sites made sacrifices to implore the gods to bring back their fo.[59] Also, during the period of mourning following the death of a reigning fo, the population prayed to the *si la'a* or *si gung* dwelling in the chuep'si to be with the successor, the new incarnation of power and authority.[60] During the fight for independence from French rule, chuep'si became sites of supplication for the gods' benevolence in the struggle for liberation from foreign rule, protection for freedom fighters evading arrest, and, after the violence, reconciliation.[61]

Certainly, the uses of major sacred sites, their role in Grassfields religious practice and political philosophy, and their significance to ordinary Grassfielders changed between the time of the chieftaincies' founding and the time of Cameroon's independence, as the inner workings of Grassfields governance adapted to European rule.[62] Colonial rule complicated Grassfields governance, widening the gap between the visible aspects of the chieftaincy's governmental institutions (such as the fo and his palace) and the secret dimensions of Grassfields political and spiritual power (chuep'si, spiritualists, and sacrificers), which were concealed from view and misunderstood, neglected, or ignored by Europeans, the region's most recent newcomers.

The Germans had only begun to occupy the Grassfields when the First World War broke out. Their rule in the Grassfields was characterized by chaos and upheaval as German administrators tried to establish regional paramount chiefdoms, such as Bali-Nyonga, that overturned the network of rivalries and alliances in place in the area.[63] Germans allied with the chiefs they deemed "paramount" to recruit laborers en masse to build roads and railways and to work on vast concessionary plantations in the Mungo River valley.[64] After the war, German Cameroon (Kamerun) became League of Nations mandate territories to be administered by the French and British, and the Grassfields were divided by the Anglo-French boundary delineated in 1919 at the Conference of Versailles.[65]

The French did not begin to administer their League of Nations mandate in the Bamileke region (as they called the eastern Grassfields) until the early 1920s. Dazzled by the royal accouterments of the fo, administrators failed to fully understand the political influence of gung's secret associations, or the balance of power among the fo, the notables, and spiritualists. They failed, too, to take into account the political significance of the landscape's spiritual potency and its importance in the administration of justice. The section that follows explores the clash of understandings between Bamileke populations and French administrators hastily erecting a stopgap government in the region.

THE FRENCH ADMINISTRATION'S ASSIMILATIVE PULL IN THE BAMILEKE REGION

Perhaps nowhere was colonial law more haphazardly applied than in Cameroon. The French arrived in French Cameroon and French Togo late, decades after colonization of their other territories in Africa. From 1919, with the delineation of the Anglo-French boundary, French administrators in French Cameroon began trying to catch up with their counterparts in other parts of Africa. The high commissioner in Cameroon relied on directives, briefs, and reports from French West Africa and French Equatorial Africa to cobble together policy in the newly acquired territory. In 1917 a landmark circular written by Governor General Joost Van Vollenhoven of Dahomey suggested the necessity of incorporating traditional chiefs into French "direct administration,"[66] and encouraged the renovation of "native command" to shape it into an instrument of collaborative rule for the French government in African territories.

Having almost no information from the German administration to aid in establishing their rule over Bamileke populations, French administrators had to begin their negotiations with Bamileke chiefs and their codification of Bamileke laws from scratch. The basis for their perceptions of Bamileke chiefs as absolute rulers was a single fragmentary ethnographic report from 1914.[67] According to the report, Grassfields society was "based on the absolute authority of the chief, master of subjects and land. Each territory is divided into quarters of unequal importance, governed by noblemen. If the chief meets with these noblemen, it is to hear their account of the execution of his orders. Each decision belongs exclusively to him."[68] The French administration's mission was clear. If they were to follow the tone implied by Van Vollenhoven's 1917 directive, they would have to shape traditional chiefs into dependable auxiliaries in a French administration. In so doing, not only would they conform to an overarching, rational French colonial policy but they would also fulfill the terms of their League of Nations mandate, demonstrating that as administering authorities they were more just than their German predecessors. They could also show up their British counterparts, who were severely understaffed and did not begin to establish an administration in the western Grassfields until 1924, and thus were unable to put a stop to slave trading in the region.[69]

In 1920, the year after the Treaty of Versailles defined the boundary between the British Cameroons and French Cameroon, French administrators began to add their own ethnographic descriptions of ritual customs and practices to the sparse information on the Grassfields. Of course these preliminary reports, based on scant observation and hearsay, conveyed little accurate understanding of Grassfields political philosophy, spirituality, or administration of power and justice. But boasting of their achievements, French administrators reported their successful liberation of the population from the "ferocious exigencies" of the "feared and cruel" chiefs. Having banished corporal punishment, they described a transformation in the attitude of the chiefs: "They are no longer the kind of feudal lords that they were, invested with absolute power, but rather they are often valuable auxiliaries of our administration, and soon they will have no other prestige than that derived from the position of functionary."[70] By 1927 the annual report to the League of Nations indicated that the French administration had, "at the request of the oppressed populations, managed to change a feudal regime into a well-controlled system of indirect administration and to transform tyrannical dynastic heirs into" delegates whose power was derived solely from the French administration.[71] But the 1927 report overstated the reality as tensions over the traditional chiefs' legitimacy and power continued to unfold, particularly in the Bamileke Region, for the duration of the period of French rule.

As French administrators "civilized" the chiefs beginning in the 1920s—primarily by eliminating their capacity to make war, changing the system of justice and punishment of crime, shifting the balance of power among notables, and reinventing the institution of marriage—they slowly began to assimilate them into the French administration as functionaries, in keeping with French policy toward chiefs who wielded a significant amount of power and authority over their subjects.[72] Throughout the 1920s the role of traditional chiefs according to French colonial policy was to assist administrators with labor recruitment, taxation, census taking, and control of settlement patterns. In the Bamileke Region, where traditional chiefs historically had wielded a great influence in these realms, the French began to depose *mfo* who did not conform to administrative policy.

Soon after the military conquest of the eastern Grassfields in the First World War, Pouokam I became fo of Baham. He succeeded the formidable fo Kamdem II, who had upheld the lepue ideal by waging three wars, thereby extending his territory to the north, west, and south, and had initially refused to submit to German rule. After his predecessor's military exploits, Pouokam I's prohibition from making war underscored the diminution of his power under foreign rule. During the first few years of mandate rule, the chief was liable to being tried in court, further diminishing his stature. As an agent of the administration, Pouokam I was required to collect taxes—ten francs per woman and fifteen francs per man—and to supply labor for European plantations in the Mungo Region.

In 1925, Pouokam I asked the French administration to intervene in Baham's favor in a land dispute with neighboring Bandjoun. The French upheld what they believed to be the status quo and did not support Pouokam I's claims. In 1927, perhaps to regain prestige in the eyes of his people, Pouokam I attacked Fo Komguem III of Bayangam,[73] and for that transgression was sentenced by the French in 1928 to three years in prison and twenty years of exile from the chieftaincy.[74] He never reigned as fo again. The same year, after negotiations between the French administration and kamveu, with Pouokam I still in prison, his son Max Kamwa began to serve as fo. Kamwa remained fo until his death in 1954.⁷⁵ Many inhabitants of Baham believe that Kamwa "sold" his father to French administrators to ensure his own succession, suggesting either that Pouokam I had not yet named his heir, or that Kamwa and his French supporters disregarded the legitimate successor.

Soon after the arrest and imprisonment of Pouokam I of Baham, the French deposed another fo, Nono Tchoutouo of Bangwa, in the Nde. Suspicious of Tchoutouo's earlier loyalty to the Germans, the French administration charged him with failing to transfer the taxes he collected to the proper authorities, and misappropriating land from its rightful occupants for his wives' fields. Tchoutouo also found it increasingly difficult to stand up to his brothers, formerly soldiers under the German regime, who sought a portion of his wealth.⁷⁶ In 1931 a young literate Christian, Jean Nana, former student of the Société des missions évangéliques de Paris, "succeeded in having the old Nono exiled and having himself named chief in his place by the administration. He is thus legally the chief, but in reality he is not [the chief]."⁷⁷

Nana had served the administration as scribe and interpreter for four years before overthrowing Fo Nono by using the administration as his leverage. However, according to medical missionary Dr. Josette Débarge, despite Nana's baptism, he "did not dare" to live in the empty chief's palace, knowing that the fo's ancestral skulls were housed there and that "the power of the totems belong[ed] to the legitimate chief Nono."⁷⁸ Furthermore, Nana was not initiated as fo with the usual ritual ceremonies since Fo Nono was still living and succession rites could take place only after his death. The inhabitants of Bangwa called the real Fo Nono "our father," and called Nana simply Jean. Villagers obeyed Jean out of fear, Débarge continued, for "behind him he has the power of the whites. But the true devotion and notion of belonging go to the old exiled chief."⁷⁹ Débarge concluded that villagers were sad and disoriented, and that the incident proved that the chief's authority came from mystical powers derived from the spirit of the land and of ancestral chiefs: "He is chief by divine right."⁸⁰

The depositions of mfo and the irregular successions left residual conflicts that smoldered beneath the surface long after the event, and French administrators overlooked the spiritual repercussions that Débarge alluded to. A successor enstooled while the legitimate ruler was still alive lacked the political and popular support required to govern the chieftaincy effectively. By disconnecting the fo from the governmental institutions that ensured his right to rule and from the notables and ritual specialists who "made" him, the French sought to replace those legitimizing institutions with their own administration. In so doing, they fostered the fo's dependence on a foreign government. While this may have increased the fo's administrative authority within the context of colonial rule, it also effectively increased the importance of the secret spiritual and magical institutions that formed a part of Grassfields governance.

French administrators became aware of mystical secret associations early in the mandate period but misunderstood their relationship to the institution of the *fo* and therefore underestimated their role in chieftaincy governance. A French administrative report from around 1920, entitled simply "Ritual Customs," described secret societies of "fetishists and free spirits, thirsting for riches and dominance,"[81] who had to commit a "ritual murder against someone close to [them] in order to be let in on the secret of the fetish medicine," and who would rather face death than reveal their secrets.[82] Despite its cursory knowledge of the existence of secret associations, the French administration deliberately excluded them from the system of indirect administration they were building,[83] in part because they misunderstood the logic of constitutional restraint imbued in these institutions. French administrators oversimplified the secret associations by equating *secret* and *mystical* with *evil*. While malefic associations did exist, the majority of secret associations served as regulatory societies whose purpose was to adjust and maintain the balance of power in gung. The associations' secret activity protected them from a potentially despotic fo—if he did not know who challenged him, he could not punish or penalize. At the same time, the members of the associations, unknown to the population at large, could not use their position to challenge or usurp power from the fo. The structure of the regulatory associations helped to relegate confrontation between powerful community leaders to the realm of secrecy, hidden from public view. The result was to preserve a public façade of strong, unified governance, while maintaining a system of checks and balances within the chieftaincy's institutions of rule.

In the early 1930s overall French colonial policy toward "native command" shifted when the governor general of French West Africa, Jules

Brévié, issued a circular opposing the assimilation of chiefs into the administration and stressing the importance of the "traditional character of the institution [of the chieftaincy]" and of the chief as "representative of the population."[84] However, in French Cameroon, the administration's intent to position itself as the source of the traditional chiefs' legitimacy continued throughout the 1930s, evolving into one of consolidation and homogenization of the category they viewed as an essential administrative class. Administrators sought to reorder rural life by adjusting structures of traditional governance, namely by limiting some chiefly powers while strengthening others, by reducing or augmenting a chief's power vis-à-vis his notables in Bamileke chieftaincies, and by establishing schools for chiefs' sons with an eye to assimilating future traditional chiefs through education. Administrators in Cameroon justified the deviation from French colonial policy in the annual report to the League of Nations in 1933 by presenting "native command" in equatorial central Africa as almost nonexistent, since "in Central Africa" there was "no history of empires," but only the "law of small tribal chiefs supported by witchcraft practices."[85]

In 1933, French administrators classified indigenous chiefs of French Cameroon hierarchically as superior chiefs (*chefs supérieurs*), settlement chiefs (*chefs de groupement*), or village chiefs (*chefs de village*), contradicting Brévié's philosophy.[86] By imposing an administrative hierarchy on chiefs in the Bamileke Region, the French implied that superior chiefs were more powerful than village chiefs. The administration used the census of the fo's subjects as a quantifying factor, but in Grassfields politics, a polity's degree of sovereignty (lepue), not the size of its population, defined a chieftaincy's power and influence within the region. The 1933 decree also gave French administrators the right to name chiefs, although "whenever possible, tradition should be respected." Nevertheless, the decree made official the administration's right to intrude on successions in Bamileke chieftaincies.[87] Also in 1933, schools for the sons of chiefs were established by administrative decree at Yaoundé, Dschang (the capital of the Bamileke Region), Domé, Edea (in the Sanaga-Maritime), and Garoua (in the north of French Cameroon).[88] The creation of special elementary schools for the sons of chiefs reflected administrators' desire to standardize the educational level of the traditional authorities, who would "become, in the future, our collaborators."[89]

Despite Brévié's stated shift in French colonial policy, which emphasized custom and tradition as the legitimate sources of traditional chiefs' authority to rule, in the Bamileke Region of French Cameroon, the administration's primary objectives remained taxation, labor recruitment, and the resettlement of populations from the Bafoussam area (Mifi) to the left bank of the Noun River (Nde). From the viewpoint of French administrators, a chief's quality as a ruler was determined by his ability to raise the requisite tax. Because of the balance of power between the mfo and the district heads in Bamileke chieftaincies, French local administrators dissatisfied with the tax revenue found that they could bypass the fo and rely directly on his mfonte and mwabo.[90] If the fo was uncooperative, the French supported a new district head of their own choosing to replace the one named by the fo. Yet their interventions did not always achieve the desired outcome.

In 1934, Fo Nganjong of Bandrefam replaced a wabo, Ouambo Nzezip, with an eight-year-old boy and his regent, and began to send his armed guards (*tchindas*) to notables' compounds to collect taxes. The fo's coercive tax collection methods caused a number of inhabitants, including titled notables, to emigrate to neighboring chieftaincies in protest. Concerned by the exodus, the administration categorized Bandrefam as a problem chieftaincy. While on tour of the subregion, French subdivision chief Robert Gentil attempted to reconcile the fo and his notables in order to encourage emigrants to return to their village. Gentil reinstated the wabo, whom he described as not quite a model leader but one capable of keeping the inhabitants of his district from leaving to other chieftaincies. Two months later, when interviewing notables about the reconciliation process, Gentil discovered that twenty-three people had returned because the fo no longer sent tchindas to their homes to collect taxes. With a touch of sarcasm, Gentil remarked in his report, "Everything runs smoothly as long as our chief does not govern," clearly articulating the relationship between "native command" and tax collection in French administrative policy.[91]

Reading between the lines of Gentil's annual report, the notables' emigration can be seen as resistance to a fo who had overstepped what they perceived as an acceptable level of taxation in that district. It could be that the "problem district" was governed by a wabo who had historically been exempt from paying tribute to the chief's palace, as was the case with the Ngougoua District in Baham.[92] However, with the increasing taxation imposed under French rule, Fo Nganjong had gambled that the administration would support his position and seized an opportunity to bring Wabo Nzezip's district firmly under his command by forcibly collecting taxes. By leaving the chieftaincy, the notables in the problem district of Bandrefam communicated their refusal to submit (lepue) to the fo's exploitative taxation methods, leaving Fo Nganjong unable to meet the required tax quota.

Subdivision chief Gentil did not take the time to evaluate the reasons for the fo's deposition of the wabo or to learn the identity of his eight-year-old successor (which would have told us a great deal about the breakdown in power and the fo's strategies for its reconstruction). Instead, Gentil simply "reinstated" the leader he believed best suited to the regime's objectives at the time—curtailing unauthorized emigration and collecting revenue. He thereby reinforced the notion that the fo was not capable of governing his chieftaincy, and increased the notables' power in relation to the fo's. Gentil's decision also displaced the source of the notables' legitimacy from the fo to the French administration. But, the French, like Fo Nganjong, overplayed their hand: restoring the wabo to his position may have stemmed the emigration from Bandrefam, but taxes remained uncollected.

In contrast to Bandrefam, Bandjoun, one of the first chieftaincies in the area to submit to European rule, was a model of successful tax collection. The cooperation of Fo Kamga of Bandjoun allowed administrators to congratulate themselves for following the French colonial policy du jour in the matter of native command. Citing his "close relationship" with Fo Kamga, Gentil reported that the fo accepted that his mfonte collect taxes for 1935. Gentil expected that that would increase Kamga's authority, since he would find himself "in the simple roles of arbitrator and guardian of customs in the chieftaincy, and no longer in that of tax collector."[93] Fo Kamga was left to govern the internal affairs of his chieftaincy unhindered by French intrusion, thus preserving the polity's autonomy to a degree.

The French administration's inability to manipulate the workings of traditional governance to their advantage was best illustrated by the failure of the resettlement project on the left bank of the Noun River. French regional chief Ripert launched the project in 1925 in Dschang to address overpopulation in the Bamileke Region, to encourage the commercial production of coffee, raffia palm and kola nut, and to channel migration toward unsettled land in the Bamileke Region, rather than toward the Mungo Region connecting the area to the port city of Douala. The administration's pet project in the Bafoussam subdivision for over a decade, resettlement proceeded slowly, and only three mfo appeared to cooperate: Fo Kamga of Bandjoun, Fo Kamwa of Baham (who owed his position to French intervention as mentioned above), and Fo Komguem of Bayangam.[94] As part of the strategy, administrators selected notables to serve as chiefs of the new settlements, arranged by chieftaincy of origin: Baham II, Bandjoun II, Bamendjou II, and so on.[95]

The new "villages" were settled by district, each with its district chief. The local French administrator soon dismissed and replaced these satellite district chiefs for being "incapable of governing," for having coffee plantations that did not conform to agricultural standards, or for being unable to maintain a minimum number of families in the new settlement.[96] The Noun project eventually fizzled out, mostly for lack of enthusiasm among the mfo.[97] Gentil remarked in his report that, should chiefs prove hostile to the project, "we should bypass them and rely on their notables in the left bank," and entice a nobility leadership to collaborate by offering them free coffee seedlings.[98] But by 1935 it became clear that the district chiefs selected to govern the new settlements had no authority over their populations.

French administrators had been certain that by building a replicate model of "traditional" structures of Bamileke governance, complete with a reigning fo and his mfonte, they could ensure the success of the settlement project. But the project's failure demonstrated French ignorance of the essential ingredients the governance of gung. For example, nothing had been done to domesticate the spiritual landscape and render it habitable. By 1935 an unusually high mortality rate due to high infection by malaria appeared to be evidence of a lack of divine benevolence in the area, and the resettled population lacked spiritual advocates or the sites on which to offer sacrifices. A massive emigration from the Noun area began after 1935. Inhabitants of Baham II actually preferred to seek refuge in chieftaincies bordering Baham rather than risk being sent back to Baham II by Fo Kamwa, a French protégé, and, not coincidentally, one of the project's most loyal supporters.[99]

The French administration played on what they perceived as a dialectic of power in gung between the fo and the notables. But it is too simple to suggest that they reinforced the fo's power to the detriment of the nobility and spiritualists in gung.[100] In many cases, they minimized the power of the fo in favor of a district head who conformed to taxation policies or who could curb unauthorized migration. At the same time, French policies opened up new political opportunities for notables and chiefs, who saw in the French administration a new variable that could affect the precarious balance of power in their chieftaincy. As French policies toward native command shifted, the malleability of chieftaincy governance afforded new political platforms on which an ambitious notable could reinvent himself and reposition his lineage vis-à-vis the chief's palace.

In 1941, French Equatorial Africa governor general Félix Eboué's circular announced a new shift in administrative policy, which amounted to an effort to restore traditional chiefs to the prestigious position they held before European occupation. Eboué wrote, "The chief is not a functionary, he is an aristocrat. The best functionary with the highest rank is not comparable to the chief."[101] Eboué's study recognized the chief's supporting religious and traditional institutions as the foundation of his authority: "No council should be omitted, no guardian overlooked, no religious taboo neglected."[102] Eboué had come to understand, as many colonial administrators did not, that French attempts to make their own administration the source of the chief's legitimacy constituted a flawed policy. In fact, there is some evidence that he had understood this for at least two decades, but had had to await his promotion to governor general before articulating his understanding as policy.[103] However, Eboué's study appeared in the twilight of colonialism, after the chieftaincy's supporting institutions had been reconfigured during decades of foreign administration. In the Bamileke Region, where French administrators had focused primarily on the fo as the figurehead of power and government in the chieftaincy, it was too late for them to retrieve and integrate his supporting religious institutions into the "traditional chieftaincy" they had conceived. The French administration had, mostly unwittingly, already separated the visible symbols of rule and its concealed, religious, or mystical forms.

The Second World War interrupted Governor General Eboué's proposed change in attitude toward "native command" before it came to fruition. In 1946, French Cameroon and the British Cameroons became United Nations trust territories, to be administered according to the UN Charter and the UN trusteeship agreements. Article 76 of the charter, the most crucial to Cameroonian nationalists, placed an expiry date on European rule by stating that the administering authorities' must lead their territories on a path of "progressive development towards self-government or independence." In 1947 the French administration in Cameroon released a decree designating chiefs as members of the public function.[104] In late 1948 the high commissioner stated that, as intermediaries, traditional chiefs were to be representatives of both their populations and the French administration. This assertion cast aside Eboué's contention that the chief's legitimacy before his people came, not from his association with colonial power, but rather from sacred institutions, relatively unknown to European administrators.

CUSTOMARY LAWS AND FRENCH LEGAL CODES

In the 1920s and 1930s the French administration wielded little influence on the justice system within Bamileke chieftaincies because most civil matters continued to be resolved at the level of chieftaincy, district, or compound. Beginning in 1921 French officials worked to integrate local justice into the newly created *tribunaux des races*, an "African" court system under French surveillance. By 1935 the "African" justice system in Cameroon was to apply "local" law in civil matters and to replace a "barbaric" penal code that allowed corporal punishment, torture, and execution with a "civilized" French penal code of prison sentences and forced labor. In the Bamileke Region in the early 1930s, local French administrators compiled a "customary penal code" describing "customary sanctions" and "customary punishments in criminal matters." The code included a list of seventy-three articles, with a second column designating the suggested equivalent "civilized" punishment.[105] The document, which became the basis for the codification of laws in administrative courts, made no mention of the truth-telling ceremony, the chuep'si, or the spiritual aspects of justice in the region. Still, whenever possible, justice continued to be administered locally within the chieftaincy. In the 1930s, Reverend R. P. Albert, a French missionary in Bandjoun, wrote that sentences were frequently "rendered at the chieftaincy, or in secret in the villages, that the administration can only suspect, and that consist of peculiar practices and unexpected punishments."[106]

After the Second World War, the French administration sought to codify "customary law" as a precursor to creating a uniform legislative structure that could be applied across the entire territory of Cameroon. A law passed on April 30, 1946 brought all penal matters into French courts. The changes imposed by the French administration removed justice from the context provided by gung's particular landscape and history and brought it into a regional judiciary space shared by the people of Bandjoun, Bamendjou, Bayangam, Bangou, and Bafoussam. The artificial separation of civil and penal affairs made little sense, since Bamileke inhabitants did not differentiate between the two, and the financial means and the identity of the accused and the accuser were no longer taken into consideration when considering the case or sentencing. The accused no longer had to fear the spiritual power of the fo, those officiating the trial, or the unseen witnesses present, but found himself free of mystical repercussions. In short, in Grassfields moral and ethical terms, it became spiritually, politically, and socially acceptable to lie at one's trial. The most dangerous of crimes, those performed in secret or at night, such as vampirism or other sorts of mystical wrongdoing, fell outside the scope of the administration's penal system.[107]

French policies in matters of administration, taxation, and justice affected the practice of traditional Grassfields power as well as the way it acted on ordinary inhabitants of the Grassfields chieftaincies. Throughout much of the colonial and mandate periods, juniors and untitled men who historically had to work hard and wait long periods before being granted a nobility title or even being allowed to establish a compound and marry, were increasingly cut off from channels to social mobility.[108] The social hierarchy throughout the region became increasingly top heavy under foreign rule as cooperative chiefs—to whom European administrators turned to impose taxes and recruit laborers—benefited most from a proximity to territorial administration.

By the 1920s, the beginning of the official mandate period of French rule, the gap between "big" notables at the top of the sociopolitical hierarchy and "small," lesser notables or untitled commoners who were excluded from access to wealth and privilege was larger than it had ever been.[109] Previous scholarship has emphasized the reaction of young men or youths to the obstacles that an ever more dominant nobility system placed in the way of their path to adulthood.[110] Certainly, a few young, untitled men did use new opportunities provided through mission or French schooling, becoming part of a Christian mission community, the implementation of a plantation economy, and urbanization—all modernizing elements of the colonial order—to resist the chiefs' appropriation of their labor and access financial and social success directly.[111] But in the interwar period, with only 1,290 students enrolled in French regional schools in 1922 and 2,074 in 1932 (out of a total population of 2,223,000), access to social mobility via education was extremely limited.[112] A series of church and mission closures swept the Bamileke chieftaincies of French Cameroon during the mid-1920s, reducing still further alternative opportunities to social advancement in the region.[113]

While social juniors' and commoners' tentative embrace of the modern institutions introduced under European rule did little to curtail the mfo's growing power, the front line of resistance against the rise in chiefly excesses during the colonial and mandate periods—especially in those chieftaincies, such as Bandjoun, where the fo had willingly allied with colonial administrators—came from the ranks of the nobility. The first wave of depositions to sweep Bamileke chieftaincies came in the 1920s as French administrators set aside newly chosen heirs that notables' associations kamveu and kungang had selected and enstooled and replaced them with mfo more suitable to their liking. In Bandjoun in 1925, for example, the notables' choice of a legitimate heir, Bopda, was removed, exiled, and replaced with Joseph Kamga, who spoke German and French, had served as interpreter to the Bamileke Region's French commanders from 1919 to 1925, and who had converted to Christianity against the will of his father, Fotso Massudom, the fo who had first resisted, then allied with the Germans.[114] The selections of the notables overseeing succession suggested a resistance to the notion of fo as colonial ally. Even more telling was the regulatory associations' barely concealed, sometimes overt confrontation of Christian missions throughout the region in the 1920s. In 1923 in Bandjoun, for instance, members of a powerful regulatory association known as Nyeleng demanded that the fo close the church built near the northern entrance of the chief's compound.[115]

French administrators' attitudes toward traditional authorities in French Cameroon necessarily differed from region to region as political institutions ranged from the *lamidats,* such as Bornu and Baghermi in the Islamized north, characterized by centralized, even bureaucratized hierarchical governments, to the decentralized or "stateless" segmentary lineage societies of the southern forest regions.[116] Grassfields chieftaincies figured in the mid-range of this spectrum but throughout the colonial, mandate, and trusteeship periods, traditional authorities mostly preserved their power over their subjects. In a general way, French administrators relied on traditional political systems to govern the territory, particularly its rural areas. But given the varying strength of traditional governance from region to region, indirect administration through the chiefs was tailor made to each locale. Where traditional authority had been weakened or undermined by foreign rule, as among Duala populations, the French administration sought to shore it up, and where it was strong, administrative policy was to assimilate it.[117] Accordingly, because Bamileke mfo maintained authority over their populations only insofar as a tenuous balance of power vis-à-vis the nobility allowed them to do so, French administrators' policy toward traditional chiefs in the Bamileke Region was necessarily ambivalent. French administrators readily assimilated those mfo, such as Fo Kamga of Bandjoun, who dominated and controlled the institutions of chieftaincy government, while they were obliged to limit their assimilation of mfo who were less effectively dominant in matters of taxation, labor recruitment, and resettlement.

In the interstice between chiefly power and that of the nobility, a wedge grew between the visible workings of traditional governance and its invisible aspects. The material, physical representations of power included the person of the fo and his manner of dress, the spatial arrangement of his dwelling, the assembly hall, his wives' kitchens, and notables' meeting houses in the palace compound, and symbols of royalty such as the leopard skin, the copper bracelet, and the three-legged stool. The invisible, metaphysical workings of traditional power were made up of the secret associations of notables, the world of ké, animal totems and sacred sites mediated by spiritualists and sacrificers, and the hidden but remembered histories of some districts' or lineages' incomplete submission to the central palace. The unseen workings of power remained concealed beneath the surface and mostly unknown to outsiders, but they nevertheless formed a part of religious and political practice, history, cultural memory, and identity for Grassfielders. Although French administrators sought to govern through the seen, material symbols of the person of the chief, the unseen formed as much a part of the collective political imaginary for those residing in Bamileke chieftaincies, whether notable or commoner.

Struggles over the chieftaincy's balance of power were not new to Grassfields traditional governance. What was new was the French administration's assimilative pull toward the visible, material, bureaucratic institutions of state rationality including taxation, penal code, remuneration, census taking, and other record keeping. The emphasis on these administrative functions of government in turn led to compliant mfo's gradual alienation from the metaphysical, invisible forms of power that became even more the preserve of various notables, regulatory associations, and spiritualists. Many noncompliant mfo whom the French deposed were also cut off from the chieftaincy's spiritual realm of governance, leaving other institutions of the chieftaincy to repair the damage. The spiritual realm and the ability to mediate between the invisible and visible worlds became ever more crucial to sustaining the lepue ideal. Faced with these changes to traditional governance imposed by foreign rulers, for truly important matters of governance, Bamileke populations began to turn toward the less visible facets of power, that is, to institutions outside the realm of the chief's palace—chuep'si, *mkamsi* (diviners or healers), regulatory societies, or district heads. These peripheral institutions maintained distance from the foreign occupying power that forced the fo to submit and to wield his executive power to impose taxes and draft laborers.

Ordinary inhabitants of Bamileke chieftaincies could access the spiritual realm as well, and could thus draw directly on various spiritual technologies to attempt to temper the growing inequalities that characterized their relationship to their mfo. Versatile and accessible, the politicospiritual realm provided an essential lubricant for the articulation between UPC nationalism and Grassfields political culture in the 1950s. As shown in the next chapter, the metaphysical aspects of Grassfields power were those that proved most essential to emigrants as they departed their home chieftaincies. Most emigrants, even those seeking to escape the restrictive social controls that allegiance to their home chieftaincies imposed on them, took care to ensure their continued access to the sacred sites and ancestral graves they had left behind. At the same time, migration to the Mungo River valley to labor in commercial agriculture or take up commerce offered more opportunities than ever before for social cadets to benefit from new pathways to wealth and social mobility generated by participation in the tangible, material reality of a colonial plantation economy.

2 ～ "Bamileke Strangers" Make the Mungo River Valley Their Home

INITIALLY RECRUITED to the Mungo River valley as laborers to build the railroad under German rule, Grassfielders began to arrive as early as the turn of the twentieth century. After the completion of the railroad, they continued to migrate to work as field hands in Duala-owned plantations around Mbanga.[1] From the 1930s, with the introduction of bananas and coffee as cash crops, Bamileke immigration to the Mungo River valley increased significantly.[2] French administrators applied the term Bamileke to Grassfielders who came from the chieftaincies of the Bamileke Region, the portion of the Grassfields that fell under French rule after the delineation of the Anglo-French boundary, in 1919. A "Bamileke identity," entirely absent before French rule, emerged during the interwar period, primarily in the Mungo Region, as a result of a fluid interplay between the administration's classification of "races" and the African populations' agency when it came to defining ethnic identity.[3] As French administrators in the Mungo Region used the term Bamileke more frequently from the 1930s onward, Bamileke populations gradually assumed this identity and began to assert themselves as belonging to a larger Bamileke collectivity when it suited them.

Language used to describe the settlement and transformation of the Mungo Region during the colonial and mandate periods must necessarily reflect the plurality and changeability of identities. Accordingly, this chapter makes use of the term Grassfielders to identify migrants to the Mungo Region before the 1930s, when the term Bamileke began to be used to designate newcomers from the Grassfields under French rule. It should be noted, however, that when speaking indigenous languages, Bamileke inhabitants of the Mungo Region today most often employ the term Grafi, derived from pidgin English, the lingua franca of the region, to refer to the ensemble of Bamileke populations. The decentralized host populations indigenous to the Mungo Region include multiple groups: Balondo, Bakaka, Mouamenam, Baneka, Miamilo, Bakossi, Abo, Elong, and others. The word *autochthonous* is used here to designate the indigenous populations of the Mungo Region, while the term Mbo is used occasionally to refer to the autochthonous populations in the area around Nkongsamba (the region's capital).[4]

By 1947, Bamileke newcomers made up roughly 33 percent of the Mungo's overall population, and by 1955, some 54 percent of Mungo inhabitants were of Grassfields origin, the majority of whom were from the Bamileke Region.[5] Their settlement of the Mungo coincided with that of European farmers during the interwar period. With one hundred and ten European-owned plantations extending over nearly twenty-three hundred square kilometers out of a total surface area of thirty-seven hundred square kilometers at the high-water mark of the white-settler presence in the reason (during and just after World War II), the Mungo Region hosted the largest number of European agricultural settlers in the territory.[6] Conflicts over the most fertile lands arose between Europeans and Africans—both those indigenous to the region and those arriving from elsewhere. During the mandate and trusteeship periods, Mungo-based planters, regardless of origin, competed over resources, and the resulting tensions were exacerbated by administrative policies that established ethnic identity as a factor determining access to land as well as by discriminatory regulations of cash-crop agriculture that favored European planters.[7] Yet by the 1950s, Richard Joseph argues that "a class of Bamileke capitalist farmers had clearly emerged," in the Mungo Region, and Bamileke planters were producing a greater amount of coffee for export than their white-settler counterparts.[8] In contrast, the landholdings and agricultural productivity of the region's autochthonous populations as well as those of the Duala, who had been first among the region's African planters in the German and early French mandate periods, had shrunk to negligible quantities.[9]

Because landholdings in the region were in constant flux throughout the twentieth century, and since much of the land in the Mungo Region—particularly portions owned or occupied by autochthonous or Bamileke planters—went unregistered, it is difficult to provide a systematically inventoried account of the gross dimensions of land commercialization, of large-scale numbers of holdings, or of the total numbers of white settlers, African landowners, and migrants in the Mungo Region throughout the years. Studies of these matters do exist but are often focused on a particular portion of the heterogeneous Mungo Region,[10] or chart a short period rather than offering a chronological overview. Although precise figures are unavailable, it is possible to piece together a general overview of the evolution of land ownership and exploitation in the Mungo Region during French rule. The holdings of white, mostly French, settlers steadily climbed during the first fifteen years of the mandate period (beginning in 1922), but peaked in 1936. A third of the European-owned plantations in the region were owned by joint-stock companies that averaged two hundred hectares, although there were several between five hundred and one thousand hectares or even larger.[11] The Company of Plantations in Njombé-Penja reached thirteen hundred hectares,[12] where the Niabang plantation, northwest of Nkongsamba, eventually reached twenty-two hundred hectares.

In 1937, Governor Pierre Boisson, newly arrived, was faced with a labor shortage that would have required intensified conscription of laborers—in violation of the terms of the mandate system—at the very time that an increasing number of Cameroonian planters were becoming involved in cash-crop agriculture.[13] Worried too about German propaganda to retake the Cameroons, voiced in the form of critiques of French exploitation, Boisson stopped granting concessions to white settlers in the Mungo Region.[14] Accordingly, the number of agricultural workers declined by 25 percent in the Mungo Region, dropping from about ten thousand in 1935 to seventy-four hundred within two years, and white settlers found the expansion of commercial agriculture enterprise in the region severely curtailed, if not halted.[15] From the late 1930s until the outbreak of World War II, Bamileke planters, who had increased their holdings in the Mungo Region during the economic crisis that swept the territory at the turn of the decade, achieved a tenuous equilibrium vis-à-vis their European counterparts in the region; but the war, which led to an intensification of forced labor justified in the name of the "war effort," again tipped the balance in favor of white settlers.[16]

In the Mungo Region, where large numbers of Africans, especially settlers of Bamileke origin, acquired landholdings and became cash-crop farmers during the mandate period, restrictive land policies and commercial agriculture regulations, together with one of the highest proportions of agricultural workers—ten thousand out of a total of twenty-one thousand in French Cameroon were employed in the Mungo Region in 1935—promoted an interest in political organization and participation in labor unions and planters' cooperatives.[17] By 1946, when the postwar age of territorial politics dawned, the Mungo Region had become a forum for political, economic, and social activism. By 1952 the Mungo River valley was home to fifty African planters' cooperatives—more than twice the number in the Nyong and Sanaga Region, around Yaoundé, the territory's capital,[18] and had the highest rate of participation in local and territorial elections of any area outside Douala, French Cameroon's port city and largest urban settlement.[19]

At the end of the trusteeship period, the Mungo Region was a diverse and potentially explosive melting pot, and, via immigrants from the Bamileke Region, the channel through which UPC nationalist ideology merged with Grassfields political culture. This chapter recounts the Mungo Region's gradual transformation into a political catalyst in independence-era Cameroon. After first discussing French administrative policies and their effects on Bamileke populations' settlement of the Mungo Region, I demonstrate how, in the early mandate period, migrants and autochthons negotiated terms of land use and occupancy largely outside the French administration's control. The second part of the chapter examines migrants' organizational strategies and their consensus that family chiefs be selected to link their Mungo settlements to their home chieftaincies in the Bamileke Region. The third section reveals how Bamileke migrants, buoyed by their semiautonomous sociopolitical organization and financial independence, familiarized themselves thoroughly with administrative policies. That knowledge allowed them to gain an edge over Mungo autochthons as the French administration imposed stricter regulations on land distribution and agricultural methods in the region, and as administrators discursively pitted "autochthonous" populations against "strangers," or "Mbo" against "Bamileke." The chapter ends with an assessment of the postwar political and economic organization that began to spread throughout Mungo Region cities and towns.

GRASSFIELDERS IN THE MUNGO RIVER VALLEY

The entire Mungo valley region, nestled between the volcanic mountains of Nlonako, Kupé, and Manenguba and extending southward to the port city of Douala, provided an ideal settlement area for white, mostly French, colonists seeking small farms and plantations after the First World War.[20] European commercial planters exploited the region's fertile land and forests along the railroad to cultivate coffee, cocoa, bananas, palm oil, and rubber for export. In desperate need of laborers to work their plantations, French administrators, like their German predecessors, rounded up laborers from the Bamileke Region and put them to work in the fields.[21] Forced labor violated the terms of the mandate system, but nevertheless it regularly occurred throughout the interwar period in French Cameroon and increased during World War II.[22]

Although laborers were required to work on European plantations for only three months of the year before being allowed to return to their home chieftaincies,[23] the fertility of the black volcanic earth encouraged many of them to make arrangements with the indigenous population in order to stay by negotiating the terms of customary arrangements regarding land use and allotment.[24] The agreements the settlers reached with their autochthonous hosts specified terms for usufruct and occupancy, not for permanent ownership. Autochthonous populations who granted use of land to newcomers assumed, according to local understandings of land use, that land could only be loaned, not permanently sold or transferred, to strangers, as they called settlers from beyond the Mungo River valley.[25] Newcomers traded fish, cloth, salt, and palm or raffia wine for plots and also offered a portion of the harvest to their host.[26] Autochthonous landowners gave Grassfielders permission to use land as a form of remuneration for labor. In the early twentieth century, African owners of small plantations throughout the Mungo Region—many of whom were ethnic Duala from the coastal region around the port city of Douala—cultivated cacao as a cash crop for export, and employed laborers from the Grassfields, paying them with a percentage of the crop sales and allowing them to work their own plots of land on which they grew food.[27] This practice was reinforced on 1 April 1927, when French administrators passed a decree making it mandatory for planters to feed their laborers.[28]

Early contracts between Grassfielders and Mbo or Duala landowners were drawn up for a limited period, usually ten to thirty years. These contracts resembled a lease, with a specified departure date. The migrant sharecroppers agreed to provide their hosts with as much as 40 percent of the revenue from cash crops grown on the land.[29] Before the 1930s the French administration did not regulate Grassfielders' settlement in the area, and agreements between autochthons and immigrants were negotiated case by case. French administrators later sought to legislate these customary arrangements, as discussed below.

Food crops grew well in the Mungo River valley, making it easy for sharecroppers to practice subsistence farming. The climate and fertile earth allowed for two planting seasons a year for certain crops such as corn (harvested in December and in June). The earth yielded tubers easily—yellow and white yams, several varieties of potatoes, cassava, macabo, and taro (types of yams), as well as vegetable greens, hot peppers, and the tree from which *nkwi*, the Grassfields dish prepared especially for women after childbirth, was made. In many ways, the Mungo Region represented a promised land for immigrants from the Grassfields, who came from a place where the best lands were already occupied and the remaining impoverished lands were not suitable for farming.

As in the Grassfields, invisible inhabitants of the Mungo Region oversaw the land, but the newcomers had no knowledge of the autochthonous populations' cosmologies.[30] Since only the region's indigenous inhabitants could mediate on their behalf in an unknown spiritual landscape, immigrants required the permission of Mungo populations before settling. For Grassfielders, the use of land rested on a conceptual worldview in which the invisible inhabitants (gods, spirits, and ancestors) played a more significant role than living, breathing human beings when it came to the accessibility and distribution of land.[31] Migrants from the Grassfields could not found new chieftaincies in the Mungo Region under French rule; nor could they plant chuep'si in their Mungo compounds, for to do so, they would have had to rely on chieftaincy nobility and spiritualists who had not accompanied them into the new territory. Grassfields spiritual technology was mostly stationary because of its material attachment to the landscape, and that fixity ensured emigrants' continued connection with their chieftaincies of origin. Migrants needed to maintain their access to ancestral compounds and chuep'si, the essential facets of Grassfields spirituality, political culture, and identity. Since customary land contracts in the Mungo Region denoted, not permanent ownership, but the right to occupancy or usufruct, newcomers from Grassfields chieftaincies lacked the sense of permanence that came with spiritual land markers, graves, chuep'si, and trees linking them to their fathers' compounds in gung. Instead, land plots in the Mungo provided the means to financial self-sufficiency and wealth and were thus primarily of economic significance.[32]

Until the 1930s this system of land use and exchange was flexible and mutually beneficial, with landholders, planters, and merchants reaching agreements that met the specific financial needs of either party as they arose. The railway, the road, and the border with British territory all served to transform the Mungo River valley into a commercial system benefiting Africans, whose trading systems were only gradually and partially integrated into a colonial capitalist economy. The railway from Douala established Nkongsamba as an essential transit point for goods and merchants traveling to and from the Bamileke Region.[33] By the late 1920s, the completion of the road from Nkongsamba to Bafang facilitated access to Douala from the Bamileke Region. The city of Nkongsamba attracted merchants and producers of the essential staples that the African inhabitants of the northern Mungo consumed, including palm oil, kola, dried fish, and food crops. Nkongsamba became an entrepôt for a flourishing regional commerce independent of economic links to European settlement. Between 1947 and 1957, the town grew from some 13,500 inhabitants to a population of nearly 30,000 (nearly 19,000 of whom were of Bamileke origin).[34]

In the late 1920s, French and British administrators began to regulate commerce and the traffic of people and goods across the Anglo-French border that ran along the Mungo River, the western border of the region. Administrators required permission tickets for the purchase of imported goods like matches, soap, and cigarettes[35] and introduced customs points along the boundary between French and British territory. In the Mungo Region, French administrators turned their attention to controlling access to land, further limiting African economic autonomy.

Although French administrators turned a blind eye to negotiations between African planters and field hands during the 1920s, they passed a number of laws favoring European settlement, both in the plantations and in burgeoning town centers. In the early 1920s High Commissioner Théodore Marchand, anxious to win the approval of the League of Nations Permanent Mandates Commission (PMC), initially avoided granting immense plantations to European settlers. Instead, he approved parcels of one hundred to four hundred hectares for the development of "small-scale European colonization."[36] The number of individually owned plantations granted increased steadily during the first ten years of the mandate (1922–32), peaking at twenty-nine in 1929, and bringing the total number of hectares allotted to Europeans to 21,730, or about 3 percent of arable land.[37]

Marchand also encouraged settlement in regions other than the fertile Mungo valley: "Most planters are hypnotized by the Douala suburbs or crowd into the land along the railroad. They request only the parcels that have already been cleared by the indigenous population or even those that are already planted."[38] Marchand recognized that this trend reflected the settlers' desire to cut installation, labor, and transport costs, but, keeping League of Nations mandate terms in mind, he reserved the right to refuse settlers' requests for land that would constitute "a revocation of the rights of the original occupants and would justify their discontent."[39]

The French report to the PMC in 1926 cited the administration's decision not to increase the number of rural plantations larger than one thousand hectares in Cameroon. The commission lauded the decision, remarking that French land policy in the Mungo reflected the spirit of the mandate.[40] Throughout the 1920s, French administrators appeared to encourage African land ownership and cultivation as a way of developing the land commercially and providing a solution to the regional labor shortage through "an ever greater intensification of individual plantations that enables an efficient use of family labor."[41] By 1928 an administrator reported, "In two years, the land bordering the railway and the road will be entirely occupied and cultivated."[42] Remarking on "the liking Europeans have taken to agriculture," the report added, "the 'native' is not far behind. He follows the same trend, as much to keep the rights to his land—he is afraid that we will grant it to Europeans if he does not cultivate it—as to become a *colon* in his own right, to make money."[43] Cash-crop agriculture in the Mungo River valley attracted white settlers and African farmers alike.

Marchand's posturing for the PMC concealed the administrative policies and practices that privileged French planters and ensured their economic advantage over African planters in the Mungo. Complex zoning laws and a variable classification system restricted African access to the best agricultural lands and grazing lands. The first land decrees, passed in 1920 and 1921, defined the private and public domains of the state. The private domain, which included vast areas that administrators described as "vacant lands without owners," was classified as either urban or rural. A zoning plan established the size and spatial arrangement of lots for public service buildings, roads, avenues, and public squares, as well as district and subdivision headquarters, and divided the urban centers into segregated European and African quarters.[44]

Urban lots were made available to settlers on a provisional basis and were divided into three graded categories: premium A lots, greater than 2,000 square meters, which sold for 10 francs per square meter; intermediate B lots, from 100–200 m^2, which sold for 5 fr/m^2; and C lots, less than 20 m^2, which cost 5 fr/m^2.[45] As Nkongsamba became an official urban center on 16 May 1923 and subdivision capital on 30 September 1923, twenty of the thirty A lots went to Europeans. Africans obtained a greater number of the 120 B lots available; Bamileke migrants held half of them, while only three were assigned to the autochthonous population.[46] Rural lands outside urban perimeters were also divided into three categories: pasturage lands, used also for the cultivation of food crops, sold for 10 fr/ha; mid-level lands, used for the cultivation of cash crops for export, sold for 20 fr/ha; and premium lands, for the cultivation of cash crops for export (cacao, oil palms, coffee, and vanilla), sold for 30 fr/ha in 1921.[47]

Problems with land distribution and classification surfaced right away. Inhabitants of the Mungo Region had historically used many of the expropriated "vacant lands" for communal purposes, such as grazing livestock or gathering wood. Furthermore, European settlers in and near Nkongsamba circumvented administrative land policies as a matter of course. In 1930, High Commissioner Marchand wrote: "The creation of the Nkongsamba center, without any compensation for the natives, and the granting of new rural concessions side by side within the borders of the village, have reduced to a bare minimum the lands available to the autochthonous collectivity."[48] Admitting the administration's failure to adhere to its own policies, Marchand warned that in future prudence was called for in "attributing lands believed, erroneously, to be dominial, from within the boundaries of the indigenous collectivity of Nkongsamba."[49] No effort was made, however, to reverse the illegal settlement patterns in place or to compensate African landowners whose property had already been expropriated.

The administration granted provisional titles for both urban and rural lots, ensuring that ownership was conditional upon compliance with the *mise en valeur* (economic development) policy that characterized French colonialism throughout the 1920s.[50] In urban areas, this entailed an obligation to build, while in rural areas, provisional permits required landholders to use the land for its stated purpose as recorded in an official deed registry. If the parcel's temporary owner did not meet the administration's terms of development, which included productivity quotas and adherence to specific agricultural procedures for cash crops, the land could be revoked.

The productivity quotas set by the clerk of agricultural works and provisional land titles worked to the advantage of French settlers, by serving to justify French expropriation of African inhabitants' land. If an African planter failed to reach established quotas, he was forced to cede his land for minimal compensation. In a 1930 decision establishing the terms for purchase of land belonging to Essoa Ewane, an African plantation owner in the northern Mungo, Marchand described Ewane's cacao trees as poorly maintained, abandoned, and almost without value. Following the recommendation of the agricultural clerk, Marchand suggested that Ewane be paid twenty francs per tree rather than the legal standard of fifty francs,[51] adding, "If he refuses [the terms], Ewane will have to appear in civil court at his own risk and expense."[52] French planters had a greater familiarity with the agricultural standards required for exported crops. They also benefited from access to conscripted labor and from the administration's provision of financial grants or loans for the purchase of industrial farming equipment. Lacking these advantages, African planters often fell short of productivity quotas and, like Ewane, were forced to sell their farms at prices well below official cost.

Administrative land policies failed to prevent European settlers from encroaching on the "native reserves" the French administration had set apart to protect the land rights of indigenous populations. In 1925, regional administrators created a reserve for Mbo populations at the Plain of the Mbo, a "swampy, uninhabitable land" between the northern Mungo Region and Dschang, the administrative capital of the Bamileke Region, just to the east of the Anglo-French boundary. In subsequent years, the administration granted a number of large concessions in the region to French commercial agricultural enterprises, which gradually overtook reserved land. In 1928 the Niabang Company received a grant of 1,027 hectares, which diminished the reserve,[53] and the Nkongsamba-based Pastoral Company was granted 1,500 hectares of fertile land, and used additional pasture lands in the reserve on the slopes of Mount Manenguba for which it did not have a grant.[54]

In 1933, Chief Fritz Pandong of Mboroko formally protested the request of a French settler named Chollier for a plot of land in the Plain of the Mbo. Administrators were obliged to investigate. Marchand's successor, High Commissioner Paul Bonnecarrère, found that "today the reserve has become insufficient," due to the number of large concessions given out over the last few years.[55] Chollier's request was denied, but administrators nevertheless continued to dole out reserved land to European plantation owners. Faced with the limitations on settlement imposed by "native reserves," European planters in the northern Mungo solicited administrators' accommodation. To overcome legal restrictions on indigenous reserves such as the Plain of the Mbo, administrators had only to demonstrate occupants' apparent neglect or disuse.

French land distribution policies led to increased economic stratification throughout the 1920s. While most African planters cultivated less lucrative cacao on the more affordable, inferior plots, Europeans acquired the richest soils, and were well situated to profit from the coffee boom that began in the 1930s.[56] The size of European plantations increased dramatically by 1930, as white settlers used conscripted laborers to maintain the levels of productivity necessary to ensure the renewal of their deeds. While Europeans' plantations in 1922 totaled only 269 hectares, their holdings had increased to eighteen thousand hectares by 1930.[57] Only three Cameroonian planters—Isaac Tchoua and Isaac Bondja, immigrants from the Bamileke Region, and Martin Moulendé from the Douala area—met a sufficient number of the contingencies in place to be able to acquire ownership of European-style plantations.[58] But their plantations were comparatively much smaller than those of European settlers, measuring less than one hundred hectares, as compared to European farms of 325, 350 and 964 hectares. Most Cameroonian planters held small, unregistered plots on lands of inferior quality throughout the region and grew both cash crops and food crops.

From 1929 to 1934 an economic crisis linked to the Great Depression swept the Mungo Region, causing a drastic fall in the price of cacao and wiping out most of the African cacao planters in the region. Planters indigenous to the Mungo Region or from the coastal region of Douala, previously the dominant African cash-crop planters in the Mungo valley, were the hardest hit by the economic upheaval. But Bamileke migrants, who had the very economic and social networks necessary to succeed despite administrative policies that disadvantaged African land ownership, were able to increase their landholdings during the economic crisis.[59] Throughout the 1920s, autochthonous and Duala cacao farmers employed Grassfields sharecroppers as laborers, paying them with a percentage of the crop sales and allowing them to work their own plots of land. When the price of cacao plummeted in 1929, autochthonous landowners who could no longer afford to pay their laborers offered portions of their land, or sometimes wives, to migrants, to make good on their debts. Planters of Bamileke origin drew on family and patronage networks in their chieftaincies of origin to attract dependants to work in their fields for social rather than monetary compensation.[60] These unpaid workers provided Bamileke planters with a labor force unavailable to indigenous landowners, who had smaller families and a lower rate of demographic reproduction, as well as fewer social restrictions that juniors had to overcome before being allowed by their elders to marry. Furthermore, the relative abundance of land in the less densely populated Mungo Region meant that land inheritance was not restricted to one sole heir—who had worked hard to prove himself worthy of succeeding his father—as it was in the Grassfields. With fewer numbers and fewer incentives to distinguish themselves through the acquisition of wealth or winning favor with elder notables, autochthonous social cadets were less motivated to work for their elders than were their Bamileke peers.[61] By the end of the crisis, in 1934, nearly all autochthonous and Duala plantation owners had been dispossessed of their plantations, while a number of migrants from the Bamileke Region had acquired land and had set about taking the necessary steps to register it as private property.[62] In so doing, they often met with legislative obstacles, however.

On 21 July 1932, when discussions of "customary law" were in vogue in French colonies across the globe, a decree was passed to protect the rights of African landowners, but it specified that the legislation be applied to "autochthonous" collectivities, according to the terms of "local customary law."[63] Increasingly conscious of their portrayal as strangers in the Mungo after the 1930s land reforms, Bamileke migrants were the first to register deeds, buy up the remaining cheap A-grade parcels of land, and try their hands at growing coffee, bananas, and cacao as cash crops. But when Bamileke landowners applied for registered deeds, French administrators often refused to recognize customary contracts negotiated between the migrants and their autochthonous hosts[64] and throughout the 1930s rendered them invalid on the grounds that immigrant settlers were "strangers."[65] At Sadrack Kamtche's request for the recognition of ownership, the district chief of the small town of Loum-Chantiers skeptically declared that, "being a stranger to the country,"

Kamtche could not have acquired the land according to local customary law. Before validating his claims to ownership of the parcel in question, Kamtche would have to produce a copy of the "deed establishing his right to the parcel he is claiming."[66]

THE ETHNICIZATION OF LAND OWNERSHIP IN THE MUNGO RIVER VALLEY

Although land ownership policies had been designed in theory to protect African landholdings, in practice they often opened up additional opportunities for European settlers to acquire land. A further result, most significantly for the Mungo Region, was that administrators' refusal to recognize customary agreements fostered tensions between Bamileke immigrants and "autochthonous" populations by overriding agreements in place and assigning immutable labels and qualities—based on ethnic identity—to African inhabitants of the Mungo River valley. In the 1930s administrators, enthused by colonial policymakers' new interest in "tribal customs and law," replaced the ambiguous term *indigène* (native) with the terms *allogène* and *autochtone*, which categorized Bamileke in the Mungo as strangers while underscoring Mbo populations' traditional rights to the land.[67] These terms could be read as reflecting French administrators' desire to minimize the dislocation of autochthonous populations in the Mungo Region, and certainly they were intended to communicate that desire to the League of Nations in the required annual reports. However, articulations of administrative policies that appear in official records of French dealings with traditional authorities in the Mungo Region reveal the mise en valeur of the fertile region's land as administrators' primary objective, as well as their pervasive and enduring notion that allowing Bamileke settlers to acquire land was the best way to increase the region's overall agricultural productivity. Over the years, French administrative terminology and ambivalent policies in the Mungo Region glossed over the heterogeneity of both Mungo and Bamileke populations and established them as polarized, homogenous categories in competition with one another.[68]

Concerned with the dwindling land resources, administrators used the newly reified ethnic categories to justify the denial of numerous Bamileke settlers' requests for registered deeds to the land they had occupied, in some cases, for decades. The 1932 decree, which specified that lands should ideally be held "by inhabitants indigenous to the territory, following the rules of local customary law," allowed administrators to dismiss Bamileke requests as having no legal or judiciary basis.[69] However, when it suited their purpose, administrators argued for Bamileke settlement by insisting that autochthonous populations failed to exploit the land to its full potential and by depicting "the Bamileke" as a "race of workers"[70] who fulfilled the economic objectives of mise en valeur: "The Bamileke presence compensates for the persistent inertia of the autochthonous population that, in many towns, leaves the land to which it holds or pretends to hold the rights of ownership completely uncultivated. The mise en valeur of those lands is due only to the work of the stranger population."[71]

In sum, by applying classification grades, productivity quotas, and ethnic categorizations, and by counting on Africans' lack of familiarity with ever-changing land laws, French administrators exercised three strategies to destabilize African land ownership in the 1930s. They could expropriate land for European settlers by "proving" that African planters had failed to meet the mise en valeur standards consistent with the parcel's classification. If it suited them, they could refuse Bamileke requests for titles and deeds to their land by claiming that they were strangers and had no valid right to land in terms of the Mungo Region's customary law. And yet, if the situation required it, they could reject autochthonous claims to land ownership by characterizing Bamileke settlers as workers who achieved higher levels of agricultural productivity.

To say that these ambiguous and paradoxical land policies worked to the advantage of European settlers would be an understatement. Despite their occasional nods to the "spirit of the mandate," by the 1930s French land policy clearly favored European acquisition of permanent land titles. The refusal to recognize the validity of African land contracts, the lack of enforcement of land reserve boundaries, the contingencies of the lands' classification, and the arbitrary undercompensation of indigenous landholders provided European settlers with first dibs on prime land and facilitated their acquisition of permanent titles. In 1936, Europeans held 94 out of 128 rural concessions in the Mungo, 26 of them with permanent deeds. By 1953, *all* European landholders had acquired permanent titles for their land and property.[72] Furthermore, despite Marchand's initial conservatism regarding the amount of land and the size of plantations granted to Europeans, the number of hectares attributed to individual European planters continued to rise throughout the mandate and trusteeship periods, peaking at 230,000 hectares at the end of World War II, and settling at 204,090 hectares by the time of official independence—the majority of the region's arable land.[73]

Ever-stricter regulations on planting methods for commercial crops enabled Europeans to maintain a production edge over African planters as well. By 1930, as robusta coffee began to boom as a cash crop, Europeans were well placed to capitalize on coffee as cacao's replacement. A regulatory provision circulated by the chief of the district required all coffee plantation owners to register and required all those who wanted to grow coffee to obtain a special permit if they were not on land for which they had a provisional or permanent deed.[74] In 1938 the regulations of coffee growing became even stricter, demanding that the owner prove he had access to the necessary number of laborers. The chief of the region declared that any plantation lacking the authorization permit would have its trees uprooted, thereby suggesting that coffee growing required care and attention that African planters were unable to provide.[75] Yet, in spite of the various advantages the administration offered to white farmers throughout the mandate period, by the 1950s, Bamileke migrants to the region had begun to outproduce European planters in coffee for commercial export, largely because of their ability to acquire laborers when their counterparts could not.[76]

BAMILEKE-NESS, SETTLEMENT, AND POLITICAL (MIS)REPRESENTATION IN THE MUNGO REGION

Despite the strict land regulations on them and their categorization as strangers, Bamileke settlers found ways to use French legislation and ethnic classifications to their advantage, while strategizing their own sociopolitical organization in the Mungo region. Arriving in the Mungo on a shoestring, Bamileke migrants relied on mutual aid networks they put in place. The fact that they maintained strong connections to their chieftaincies of origin enabled them to recruit additional laborers from their home chieftaincies. As hired laborers themselves, Bamileke planters rubbed elbows with European settlers, acquiring language skills and perhaps some familiarity with the complicated and elusive land policies publicized in the *Journal officiel du Cameroun*. As European plantations became larger, white settlers experienced more acute labor shortages and encouraged Bamileke workers to remain in the Mungo by sharing information about land acquisition and planting techniques. As migrants from the Bamileke Region began to cultivate their own land, they used the labor shortage to negotiate wage increases or fewer working hours.[77] Finally, Bamileke settlers gradually assumed the collective "Bamileke" identity through which French administrators portrayed them as hard-working, in contrast to the "laziness" of indigenous Mungo inhabitants.

Early in their mandate, the French recognized the Mungo River valley's artificiality as an administrative region. The chief of the Bureau of Economic Affairs remarked that the Mungo Region was, in essence, an economic unit with an elevated sense of independence, characterized by a lack of native command due to the high percentage of immigrants from elsewhere. The autochthonous populations were socially organized as acephalous segmentary lineages governed by a counsel of elders rather than as centralized polities under chiefly rule.[78] The lack of a functional "native command" in the region necessitated "unity in command and uniformity in the decisions to be made."[79] In the 1920s, the decade during which French colonial policies established traditional rulers as administrative auxiliaries, administrators attempted to fabricate a "native command" in the Mungo by naming traditional chiefs for autochthonous populations and settlement chiefs for immigrant populations in the Mungo.[80]

In 1924, seeking to establish a "traditional" government in the increasingly cosmopolitan town of Nkongsamba, French administrators in the Mungo officially recognized Adam Arab, of mixed Moroccan and Chadian parentage, as superior chief of [African] strangers for the region from Nkongsamba to Nlohé, on the banks of the Nkam River.[81] In collaboration with the French administration, Arab eventually selected three assistants: a chief of Bamileke populations, Jean Saah (from Bangangte); a chief of Hausa and Fulbé populations, Mama Issoufou; and a chief of Bamun populations, Arouna Njoya.[82] The autochthonous superior chief of Baneka, on whose terrain the urban center of Nkongsamba was built, resented the "stranger" chiefs' apparent challenge to his rule, especially as the number of immigrants began to surpass the number of autochthonous inhabitants under his command.

On 9 October 1925, the French administration created the Council of Notables to serve as a liaison with the population. Convening for the first time on 16 February 1926 in Yaoundé, council members discussed taxes and conscripted labor, the construction of the railroads, roads, and commercial centers, and the maintenance of indigenous "customs." On 29 July 1933, the administration modified the makeup of the council to achieve an ethnic balance of power that suited their objectives. The council was to consist of "representatives of diverse ethnic settlements [*groupements ethniques*] within the district's territory, chosen among superior chiefs and [lesser chiefs], as well as among the most influential notables. The selection *should be proportionate to the population of each ethnic settlement.*"[83]

In the Mungo, the council was to be made up of ten to thirty members, "natives, *indigenous to the territory*, well-established in the district, and possessing agricultural, industrial, or commercial interests."[84] The Nkongsamba council was made up of twenty-four "autochthons" of the Mungo Region, and one representative each for "Bamileke," "stranger," and "Yaoundé" populations.[85] But the makeup of the Nkongsamba council was anything but proportional to "the population of each ethnic settlement." It privileged autochthonous populations and dramatically underrepresented Bamileke inhabitants of the Mungo Region. By 1936, Bamileke immigrants made up 10,727 of the 21,876 inhabitants of the Nkongsamba subdivision.[86] Furthermore, Bamileke migrants did not necessarily respect or recognize the representative that administrators named as their spokesperson, nor did they allow the chief of the Bamileke to govern their daily affairs. Selected by the French, the "superior chief of the Bamileke" had a foreign administration as the source of his authority, and French-appointed chiefs were not the ones who mattered to Bamileke populations in the Mungo Region.[87]

When it became clear that administrative policies barred them from equitable political representation, Bamileke migrants took matters into their own hands by following their own criteria to construct the sort of "traditional" government that better represented their interests in the Mungo Region. In 1935 a report from Loum highlighted French administrators' inability to select and impose a "native command" on Bamileke migrants who preferred to follow their own chosen leaders. The greater Loum area in the Mbanga Subdivision, south of Nkongsamba (made up of Njombé, Penja, Loum, and Babong settlements) hosted the highest proportion of Bamileke immigrants in the Mungo Region. In 1932, a Mr. Raynaud, French chief of the Mbanga subdivision, named one settlement chief, Njiké Lakondji of Loum, to preside over all "Bamileke" populations in Njombé, Penja, Loum-Chantiers, and Loum. Raynaud no longer recognized the Bamileke leaders who had previously been responsible for their communities in the towns of Njombé, Penja, and Loum-Chantiers, although he encouraged Njiké Lakondji to rely on them as headmen to facilitate tax collection.

Within three years, tax revenue plummeted and it became obvious that Njiké Lakondji did not even know how many taxable Bamileke inhabitants lived in the region, much less how to get his "headmen" to respect his authority. Mr. Henry, assistant to Raynaud, made the decision to reinstate those who had originally been popularly recognized as community leaders in the various settlements, assigning each the title of village chief,[88] and allowed Njiké Lakondji to preside over Loum alone. Henry remarked, "the proposed chiefs, even if they do not bear the title, are considered as such by the inhabitants."[89] He added that it was necessary to have a village chief in each town to facilitate the collection of taxes, to fill conscripted labor demands, to maintain order, to keep track of arrivals and departures, and to deal with any other "village-related incident." Henry then placed all village chiefs in the subdivision under the official surveillance of a superior chief of Bamileke in the Mbanga subdivision, "Feinboy" Nkette, who earned a bonus on the taxes collected in the area. But Chief Nkette had been the Bamileke settlers' leader of choice several years before the French recognized him as such.

Nkette had acted as a Grassfields community chief in Nkappa (Mbanga subdivision) since the 1929 economic crisis. He had managed to acquire a significant amount of land, which he distributed to destitute sharecroppers and laborers of Grassfields origin after the onset of the Depression. Although the lands surrounding Nkappa had been classified as low-grade pasturage lands, undesirable to European settlers who sought the prime lands for planting, the newcomer planters found the lands around Nkappa profitable for cacao growing and thus found their niche in the cash-crop economy after 1930. Gradually, an increasing number of Grassfields migrants settled on the periphery of Nkette's land and recognized him as their leader. The settlers themselves bestowed Nkappa's position on him, and it was only several years later, after the French-named settlement chief's failure to bring in taxes, that French functionaries in the Mungo recognized him as an official part of regional "native command."[90] The Loum-Mbanga situation demonstrates the way Bamileke settlers selected their leaders according to their own criteria, leaving French administrators little choice but to work with those who had achieved prominence and wielded influence in their communities.[91]

Although the administration was concerned primarily with tax collection and conscripted labor, Bamileke settlers had other motives for choosing their own leaders in their new world. They largely ignored the French administrators' handpicked representatives for the artificial native command. Instead, they prioritized their ties to gung and organized themselves by chieftaincy of origin. For example, in 1950s Nkongsamba the administration required the Baham community to submit to Jean Saah, chief of the Bamileke settlement, in matters of taxation and conscripted labor. But the community relied on their own "family chief," Emil Tchuenkam, to regulate their relations with the Baham chieftaincy and their economic investment strategy, or mutual-aid, associations. In Nkongsamba, Douala, and Yaoundé, Baham "family chiefs" governed external Baham communities in much the same way that mfonte and wabo did within the chieftaincy borders, by serving as intermediaries between the fo and his population.[92] By the 1930s in Mungo towns like Nkongsamba, Mbanga, and Loum, Bamileke communities had the political and economic power to set their own terms of political representation.[93] At the same time, emigrants carved out their role in governance in the Bamileke chieftaincies they had moved away from but refused to leave behind, thus reifying the mode of identification that remained important to them—that of belonging to a particular chieftaincy.

During the interwar period, Bamileke emigrants began to gain purchase in chieftaincy governance in their villages of origin. Family chiefs were not mentioned in French records until the late 1950s, but they had largely preceded that period. Each "family" of emigrants assembled to unanimously agree on their leader.[94] In short, Grassfields migrants in the Mungo recreated structures of governance similar to those they had left behind. Nothing demonstrated more clearly the continued importance of Grassfields political culture to Bamileke communities residing outside the chieftaincies, in the Mungo Region and other urban areas of French Cameroon.

BECOMING BAMILEKE BEYOND CHIEFTAINCY BORDERS

The existing scholarship has often depicted young emigrants from the Bamileke Region as breaking free of the restrictive controls of their hierarchically structured home chieftaincies and revolting against the status quo.[95] Nicolas Argenti posits a "century of youth" for Grassfields males beginning with German colonialism and the arrival of missionaries, in the late 1890s. He describes the mission-educated "interpreters"—*tapenta* in pidgin English—as a generation of youth who appropriated literacy and European-language training from the colonial administration, and used their newly acquired skills to profit from economic opportunities, "severing their kinship and hierarchical ties to their kingdom of origin."[96] These subversive social cadets were succeeded by a generation of "free boys," who learned trades, moved to coastal regions and urban areas in the early 1900s and became independent of their chiefs.[97] They held "no accountability" to chieftaincy governments, and, "pledging allegiance to no chiefdom," they "threatened authority structures."[98] According to Argenti, who draws heavily on Jean-Pierre Warnier on this point, throughout the twentieth century, the chief's palace and nobility circles lost their monopoly on power and their control over labor, and their dominance of disenfranchised cadets was thus breeched.

It was true that by the 1930s—when Bamileke planters emerged as dominant players in the Mungo Region's plantation economy—nobility and chiefs did not hold the same sway over young emigrants, who had not inherited land or titles from their fathers. But the new planters, shopkeepers, and traders in the Mungo Region certainly did not sever ties with their chieftaincies of origin, nor can they be accurately described as social rebels. Successful emigrants who excelled in their new circumstances and managed, at the same time, to penetrate the echelons of wealth, status, and nobility in their home chieftaincies might better be understood as social innovators. They conserved, rather than overturned, the chieftaincy norms and protocols that rendered their achievements meaningful in Grassfields sociopolitical terms—but found ways to leverage their own inclusion in traditional chieftaincy structures, thus increasing their flexibility and engendering their redefinition.

Like Warnier and Argenti, Andreas Eckert describes Bamileke migration to the Mungo as a "migration away from a highly centralized and unequal system of disinherited groups" that was present in Grassfields chieftaincies.[99] Indeed, young migrants sought opportunities for economic advancement, wanting to escape the rigorous labor demands that elders and notables placed on them. But it was the "highly centralized and unequal system" of chieftaincy governance that continued to give their social status meaning. Mfo's eventual bestowal of nobility titles to successful emigrants may have clinched the deal, but even those who did not achieve titles remained bound by their cosmology to sacred sites of the chieftaincy, and depended on the approval of their elders, ancestors, and mfo to ensure their success in their new world.

An investment in their chieftaincy of origin was necessary in order for them to carry out sacrifices to ancestors and spirits, fulfill their duties as good children, increase their social status, and ensure their own honorable entry into the ancestral world upon their death. Emigrants returned regularly to benefit from the fixed attributes of gung: the sacred sites (cheup'si), the fo, their fathers' compound, and ancestral skulls. In this way, emigrants continued to uphold the spiritual alliance between the visible world of the living and the unseen world of ancestors, spirits, and gods that underwrote governance in their chieftaincies of origin.[100]

In a time before European rule, emigrants to the Mungo River valley might have established their own chieftaincies with ties to home echoing only in remnant oral histories. Historically, ambitious Grassfielders had broken away from their chieftaincies of origin and founded new polities.[101] But under colonial rule, when boundaries between polities and populations were no longer in flux, and battles over territory could no longer be fought, the French administration's reification of territorialized ethnic categories prevented Mungo autochthons from being co-opted into the migrants' sociopolitical structure—or vice versa. Bamileke immigrants to the Mungo Region had little choice but to continue to turn to their specific chieftaincies in instances where traditional governance and spirituality remained important, submitting—albeit from a distance—to the authority of the mfo they had left behind in ways they expected would increase their social standing and enhance their success. Somewhat paradoxically, it was their choice to leave their home chieftaincies that opened up avenues to the economic successes that enabled them to symbolically return having attained a level of recognition and status that would have remained out of reach for most had they never left. Migration and exile thus became a cornerstone of a twentieth-century Bamileke moral economy and identity.

While the fertility of the land in the Mungo River valley was undeniably attractive to Bamileke farmers used to working the hard, sometimes rocky, red soil of the eastern Grassfields, it was not this alone that caused them to settle.[102] The promise of greater commercial opportunities and wage labor—whether in fields, factories, slaughterhouses, or homes—and the simultaneous growth of European settlement were factors in providing a financial safety net for immigrants. But it was the Bamileke migrants' demographic makeup—mostly young men and foster children during the mandate and early trusteeship periods—that accounted for their level of activity and economic success. In 1935 an administrator at Mbanga remarked in exasperation that only a third of Bamileke men in his subdivision were married, and that they brought boys and girls from their villages to cook and clean for them.[103] These young men sought to surpass the expectations of the families they left behind in their home chieftaincies.

Young Bamileke men in the Mungo Region used their access to cash to gain social and political standing back home as well as to gain recognition for their new pursuits in their chieftaincies of origin. European settlers and administrators mostly viewed Bamileke as second-class citizens, and autochthonous populations increasingly resented their intrusion and appropriation of lands. As Bamileke migrants fell through the administrative cracks or faced restrictions due to their categorization as strangers in their new land, they began to organize themselves in self-government associations based on chieftaincy of origin and which followed the principles of Grassfields governance. They also established elaborate networks of cultural associations and mutual financial-aid and credit societies. As a result they gained the security of social networks in the Mungo Region, while at the same time preserving and even increasing their influence and importance in their home chieftaincies. Since their successes in the Mungo Region had little social significance in their new surroundings, bringing economic resources back to the chieftaincy increased their status in the eyes of their elders.

The mfo in the Bamileke Region, in turn, recognized the importance of preserving connections with their emigrant communities and soon realized that the chieftaincy's emigrant communities represented a source of revenue for the palace treasury. As rewards, successful emigrants were sometimes "given" plots of land, or wives—gifts that incurred allegiance and obligations to the fo. Most important, beginning in the 1950s if not before, the most successful emigrants could obtain a nobility title. In bestowing traditional nobility titles to youths who had moved away, mfo acknowledged the achievements of cadets, while continuing to benefit indirectly from their labor and keeping them an integral part of the polity. The inclusion of emigrants in the ranks of chieftaincy nobility ushered in an era of young urban Bamileke working *with*—rather than against—traditional palace elite.[104]

As the connection between home chieftaincies and emigrant communities evolved, it became clear that, by the late 1930s, the chieftaincy was no longer the hegemonic seat of power it had been at the turn of the twentieth century. The mfo had no say in the selection of the family chiefs, who essentially served as their representatives in emigrant communities throughout Cameroon's urban areas. Instead, they relied increasingly on their emigrant intermediaries to keep them informed of territorial affairs, economic trends, and, after World War II, political processes. The Mungo River valley—and other sites of Bamileke settlement throughout the territory—became the locations in which the ranks of modern Bamileke nobility could expand despite a finite supply of land within the bounds of home chieftaincies.

Although a majority of Bamileke migrants to the Mungo maintained active links to their chieftaincies of origin, a few who achieved a degree of financial success so complete that they felt no need for the social or spiritual currency provided by the chieftaincy did sever ties, opting for a more permanent emigration. Isaac Bondja, for instance, originally from the area of Bangangte in the Nde Subdivision of Bamileke country, had by 1927 acquired European-style plantations of eighty hectares near Melong, at the northernmost edge of the Mungo Region.[105] Bondja was one of three Africans claiming the desirable A lots within the urban perimeter of Nkongsamba in 1923.[106] Agar Ndenmen, one of Bondja's eight children from his monogamous marriage, explains that her father believed his arrival in Nkongsamba to be sanctioned by a Christian God. Bondja modeled his resettlement in northern Mungo territory on the biblical story of Abraham and told his children that when he arrived, "there was no one." He and his wife created the village surrounding his plantation, and he believed "it was his country that God had given him." In 1983, Bondja was buried on his plantation, followed by his wife in 1988. During his lifetime, he had expressed his wish that his wife and all his sons be buried on the plantation as well.[107]

Bondja was one of the first converts to Protestantism from the Bamileke Region under French rule. He founded the Protestant church at Melong and served as the earliest catechist in the region. Bondja expressed a Bamileke convert's perspective on the Grassfields spiritual alliance. He taught his children to respect their elders and give them everything they could during their lifetime, such that after death they would have no complaints.[108] He told his children that a guilty conscience was what inspired sacrifices to the dead, and that if one treated others well, such sacrifices were unnecessary. Bondja's proximity to the administration, his conversion, and his wealth enabled him to finalize a separation from his chieftaincy of origin, but such a rupture was exceptional among Bamileke settlers in the Mungo Region at the time.

French administrators sought out African planters like Bondja in the early years of the League of Nations mandate before the competition over fertile lands increased in the late 1930s. An educated Christian and monogamist, Bondja received the grant for his plantation at Nkongsoung four years after occupying one of the prime urban lots of Nkongsamba. The French fertilizer company Potasse d'Alsace funded Bondja's plantation and the nearby massive Niabang Company, both located on the periphery of the Plain of the Mbo.[109] Bondja most likely used the funds to build up labor barracks for workers, storehouses and courtyards for sorting coffee, livestock shelters, and perhaps to purchase a tractor and fertilizers. By connecting Bondja with Potasse d'Alsace and granting him the eighty hectares that encroached on the Plain of the Mbo's native reserve, French administrators facilitated the settlement of a Bamileke planter on a European-style plantation.

In emigrant Bamileke communities a polarity emerged between those who viewed home as situated within the geographical borders of their chieftaincies of origin and those who considered the new frontier they settled to be home. For settlers like Bondja who achieved a social foundation in Christianity and economic success in the Mungo valley's plantation economy, home chieftaincies faded in importance and the process of entitlement in the chieftaincy held no allure. In contrast, social and spiritual connections to home chieftaincies remained essential for Bamileke migrants who had only small parcels of land and continued to be viewed as "strangers" in the region. In other words, it was not the wealthiest and most successful of Bamileke migrants to the Mungo Region who felt the greatest need to prove themselves through the acquisition of nobility titles and an ongoing connection to the home chieftaincy. Identification with chieftaincy of origin and the nobility system proved most important to emigrants who achieved more modest successes, in other words, to the very "social cadets" that Warnier and others have portrayed as severing ties and revolting against oppressive strictures of traditional governance. Similarly, the historical evidence reveals that during the 1950s nationalist era, the "disenfranchised commoners" who turned to the UPC did not always do so in a rebellious attempt to overthrow Bamileke traditional chiefs and nobility as the conventional literature maintains (see chapter 4).[110] Instead, young Bamileke emigrants often became upécistes at the same time that they sought to restore lepue to traditional chieftaincies, thus attempting to free them from their auxiliary role as an integral part of the French administration.

ETHNICITY AND POLITICAL PROCESSES: POSTWAR DISSONANCES

After the Second World War, territorial politics became a salient factor interacting with ethnicity, labor, land distribution, and commercial agriculture in the lives of Mungo Region inhabitants. Bamileke settlers established themselves as dominant cash-crop producers in the region, particularly after the abolition of forced labor, in April 1946, leveled the playing field vis-à-vis white planters. In the 1950s, French administrators seemed to accept as truth their predecessors' earlier portrayals of Bamileke as hardworking and Mungo populations as lazy: if autochthons had lost their land, it was because they deserved to. Land ownership in the Mungo Region under French rule had thus become, in part, a corollary of ethnic identity as administrators seemed to posit a Bamileke work ethic in order to reverse their earlier position—that as strangers, Bamileke settlers had no rights to Mungo land. Nurtured by such French administrative policies, ethnic tensions between Bamileke and Mbo inhabitants of the northern Mungo Region came to a head just as political parties, planters, cooperatives, and trade unions began to form in French Cameroon after the Second World War.

In the 1950s administrators organized "palavers"—town-hall meetings to inform African chiefs of administrative land policies and give them a chance to air their differences. Such assemblies were attended by the French chiefs of the region and of the subdivision, the superior chief of strangers, the chief of the Elong, chief of the Bamileke, and the chief of the Mbo in Nkongsamba, as well as the superior chiefs of the Balong, Abo-Sud, Abo-Nord, and Bamileke in Mbanga. In one assembly held on 29 April 1950, Ewane, the superior chief of the Elong, speaking as a representative of autochthons in the Mungo, explained their understanding of land ownership: "My forefathers, my ancestors, never sold their land, I will not do so either, but I am willing to give land. . . . If I hosted a foreigner that wanted to settle, I would grant him a parcel of land and the day he departed he would have to return the parcel to me exactly as it was when he settled it."[111] As Ewane explained, a prevalent belief that unoccupied and uncultivated land belonged to them and that land was not transferable by sale or gift had kept many autochthons from registering for official land deeds.

The chief of the region's response reveals the extent to which French administrators openly voiced their ethnic prejudices underwritten by racism. He deplored the autochthonous populations' ideas about land, stating that they had a market boy's mentality, "even worse than the Bamileke." Connecting the right to own property with the ability to exploit the land, the chief of the region haughtily remarked, "Well, I think that work is not such a bad basis for legislation, because the autochthonous populations are nice enough, but they are lazy as dogs. . . . For the administration to grant property rights one has to work, cultivate the land, that's what has value and warrants the right to ownership."[112]

Autochthonous representatives retorted that they lacked the resources to employ laborers to work the land. Indeed, recruitment of field hands posed challenges even for the most successful and well established planters in the 1950s, and Bamileke settlers held an advantage over both autochthons and Europeans. By the 1950s widespread settlement and the sharecropping system had funneled new arrivals into Bamileke households and plantations, and Bamileke settlers used every means at their disposal to remain financially independent both of Europeans and of their autochthonous hosts. It was common for Bamileke planters in the Mungo Region to recruit "juniors" from their home chieftaincies as additional laborers. As a result, Bamileke planters benefited from a seemingly unlimited supply of laborers who worked for little compensation beyond food, lodging, and the elder hosts' promise of social and financial support if and when the need arose.[113] As the number of Bamileke settlers increased in the Mungo Region, new arrivals had little reason to hire out their labor to indigenous farmers. Furthermore, while many did work for European settlers to supplement their sharecropping activity with cash wages, by the 1950s, Bamileke laborers proved themselves able to negotiate their terms of employment with white plantation owners.

Bamileke laborers desired to limit working hours in order to spend more time on their own plantations. In a 1952 letter to the high commissioner, A. Viossat, president of the Mungo Region Coffee Planters' Union, wrote, "Bamileke workers have tacitly agreed among themselves to refuse to work in any plantation where the workday surpasses three or four hours." In exasperation, he added that even when working for only a short period of time, they did not execute the task properly:

"Our workers consider themselves masters, not only of the length of the workday, but even of the work method, which is deplorable."[114] Marchand, the chief of the Mungo Region, underwrote Viossat's complaint in his report on Bamileke labor: "The Bamileke labor forces feel as though they are in control of the situation, because they know that the European planter hesitates to part ways with one of his few field hands, and the field hand who has been laid off will be immediately rehired by the neighboring plantation."[115]

Just as the coffee boom began in the postwar period, autochthonous populations, all but dispossessed of their land, were mostly unable to compete with Bamileke farmers in the Mungo Region's plantation economy, and European planters, despite the discriminatory export quotas that favored them, found it increasingly difficult to match their Bamileke counterparts in productivity. By the 1950s, Bamileke settlers made up 77 percent of the population of Nkongsamba (the Mungo Region's capital and terminus of the railroad to Douala) and accounted for 54 percent of all Mungo inhabitants.[116] From north to south, all along the railroad, a majority of Mungo land legally and irrevocably belonged to European and Bamileke planters. Although autochthonous inhabitants became part of the Ngondo, the "traditional assembly of the Duala people,"[117] in an effort to forge an ethnic solidarity to counterbalance the growing "Bamileke identity," their relative degree of decentralization prevented them from mobilizing collective resources to prevent encroachment on their land.

In contrast, Bamileke migrants' economic success in the Mungo Region can be partially explained by their ability to organize. In Nkongsamba and in smaller Mungo towns dotting the railroad, the family chiefs selected by Bamileke communities helped them maintain links to their respective chieftaincies, provide credit and financial support to fellow migrants in times of need, and create savings and loans associations known today as tontines.[118] Although organized by chieftaincy of origin, Bamileke migrants recognized the link between the administration's ethnic categories and political representation, and began to accept and utilize the larger category the administration assigned to them—Bamileke. The collective Bamileke identity became increasingly important as the political terrain took shape in the Mungo Region and throughout the territory of French Cameroon after the Second World War.

As postwar anti-imperial currents swept the globe, the issues that mobilized inhabitants of the Mungo Region included ethnicity, the distribution of land, export policies, wages, and labor conditions. Most Bamileke settlers supplied forced labor or paid taxes (or both) that profited areas outside their chieftaincies of origin even as the administration limited their political representation in structures of "native command," subjected them to unpredictable and ambiguous land policies, and continued to depict them as hard-working strangers as though to stoke autochthons' animosity against them. In response to these challenges, Bamileke settlers created for themselves a mode of self-governance to meet the new challenges posed by a foreign administration and the expansion of the chieftaincy to an unfamiliar landscape, as described above. But in the postwar era, a number of Bamileke settlers began to turn to territorial politics, as though convinced that sociopolitical organization within their own communities was not enough to protect their interests as emigrants to the Mungo River valley.

Several things happened in the late 1940s in the Mungo Region to galvanize Bamileke political initiatives and their participation in territorial politics of the late trusteeship period. Empirewide labor reforms enabled the rapid diffusion of these labor and political organizations throughout the Mungo Region, as well as the Sanaga-Maritime Region, the Douala area (or Wouri Region), and other regions of French Cameroon. Soon after the reforms discussed at the Conference of Brazzaville, in early 1944, the French government passed a decree on 7 August 1944 that authorized labor unions in French territories, including Cameroon, and a confederation of Cameroonian labor unions, the Union des syndicats confédérés du Cameroun (USCC), was founded on 18 December 1944.[119] The French Communist founders included Maurice Soulier, Ernest Fines (a railroad station manager based in Nkongsamba), and Gaston Donnat, who traveled throughout African territories under French control after the war.[120] Soulier, a member of the French Communist trade union, the Confédération générale du travail (CGT), had been in Cameroon since the early 1930s and as early as 1932, had founded the Associated Union of Functionaries and Agents of Cameroon (Association syndicale des fonctionnaires et des agents du Cameroun) to protect the rights of French workers.[121] Donnat left the country in April 1945, while Fines, a Communist councillor in the French union, remained in Nkongsamba. The presence of French Communists such as Fines led to the implantation of the CGT, which supported the USCC and the UPC in the Mungo Region.

Labor reforms begun within the empire were soon reinforced internationally. On 17 June 1948, following the General Conference on International Labor Organization held in San Francisco, a UN convention was passed designating participation in labor unions as a human right. On 28 January 1954, a decree in the spirit of the convention was applied in French Cameroon, allowing workers and employers to belong to the labor organizations of their choice without authorization. Thereafter, labor organizations could no longer be dissolved, suspended, or disrupted by public authorities.[122]

As Cameroonian planters in the Mungo Region increased cash-crop exports, particularly bananas, they took advantage of the new labor legislation to organize planters' cooperatives and labor unions to promote the economic interests of African planters and workers. As many as fifty cooperatives and trade unions, some linked with the CGT, others independent, sprang up throughout the Mungo Region from the late 1940s to the mid-1950s.[123] One that launched the most direct challenge to regional standards regulating commercial agriculture was the African banana planters' cooperative, the Syndicat de défense des interêts bananiers africains (SDIBA). By 1950, African planters produced 51 percent of the country's total bananas for export, but were only allotted 27.50 percent of the available space on transport due to the freight quotas established by the powerful European banana planters' cooperative, the Syndicat de défense des interêts bananiers du Cameroun (SDIBC). The SDIBA challenged the quota by negotiating the export of their 1950s crop with an Italian shipping company, Guiba, which had not signed a contract with SDIBC. Although the multiethnic SDIBA never obtained a legal permit to organize as a union or cooperative and its presence was short lived, the cooperative foresaw the struggles to come.[124]

Led by the USCC and supported by the CGT, labor unions prioritized equality between Africans and Europeans, sought to minimize economic disparity between évolués and less fortunate urban and rural populations, and challenged European monopolization of import-export trade. In the Mungo Region, where planters and laborers alike were well aware of the monetary value of cash crops, it was the agricultural economy that drew people into labor activism.[125] Significant strikes like the one that began at the Company of Plantations in Njombé-Penja in 1954 threatened European commercial agriculture. Over a thousand workers joined the strike to demand paid vacations, bonuses for seniority and productivity, free medical care, workers' compensation, janitorial services for workers' quarters, elections for workers' representatives, and the revaluation of their salaries in step with the rising cost of living. The movement spread to European-owned plantations throughout the banana belt, such as the Nassif plantation at Loum-Chantiers, Fourés at Loum, and Marcaa at Melong.[126] Through the USCC, which challenged European economic dominance in the fertile plantation zone, the UPC began to put down roots in the region into a soil made up of old and new political influences. Although in the Bamileke Region, the UPC took root via a "traditional" secret association known as Kumsze (see chapter 3), in the Mungo, Marxist study circles and labor politics prepared the way for the nationalist party.

Some trade unions, cooperatives, and parties attracted a multiethnic membership, yet ethnic cleavages were present from the beginning of workers' and planters' political mobilization in the Mungo Region, and became increasingly evident. A few trade unions, such as the Syndicat des planteurs autochthones de la région du Mungo (SPARM), which formed in 1948, were founded on ethnic or racial affinities.[127] Chief of the Mbo, Fritz Pandong's anti-Bamileke politics took shape as a reaction against the UPC following a meeting of the directors' committee near his home in Mboroukou on 20 December 1949. In attendance was the stationmaster of Nkongsamba, Ernest Fines, a French Communist and ardent CGT activist, who served as counselor to the young party.[128] Following the meeting, Pandong appealed to the French administration to help him defend against the immigration of "these races that populate a country that does not belong to them."[129] His words revealed the growing organized resistance of autochthons to Bamileke encroachment on their land. Pandong complained that elections favored Bamileke as representatives of the Mungo Region and asked that only candidates "autochthonous to the region" be allowed to run in elections to the Assemblée representative du Cameroun, reminding administrators that "a rooster cannot crow in a strange village."[130] Pandong deplored the importation of political parties, particularly the upécistes, who "ate away at the country" and undermined the authority of autochthonous chiefs in the Mungo.

Bamileke immigrants, on the other hand, saw in territorial elections an opportunity to gain political seats on the basis of demographics. The collective Bamileke identity first applied to them by French administrators in the region served them well in the issue of political representation. Whereas French administrators had previously set quotas limiting the political representation of "strangers" in the Mungo, as in the composition of the Council of Notables, formed in the 1920s, in the postwar era, Bamileke Mungo-dwellers began to go to the polls. Although they did not always vote uniformly, Bamileke settlers outnumbered autochthonous inhabitants and, as a result, wielded greater political influence in elections.

⁓

By the 1950s, via migrant communities, Bamileke chieftaincies extended beyond their physical boundaries into new urban areas such as Nkongsamba, Douala, and Yaoundé, underscoring a notion of gung as a nation of people rather than one defined primarily by its physical borders. After several years in the Mungo Region, emigrants from Bamileke chieftaincies—who had left as social cadets, to whom opportunities for social advancement were largely denied as a result of chiefs' and notables' monopolization of wealth and wives—had the socioeconomic leverage to position themselves more favorably vis-à-vis their home chieftaincies. The actions of these successful emigrants, together with the willingness of their mfo to incorporate them into the ranks of chieftaincy nobility, forged a new social category in traditional Bamileke society—that of the titled emigrant. These new, emigrant notables generally received their titles when they were much younger than notables in the home chieftaincies. They were involved as active participants in the colonial economy, and many had acquired some education in French or mission schools. As such they might be seen as intermediaries between traditional chieftaincy governance and the Bamileke population of the Mungo River valley, the site of the convergence of the traits of a French colonial modernity in the territory.

Bamileke settlers in the Mungo Region went further than merely participating in traditional chieftaincy politics, however. Their promptness to register the lands they acquired from autochthons demonstrated their familiarity with administrative legislation and the advantages it could afford them. Against administrators' rhetoric depicting them as strangers to the land, Bamileke migrants fought for a right to settle in the Mungo Region through official, legal means. They were poised to take advantage of imperial reforms in the arena of labor reform and political organization after the Second World War, and as either part of or on the periphery of a Cameroonian "capitalist bourgeoisie," they were heavily invested in the outcome of postwar political processes that they understood would influence land distribution, commercial agriculture, labor conditions, and their degree of belonging in the Mungo River valley.

The Mungo Region, which hosted the highest percentage of white settlers in French Cameroon as well as large numbers of migrants from elsewhere in the territory, was the site of competition over the new economic resources introduced under European rule. The resulting tensions exposed weaknesses and inconsistencies in French rule, which fed a growing animosity between the Bamileke migrants and their autochthonous hosts. New political influences provided organizational grounds for the discontented, and labor unions and planters' cooperatives channeled economically marginalized populations into the UPC. In the 1950s, French administrators, Bamileke chiefs, and UPC leaders all courted the Mungo Region's politically unpredictable bourgeois planters—a new economic elite in the territory—sensing that they could greatly influence decolonization processes. But the Mungo River valley elite did not behave as a cohesive body, and their opinions on traditional governance varied greatly, although their influential role in the nationalist era is undeniable. In the Mungo Region, political processes did not simply conform to broad categories. It was, after all, a region where the interests of planters and laborers could and did surmount ethnic cleavages, and political actors often transgressed the apparent boundaries. The earliest Marxist study circle in Nkongsamba attracted Mbo and Bamileke alike, and anticolonial activists forged alliances across ethnic lines.

News of the postwar formation of trade unions, planters' cooperatives and political parties in Douala and the river valley's plantation towns spread along the railway corridor through the Mungo Region. The news did not stop in Nkongsamba but, via Bamileke emigrant communities, reached chiefs' palaces and the compounds of commoners and nobility throughout the Bamileke Region. But the spread of political movements was not unidirectional. Even as anticolonial politics became prominent, thanks to the extension of chieftaincies throughout the Mungo and into Douala, chieftaincy politics also penetrated emigrant Bamileke communities to a greater and greater degree, eventually becoming imbricated with the politics of nationalism and decolonization.[131]

As independence politics began to take shape in the territory, the fertile Mungo Region—connecting the Bamileke Region to Douala and stretching along the Anglo-French boundary—carried a political influence disproportionate to its size. In 1952 the Mungo Region boasted the second-highest percentage of voters per capita, second only to the Wouri Region, home to the port city of Douala.[132] With its mostly European-controlled cash-crop economy, political complexity, and heterogeneous population, the Mungo river valley had all the accumulated tensions of a future nation-state. The Mungo Region was a midpoint between state administration and Bamileke chieftaincies, and its influence permeated the politics of both in the era of decolonization.

PART TWO

Bamileke Nationalists Claim Independence (*Lepue*) for the Nation (*Gung*)

3 ∽ Troublesome, Rebellious, Outlawed

International Politics and UPC Nationalism in the Bamileke and Mungo Regions

> The African peoples want no other liberty than that of France.
> —Minister of the Colonies René Pleven, 1944[1]

> It [is] impossible to speak of a national consciousness in the Cameroons, since that would presuppose a common origin, common traditions, culture and interests, and the memory of ordeals endured together as well as a minimum of common geographical historical and economic factors, all of which are lacking.
> —French representative to the United Nations, as quoted by Ruben Um Nyobé speaking before the Fourth Committee of the UN General Assembly, 1952[2]

> Forced labor and the *indigénat*, . . . the First World War, . . . the anti-Hitler . . . victory of 1945, . . . and the colonial regime constitute ordeals endured together that Cameroonians will never forget.
> —Ruben Um Nyobé, speaking before the Fourth Committee of the UN General Assembly, 1952[3]

STOKED BY the leaders and members of the UPC and its affiliate trade union, the USCC, its youth wing, the JDC, and its women's party, UDEFEC, anticolonial sentiment spread rapidly from the political and socioeconomic landscape of Douala and the Mungo Region into other areas of French Cameroon. From April 1948, the date of the UPC's formation in Douala, to December 1956, when the first territorial elections that allowed universal suffrage were held, the story of Cameroonian nationalism is necessarily a story of the UPC. During the early 1950s the UPC and its affiliated parties developed into a movement with grassroots foundations throughout the Mungo, Bamileke, Wouri (Douala), and Sanaga-Maritime Regions, and established a significant presence in

Yaoundé as well as throughout the southern regions of the territory. The movement even made inroads into the northern part of Islamic French Cameroon. During the first half of the 1950s, while the UPC and its affiliates were still legal, leaders deliberately opposed the pattern of progressive steps to independence being implemented throughout the French empire. Instead, upécistes emphasized the fact that the Cameroons were trust territories, rather than colonies, and as such could not be integrated as internally autonomous territories into a greater France made up of France and its colonial territories.

By 1955—the year that French administrators officially proscribed the UPC, the JDC, UDEFEC, and the USCC—the movement had more followers, by far, than any other political party. French administrators estimated that members and sympathizers of the UPC numbered some one hundred thousand out of a total electorate of just over 747,000—a number that High Commissioner Roland Pré knew to be large "relative to other political movements."[4] In fact, no other political party managed to mobilize comparable numbers. Most of the UPC's contemporaries—such as Évolution sociale du Cameroun (ESOCAM) or the Coordination des indépendants camerounais (INDECAM), both sponsored by the French administration in the Sanaga-Maritime Region—failed to get beyond a regional or ethnic base, while the few that did proved unable to rally the population at large.[5] Until the nationalist parties' official ban by decree, on 13 July 1955, only the UPC could draw crowds of thousands to political rallies, speeches, and events. After the proscription, only the nationalist coalition, the Mouvement d'action national (MACNA), which filled the political vacuum and drew large numbers of upécistes into its ranks, could do so.[6]

In the months after the proscription and leading up to the December 1956 territorial elections, UPC leaders and members proved most adept at shaping the nationalist rhetoric in French Cameroon, essentially creating a new political repertoire that outlasted the official proscription. The main elements of the UPC's political discourse included severing from France; building an economically and culturally independent nation; relying on the UN to serve as an advocate in the global political arena; and establishing a clear timeline for progression to total independence and reunification with the British Cameroons. After the movement's ban, members fled into the underground, or maquis, to escape arrest, and the party's front line shifted to rural areas.

Accordingly, the movement's political repertoire began to incorporate culturally particular elements as it blended with local political cultures in various rural regions. Paradoxically, the party's ban resulted concurrently in its wider diffusion at the grassroots level, where it seized the popular imaginary and took root in local political practice in the latter half of the 1950s *and* in its greater international visibility. This chapter traces the UPC's trajectory from the time of the party's formation, in the late 1940s, to the moment of its proscription, in mid-1955, and focuses on its international support networks, while the next examines the nationalist movement's articulation with local political vernacular in the Mungo and Bamileke Regions.

GREATER FRANCE OR SOVEREIGN NATION? CONTESTED MEANINGS, RIVAL CONSTITUENCIES

Even before the UPC's founding, in April 1948, the party's future leaders had made connections with the Rassemblement démocratique africain (RDA), an interterritorial association with affiliates throughout French Africa and the UN trusteeships under French supervision that lobbied for independence for African territories under French rule, and to that end encouraged the formation of territorial branches of the RDA throughout Africa under French administration.[7] In October 1946 five "unofficial" Cameroonian delegates attended the RDA's founding conference in Bamako.[8] Ruben Um Nyobé and Félix Moumié, who would later become secretary general and president of the UPC, respectively, met for the first time in 1947 at an RDA congress in Dakar, Senegal.[9] Soon after its formation, the UPC officially became a territorial branch of the RDA precisely when the interterritorial organization was at the height of its association with the French Communist Party (PCF), a period lasting from 1948 to 1950. The UPC refused to sever ties with the PCF even after a number of RDA parliamentarians—following the lead of Félix Houphouët-Boigny of Côte d'Ivoire, who served as the RDA's interterritorial president—elected to break with the PCF in 1950.[10] The UPC and the other territorial branches that preserved an alliance with the PCF—including the Union démocratique nigérienne (UDN) and the Union démocratique sénégalaise (UDS)—were officially expelled from the RDA at the Conakry congress in July 1955.[11] The early anticolonialist UPC, influenced by the Marxist study circles that French Communists organized in Yaoundé, Douala, and Nkongsamba and fueled by its early affiliation with the

RDA, was oriented toward a francophone, leftist solidarity among postwar anti-imperialists.[12] Um Nyobé soon began to publish in progressive or communist French periodicals, including *Cahiers internationaux: Revue internationale du monde du travail*. The UPC and Um Nyobé were featured in the PCF's newspaper, *L'humanité*, as early as 1955. The UPC's political alliance with the PCF, as well as its origins in Marxist study circles and trade unions outlined in the previous chapter resulted in French administrators' portrayal of the party as communist and hence their justification for its suppression.[13]

By the mid-1950s and throughout the empire, French administrators sought to position the African leaders they could rely on to promote the project of integrating colonial territories into a greater France.[14] In 1956 the French Assembly passed the loi-cadre—legislation granting internal autonomy to colonial territories—which established elected local institutions and Africanized the civil service to a large degree. Yet these reforms ensured continued metropolitan dominance over diplomatic relations, access to international markets, and military and security forces. While some African politicians viewed the loi-cadre reforms as tantamount to France's bestowal of self-determination on her colonial territories, others, including upécistes, who advocated total and immediate independence from French rule, viewed the reforms as neocolonialism on the make.[15]

In French Cameroon, French administrators and UPC leaders actively competed to recruit the political cadres who would advance their diametrically opposed political agendas for the territory's future. The French administration failed to consider Cameroon's particular jurisdictional status as a UN trust territory when it came to applying loi-cadre there.[16] Accordingly, the French agenda promoted the interdependence of France and French Cameroon, which was to become an internally autonomous territory while at the same time being integrated into a greater France. In contrast, the UPC's political platform underscored the differences between UN trust territories and French colonies. Upécistes advanced a nationalist vision of the territory as an economically, politically, and culturally independent, sovereign nation-state. They viewed loi-cadre as an impediment to the achievement of total independence, rather than a step along the way.

Both the French administration and the UPC leadership drew on the same political field to increase the numbers of their supporters. They differed only in the extent to which they cast their respective nets when recruiting the nation's future leaders. French administrators chose their allies from a narrowly defined field, made up of those who had attended school, spoke French, and agreed to send their potential successors to French schools; landowners who cultivated cash-crops according to official agricultural policy; and traditional chiefs who had consistently aided in tax collection.

Directors of the UPC drew supporters from this narrow field of the territory's elite, but expanded it considerably. Simply put, a person did not have to be elite or in any way évolué or "assimilated"[17] to be an upéciste. Although UPC leadership consisted mostly of men and women who had been schooled in French or mission schools, the ranks remained open to men, women, and youth who were nonliterate, did not speak French, were not property owners, and so on. Whereas French colonial governance had been premised, since its inception, on creating a distinction between an elite minority and the "native masses," upécistes emphasized the commonalities between the elite and the nonelite, the nonliterate, the nonfrancophone, the poor, and the "unassimilated"—they were all Cameroonians.[18] Furthermore, UPC leaders undertook a political strategy that French administrators and their allies did not: that of teaching a political practice and discourse. In stressing the commonalities between elite and nonelite and making the political field popularly accessible, UPC leaders deliberately undermined the distinction between citizen and subject that had served as the foundation for French colonial administration since the late nineteenth century.[19]

In the 1950s, Nkongsamba, the capital of the Mungo Region, became a site of the nationalization of politics as French administrators and upécistes competed for the allegiance of the territory's future political "cadres." By the late trusteeship period, the Mungo Region—filled with plantations, factories, markets, and a railway and road linking all its towns to the economic capital, Douala—had become an essential part of the colonial economy, and no region exhibited greater ethnic plurality. As a geographical and commercial crossroads between the Bamileke Region, the Mbam, the Nkam, the Sanaga-Maritime, and British territory, the Mungo also facilitated the diffusion of the UPC throughout the southern region beginning in the mid-1950s. As seen in chapter 2, the foundations of the nationalist movement in the Mungo rested on issues of land and labor, and on the terms of export and sale of cash crops. Since Bamileke populations dominated these economic activities, they served as the party's backbone. It was logical that the UPC in the Bamileke Region had the Mungo River valley as its anchor.

The key to the UPC's success as a popular nationalist party even after its official proscription was its members' ability to articulate UPC nationalism with an international and Pan-Africanist anticolonialism on the one hand and people's local and regional concerns within the territory on the other. The party thus created a dual nationalist front: one located within the territories, and the other beyond its borders. This dual front—one part external and Pan-African, the other internal and supported by farmers, laborers, and political activists in the Mungo and Bamileke Regions—became the UPC nationalist movement's trademark. The following exploration of the UPC's multilayered foundation illustrates its ability to reach from the international to the local, joining these different political spheres.

THE UPC'S (INTER)NATIONAL POLITICAL PLATFORM AND STRUCTURE, 1947–55

As French administrators targeted UPC assemblies with increasing vehemence, UPC leaders' purpose and vision would soon shift from metropolitan political processes to transregional, Pan-African, and Third World affinities and solidarities. In other words, upécistes worked hard to raise awareness of "the Cameroon question" in international political arenas. Key to the UPC's political platform was, after all, the reunification of portions under British and French rule, and as a result the movement naturally crossed colonial boundaries. The international forum of the United Nations, with its promise of global equality for member states, its charter and declaration of human rights, and its representation, in the early years, of a Third World optimism, also became a powerful political symbol for upécistes.[20] The leaders of the UPC and its affiliates began to establish transregional bases of support early on: Um Nyobé, a court clerk and record keeper in Edea, and Moumié, a medical doctor, were archetypal nationalist "pilgrims" of the sort Benedict Anderson calls the "bilingual intelligentsia" of a nation.[21] Um Nyobé and Moumié's meeting in Dakar foreshadowed the later Pan-African circuit of UPC nationalists in exile, many of whom traveled to Ghana, Guinea, North Africa, Congo-Brazzaville, Angola, and beyond after the movement's official ban.[22]

From the party's inception, the UPC and its affiliates (UDEFEC, the JDC, and the USCC) broadcast the fact that the territories of

Cameroon were not colonies but trust territories, administered jointly by the French and British.[23] The UPC promoted a popular awareness of that international status along with its nationalist and anticolonialist message, adding another layer to the party's global foundation. Um Nyobé and other party leaders explained the UN Charter's Article 76, which promised eventual autonomy to the trust territories.[24] The women of UDEFEC distributed copies of the UDHR and read them aloud in local committee meetings.[25] Beginning in 1952, Um Nyobé traveled annually, until the UPC's proscription in 1955, to New York to speak before the UN General Assembly's Fourth Committee.[26] Upon his return from trips abroad, he gave accounts of his visits in public gatherings and UPC congressional meetings and distributed copies of his speeches as tracts in local meetings.

While the UN facilitated political mobilization within the Cameroonian trust territories, it also promoted the formation of Pan-African and anticolonial networks. In 1952, as Um Nyobé and Abel Kingué, the president of the JDC, went to the meeting of the UN's Fourth Committee, they traveled under a class-C visa, which allowed them only to go between the Tudor Hotel and the UN building for daily meetings. Harlem was specifically off-limits. Already isolated due to their visa restrictions, Kingue and Um Nyobé found the winter weather unbearable and rarely ventured outside except to attend meetings at the UN. However, at the UN they met with a few African anticolonialists such as the Tunisian representative of Algerian nationalist Ahmed Ben Messali Hadj in the United States and secretary general of the Liberation Movement of North Africa. At meetings such as the International League for the Rights of Man (ILRM) and the American Committee on Africa, also held at the UN, since the ILRM had an office there, Um Nyobé met the future first president of Togo, Sylvanus Olympio.[27]

In its formative years, the young nationalist party received the support of several international organizations, mostly communist or socialist. From 1950 to 1952, UPC representatives attended the Second World Congress of Partisans of Peace, in Warsaw (November 1951); the World Youth Festival, in East Berlin (August 1951); the International Conference for the Defence of Children, in Vienna (April 1952); the International Student Union, in Bucharest (1952); and the assembly of Partisans of Peace in Montecatini, Italy (October 1952).[28] UPC, JDC, and UDEFEC leaders received invitations to these world conferences, traveling, as Ernest Ouandié did in 1954, to the communist centers of

Moscow and Peking as pilgrims, not as much of communism as of anticolonialism, now one of the key principles of Pan-Africanist thought.[29]

In light of the Cold War, Western powers viewed African nationalists' participation in these meetings and congresses as a cause for concern. But for African anticolonial activists, they provided an international forum in which to discuss nationalist, anti-imperial, and Pan-Africanist ideologies that could galvanize liberation movements "back home." The transregional networks that party leaders cultivated throughout Africa and France, at the UN in New York, and in Communist bloc countries—particularly China and Russia—proved crucial to the UPC after its official ban in French territory, in 1955, then in the British Cameroons, in 1957.

From the moment of the UPC's foundation, international connections—across metropolitan axes, from West to East—became essential to popular conceptions of nationalism and set in motion the alliances that nationalist leaders would rely on for support after the party's ban. Because UPC activists cultivated an awareness of the international dimensions of their nationalist struggle, a global perspective increasingly became part of everyday knowledge, from urban to rural areas, and especially in nationalist circles. The collective national identity that nationalist leaders promoted was one that contained equal parts local concerns and consciousness of a world beyond.

Territorial Organization, Leadership and the Creation of a Political Repertoire

UPC leaders deliberately educated people about worker solidarity, human rights, and anti-imperialism and encouraged them to integrate these ideas into local vernaculars. The pyramidal organization of the movement helped the diffusion of these ideas, as did the inclusion of youth and women in party activities.[30] The UPC directors' bureau, composed of elected members of the party, was formed in April 1948, at the party's inception. The following year, the JDC was founded, with its own directors' bureau, and in 1952, the women's party, UDEFEC, followed suit. Central and regional committees provided the link between the directors' bureaus and the local committees on which the party's dynamism depended. Um Nyobé believed that the strength of the party came from the grassroots and declared, "Nothing valuable or constructive can be realized if we operate from the summit like the colonialists. . . . The leaders of the local committees should consider themselves catechists of the villages or quarters in which they assume political responsibilities and in this capacity render periodic visits to the members and sympathizers of their committee."[31] The nationalist parties' structure, like that of the Democratic Party of Guinea (PDG) and other RDA branches, was modeled on the structure of the PCF.[32]

The French soon understood the crucial role local committees played in increasing the party's popularity, and a metropolitan journalist reported, "What explains the strength of the UPC is its organization, its structure, its roots, which extend to every milieu."[33] Ideally, local committees were to have at least ten members; a secretary for keeping records, taking minutes, and writing petitions to the UN was required for each meeting. As local meetings grew to over twenty members, they were to divide and continue recruiting members. Local members elected delegates to travel to scheduled regional meetings or general congresses, where party matters were discussed and officers elected.

The UPC leaders at the national, regional, and central-committee levels shared common traits. The most prevalent characteristic, and one actively sought out by the party leadership, was not age, ethnic origin, or an urban or rural locale, but a cosmopolitan identity (in Kwame Appiah's meaning) derived from a high degree of mobility.[34] From the upper echelons of party leadership to the grassroots local committees, upécistes in leadership positions were polyglots with ties to multiple communities. The UPC committee leaders, for the most part, had grown up far from their birth parents (and therefore had multiple "adopted" or "foster" families), were highly mobile, and had close relationships with European missionaries, planters, or entrepreneurs, most often through school or work. They had an intimate knowledge, not only of their place of origin but also of the places where they had lived, which afforded them both local roots and transregional exposure. Many of them lacked one or both parents and had been raised by relatives; the mother of Secretary General Ruben Um Nyobé, for instance, had died in childbirth in 1913 and his mother's co-wife brought him up. Um Nyobé became a *moniteur indigène* (native teacher) after being educated at the American Presbyterian Mission school at Foulassi. He then passed a territorial secretary-interpreters' examination and worked at the Department of Finance, in Yaoundé, after which he was transferred to the position of court clerk at Edea.[35]

Félix Moumié, president of the UPC, born of noble blood in Bamoun in 1925, received his primary and secondary schooling in Bandjoun, Bafoussam, and Dschang. Moumié's father, Samuel Mekou, himself a

UPC activist throughout the 1950s, sent his son to live with a friend of his, Esaïe Moumbain, a schoolteacher in Bandjoun, so that Moumié could embark on his education.[36] He attended the École supérieure Édouard Renard in Brazzaville from 1941 to 1944, and then continued on to the École de médecine et pharmacie de Dakar from 1944 to 1947.[37] He returned to Cameroon as a *médecin africain* (African doctor), and practiced first in Kribi and Lolodorf, on the southwestern coast, then in the extreme north, in Maroua, from 1950 to 1955, and finally in Douala.[38]

Mathieu Tagny, one of the UPC's most outspoken intellectuals from the Bamileke Region and who led the party in Yaoundé, attended primary school in Bafoussam, where Ernest Ouandié, the party's vice president, was his classmate, and later underwent medical training at both the French protestant mission at Bangwa and the American Presbyterian Mission in the Sanaga-Maritime.[39] Like Moumié, Tagny eventually studied in the École de médecine et pharmacie de Dakar before returning to Cameroon to practice medicine.

Ernest Ouandié, who became UPC president after Moumié's assassination, in November 1960, and later served as commander in chief of the UPC army in the maquis from 1962 until his arrest in 1970, was born in 1924 near Bana to parents from Bangou (a village bordering Baham). He lived in Bangwa (near Bangangte) with his parents before they sent him to stay with his uncle, Kamdeu Sango, so that he could attend primary school in Bafoussam.[40] Ouandié attended school in Dschang in 1937 and moved on to Yaoundé in 1940. By 1944, like Um Nyobé, he had finished training as a certified moniteur indigène. His first teaching job took him to Edea, in the Sanaga-Maritime. In 1948, he began a five-year position in the École publique de New Bell Bamiléké in the "African quarter" of Douala.[41] However, administrators transferred him to the remote town of Yoko, in the extreme northern region, as part of the effort to isolate UPC activists. In early 1955, when High Commissioner Pré decided to bring UPC leaders under closer surveillance, Ouandié was transferred back to Douala. There he crossed paths with Job Ngapeth, who would serve as UPC treasurer for a number of years, and his wife, Marie-Irène Ngapeth-Biyong, also teachers.[42] An advocate of women's rights as much as nationalism, Ngapeth-Biyong, secretary general of UDEFEC, was one of the first Cameroonian women to obtain teaching certification.[43]

Experience with French policies and legislation of the sort that Bamileke migrants gained in the Mungo Region gave leading upécistes an acute understanding of the inner workings of the French administration. By living, working, and even marrying outside their place of origin, they crossed geographical and cultural borders and became capable of tailoring their nationalist message to audiences throughout the territory. The mobility of activists was characteristic of popular nationalist movements in many parts of colonial Africa, including Algeria, Tanganyika, and in territories under French rule where RDA branches were active.[44] Being part of a relatively small cadre of literate elites educated through the secondary level, these teachers, medical practitioners, and secretary-interpreters had occasion to meet each other in the public spaces of the civil service, schools, or clinics.[45] "Less socially anchored and hence more autonomous,"[46] they were not bound solely by the sociocultural conventions of their families and villages but served as cultural brokers linking different regions in the early era of anticolonial activism. The sort of cultural brokers who proved most skilled at diffusing nationalist ideas were especially prevalent among Bamileke migrants seeking their fortunes in the prosperous Mungo or the economic capital of Douala.[47]

For many Bamileke nationalists, especially emigrants far from their villages, mobility was nothing new. They were already in the habit of traveling back and forth from their chieftaincies of origin. Many Bamileke members joined the UPC in their host communities and were then recruited by the directors' bureau to make up the traveling delegations sent into the Bamileke Region to give accounts of Um Nyobé's trips to the UN and the importance of the petitioning.[48] Although they held public demonstrations during the day, far more important was the solidarity created behind closed doors at night in the homes of local UPC members. Among nationalists, a code of conduct emerged based on generosity, sharing, assisting one another in crisis, and creating information networks.[49] The activity and mobility of nationalists in the early 1950s must have smoothed their ultimate transition from translocals in Cameroon to transnationals beyond its borders, as thousands went into exile after French and British administrators proscribed the movement in their respective territories.

On 7 March 1955, UPC directors decided to formalize the training that already characterized the party leadership by founding an *école des cadres* to prepare the nation's future administrators,[50] in New Bell, Douala. The courses promoted knowledge of international politics as well as a nationalist political consciousness. Classes such as Public

Rights and Law and From Colonial Administration to National Government, shaped nationalist ideology; and training on how to use cameras and shortwave radios, to lay out and edit copy for print, to operate mimeographs, and to organize archives and books into libraries taught nationalists the technical expertise needed for its dissemination. The class on colonial administration clarified the definition of *nation* by underscoring "the difference between a national government, institution of a sovereign state, and a colonial administration, the apparatus of a foreign power's oppression of a subjugated people."[51] Furthermore, it familiarized students with the history of anticolonial revolutions in other parts of the world, including Haiti and India. The program educated nationalists in six-week sessions, in classes of some thirty students selected by their central committees. For homework, students were encouraged to think like radical political activists, familiarize themselves with administrative law, and conceive of defense strategies in case of arrest. Party directors and leaders drew comparisons between UPC nationalism and anticolonial political activism on an international scale, and familiarized students with historical precedents for anticolonial rebellions, from Toussaint l'Ouverture to Indochina, as well as with the current priorities of the global anti-imperialist movement. Although only one or two classes completed the école des cadres before the party's ban, in July 1955, the school demonstrated the UPC's multidimensional approach to teaching the discourse and practice of politics.[52]

The first class of the école des cadres, which lasted from 18 March until 21 April 1955, included among its graduates Elias Tchuente of Nkongsamba, Marthe Ouandié, Gertrude Omog, and Marthe Moumié of UDEFEC, and Chrétien Dzukam of Bandjoun, who became one of the most dynamic activists in the Bamileke and Mungo Regions.[53] These men and women, together with those who participated in the creation of the school and the education of its students in New Bell, Douala, formed the centrifugal force of the nationalist party.[54] Guided by their common understanding of the party's objectives and their familiarity with local political cultures and global currents of anti-imperialism, these leaders spread through the territory, educating others in UPC ideology and planting nationalist ideas in the fertile grassroots of rural areas. In this way, they facilitated the cultural translation of UPC nationalism in various locales throughout the territory.

Political Repertoire

The UPC's traveling leaders, the école des cadres, and the tracts, newspapers, and petitions authored by party members all contributed to an independence-era political repertoire. A political repertoire "is first of all one of utterance or enunciation," argues political scientist Jean-François Bayart, and various utterances—written and oral, formal and informal—together form discursive genres, or political repertoires, that are contextually and historically constituted. In other words, a discursive genre can appear or disappear along with a change or shift in a given political culture. A period of dynamic change such as decolonization is more apt to bring a new political repertoire into widespread use, because the emergence of a new discursive pattern facilitates collective participation and a shared understanding of reality.[55] Furthermore, a discursive genre builds on those that preceded it and can be a hybridization of autochthonous and imported manners of speaking.[56]

Drawing on both local and global resistance ideologies, upécistes created a new discursive genre; but, paradoxically, they were aided also by contributions from French colonial administrators. When High Commissioner Pré arrived in the territory in late 1954, despite all evidence to the contrary, he viewed the UPC as a local organization launched and directed by the international communist movement.[57] Pré's objective was to eradicate the UPC through counterrevolutionary propaganda and various rollback strategies, which included the creation of alternative political parties and social associations.[58] Through their efforts to minimize the growing influence of the USCC, the UPC, UDEFEC, and the JDC, the French administration contributed language to the territory's ongoing debates about political sovereignty, decolonization, and nation building. Upécistes deliberately appropriated French references to enlightenment, liberty, and reason, as well as the international texts of the UN, and inverted these historical references to support their goals and expose the hypocrisy of French administrative policy.[59]

In early 1955, Pré decided that, in order to comply with the terms of the UN Trusteeship Charter, the administration must fight UPC political activity in the courts. After consulting with the minister of overseas France, Pierre-Henri Teitgen, Pré wagered that the UN would not contest court decisions as vehemently as they would administrative sanctions. The high commissioner ordered administrators and law enforcement officers to take court action against all those who disturbed public order by their activities, speech, or writings. The new administrative strategy was based on the law of 10 January 1936 permitting the dissolution of political parties linked with militias or paramilitary groups, and on the decree of 23 October 1935, which prohibited public demonstrations.[60] UPC public speakers appropriated French legal discourse to fit their own political agenda, citing metropolitan law and the UN Charter to make the nationalists' case against the injustice of the administration's suppression of civil and political liberties. Anticolonial activists in other French territories also made references to the French constitution, the French revolution, and African support for France during World War II. Upécistes applied this broader trend, but, due to the Cameroons' particular status as UN trust territories, also went beyond arguments centered on French history, by invoking UN documents and the UDHR.[61]

UPC leaders took every chance they could to reject French administrators' definition of independence for Cameroon, which rested on the broader supposition that a national identity for former colonies, even after they had gained some degree of internal autonomy, would be rooted in France. In 1954 the French representative of Cameroon at the UN's Fourth Committee argued that the lack of a common national language precluded national unification and independence. But Um Nyobé refuted that argument before the Fourth Committee, stating that once national sovereignty had been achieved, Cameroonians could "concentrate on developing a national language."[62] If Cameroonians lacked a common tongue, Um Nyobé continued, they were bound in its stead by their common experience under colonialism, and collectively linked by the hardship and discrimination they had withstood since the late nineteenth century.

Um Nyobé's speeches before the General Assembly may have set the tone of the UPC, but he was not alone in inverting French laws, actions, and rhetoric for the nationalist cause. References to the French constitution, the French revolution, Cameroonian support of France in the Second World War, and the status of the territory as a trusteeship rather than a colony surfaced in petitions to the UN, and in later speeches made by pronationalist politicians.[63] The appropriation of colonial discourse also appeared in a growing nationalist print culture composed of newspapers, tracts, and petitions to the UN.[64] As the movement spread, the strategies learned in the halls of the école des cadres radiated outward into local committee meetings, until most members became familiar with the act of petitioning and the importance of newspapers and tracts.

This print culture arose from the UPC's reaction to Pré's repression of public meetings and demonstrations. Félix Moumié, the UPC's president, authored tracts that the French chief of the Mungo Region described as "inflamed articles" filled with "passion and indignation."[65] Contributions to nationalist writings throughout Cameroon poured forth from UPC, JDC, or UDEFEC members with an adequate command of French, and students in France added their written words to the anticolonial current as well.[66] Regional UPC newspapers cropped up throughout the territory: *L'étoile,* in the southern part of the territory; *Lumière,* in the north; and the standard *La voix du Cameroun,* edited by Abel Kingué, published in Douala. Um Nyobé and other UPC, JDC, and UDEFEC nationalists visible in the international political arena began to give interviews to metropolitan newspapers. From these writings, an upéciste archive took shape. Like Land and Freedom Army soldiers in Kenya, FLN fighters in Algeria, and the Zimbabwe African National Liberation Army,[67] members of the UPC, UDEFEC, and the JDC kept meticulous records of local meeting minutes as if constructing an official archive that would later become part of national history. Upéciste activists also distributed tracts, carbon copies of leaders' speeches to the UN and party newspapers.

The Act of Petitioning—A Blend of Written and Oral Voices

Ordinary upécistes added their voices to this stream of writing, as party members took up the act of petitioning in their local committee meetings. As party ideology spread into rural zones, the combination of oral transmission with written distribution facilitated the widespread dissemination of the UPC's nationalist message. Although the UPC's central message was standardized in written form, the party's popularity arose out of the oral distribution of information about the party. This distribution occurred primarily through oral accounts, whether in committee meetings, in public places, or by word of mouth, and even through gossip, hearsay, and rumor—the means of information exchange available to nonliterate populations.[68] The mandatory presence of a literate scribe at every local meeting ensured the transfer of ideas from their oral form to the written documents of meeting minutes and petitions and ensured the oral transmission of party literature read aloud at meetings.

Directors' bureau members and central committee leaders had been petitioning the UN on behalf of the Cameroonian population since 1949. But in 1955 the UPC leadership urged nationalists to write to the UN directly from their own locales. Memoranda circulated from one local meeting to the next announcing "the new articles of faith of UPC ideology" for 1955.[69] One of these circulars, distributed to all local and central committees, contained Um Nyobé's call for popular petitions to be sent to the UN requesting that the violence unleashed by the Pré regime be investigated.[70]

The act of writing down individuals' spoken accounts promoted the diffusion of stories about UDEFEC and UPC members on a national scale, eventually permitting their stories to reach the international audience of the Trusteeship Council. The act of petitioning helped to construct the collective nationalism that petitioners signed on to. Through the process of petitioning, individual complaints against the French and British administrations contributed to a growing collection of such stories, which in turn established the bedrock of new political ideas and new ways of articulating them.[71] Individuals committed their stories to writing in the form of petitions, which were sometimes used as illustrations in the party's tracts that were then circulated and read aloud at meetings. The personal nature of these stories encouraged more stories to be shared, allowing members to identify with people outside their own locale, whom they may not have met. Through this exchange, the UPC message and ideology became personalized and more widely credible.[72]

Although Cameroonian nationalists began to petition the UN soon after the founding of the UPC, anticolonial activists from other trust territories had already established the precedent of petitioning. In 1947, Sylvanus Olympio of Togoland became the first African politician from a trust territory to appear personally before the General Assembly.[73] Following Olympio's lead, "political leaders and spokesmen from Somaliland, the French Cameroons, and Tanganyika" regularly addressed the General Assembly.[74] The same year, Reverend Michael Scott, a renegade Anglican priest of British origin residing in Tobruk, an African shantytown just outside Johannesburg, became the first nongovernmental representative to speak at the UN on behalf of subject populations. He described the hardships of the Herero, Berg-Damara, and Nama populations of South-West Africa just as the Union of South Africa expressed its intent to annex the territory.[75] Thereafter appearing every two years before the Fourth Committee, Scott eventually persuaded the UN body to vote in November 1951 to invite the traditional leaders of South-West Africa to speak before the committee as representatives of the indigenous peoples.[76] The Union of South Africa government refused passports to the delegation of traditional chiefs, thereby preventing them from traveling. But the Fourth Committee's vote opened the door to allowing nongovernmental representatives of the "indigenous peoples" of other territories to address the General Assembly. It was a precedent on which Cameroonian nationalists built in order to be heard in the international forum of the United Nations. Yet a few things made the petitions from Cameroonian nationalists unique among those received by the Trusteeship Council from 1946 to 1960.

First, their sheer number rendered the petitions from the Cameroons exceptional among those emanating from the trust territories. The largest number of petitions in UN Trusteeship Council files from 1946 to 1960 originated in the French and British Cameroons. During that period, Cameroonians, most of them affiliated with one of the nationalist parties, the UPC, UDEFEC, the JDC, or the USCC, sent some fifty thousand petitions to the Trusteeship Council.[77] In 1952, after Um Nyobé spoke before the Fourth Committee in the UN General Assembly, the Belgian representative, Pierre Ryckmans, stated that since Um Nyobé had not submitted a written petition before his request for an oral hearing, he was not following the proper rules of procedure.[78] Those in favor of hearing Um Nyobé outnumbered those opposed, and so the UPC leader was allowed to address the Fourth Committee. But tactical objections such as this, voiced by members of the Fourth Committee, prompted even more petitions. In the ensuing years, the number of petitions sent to the UN by UPC nationalists increased, peaking in 1955 and 1958, the years of the UN visiting mission's tour of the Cameroonian territories under French and British administration.

Cameroonian women, too, took up the act of petitioning to a greater extent than women in other trust territories. The Women's Committee of the UPC sent its first petition in 1949, even before the women's party—UDEFEC—was formed, in 1952.[79] Soon thereafter, a Fourth Committee representative's query prompted a rise in women's participation in the nationalist movement. During Um Nyobé's second trip to New York, in 1953, to address the General Assembly, Mrs. Lakshmi Menon, representing India in the Fourth Committee, pointedly asked "whether some of the petitions received by the UN from the Cameroons under

French administration emanated from women's organizations affiliated with the UPC, . . . whether women showed an interest in the country's political life and what part they took in the movement."[80] Upon his return to Cameroon, Um Nyobé encouraged the women of UDEFEC, which he had described to the Fourth Committee as the only women's organization in the territory,[81] to increase their visibility before the UN by taking up their pens to write petitions as well.[82] Of the thousands of petitions on record from Cameroonian nationalists, approximately one in six came from women. They provide a rare written record of everyday African women's political involvement in anticolonialism.[83]

Finally, unlike petitions from other territories that petitioners attempted to articulate in terms they believed suitable for a UN audience, the Cameroonian petitions must be read as a part of the new nationalist narrative composed of both a postwar international anticolonial rhetoric and local vernaculars.[84] Recognizing the importance of word of mouth in conveying information, and not wanting the party message to be available only to educated and literate members, party leaders stressed the importance of local committees in facilitating the oral transmission of nationalist ideology. The committees played a key role in this transmission, as traveling activists used skits, songs, stories, and even biblical parables to convey party objectives. As the act of petitioning gained in popularity, a narrative style that closely resembled the oral became more common in the missives sent to the UN, and the UPC, JDC, and UDEFEC petitions sent after the 1955 proscription can be read as a genre consistent with oral transmission that is then committed to writing.[85] On reading the petitions together, their contribution to an emerging anticolonial, proindependence political repertoire—created, popularized, and disseminated, in part, through the act of petitioning—becomes clear. Like the practice of petitioning, the adoption of a national flag and anthem galvanized the UPC movement among the population at large.

The Joint Proclamation and the Symbols of UPC Nationalism

UPC leaders built on the new political repertoire to unveil their plan for "immediate" independence before crowds of people in Yaoundé and Douala in an atmosphere of heightened political consciousness. On 22 April 1955, nationalist leaders in Douala and Yaoundé coordinated a public reading of the Joint Proclamation, declaring solidarity among the UPC, UDEFEC, the JDC, and the USCC, foretelling the end of the trusteeship, and calling for general elections before 1 December 1955, to be followed by the UN-supervised establishment of a sovereign state of Cameroon by 1956.[86] Before thousands of people dressed in red and black, the colors of the UPC, the directors unveiled the "Cameroonian" flag (a black crab on a red background), and performed the "national anthem." The crab symbolized the crustaceans for which the territory was named, while the color black stood for solidarity among black populations under colonialism, and red for the blood spilled in the struggle for independence.[87] The Joint Proclamation served to highlight the distinction between the UPC's call for immediate and total independence accompanied by the reunification of the territories under British and French rule, and the French administration's promise of a gradual decolonization process that would grant independence progressively, with France overseeing each step.[88] Combining the symbols of official statehood (flag and national anthem) with a precise political plan of action to achieve independence, the UPC and its affiliates claimed the task of nation building on behalf of Cameroonian populations.

After the Joint Proclamation, the attitude of upécistes toward the Pré administration's repressive campaign against the nationalist movement shifted. Despite the regular disruption of their meetings, upécistes in Douala, Yaoundé, and throughout the Mungo Region organized ever-larger assemblies. As seen above, by 1955, the ranks of upéciste members and sympathizers had grown to at least one hundred thousand, outnumbering the supporters of any other political movement in the territory.[89] By May of that year, the UPC clearly wielded the greatest and most widespread political influence in the territory. In a report on the UPC's establishment in the territory, Pré informed the minister of overseas France that the movement "forced its adversaries to take the UPC's political position into account" and, by imposing the engagement with its nationalistic ideals, had "changed the general atmosphere" throughout French Cameroon.[90]

The UPC's dominance of the political landscape became publicly apparent during an official event soon after the Joint Proclamation was unveiled. In 1955, Minister of Overseas France Teitgen scheduled a visit to the territory to coincide with the inauguration of the new bridge across the Wouri River connecting Douala to the Mungo Region. In honor of Teitgen's visit, the administration planned a parade that was to feature veterans of the Second World War. The administration had issued khaki cloth and berets for their uniforms. But for upécistes, particularly the war veterans among them, the inaugural visit provided the opportunity to organize an en masse boycott of the official ceremonies.[91] On 10 May 1955, five days before the scheduled event, François Fosso, an active member of the UPC and vice president of the Amicale des anciens combattants et ex-militaires, addressed eight hundred assembled supporters. He described the neglect and disrespect veterans faced at the hands of the administration in French Cameroon—a stark contrast with how veterans in France were treated.[92] He dissuaded veterans from wearing the khaki uniforms and asked them not to participate in the parade: "Why haven't the veterans ever been invited to participate in such a parade in the last ten years?" He ended his speech with a threat: "We say to those who participate on 15 May that they carry the stench of high treason in the pockets and creases of their khaki uniforms . . . a betrayal not only of our interests, but of those of our entire country."[93] On the day of the minister's inaugural visit, UPC leaders organized an alternative assembly attended by some fifteen hundred people,[94] many of whom wore red clothing or scarves and neckties bearing the party's insignia, the black crab.

For Bayart, gestures, music, clothing, and performance, as well as oral and written discourse, are the elements that constitute a political repertoire.[95] Cameroonian nationalists fashioned their independence-era political repertoire out of a combination of public discourse, print culture, symbols, political cartoons, clothing, religiosity, and the political symbolism of the UN in an international arena. Many of these media had previously been used to speak for the "colonial modernity" introduced by European administration, but within the context of nationalism they were appropriated by the UPC, as "the colonized, [in order] to speak against the colonizer, [used] the tools of the latter."[96] As the UPC gained experience as a political party, it applied more and more of these discursive strategies to refute the administering authority's claims of preparing the trusteeship inhabitants for autonomy.

While administrators tried to shape political discourse through supporters of the French project for Cameroon's integration into a greater France (the French Union of 1946 and the French Community of 1958), and through their sponsorship and financial support of alternative political parties, newspapers, and other media,[97] Cameroonians had a greater discursive range available to them. They actively drew on the arsenal of linguistic expression located in local cultural reservoirs as they increasingly incorporated local political philosophies and indigenous discourses into the repertoire. Employing language and narrative as a social and political practice, they rejected the European administration's self-proclaimed "authority to designate what would count as reason," and instead constructed their own "reasonable" political expression.[98] Through language and the construction of political discourse, colonial subjects "reactivated" a political imaginary that not only rejected colonialism but also created a separate ideological terrain in which they imagined a nation free of any sort of foreign administration.[99] Historian Achille Mbembe has analyzed the local political philosophies particular to the Bassaa-speaking populations of the Sanaga-Maritime at length in his account of the quest for independence in the region.[100] The intersection of UPC nationalism with Grassfields political philosophies and practices—including traditional chieftaincy and biological reproduction—is examined in the following chapters.

THE MUNGO REGION AS A POLITICAL AND CULTURAL EPICENTER OF UPC NATIONALISM

It took a few years for the UPC to fully take root in the culturally diverse and economically dynamic Mungo Region, which served as terrain of postwar political experimentation. From the late 1940s and throughout the early 1950s, the Mungo Region witnessed the rise and fall of various planters' cooperatives, trade unions, and political parties. In the Mungo River valley—the land of cash crops, railroads, plantation labor, and factories—the UPC was born of the USCC, a communist labor union associated with the French Confédération générale du travail (CGT).[101] In this varied political landscape UPC membership fluctuated. The first UPC committee was created in 1949 and included both Mbo and Bamileke members, but it had completely disintegrated by 1952.[102] Alfred Elong, a founding member of the UPC in Nkongsamba, later became president of the Nkongsamba section of ESOCAM, a pro-French political party established with the administration's support as an antidote to the UPC.[103]

Three years after the dissolution of the multiethnic local committee, the UPC had re-formed in Nkongsamba with Bamileke migrants at the helm. A UPC central committee was formed in Nkongsamba in 1952 and its members remained active in the region until the party's ban, in July 1955. Sakéo Kamen was president; Abel Kingué, secretary-general;

école des cadres graduate Elias Tchuente, secretary; and Mathias Kom Kamgaing, treasurer.

Tchuente and Kamgaing had come to political activism through community organizing in Nkongsamba. They left their home chieftaincy of Bayangam in the Bamileke Region to settle in Nkongsamba in the 1930s and became involved in labor unions in the late 1940s. Tchuente, a Second World War veteran who had fought at Tripoli, worked for the French-Armenian coffee exporter Kourgen Gortzounian. In 1947 Tchuente led commercial agents and merchants in a citywide strike that resulted in his dismissal from Gortzounian's coffee-bean factory. On 11 November 1948 the two emigrants from Bayangam founded a cultural association called the Foyer de progrès de la jeunesse de Bayangam (FOPROJEUBA) for Bayangam youth. Like many Bamileke chiefs who sought to incorporate the activities of their emigrant communities into the chieftaincy, the fo of Bayangam recognized the association in 1950, and by 1952 its statutes were officially registered with the French administration.[104] Tchuente and Kamgaing's Bayangam youth association promised mutual aid to members in need, provided financial support for funeral celebrations in Bayangam, and promoted and defended Bayangam interests in Nkongsamba.[105]

As the case of Bayangam demonstrates, the UPC spread to the Bamileke Region primarily through the political and social alliances connecting a given home chieftaincy to its emigrant community in the Mungo Region. After the fo formally acknowledged the youth association, Tchuente and Kamgaing collaborated with two Protestant catechists in Bayangam, Lucas Kamdjom and Marcus Tchatchueng, to establish local FOPROJEUBA meetings throughout the chieftaincy. These meetings broadcast the UPC's political message of political and economic emancipation from French rule. In 1954, Kamdjom and Tchatchueng became president and secretary general of the UPC central committee of Bayangam, respectively, overseeing local committees throughout the chieftaincy.[106] The UPC took root in the Bamileke chieftaincy of Bayangam through the FOPROJEUBA initially founded in Nkongsamba.

Central committee president Lucas Kamdjom embodied Um Nyobé's insistence that "the leaders of the local committees should consider themselves catechists of the villages or quarters in which they assume political responsibilities."[107] He had attended the Protestant seminary of Ndoungue, ten kilometers outside Nkongsamba and had served as a catechist throughout the Bafoussam and Bangangte Subdivisions and in the resettlement villages along the Noun's left bank. A polyglot with strong communal ties to more than one locale, Kamdjom had the kind of education and transregional upbringing that the UPC directors wanted in their leaders. Born in 1895, he was older than many upécistes.[108] His participation calls into question the conventional scholarly assertion that the UPC membership in the Bamileke Region was made up solely of young, disenfranchised "social cadets."[109] In 1957 the sixty-two-year-old Kamdjom stood trial with the twenty-something chief of Baham, Pierre Kamdem Ninyim (whose story will be recounted in the next chapter), and was sentenced to two years in prison for his role in the proscribed UPC. He died in prison on 13 January 1959.[110]

FOPROJEUBA exemplified the overlap between city-based cultural associations and political mobilization in associated chieftaincies, a combination that strengthened the UPC's popular appeal in both urban and rural areas. Through the channels forged between rural and urban political activists, UPC local committees spread from the Bamileke communities settled in the Mungo River valley to the Bamileke Region. In Baham, which shared a border with Bayangam, three local committees were established by 1954 in the quarters of Chiala, Pumsze, and La'agweu. Members met clandestinely twice a month. Ignace Néguin Djoko, an ardent UPC activist in Baham, explained: "It wasn't very public; everyone had the idea that it was like a secret association. Each local committee did its own thing."[111]

When a significant number of local committees had cropped up in a region, the UPC leadership could designate a regional section to serve as an intermediary between the central committees and the directors' bureau. To be classified a "regional section," an area had to have at least three thousand UPC members, to be financially self-sufficient, and to maintain a permanent office equipped with a typewriter, a radio, a camera, and subscriptions to a selection of local and international newspapers. UPC leaders strongly recommended the French Communist *L'humanité* as one of the subscriptions. Regional sections were also required to have liaison couriers and messengers, a mailbox, an accounting ledger, and an adult literacy program. A regional section was established in the Mungo Region in 1953.[112]

There were eight permanent bureaus within the Mungo regional section: two in Nkongsamba, one in Mbanga, two in Dschang, one in Bafang, one in Bafoussam, and one in Ndikinimeki, in the Mbam. The regional section had an annual budget of two million francs in 1955 and oversaw a number of local committees throughout the Mungo Region, including eight in Nkongsamba, eleven in Mbanga, eleven in Manjo, nine in Mbouroukou, and so on, all the way down to Loum. Five of the Mungo leaders, including JDC president Abel Kingué, regularly crossed the Anglo-French boundary to organize UPC local committees in British territory. By 1955 the French estimated the UPC to have some twelve hundred dues-paying members in the Mungo alone and an additional three hundred in British territory.[113] Significantly, the UPC's Mungo regional section included the Bamileke Region, as upéciste organizers understood that the two administrative regions were interlinked.

BAMILEKE CHIEFS AT HOME AND BEYOND

In 1955 there were three UPC central committees in the Bamileke Region, and nearly a hundred local committees known to the French administration at Bafoussam, Dschang, and Bafang.[114] In a rare moment of truth, the report on UPC politics referred to the number of "traditional chiefs, such as those of Bafoussam, Bamendjou, Bameka, Batcham, Fokwe and Fomopea, who openly sympathize with the movement,"[115] adding that there were "more than fifteen hundred active members" of the UPC in the Bamileke Region, and an estimated ten thousand supporters.[116]

French policy toward the UPC in Bamileke communities rested on the fallacious belief that Bamileke chiefs were their allies in suppressing the nationalist movement. In 1954 the French chief of the Bafoussam Subdivision wrote, "The administration and traditional chiefs must be vigilant and firm each time the troublemakers want to create disorder."[117] In 1955 administrators emphasized the opposition "of most traditional chiefs" to the movement in the Bamileke Region.[118] When describing the leaders of UPC local committees, administrative reports suggested that they were selected, not for their political ideology, but "because of their natural disposition toward opposition, whether carried out against the administration or against the traditional representatives or European employers."[119] Each of these reports reflected the failure of French administrators to acknowledge on the record the fact that a number of young Bamileke chiefs had emerged as strong supporters of the UPC movement.

In the 1950s, French administrators tended to view Bamileke chiefs as part of a regional, homogenous "native command" made up of static, authoritative instruments of government. That perception was a throwback to 1930s French policy in French Cameroon when, under Bonnecarrère, territorial administrators, especially in the Bamileke Region, were urged to "reorganize native command" by reassembling and reinforcing the chiefs' power and authority,[120] and to create "in the absence of unity based on organization or attribution, a unity based on methods."[121] In assuming that mfo in the Bamileke Region still believed, as they supposedly had in the 1930s, that their power was derived from "the administration's endorsement,"[122] administrators overlooked two contemporary political trends in Bamileke governance. The first took shape within the chieftaincy and consisted of a younger, anti-French generation of chiefs inheriting power and supporting the UPC. The other took place among Bamileke emigrant communities and had to do with the growing influence of family chiefs chosen as representatives of the fo in urban areas, and with their degree of influence on the politics of home chieftaincies.

Within the Bamileke Region, Fo Mathias Djoumessi of Foreke-Dschang represented a new generation of Bamileke chiefs who recognized the waning popularity of the traditional institution of chieftaincy and the mfo's need to reinvent themselves as leaders with popular support.[123] In 1953 fourteen-year-old Fo Sokodjou succeeded his father at Bamendjou, followed by eighteen-year-old Fo Feze of Bandenkop and Fo Kamdem Ninyim of Baham in 1954, and twenty-year old Fo Kemajou of Bangou.[124] As if following Fo Djoumessi's lead, these mfo and others like them would emerge as a new type of traditional ruler, who kept informed about the political realities of the day, who catered to the demands of their emigrant populations while seeking access to their wealth, and who took direction from the secret institutions and politicospiritual councils such as kamveu and kungang that had witnessed the political errors of their fathers. These mfo provided the UPC with the support it needed to take root among their populations. But they were few enough and their chieftaincies small enough that French administrators believed they could be easily eradicated and then replaced with traditional chiefs more favorable to the administration's political project.

As the UPC took root throughout the Bamileke Region, the party became engaged with the politics of chieftaincy, which gradually became a part of its political platform. In April 1955 the UPC central committee of Bafang wrote a petition accusing René Borne, the

French chief of the Bamileke Region, and François Orabona, fo and mayor of Bafang, of instigating hostilities between the chieftaincies of Banka and Badoumjia. The petition stated that Fo Kamga of Bandjoun had, on the authority of the French administration, sent mercenaries to Bafang in military vehicles to launch a civil war. According to the petitioners, the operation was a French strategy to instill an atmosphere of fear before the arrival of the UN visiting mission scheduled for later that year. The central committee also complained that "Borne and Orabona oppress the population by delimiting parcels of land without soliciting the opinion of the occupants, and some parcels are delimited twice."[125] The petition from Bafang demonstrated a growing popular distrust of mfo who held both a traditional title and an administrative function. Increasingly, Bamileke populations perceived mfo such as Fo Kamga of Bandjoun and Fo Orabona of Bafang as auxiliaries of the administration, complicit in French oppression of Bamileke populations. The equitable distribution of land became once again a prime political issue defining the legitimacy and accountability of the fo, as it had been when Grassfields chieftaincies were founded and centralized during the eighteenth and nineteenth centuries.

The second trend in Bamileke government that administrators overlooked was the importance of the leadership of family chiefs for emigrant communities in the Mungo Region, in Yaoundé and Douala and other towns. These community leaders very often remained unknown to French administrators and governed with the popular consent of fellow villagers as their primary source of legitimacy and authority.[126] As the fifties brought falling coffee and cacao prices and urban unemployment to the Mungo Region, the urban-based representatives of gung allied themselves with the new generation of Bamileke mfo, who were born and came of age during the French mandate period. Emigrants served as informants who helped their rulers understand the changing political and economic climate beyond chieftaincy borders.

UPC activists worked with Bamileke chiefs at home and with the family chiefs governing urban communities to bring village and city together. This triangular alliance among upécistes, mfo, and city-based family chiefs seemed to go largely unnoticed by French administrators (see chapter 4). As the importance of Bamileke migrant communities' autonomously selected family chiefs increased, the influence of those selected by the French administration waned. By 1950, Adam Arab, Nkongsamba's first chief of strangers, passed away and was not replaced.[127]

The symbiosis between Bamileke chieftaincies and Bamileke migrant communities in cities and towns superseded the very administrative boundaries of the Bamileke Region. Just as UPC nationalists paid little attention to official regional borders when establishing the regional sections of the party, the political and cultural organization of Bamileke populations spread beyond the region's geographic boundaries.

FRENCH STRATEGIES TO ERADICATE THE UPC

In the interwar period, the French administration in Cameroon, as colonial administrators elsewhere, began to cultivate an elite, intelligentsia class composed of scribes, interpreters, clerks, nurses, doctors, schoolteachers, plantation owners, and entrepreneurs. French administrators promoted the assimilation of traditional rulers into this class by ensuring the literacy of chiefs' potential heirs, offering bonuses for chiefs who followed administrative policy to the letter and brought in the requisite amount of taxes, and keeping track of chiefs' performances in an annual report card system.[128] In the 1950s, as the UPC expanded its base, its leadership sought out the same sort of people. French administrators, observing the number of persons in the elite class they had courted for decades who joined the ranks of UPC supporters, scrambled to establish political parties throughout the southern region, in the hope that these new parties would staunch the flow of the elite into the UPC. Most notable among these parties were the ESOCAM, in the Sanaga-Maritime,[129] and the BDC, under the tutelage of the French Catholic missionary doctor turned politician, Louis-Paul Aujoulat.[130] In the Bamileke Region, the French administration sponsored and oversaw the formation of the antidotal political party, Rassemblement du peuple camerounais (RPC), led by André Mouthemy of Bafoussam, but overseen behind the scenes by French chiefs of region and subdivision.[131]

In April 1955, Um Nyobé, Kingué, and Mathieu Tagny traveled throughout the Bamileke Region to spread news of Um and Kingué's December 1954 trip to France and the United States. At Bansoa and Babete, on 7 April 1955, RPC members prevented public meetings from being held. The next day, Kingué organized a meeting in nearby Bafoussam, but RPC members stole the UPC flag and its pole and filled the meetinghouse, causing the meeting to dissolve. That afternoon, the delegation arrived in Bamena, only to be asked by the fo to leave. Meetings scheduled to take place in Bangangte, Bandjoun,

Batoula, and Bafoussam in the following days were canceled. On 10 April, two meetings took place without mishap at Bafang and nearby Fonkouakem, in the presence of Um Nyobé, but the mayor of Bafoussam prohibited the meeting scheduled there on 24 April.[132]

Village populations in the Bamileke Region recognized the RPC as a French creation. A nobleman and coffee planter in Baham today describes the party as a guise to prevent harassment by French administrators: "Here, we became members of the RPC. But it was a ruse; in order to have something to eat from the French, we duped the French governor. It was a way of being sheltered. In the UPC, you were noticed."[133] Lacking the grassroots support of the UPC, the RPC all but disappeared before the territorial elections of 1956. In February 1956 the French recognized that "André Mouthemy, of the RPC, has given up on political activity," as his house had been burned down while "he was drunk in town."[134]

The parties founded with French encouragement never gained large numbers of supporters or crossed ethnic divides, with the exception of the BDC, which was linked with Catholic lay activity and already enjoyed a multiethnic base.[135] But a number of elite political actors did cast their lot with the administration. In the new postwar era of the coffee and banana boom, wealthy African landowners and merchants began to rub elbows with French settlers, or colons, as upécistes called them. The expatriate community of Nkongsamba worked hard to co-opt these elite into the echelons of the administration, hoping that they would protect French economic interests during and after decolonization.

In the Mungo, the most well known and successful of these assimilated évolués was "Prince" Daniel Kemajou, a wealthy Bamileke resident of Nkongsamba who served as an elected representative of the Mungo in the Cameroon assembly from 1946 to 1956, and as one of five Cameroonian counselors to the French Union from 1947 to 1959. Kemajou also succeeded his father as fo of the Bamileke chieftaincy of Bazou in 1953, becoming the first fo to govern from beyond chieftaincy boundaries. In December 1956, Kemajou, running his campaign from Bazou in the Bamileke Region after his defeat in Nkongsamba earlier that year, was reelected to the assembly, and in 1957 he was chosen to serve as the assembly's president.[136]

It was contradictory for the conservative French community of the Mungo Region to politically support Bamileke elite such as "Prince"

Kemajou while casting other Bamileke settlers in the Mungo as strangers, troublemakers, and land swindlers.[137] On the other hand, upécistes painted évolués such as Kemajou as collaborators, the French administration's valets, and thus traitors or mfingung. After the movement's official ban in French Cameroon, political rhetoric became increasingly polarized as upécistes pitted "nationalists" and "patriots" against "lackeys" and "traitors," thus reducing the political landscape to two dimensions.[138]

An administration-sponsored party never took shape in the Mungo Region, perhaps because administrators had another strategy they hoped would prevent the mobilization of upécistes. As their predecessors had done since the late 1920s, French administrators and colons played on Mbo-Bamileke tensions over landownership and usufruct as a way to undermine the party's interethnic influence in the Mungo. By the early 1950s, landownership had become increasingly ethnicized. In 1955 the central committee of the UPC in Manjo opposed French expropriation of four thousand hectares of land by submitting to the high commissioner a registry of deeds that designated fifty-three parcels as belonging to African owners. The registry had a clear record of the description of the parcels, their state of cultivation, the crops planted on them, and the date of the customary agreement reached between occupant and owner.[139] On the Ngol-Manjo land registry, Bamileke planters submitted the majority of the claims to plots of land, all of which included coffee as a crop.[140]

The Ngol-Manjo case demonstrated that Bamileke planters in the Mungo had actively obtained titles for the land they occupied. As such, Bamileke planters had the required legal documentation to protest the French administration's expropriation of land. The UPC sought to support the claims of landowners in the Mungo, but, since fewer autochthons legally owned land, and still fewer had officially registered their holdings, Bamileke planters received the greatest benefit from UPC involvement in the politics of land distribution. Administrators and French planters were already depicting Bamileke in the Mungo as cunning swindlers of land. Using the same ethnic discourse, they now portrayed the UPC as a political party furthering a Bamileke "colonization" project. Autochthonous populations who mobilized in the 1950s to resist the expropriation of their land initiated the nullification of the customary contracts that had granted the right of occupancy to Bamileke farmers.[141]

By placing itself at the forefront of the prevailing economic issues in the Mungo Region, the UPC acted as an advocate for workers' rights, Cameroonian planters' export initiatives, and Cameroonian landowners. Those who held officially registered deeds to Mungo Region land were primarily Bamileke immigrants. As a result, the UPC appeared to advocate more for Bamileke populations than for autochthons in the Mungo River valley, enabling French administrators and colons to use ethnicity as a way to undermine the party's influence.

THE UPRISINGS OF MAY 1955 AND THE FRENCH PROSCRIPTION OF THE UPC

On 22 May 1955, the frequent skirmishes between the French administration and the upécistes erupted into full-fledged violent confrontation.[142] Campaigning throughout the Mungo Region in the weeks leading up to the UPC's Joint Proclamation, announced on 22 April (see above), Moumié, Ouandié, and Kingué regularly drew crowds from Loum to Nkongsamba.[143] On 15 May in Mbanga, fifty kilometers north of Douala in the Mungo Region, troops forcibly dispersed a UPC assembly. Before disbanding, UPC leaders promised to hold another meeting the following week.[144]

On Sunday, 22 May 1955, UPC delegations from Douala, the southern Mungo Region plantation towns of Njombé and Penja, as well as Tombel, a plantation town just across the border in British territory, arrived in Mbanga for the 11:00 a.m. meeting that drew about fifteen hundred upécistes. The French chief of the Mbanga Subdivision arrived with his assistant, the commander of the police force, eleven Cameroonian guards, and seventeen regional guards to break up the assembly. The French officials and guards headed to the neighborhood of Mbanga's UPC central committee president, André Tchomte. As they approached, a crowd surged forth from the surrounding houses, encircled the gendarmes and guards, attacked them with bottles, stones, and clubs, and wounded a gendarme in the leg. The guards, whose weapons were not loaded, retreated, and the chief of the subdivision and his entourage fled. The nationalists destroyed five vehicles, and, after the administration's retreat, continued the meeting. Reinforcements of the guard arrived at 3:30 p.m., but the upécistes had already disbanded and left town. During the fracas at Mbanga, nationalists severely injured one French gendarme, two Cameroonian guards, one of whom would die in the hospital, and one regional guard, and managed to collect several of their weapons. The UPC's victory was broadcast throughout the northern Mungo, and the news reached Nkongsamba and Douala that same evening.

The incident at the Mbanga meeting sparked uprisings that wracked the region for the next several days. Throughout the morning of 23 May 1955, French security forces arrested those who had participated in the Mbanga ambush. At Loum, upécistes attacked the chief of the administrative post, a Mr. Monnier, inflicting severe injuries and stealing his weapon and those of two of his guards. The arrival of a mobile unit saved Monnier's life by dispatching him to Douala for medical treatment. The next day, police reinforcements arrived in Loum, evacuated Mrs. Monnier and their three children, and forced the dispersal of the nationalists. The following day, by some accounts, upécistes at Loum marched on the prison to free those arrested in the previous days. Security forces fired into the melee, killing six and wounding five of the demonstrators.[145]

The chief of the Mungo Region, Michel Vallée, traveled to Loum from Nkongsamba on 24 May, only to return the same day to insurrection and revolt in his own town. On the order of JDC president Abel Kingué, a group of nationalists armed with clubs, iron bars, and machetes stormed the Nkongsamba administrative buildings. The assistant chief of the region ordered the demonstrators to return to their homes. Instead, eight hundred of them proceeded to the neighborhood of David Tchoupo, where they held an impromptu outdoor assembly. One speaker announced, "Now all the upécistes have decided to no longer submit to administrative disruptions and the intrusion of an administrative representative in any meeting shall be opposed by force."[146]

That afternoon, upéciste delegations from surrounding towns began to arrive in Nkongsamba. Many of the new arrivals, including an UDEFEC group, came by dump truck and made their way to the prefect's residence. Police forces and mobile units dispersed the crowd, but at around 5:30 p.m., they marched on the prison, pelting the Cameroonian guards with stones and then engaging them in hand-to-hand combat. Several law enforcement agents suffered stab wounds.[147] The nationalists captured a French guard, knocked him to the ground, and pelted him with sticks and stones. Managing to regain his footing, the guard fired three shots into the air, and the nationalists retreated toward the center of town, destroying cars and raiding European shops along the way.

On 25 May the train from Douala brought fresh reinforcements for nationalists in Nkongsamba. They had been spotted on the train without baggage, carrying clubs and other makeshift weapons, and wearing bandanas across their faces. When the train reached the station in Nkongsamba, police and gendarmes awaited them with a paddy wagon. Security forces herded them into the vehicle, but one threw hot pepper in the face of the gendarme closing the door on the prisoners.[148] Many of the nationalists, armed with crowbars, tire irons, and knives, escaped and attacked the guards. The gendarmes retaliated with gunfire, injuring several demonstrators, including Abraham Tchembiap, the first Cameroonian baker in Nkongsamba, who would die from his wounds a few hours later. On the same day in Douala, French troops fired on prisoners who revolted in the jail in New Bell, the "African quarter" of the city, killing seven and wounding sixty.[149]

Later in the day, administrative security intensified and the chief of the region, Vallée, gathered neighborhood chiefs and other town leaders to request that they denounce those who had participated in the riots. In an official statement Vallée solicited the population's aid in the hunt for the wrongdoers:

> A person who hosts a UPC leader in flight or helps one of them in any way will be immediately arrested for collaborating with a criminal and will be brought to justice. All chiefs who fail to alert the administration within 24 hours of the passage of a criminal in flight or a clandestine meeting can also be arrested and brought to justice. Any citizen can apprehend a person who has a warrant out for his arrest.[150]

The warning was circulated in other regions as well and would later become part of the emergency legislation passed to suppress the nationalist movement. The official calls for denunciation led to the suspicion, distrust, and resentment that would characterize the Mungo Region during the next two decades.

In the wake of the uprisings of May 1955, the administration arrested a number of upécistes, but most of the leaders fled Nkongsamba to take refuge across the border in British territory. In Bamileke the region's chief, Maurice Delauney, assembled the mfo and instructed them to denounce any upécistes in their chieftaincies. He also authorized the chiefs' use of "customary law" for rounding up criminals and expelling them from the village.[151] In a few villages, the fo's overzealous application of the French version of customary law led to the burning of suspected nationalists' compounds or the forced exile of those who were not a part of the UPC movement. Bamileke inhabitants exiled in this way joined the ranks of those hiding out in the hills of the Bamileke Region and the forests and mountainous zones of the Mungo Region as the maquis—or underground resistance—was formed. Without resources, banned from their chieftaincies, and prevented by administrative roadblocks from traveling freely, many of these exiles were trapped in the maquis and became upécistes by default. Significantly, however, despite Delauney's pressures to involve Bamileke chiefs in the roundup of nationalists, of the seven chieftaincies bordering Baham, only two mfo established themselves as anti-UPC leaders: Fo Joseph Kamga of Bandjoun, and the fo of Bahouan, a small chieftaincy situated between Bandjoun and Baham.

On 13 July 1955, approximately seven months after his arrival in French Cameroon, Pré's regime passed a decree proscribing the UPC and its affiliated parties, turning upécistes into outlaws with the stroke of his pen. It was the first political party to be banned in a UN trust territory.[152] The decree violated the UN Charter, the Trusteeship Agreement, and the UDHR, particularly Article 19, which ensured the right to freedom of opinion and expression, and Article 20, which defined freedom of peaceful assembly and association as a human right. Soon after the French administration's ban of the party, Joseph Mballa, a member of the UPC's central committee in Yaoundé, wrote to the public prosecutor, the high commissioner, the president of the French National Council, the secretary general of the United Nations, and the territory's highest magistrate. As other upéciste comrades had throughout the year leading up to the ban, Mballa referred to France's own history while calling for the restoration of political liberty in Cameroon:

> It is regrettable that the French rob themselves of the spirit that caused absolutism to surrender to democracy in 1789 and have turned leaders of the UPC into outlaws. It is inconceivable that representatives of the France of 1789, of 1848, and of 1940–44 have shown themselves to be hostile to liberalism . . . , the only measure of lasting peace. We ask you to conform to the spirit of universal brotherhood promoted in the French constitution of 1946.[153]

In the years after the 1955 proscription of the UPC in French Cameroon, references such as Mballa's to French constitutional history became scarce. Instead, party rhetoric and philosophy centered on French political processes gave way to a greater emphasis on the UN, human rights, and Afro-Asian liberation politics.

⁌

The first months of Pré's reign as high commissioner of French Cameroon set the political tone for the remaining trusteeship period. By the time of the party's official ban, the UPC dominated the political landscape in Cameroon and defined nationalist rhetoric in the territory. In the months leading up to the July 1955 proscription, UPC leaders mobilized supporters en masse, holding public assemblies with a turnout in the thousands. The synchronized demonstrations that took place during April and May 1955 revealed the strong communications network upécistes had in place, one that relied on party members and local committees as links in a word-of-mouth relay system crisscrossing the territory.

The UPC, UDEFEC, JDC, and USCC organized the Joint Proclamation of April 1955 to coincide with the ten-year anniversary of the San Francisco Conference, during which the United Nations was formed (25 April–26 June 1945).[154] With the national anthem, flag, and date setting for official independence, upéciste leaders positioned the movement to represent the independent, reunified nation-state of Cameroon. Due to their familiarity with other anticolonial resistance movements—particularly the PDG in Guinea-Conakry, where Pré had served as governor before his arrival in French Cameroon—UPC leaders had anticipated the arrests that would follow the Joint Proclamation and the uprisings of May 1955. They undoubtedly hoped that the arrests would increase the UPC's international visibility, but they could not have expected that the movement would be proscribed by official decree. Although he had orchestrated punitive lawsuits, arrests, imprisonments, and the transfers and dismissals of civil service employees of PDG members in Guinea during the early 1950s, Roland Pré had not banned the PDG-RDA during his time as governor in Guinea.[155] Furthermore, the UN documents clearly protected the political and civil liberties of trust territory inhabitants and specifically prohibited the administering authorities from banning political parties.

It would not be the last time that upécistes would overestimate the UN's ability to uphold the rules and principles outlined in its charters, agreements, conventions, and declarations. Cameroonian nationalists came to rely more heavily on the UN principles as well as on their anti-imperialist international supporters after the proscription of the movement. International political leverage was crucial to upécistes, particularly as the UPC and its affiliates, being outlawed, were excluded from the territorial elections of late 1956—the first within which universal suffrage applied and the last to be held before official independence. Shut out of territorial politics tightly managed by the French administration and its Cameroonian supporters, upécistes' expectation that the UN would intervene to rectify French violations of the international rule of law increased. But the UN's failure to enforce the trusteeship agreements amplified upécistes' disappointment in the international body.

In its simplest terms, the confrontation between UPC nationalists and French administrators in 1955 amounted to a fight for control of the process of decolonization, a process on which France's postcolonial relationship with independent Cameroon would build. French administrators conceived a French Union and French Cameroon's role within a greater France after independence. In March 1955 the minister of overseas France wrote to the high commissioner of French Cameroon, Roland Pré, "[We must] redouble our efforts to reassemble nonextremist movements locally and to reanimate Cameroonian political life by strengthening ties to the metropole. [This] should enable Cameroon, when she exits the trusteeship, to have at her disposal responsible men who . . . will win acceptance for the solutions we desire for a definitive association with the French community."[156]

On the other hand, UPC nationalists eschewed the territory's potential integration into a greater France; spoke of independence, liberty, sovereignty, and human rights in their own terms; and pursued alternative, extrametropolitan routes to constructing a national political community. Gradually, upécistes shaped a Cameroonian nationalist movement that deliberately bypassed inclusion in or collaboration with metropolitan political institutions and frameworks. Although the UPC movement was founded in part on the principles of liberty embedded in the French constitution, its political vision came to include a world far beyond one centered on the French metropole and bounded by the empire's borders. Nationalists' refusal of the greater-France project hinged, first and foremost, on the Cameroon territories' status as UN trusteeships, a status that upécistes used as the legal argument for rejecting a continued association with the

French government. From the viewpoint of Cameroonian nationalists, France's attempts to integrate its Cameroonian trust territory into the French Union amounted to as grave a violation of the UN Charter as the Union of South Africa's outright refusal to sign a trusteeship agreement for the former League of Nations mandate territory of South-West Africa in 1946.[157] After the 1955 proscription, upécistes continued to construct their three-dimensional movement—part international, part territorial, and part local. They drew on the global foundations of anti-imperialism, symbolized by the UN and articulated in the Bandung Conference of 1955. They also grounded the movement in local political philosophies such as the lepue ideal still present in chieftaincy governance despite decades of foreign rule—the indigenous elements of nationalism explored in the next chapter.

At first glance, the history of the UPC in French Cameroon might seem exceptional within the larger framework of French Africa's decolonization. In a historical analysis of French West African attitudes toward inclusion in a greater French Community, Frederick Cooper has argued that Africans under French rule found the prospect of postcolonial federation and citizenship in the French Union very appealing as an alternative to national independence in the era of Africa's decolonization.[158] Other detailed histories of decolonization in France's African territories suggest that French colonial administrators used political machinations and coercion to push significant portions of the population to vote in favor of inclusion in the French Community.[159] Conflicting attitudes toward a continuing political, cultural, and economic relationship with France came to a head throughout French West and French Equatorial Africa and the UN trust territories under French rule (French Cameroon and French Togo) in the referendum of September 1958, when Africans in France's colonial territories voted for or against inclusion in a French Community. Guinea's singular vote of no has been noted for its exceptionalism.[160] Yet arguably, what was truly exceptional about Guinea was the survival of its progressive nationalist party, the PDG, in the face of heavy-handed and often brutal French repression of political freedoms throughout its disintegrating empire. Guinea's vote of no may be more illustrative of an exceptional French policy (that of not banning the PDG) than of the uniqueness of the Guinean populations on the eve of decolonization. The outcome of the 1958 referendum in French Africa could very well have been quite different, had civil and political liberties not been suppressed throughout

French territories in 1958 to the degree that they were in Niger, French Congo, Gabon, Côte d'Ivoire, and French Cameroon.[161]

In French Cameroon, tactics of political manipulation through the fabrication of anti-UPC political parties, the arrest of upécistes on trumped-up charges, and counterpropaganda—all designed to further the greater France project—were in place by early 1955, even before the administration outlawed the UPC movement by official decree on 13 July 1955.[162] After the ban, the French administration remained committed to Cameroon's integration into the French community in formation. The purges, arrests, and imprisonments of UPC members and sympathizers undertaken after the official proscription of the party set in place the political strategies—martial law and emergency legislation— to be used thereafter to govern the territory. In categorizing upécistes as outlaws, the administration also stigmatized the Sanaga-Maritime, the Mungo, and the Bamileke Regions, which hosted the greatest number of nationalists, as particularly troublesome and rebellious.

UPC leaders knew that, faced with the French administration's effort to eradicate the movement within the territory, they had to rely on international support for it to survive, particularly after the proscription. They also knew that global political networks were only important insofar as they could be transplanted to every region, in the smallest locales. Upécistes appropriated global anti-imperialist discourse emerging from the UN, from India's independence, and from other anticolonial movements, as well as the enlightenment discourse that had once driven the French Revolution, and despite these diverse ideological bases, they remained connected to local and regional concerns in cities and villages throughout Cameroon. In 1956, the year after the ban and the year of the first single-college territory-wide elections open to all men and women of voting age, chieftaincy in the Bamileke Region took center stage in the political theater of French Cameroon's decolonization.

4 ⇒ Nationalists or Traitors?
Bamileke Chiefs and Electoral Politics in the Year of Loi-Cadre

IT WAS market day in the Bamileke chieftaincy of Baham on 22 November 1956, about a month before the first territorial elections of the deputies who would make up Legislative Assembly of Cameroon (ALCAM).[1] A mobile unit of French troops descended on vendors and marketgoers in Baham, checking for official identification and proof of the payment of taxes. A riot erupted as market women pelted the foreign troops with their goods and tried to shame them by disrobing. Other villagers threw rocks and sand at the armed forces. Fo Kamdem Ninyim, who had inherited the seat of power from his father, Fo Max Kamwa, only three years earlier, was very young: by some accounts and official documents, he was twenty-three, while others said he was only twenty. Himself a candidate in the upcoming elections, he observed the scene with interest. He made no attempt to calm his people or to intervene in their ad hoc retaliation against the French soldiers. Military reinforcements soon arrived to disperse the crowd and evacuate the market. Two days later, Fo Kamdem Ninyim was summoned to Yaoundé, where he was arrested for assault, illegal ownership of firearms, incitement of the population of Baham to refuse to pay taxes, and participation "in the maintenance of a dissolved league," the UPC. The young fo was imprisoned at the Bamileke Region's administrative capital, Dschang, to await trial. Three months after his arrest, Kamdem Ninyim was sentenced to two years in prison, to be followed by a five-year exile in Yokadouma, at the extreme eastern edge of Cameroon. French administrators declared him deposed and, collaborating with

Samuel Kamé, a notable from Baham who was also assistant to the chief of the Bamileke Region and presiding judge of the Court of Appeals, named Kamdem Ninyim's half-brother, Jean-Marie Teguia, as the legitimate fo.

The night of Kamdem Ninyim's trial, 12–13 March 1957, violence erupted in Baham, setting off three years of arson, murder, and looting both within chieftaincy borders and in Baham's urban emigrant communities throughout the Mungo Region, in Douala, and in Yaoundé. But the repercussions of Kamdem Ninyim's deposition rippled out beyond Baham communities. The "Baham affair" was soon taken up by territorial politicians and educated elite of Bamileke origin, who analyzed Kamdem Ninyim's deposition in terms of nationalist politics. Other depositions followed in the wake of Kamdem Ninyim's. Like Pierre Kamdem Ninyim, two young mfo, Marcel Ngandjong Feze, and Jean-Philippe Rameau Sokodjou, inherited the chieftaincy from their fathers in the early to mid-1950s, in the neighboring chieftaincies of Bandenkop and Bamendjou, respectively. They too became UPC supporters. Following the unseating of these and a number of other young, nationalist chiefs throughout the Bamileke Region, chieftaincy became an idiom through which people in late-colonial Cameroon spoke politics, adding another layer to discussions of the meaning of independence and nation.

The depositions of Kamdem Ninyim and other young, nationalist mfo drew significant portions of the Bamileke population into political action on a territorial scale for many reasons. Many of those residing in the affected chieftaincies, as well as emigrants who remained spiritually, culturally, economically, and politically tied to chieftaincy governance, viewed the mfo's depositions as a violation of the spiritual alliance underwriting Grassfields political culture.[2] As the legitimately enstooled successor of the previous chief, Fo Kamdem Ninyim was the only fo entitled to reign in Baham until his death. But after sentencing Kamdem Ninyim, in 1957, French administrators replaced him with his half-brother Teguia, thus exposing Baham to dangerous mystical repercussions.

A number of Bamileke intellectuals, perhaps somewhat less concerned with the politicospiritual workings of chieftaincy governance, also were incensed at Kamdem Ninyim's deposition, resenting French intrusion into the affairs of "traditional" chieftaincy, particularly in a matter as crucial as succession in the chief's palace. Upécistes of Bamileke origin, as well as nationalists from other regions of French

Cameroon, viewed the deposition of a pro-UPC electoral candidate as a tactic in the French administration's continuing war against UPC nationalists. For the Baham inhabitants most familiar with the genealogical histories of the chieftaincy's dynastic lineages, Kamdem Ninyim's removal recalled illegitimate successions that had occurred in previous generations, as in 1928 when Fo Kamwa began to govern after the reigning fo, Pouokam I, was imprisoned and exiled from Baham.[3] A combination of factors provoked deep-seated reactions among those who lived through the Baham affair. But the depositions of Bamileke chiefs, coinciding as they did with the implementation of internally autonomous governments throughout the colonial territories under French rule, forced a convergence of colonial, nationalist, and chieftaincy politics, drawing a greater proportion of the Bamileke population than ever before into local, territorial, and international political processes.

Throughout much of colonial Africa, as decolonization processes began, traditional chieftaincy rested at the intersection of local and territorial politics. European administrators and African politicians alike had to decide whether and how to integrate "native authority" structures such as chieftaincy and notables' councils into nascent national governments. In many territories, chieftaincy had been variously "invented" during colonial rule, and the institution's historical roots were tenuous or altogether nonexistent before colonization. But in other places, as in the Grassfields of the British and French Cameroons, chieftaincy had roots primarily in the precolonial past, although these had become intertwined with the more recent, shallow roots of the institution as an extension of colonial administration.[4]

Historians, political scientists, and anthropologists have written extensively on the parochialism introduced into governance in British colonial territories via indirect rule and the administration's reliance on native authorities and traditional chiefs to represent them.[5] In contrast, French colonial policy toward traditional governance has often been portrayed as centralized rather than parochial, and in this "direct administration" chiefs and notables figured as administrative auxiliaries. But in practice, as the case of French Cameroon clearly demonstrates, the French administrative apparatus was also fragmented by parochialism. Race tribunals, discourses that separated "strangers" from "autochthons" or reified ethnic classifications, and the administrative boundaries dividing the territory into regions and regions into subdivisions were all French policies that engendered a fragmentation of populations into what Achille Mbembe has designated *terroirs*—administrative units that were at the same time linked to the overarching colonial economy.[6]

In this mosaic of localities, chieftaincy as a mode of traditional governance operated differently from place to place. The northern, Islamic lamidates established by Fulbe populations were historically the largest and most hierarchically organized, while Bamileke polities were smaller, yet centralized by a well-defined, if flexible and sometimes changing government directed by the fo, spiritualists, and notables.[7] Throughout the central, southern, and eastern regions, traditional governance was much more decentralized. The sociopolitical leaders in Douala were lineage heads who wielded a great deal of power over those belonging to the group but whose governing reach was lineage specific and therefore limited.[8] Elsewhere, those whom French administrators designated as chiefs had little to no historic legitimacy as community leaders.[9] In sum, the role of traditional chiefs, especially in a territory as diverse as Cameroon, was far more varied and ambiguous than written French administrative policies implied. And, as events of the late 1950s made clear, local political histories and cultural practices, more than administrative policy, dictated the chiefs' position in administration. In the era of decolonization, various actors of Bamileke origin used the opening afforded by political shifts to redefine the place of chieftaincy in the soon-to-be-independent nation of Cameroon.

The loi-cadre legislative reforms passed in the French Assembly in June 1956 set the stage for territorial elections to put African administrations in place throughout French Africa. As the new age of internal autonomy dawned in Cameroon, French administrators sought to use electoral processes to exclude chiefs who did not represent their vision of the territory's future, while integrating chiefs who complied with their vision into the ranks of government bureaucracy, thereby phasing chieftaincy out of governance altogether.[10] In the first local elections of municipal councillors, held in 1955, two-thirds of those elected in the Bamileke Region were traditional chiefs.[11] In regions of French Cameroon where strong chieftaincies had not existed before colonial occupation, the French policy of replacing chieftaincy with an elected bureaucracy was even more obvious. For example, in Maka, where chieftaincy was largely a colonial invention, "traditional" chiefs lost in elections to French Cameroon's territorial assembly as early as 1952 and were replaced as local administrators by educated elites who ended the Maka chiefs' "role in modern politics."[12]

The December 1956 elections to French Cameroon's assembly were the first in which every Cameroonian man and woman of voting age (twenty-one years and above) would be allowed to vote for the candidate of their choice in a single electoral college. The territorial elections gave French administrators the opportunity to definitively exclude troublesome chiefs from official politics, while assimilating those who represented French ideals into the growing structure of territorial government. A number of chiefs whom French administrators deemed to be francophiles were candidates for election or reelection to the assembly in 1956. If they were elected, French administrators labeled them *interlocuteurs valables*—a phrase used throughout French-ruled territories in the time of loi-cadre to designate political representatives who promoted the project of a greater France. Cameroonian nationalists, largely excluded from French-controlled political processes in the territory since the UPC's ban, deliberately selected their own representatives in lieu of those designated as such by French administrators.

In the Bamileke Region, upéciste notions of legitimate political representatives overlapped with a regional initiative to recuperate chieftaincy from its submission to a foreign administration. As *chieftaincy* became articulated with *nation* in the political imaginary of Bamileke nationalists, *lepue*, the term designating a sovereign polity that paid tribute to no ruler outside its borders,[13] was recycled and redefined to mean "independence from European rule." By engaging in discussions about chieftaincy and the French administration's unlawful depositions of chiefs, Bamileke populations found a way of expressing their anxieties about various issues related to the nation's future: the degree of political representation and autonomy afforded to Cameroonians within the French Union; the degree of national unity that could be achieved and at what expense to "traditional" forms of local governance; the political implications of sustaining or rupturing Cameroon's ties to France; and the meaning of modernity for local communities. The debate about chieftaincy, particular to the Bamileke Region, coincided with a concurrent, territory-wide discussion of the legitimacy of political representatives after the UPC's proscription (July 1955) and the establishment of loi-cadre (June 1956). Joined by common concerns about the place of chieftaincy in the nascent nation, Bamileke populations varied in their degree of anticolonial, nationalist, or pro–French Union activity. At stake for Bamileke political actors was not only Cameroon's political future as an independent nation but also the role and identity of Bamileke populations within it.

AN OUTLAWED POLITICAL PARTY AND THE LOI-CADRE ELECTIONS

After the proscription of the UPC, the movement's leaders pursued a variety of strategies to ensure its political survival, to recruit upécistes, and to continue to wield political influence despite the ban. Clearly, they believed that the proscription was temporary and would be rectified, either by the supervisory body of the UN or once the territory achieved self-determination; upécistes had only to remain organized and be ready to reenter the political field once the ban was lifted. This notion of the UPC's illegal status being a temporary setback was clearly articulated in the New Year's memorandum that Ruben Um Nyobé released in early 1956.[14] In it, Um Nyobé promised that 1956, the tenth anniversary of the UN Charter, would bring the Cameroon territories' liberation from foreign domination. The memorandum also contained a Program in Six Points, which upécistes were to put into action over the coming months. The program emphasized cooperation among all anticolonial forces in the country, the reinforcement of fraternal relations between Cameroonians of both territories, and the need to appeal to the UN and other international entities (whether political parties or NGOs such as the International League of the Rights of Man) for support in solving what upécistes in international forums presented as "the Cameroon question."[15]

Soon after the release of the Program in Six Points, Paul Soppo Priso, a popular and dynamic politician from Douala and president of the Territorial Assembly of Cameroon (ATCAM) since 1954, met with Um Nyobé in the Sanaga-Maritime maquis. The two men had collaborated politically as early as 1938, as members of Jeunesse camerounaise française (JEUCAFRA), one of the first political organizations formed in French Cameroon.[16] Upon meeting in the maquis nearly twenty years later, Um Nyobé gave Soppo Priso a copy of the Program in Six Points and promised him the upécistes' continuing political support.[17] In return, Soppo Priso agreed to act as a liaison between the legal opposition to Cameroon's inclusion, via loi-cadre, in the French Union, and the now illegal nationalist movement, the UPC. Specifically, Soppo Priso would use his position as ATCAM president to enact the UPC's six-point program and facilitate the UPC's restoration to legality.

During the first half of 1956, Soppo Priso made two important political moves that sealed his alliance with the UPC's nationalist politics. He publicly declared his opposition to France's loi-cadre plan and abstained from voting on the bill in the assembly of the French Union, of which he was a member. Instead, he drafted a motion requesting amnesty for the upécistes arrested after the events of May 1955.[18] When loi-cadre passed in June 1956 and began to be implemented throughout French Africa, Soppo Priso launched a legal nationalist, transethnic, anticolonial coalition, MACNA. The Sacred Union or National Union, as its adherents called it, drew progressive nationalists who opposed Cameroon's integration into the French Union, advocated for "immediate independence" over the gradual process of progressive autonomy enabled through loi-cadre, accepted upécistes into the movement's ranks, and demanded amnesty for those imprisoned, in exile, or in hiding.[19] To recruit supporters, upécistes among them, Soppo Priso held political rallies in the main towns and cities of southern French Cameroon, including Yaoundé, Bafia, Edea (in Um Nyobé's native Sanaga-Maritime Region), Douala, and the Mungo Region towns of Loum, Mbanga, and Nkongsamba, where he drew crowds in excess of two thousand.[20] Soppo Priso proclaimed that he spoke "as a Cameroonian, not as president of the assembly." Like upéciste leaders in 1955, he referred to Cameroon's particular history in his arguments against loi-cadre, reminding his audience that Cameroon had never been a colony, but a protectorate under the Germans, and then divided into mandate and trust territories under British and French administration. As a UN trust territory, French Cameroon could not be integrated into the French Union. He expressed his hope that the National Union would promote dialogue with France on Cameroon's future statutes, but he stopped short of demanding total, immediate independence.[21]

Soppo Priso invited the participation of traditional authorities in his political campaigns. It was an invitation to which a number of nationalist Bamileke political activists responded. Pierre Kamdem Ninyim, Marcel Ngandjong Feze, and Jean Philippe Rameau Sokodjou, the nationalist mfo of Baham, Bandenkop and Bamendjou, campaigned with Soppo Priso throughout 1956. Like many of their chiefs, Bamileke nationalists straddled the divide between legality and illegality, using National Union membership as a legal cover for their nationalist activity, while at the same time maintaining active ties with UPC leaders in exile or in the maquis. In contrast, other Bamileke elite, whether mfo, emigrant planters in the Mungo Region, or civil servants, collaborated with French administrators and Franco-Cameroonian security forces to supplant nationalist activity in the Bamileke Region and emigrant Bamileke communities.

Although the National Union coalition set the political stage for nationalists in 1956, the politicians and activists who became a part of it ranged from radical to moderate in their degree of anti-French nationalism. National Union members agreed on demanding amnesty for the UPC and refusing the implementation of loi-cadre. But they differed on how to proceed in the event that the French administration maintained the ban against the UPC or continued with the loi-cadre project. Some National Union nationalists believed that legal political procedures should be followed, even though the French administration had established those procedures in ways that seemed unjust.[22] But others insisted on boycotting elections as a way to break free of French control of political processes if administrators refused to meet their terms, and they planned to appeal to international supporters and the UN. Differences over political strategy came to a head as the year-end legislative assembly elections approached. After Soppo Priso refused to endorse a boycott of the elections despite the French administration's failure to lift the ban on the UPC, many upécistes harbored suspicions that he was merely an opportunist who would "confiscate for his profit the popularity of the UPC" in order to be elected president of an independent Cameroon.[23]

BAHAM AS A THEATER OF FRENCH CAMEROON'S DECOLONIZATION

In 1956 and 1957 the Bamileke chieftaincy of Baham became a theater of French Cameroon's polarized political landscape after the UPC's ban, with Kamdem Ninyim and Samuel Kamé playing center stage. The young nationalist fo of Baham contributed to the vernacularization of nationalist ideology by bringing it into chieftaincy governance. Samuel Kamé, a descendant of one of the chiefly lineages of Baham who became an administrator in the Franco-Cameroonian government of the late 1950s, used territorial legislation to integrate chiefs who were allies of the greater France vision into the administration, while eliminating those who, like Kamdem Ninyim, viewed a total rupture with France as the only route to political independence. The figures of Kamdem Ninyim and Kamé, as well as other political actors who became involved in the Baham affair during 1956 and 1957 help to shed light on the articulation between territorial and chieftaincy politics for Bamileke communities on the eve of Cameroon's independence.

Fo Kamdem Ninyim

The young Fo Pierre Kamdem Ninyim inherited the chieftaincy from his father, Fo Max Kamwa, in 1954. Fo Kamwa, who had come to the stool of power in the 1930s, had profited financially from his proximity to French administrators, since he was one of the mfo to comply with the Noun settlement project.[24] As such, Kamwa had taken his role as administrative auxiliary seriously, as did most of the Bamileke chiefs of his generation. He followed French administrators' recommendation to provide the sons of the chieftaincy with a French education, and sent his selected heir, Kamdem Ninyim, to study in Paris at Lycée Pascal, in the Sixteenth Arrondissement, the school attended also by the sons of Fo Kamga of Bandjoun and Sultan Njoya of Bamoun.[25]

In choosing his successor, Fo Kamwa had consulted with the requisite councillors and diviners.[26] According to one commonly recounted version of the Kamwa-Kamdem Ninyim succession, Kamwa learned through spider divination that one of his sons would govern Baham, and another would rule all of Cameroon. Other accounts claim that Kamwa knew Kamdem Ninyim, who was born with a copper bracelet around his wrist, to be the successor from the time of his birth. Yet some say that more than one child of the fo can be born with the copper bracelet. Many elders insist that Kamwa had obviously decided that his successor would be Kamdem Ninyim and for that reason chose him alone to study in France, while others say the reason Kamdem Ninyim was chosen is that he showed the most promise in school. Kamdem Ninyim's brother, Michel Debonnaire Kamguia, remembers that Kamwa had a photograph taken with Kamdem Ninyim in which father and son posed cheek to cheek, a sure sign that the boy was his chosen heir.[27]

Kamdem Ninyim first attended the Catholic mission primary school in Baham, and he developed a close relationship with his maternal uncle Benoît Domtchueng, who lived in Nkongsamba and was immersed in UPC politics. It is certainly possible that, if Kamdem Ninyim visited Nkongsamba before leaving for France, Domtchueng taught him about labor unions and political parties in Nkongsamba, exposed him to political discussions, and arranged for him to connect with student upécistes in Paris.[28] At the very least, Kamdem Ninyim's perception of whites, derived in Nkongsamba at an early age, would have been different than that of a future fo who had never traveled far beyond his chieftaincy. He would have seen Nkongsamba's white population as farmers, butchers, factory owners, and merchants interacting with African businessmen, family chiefs, and planters in similar positions.

Shortly before his departure, Kamdem Ninyim went to see his father, Fo Kamwa, for his parting blessing. A mwala may have made sacrifices at the chief's palace tchuep'si and to the ancestral skulls to incur the blessings of the mbem and the royal ancestors for Kamdem Ninyim before his travels.[29] Certainly, he did not leave Cameroon without notifying the gods, spirits, and ancestors of Baham.

In France, Kamdem Ninyim gained a new perspective on the status of white Europeans in the world. He probably had a white maid empty the wastebasket and mop the floor in his dormitory room, white French waiters served him coffee in cafés, and he must have witnessed white janitors cleaning the subway station near the high school. Not to be outdone by his compatriot, Njoya, the son of the sultan of Bamun, Kamdem Ninyim introduced himself at his school as a prince. The principal of the Lycée Pascal, a M. Ritz, remembered Kamdem Ninyim's sullen posturing and avid interest in "leftist politics."[30] When Kamdem Ninyim joined the student group of Cameroonian nationalists based in France, the Union nationale des étudiants kamerunais, he had already learned that French administrators in Cameroon were only low-level players in French government. If he had time to confer with his fellow student compatriots before returning to Baham after he received news of his father's death, surely they instilled in him a duty to the nationalist cause and convinced him to use his position as a traditional ruler to liberate his people from French rule and awaken a desire for political independence among his population.

Kamdem Ninyim returned to Baham from France to be "arrested" and then prepared to succeed his father. He went back to Lycée Pascal at the beginning of the academic year (1954–55), only to travel home definitively in March 1955, when funds ran out for his schooling. The associations of nobility, kamveu and kungang, oversaw his initiation and enthronement as fo. Baham notables were well aware that Kamdem Ninyim was the first fo of Baham to have studied abroad. Notables and commoners alike, both at the time of his succession and long after his death, referred to him as an intellectual.[31] Fo Kamdem Ninyim's political actions during 1956 dashed administrators' hopes for an ally in the new generation of Bamileke chiefs coming to power in the 1950s.

Samuel Kamé

Samuel Kamé was the sort of person to be featured in *Le Bamiléké: Organe mensuel de liaison des chefferies de la région Bamiléké et des Bamilékés de l'extérieur*, the French-sponsored newspaper targeting elite Bamileke readers.[32] In fact, the paper published his curriculum vitae in the fifth issue, September 1955. Kamé had served as a secretary-interpreter to the French administration from 1942 to 1946, when he obtained a scholarship to finish secondary school in France. After high school, he graduated from the Institut d'études politiques de Paris in 1952 and then obtained a law degree. In 1955 he gained admission to the École nationale de la France d'outre-mer, which trained future administrators of France's overseas territories. In 1957, Kamé was named assistant to the chief of the Bamileke Region and presiding judge of the Court of Appeals, becoming the highest-level Cameroonian administrator in the territory.[33] In 1960 he would be appointed inspector of administrative affairs, an essential role in the Cameroonian intelligence agency, the Service des études de la documentation (SEDOC). Kamé proved instrumental in the deposition and replacement of Bamileke chiefs in the late 1950s, beginning with his own, Fo Kamdem Ninyim.

THE NATIONAL UNION, BAMILEKE CHIEFS, AND TERRITORIAL POLITICS

Beginning in January 1956, Kamdem Ninyim, often in the company of his friend and peer Fo Feze of Bandenkop, traveled throughout the Bamileke and Mungo Regions and to Douala and Yaoundé as a UPC spokesman for Bamileke communities. In March that year, in his first explicitly antiadministration political action, Kamdem Ninyim popularized a tax strike mandated by UPC leaders in exile. Initially, Bamileke populations had largely ignored the so-called Kumba Resolution, by which the UPC directors' bureau requested that nationalists substitute membership dues for taxes.[34] But Fo Kamdem Ninyim's enthusiasm for the tax boycott soon bolstered its popularity throughout the Bamileke Region. In upholding the boycott, Fo Kamdem Ninyim and the other mfo who participated not only reduced administrative revenue but also irreparably undermined the French ideal of the traditional chief as administrative auxiliary. When M. Cognet, assistant to the chief of the Bafoussam Subdivision, arrived in Baham on 30 March to distribute tax receipts to Baham quarterheads, he was met with such "hotheaded jeers" from young people that he feared for his safety and left the chieftaincy.[35]

Baham's example encouraged the people of other Bamileke chieftaincies to resist taxation throughout 1956. In Bamougoum on 9 June, gendarmes stopped a villager on his way to market and arrested him for failing to produce his tax receipt. Fifty bystanders followed the tax delinquent and his arresting officers to see the chief of the subdivision. The following day, the commander of the Bafoussam gendarmerie, M. Godot, went to the market of Bamougoum to "investigate" the matter and purchase provisions for the prison. Upon his arrival, a crowd of nearly three hundred villagers armed with clubs surrounded him. The chief of the subdivision was called, but a sabotaged bridge on the road to Bamougoum delayed his arrival by several hours. When he reached the market at noon, accompanied by two units of mobile troops, twenty people carrying knives and machetes were arrested, one of whom had tried to stab him. Following the skirmish, 180 people gathered in the Bentchow quarter of Bamougoum for a local UPC committee meeting.

The Bamougoum dissenters faced trial at Dschang the following week, and five of the leaders were sentenced to three years in prison and a fine of FCFA 50,000 (worth 1,000 French francs at the time). Joseph Nde, convicted of assaulting an administrator, received five additional years and a ten-year exile from Bamougoum. The others faced two to three years in prison and a fine of FCFA 30,000 (600 French francs). Some time later, the fo of Bamougoum sent his security forces (tchindas)[36] to arrest UPC member Henri Fongang, who was allegedly associated with the tax boycott. Suspected of killing a tchinda, Fongang was taken into custody by police and he died while under interrogation in the security chamber at the Bafoussam gendarmerie.[37] Fongang's son, Anatole Naoussi, also a member of the UPC, explained that his father was killed by an intravenous injection and called his father's death a disguised elimination. For Bamileke upécistes, Fongang's death sealed a pact of vengeance against mfingung, tax collectors, and administrative auxiliaries. At a meeting held in Bafoussam in early November 1956, members pledged to sabotage administrative vehicles and to attack gendarmes and any other antiupéciste functionaries or informants.[38] As they pledged to avenge Fongang's death, upécistes cited Point Four of Um Nyobé's 1956 Program in Six Points—"Isolation and denunciation of colonialism's lackeys and mercenaries"—as their political justification. While the fo of Baham allied himself with the nationalists by upholding the tax boycott, the fo of Bamougoum, by facilitating Fongang's arrest, placed himself squarely on the upécistes' list of those they referred to as *valets du colonialisme* (colonialism's lackeys), who became the UPC militias' targets as the movement turned violent.[39]

Fongang's death became a political and material symbol for Bamileke nationalists, causing them to reaffirm their desire for freedom from economic and political domination and bringing them a step closer to adopting violence as the method to achieve it. Throughout 1956, UPC leaders simplified their political message, effectively painting anyone who was not a supporter of the UPC as a traitor, while claiming to be Cameroon's true patriots. The polarization of upéciste attitudes toward territorial politics shaped electoral processes throughout 1956 and flattened the political landscape into two opposing and confrontational sides.[40] In the regions where the UPC had become most deeply implanted—the Sanaga-Maritime, Mungo, and Bamileke Regions—people had little choice but to join the UPC or face being labeled a traitor or a lackey.

Kamdem Ninyim did not haphazardly choose the tax boycott as the way to signal his nationalist convictions. During the late-colonial period, metropolitan powers spent growing sums on development, and traditional chiefs were expected to bear their share of the economic burden by overseeing taxation.[41] A simple way to ascertain whether a Bamileke chief fulfilled his role as "auxiliary" to the French administration during the trusteeship period was to measure his effectiveness as a tax collector. Upécistes, who considered 1956 to be the year of Cameroon's independence and began to "administer" populations as if they had created a state within a state, called on inhabitants to buy a "subscription" to the nationalist party instead of paying yearly taxes. In the historical and cultural Grassfields worldview that Bamileke upécistes sought to reawaken, taxation amounted to paying tribute to a dominant power. Recalling Grassfields history, nationalists viewed chiefs who collected and paid the requisite taxes as impeding the restoration of lepue to their chieftaincies. The nationalist Bamileke chiefs who impeded tax collection rejected French control, openly sympathized with the UPC, and actively sought to restore their polities' sovereignty.

Through the issue of taxation, nationalist politics rekindled and popularized the political notion of lepue as an autonomous, sovereign status manifested by a refusal to accept outsiders' control of chieftaincy affairs. Local songs lauded the chiefs who upheld the tax boycott as protectors and defenders, while depicting those who collaborated with the French as coercive rulers who consumed the territory's wealth to excess. A farmer from the Bafang Subdivision, Chrestine Emachoua, described administrative taxation as an unjust consumption of material goods in a petition she sent to the UN. Thanks to its repetitive refrain, the narrative form of her petition more closely resembles that of a song, indicating that a Ms. Emachoua, unschooled in letter writing, most likely dictated an orally transmitted song to a scribe, who framed it with the greeting and closing of a petition:

> To the President of the General Assembly, New York:
>
> Sir:
>
> When I left for Bafang with a bundle of wood, they beat me and took my wood away from me without reason.
>
> They did the same when I had a basket of cassava.
>
> They beat me and took a basket of cassava meal without reason.
>
> When I was carrying a basket of macabo [a variety of cocoyam],
>
> they sent the police, beat me, and took away the macabo.
>
> When I had a basket of taro, they sent it to the police and it was the same story . . . .
>
> Long live the United Nations!
>
> Long live a unified and independent Cameroon!
>
> —Emachoua Chrestine[42]

Although Ms. Emachoua was from Baboucha, the petition recounted her journey to Bafang, which she recognized as the administrative capital of the subdivision, the site of excessive taxation, or, in her words, the site of her encounter with those who robbed her, violently, and without reason. She signed and sent her petition—which joined hundreds of others from the Grassfields region in late 1956—during the height of the tax boycott throughout the Bamileke Region.

Having galvanized the population through the tax strike, in May 1956, Kamdem Ninyim began to hold meetings in the area around Baham to plan the commemoration of the events of May 1955, prompting the reestablishment of UPC local committees in the Bamileke and Mungo

Regions. At the same time, he announced his plan to run in the December 1956 elections.[43] Nationalists began to address threatening petitions to municipal councillors, francophile notables' associations, and collaborationist chiefs. They posted tracts throughout the Dschang market warning that the day of reckoning was coming for colonialism's "lackeys," especially those guilty of "perfidious maneuvers."[44] Throughout the Mungo River valley, in Mbanga, Loum, Loum-Chantiers, and Penja, rumors spread that the UPC had been legalized and administrators had received orders not to interfere with its activities. All the local committees in the Mungo and Bamileke Regions responded to exiled UPC president Moumié's convocation of "Bamileke committees" to Bamenda, scheduled for 3 June 1956, in the Grassfields under British rule.[45] The number in attendance revealed the permeability of the Anglo-French boundary and the ease with which nationalists could circulate between the two zones. Such gatherings strengthened ties between the UPC leadership in exile and nationalists in the Mungo and Bamileke Regions, and between Cameroonians under British and French rule.

The planned commemoration of the May 1955 casualties took place in Baham on the anniversary of the party's dissolution, 13 July 1956. Over five hundred delegates and members poured into Chiala, the chiefly quarter of Baham, and assembled in the meeting place of the *tsa* (the chief's compound). The event was presided over by Fo Kamdem Ninyim, Fo Feze, and Chrétien Dzukam—a JDC activist and école des cadres graduate from the Bandjoun chieftaincy who led the initiative to recruit mfo, notables, and urban family chiefs to the nationalist movement.[46] Born in 1932, Dzukam was of the same generation as Fo Kamdem Ninyim and Fo Feze. Being a resident of the New Bell neighborhood of Douala, he had a cosmopolitan outlook and an extensive network of ties with upécistes throughout the territory.[47] During 1956, Dzukam visited the Sanaga-Maritime maquis and frequently crossed the Anglo-French boundary to meet with the exiled UPC directors in Kumba and Bamenda. He traveled back and forth between Douala and the Bamileke chieftaincies in the Bafoussam and Mbouda Subdivisions, where he worked with local committees. He campaigned with the National Union and attended every UPC or JDC assembly that year. In the evening, after the assembly, a private meeting of seventy-five delegates from local committees in the Mungo and the Bamileke Regions began just after dark in the chiefly assembly hall. Dzukam spoke about the UPC's reorganization in the Bamileke Region, and the founding of a regional UPC bureau, complete with a typewriter and mimeograph, as per section headquarter standards, within the Baham chief's palace itself. Delegates contributed FCFA 31,500 in a collection of funds for the establishment of the UPC bureau.[48]

On 8 August 1956, soon after Fongang's "elimination" and while the tax strike was at its height, Kamdem Ninyim convened a second transregional assembly at Chiala in Baham. Nearly 200 delegates, representing 102 local committees on both sides of the Anglo-French border, and the Mungo and the Mbam Regions assembled on that morning. Representatives from the UPC directors' bureau in British territory arrived to inspect the UPC regional and local committees in attendance. The first signs of a political fault line between exiled upécistes and those in French territory emerged during the morning session when delegates based in British territory suggested that their comrades were selling out to Soppo Priso. Dzukam, who often mediated between the exiled upécistes and those who remained in French territory, countered with accusations of sabotage and called for a recess. Kamdem Ninyim took the floor after the break, defended Dzukam, and urged upécistes to support the National Union. At the meeting's close, each delegation paid its respects to the fo, following "traditional" protocol for associations at the end of a chieftaincy festival. In return, Kamdem Ninyim provided each leader with a copy of an "Open Letter to M. André-Marie Mbida," written by a group of Cameroonian students in Toulouse, France. Through the cosmopolitan Fo Kamdem Ninyim, the exiled upécistes, and nationalist students, the Baham chieftaincy began to develop a transnational reach. In presenting the students' letter to the delegates, Fo Kamdem Ninyim brought Cameroonian students abroad into the chieftaincy and provided conference attendees with a fragment of the French student world. On 19 August, at a meeting held in Dschang, Fo Kamdem Ninyim declared himself to be the protector of the UPC in the Bamileke Region.[49]

Also during the month of August 1956, Bamileke emigrants established a UPC central committee in Nkongsamba to oversee the local committee meetings in the Mungo and Bamileke Regions. Thereafter, Nkongsamba became an outpost for UPC activity in the Bamileke Region and a stopover for nationalists coming from British territory. The UDEFEC women of Nkongsamba met in the home of Joseph Kamgang on 31 August 1956, where Victor Djimi, a young émigré from Baham, encouraged them to spread the nationalist message, organize themselves, and provide food, writing materials, and newspapers to political detainees in Nkongsamba's prison.[50] The following month, Martin Singap, who in 1957 would be named commanding officer of the UPC's Bamileke Region army, the Sinistre de la défense nationale du Kamerun (SDNK),[51] crossed the Anglo-French border to meet with nationalists at Kamgang's house in Nkongsamba. He spent the night at the home of UDEFEC member Elisabeth Mapondjou, originally of Bamendjou, who had hosted other traveling nationalist leaders, including Ernest Ouandié, over the years.[52] Singap brought news of the JDC's reorganization in British territory, the UPC candidates' intention to participate in elections for the Buea assembly in the British Cameroons, and the directors' decision to divide the UPC in the Bamileke Region into two sections—one based in Bafoussam, the other in Bafang. The next day, Singap continued on to the Bamileke Region.[53] A descendant of one of the many chiefly dynasties of Bandenkop, Singap worked closely with Dzukam, Kamdem Ninyim, and Feze to lay the foundations of what would soon become the general headquarters of the SDNK (near the border between the Baham and Bandenkop chieftaincies), and to recruit the fighters who would fill its ranks.[54]

The political valence of nationalist Bamileke chiefs became apparent during the first National Union assemblies, which took place in July 1956. Soppo Priso and other politicians recognized the "organizational and mass strength of the UPC and the need to establish the basis for dialogue and cooperation between themselves and their more radical and extraparliamentary opponents."[55] The coalition leaders drew on the political networks and infrastructure that upécistes had kept in place and even strengthened over the year since the official proscription of the movement. In the Bamileke and Mungo Regions, this meant that the National Union placed the nationalist chiefs such as Fo Kamdem Ninyim, Fo Feze, and Fo Sokodjou at the forefront of campaigns and rallies.

On 1 July, Soppo Priso made his first tour of the Bamileke Region as head of the National Union. He was accompanied by Fo Kamdem Ninyim of Baham, and by the Nkongsamba-based leader of the politicocultural association Autochthons of the Mungo, Jean Ekwabi, who had won a seat in Cameroon's Territorial Assembly (ATCAM) during partial elections held in April 1954.[56] The tour of the Bamileke Region set the stage for a mass assembly of nationalists in Douala on 8 July. Soppo Priso invited all superior chiefs of Cameroon to attend the gathering and requested that they each inform their populations of the event. He also wrote to the bishop of Douala, suggesting Cameroonian unity as the theme for all homilies given in the diocese that Sunday.

On the day of the scheduled assembly, over five thousand people marched from the Place of the Mosque down Resistance and Bonnecarrère Avenues to the Festival Hall in Akwa quarter. Cyclists headed the parade of delegations carrying banners announcing the towns they represented: Bafoussam, Dschang, Mbouda, Bafang, and Bangangte from the Bamileke Region; Eseka, Edea, and Ngambe, from the Sanaga-Maritime; and groups from the capital region of Yaoundé and from the coastal area of Kribi. All the associations displayed signs against loi-cadre. Women wearing red dresses or scarves, and men in red ties—the upécistes—seemed to dominate the crowd. In New Bell, a vendor set up a booth where attendees could have their headscarves and ties stamped with the black crab, the symbol of UPC nationalism. Marching together, those wearing red chanted, "Long live the UPC, down with the 'kolos [colons]'!" And, foreshadowing the violence to come, they shouted, "General Moumié has 500,000 soldiers!" A crowd of nearly two thousand more assemblygoers awaited the parade at the Salle des Fêtes.[57] They knew their sheer numbers offered them protection.

Soppo Priso, the first to address the crowd, began by stressing the importance of Franco-Cameroonian collaboration but insisted that Cameroonians should be the ones to define the statutes for the nation's future government. He was followed by a range of politicians demonstrating the National Union's broad reach, including Victor Kanga, leader of the Association of the Cameroonian Students of France, and Fo Kamdem Ninyim. A number of political actors from Nkongsamba took the floor, among whom were Jean Ekwabi, who would be reelected on the Autochthons of the Mungo ticket in December 1956, and Joseph Massing, who had organized a study circle to facilitate political discussion.[58] Dr. Mathieu Tagny, who worked as a physician at a hospital in Yaoundé and headed the UPC in Yaoundé before the ban, concluded the speeches.[59] After the assembly, Soppo Priso continued to work closely with Fo Kamdem Ninyim, whom he designated the National Union delegate in the Bamileke Region. The two men agreed that Chrétien Dzukam would serve as their liaison.[60]

PARLIAMENTARY ELECTIONS AND THE STATE OF CHIEFTAINCY

In December 1956 it was clear that attempted negotiations in the maquis between Ruben Um Nyobé and French administrators (under the command of High Commissioner Pierre Messmer since April 1956) had failed. The French had not made good on their promise of amnesty to those upécistes who had been involved in the May uprisings and had not restored the UPC and its affiliated parties to legality. Since the nationalists' terms had not been met, Um Nyobé and the Kumba directors' bureau issued a directive barring UPC and National Union members or sympathizers from participating in the parliamentary elections as candidates or as voters, and committee leaders selected loyal upécistes to organize action groups to sabotage the elections.[61]

Despite the fact that he had campaigned on a criticism of UPC politicians' absence from the assembly and on warnings that the ban jeopardized the future of the country, Soppo Priso did not heed UPC leaders' call for a boycott. In December 1956, Um Nyobé called Soppo Priso a traitor for continuing to run his electoral campaign even though upécistes had not been granted amnesty and the party was still proscribed. In response, Soppo Priso entreated Um Nyobé to break with the exiled UPC president Moumié, who "led the UPC, and with it the territory, down the disorderly path of chimerical claims."[62]

UPC leaders, even those who, like Dr. Tagny, were affiliated with the National Union throughout 1956 and had planned to run as candidates in the elections to the assembly, upheld the vote boycott.[63] The UPC leaders' decision filtered down to the grassroots in Um Nyobé's Sanaga-Maritime Region, where only 14 percent of the registered voters went to the polls.[64] But elsewhere voter turnout reached record highs, with 66 percent of the 61,868 registered voters going to the polls in the Mungo Region and 54 percent of the 223,850 registered in the Bamileke Region casting their ballots.[65] The boycott's unenforceability in the Bamileke and Mungo Regions can be attributed to the National Union's popularity there and to the success of Soppo Priso's political campaigning. The expectation that Fo Kamdem Ninyim would be an electoral candidate also may have drawn Bamileke nationalists to the polls.

Of the pro-UPC Bamileke politicians who had campaigned with the National Union during 1956, Kamdem Ninyim was the only one to deviate from the UPC party line when it came to the electoral boycott. Even after UPC and JDC leaders had resolved to boycott elections, the young fo of Baham remained a candidate for a seat in Cameroon's assembly, representing the Bafoussam Subdivision.[66] French administrators had observed that, during previous elections, the Bamileke chiefs who presented themselves as political candidates were successful in their candidacy. Fearing the electoral victory of one of the most zealous UPC supporters in the Bamileke Region, they had to find a way to expel Kamdem Ninyim from the political field.

On 24 November 1956, a month before the elections, as earlier recounted, Fo Kamdem Ninyim was arrested and charged with, among other things, inciting the population of Baham to refuse to pay taxes and "participating in the maintenance of a disbanded league," the UPC.[67] Despite his legal troubles, Kamdem Ninyim continued to present himself as a candidate in the upcoming elections. French administrators kept him in custody and then took steps to ensure his disqualification from electoral processes by annulling his candidacy because he was under the age of twenty-one.[68] Lacking the requisite three candidates after Kamdem Ninyim's disqualification, the National Union ticket from the Bamileke Region was completely thrown out on the eve of the elections.

The loi-cadre election results demonstrated that French administrators successfully excluded the nationalists from French Cameroon's political terrain, although the upécistes' decision to boycott the vote once it became clear that the UPC ban would not be lifted certainly contributed to the nationalists' defeat at the polls. The National Union ticket obtained only 6.5 percent of the vote and eight seats in the assembly. Moderate conservatives—a coalition of those who advocated gradual progression toward independence and a continued French presence—took 64 percent of the vote and obtained a majority in the assembly with fifty-nine out of seventy seats. The remaining seats went to independent candidates, including the committed nationalist Dr. Marcel Bebey-Eyidi, a Second World War veteran and physician from Douala, and Charles Okala, leader of the Social Union of Cameroon party.[69]

Of the sixty-three Cameroonians elected, twenty-two were traditional chiefs, and twenty of those hailed from the northern and western regions of the territory. In the northern Islamic lamidates and in the Bamileke Region, where the political weight of "customary rulers" remained significant despite decades of European administration, traditional chiefs outnumbered civil servants among the deputies elected. Thirteen chiefs and notables from the northern region took seats in the assembly, while civil servants won only ten. In the Bamileke and Bamun Regions, traditional chiefs took six of the nine parliamentary seats occupied by Cameroonians, while the son of the chief of Batie, Pierre Ngayewang, filled a seventh seat. The 1956 electoral results revealed the continuing political valence of chiefs in the two regions where strong, organized chieftaincies had served an important role in governance before colonization. In contrast, the political influence of "traditional chiefs" in the Littoral, Centre, and East Regions was by 1956 virtually nil.[70]

With Fo Kamdem Ninyim, the nationalist candidate, barred from the electoral process, the Bamileke mfo who became or were reelected as deputies in December 1956 fit the profile of the assimilated traditional chief that French administrators hoped would facilitate the chieftaincies' integration into state governance. Fo Michel Njine of a small chieftaincy in the Bafang Subdivision had become a municipal councillor in 1955 and had been one of several to tour France after his election.[71] Although he participated in National Union campaigns throughout July 1956, he eventually cast his lot with Mathias Djoumessi, fo of Foreke-Dschang, who had been the first UPC president and head of the secret organization Kumsze. After distancing himself from the UPC, Djoumessi became a parliamentary deputy in ATCAM, the territorial assembly formed in 1952. In 1956 he headed the Defense of Bamileke Interests ticket, which included Marcel Lagarde, the only Frenchman from the Bamileke Region to be elected.[72] Fo Etienne Djuatio of Batcham, in the Mbouda Subdivision, led the Defense of Mbouda Interests ticket.[73]

French administrators' ideal Bamileke fo as politician was undoubtedly Daniel Kemajou, parliamentary deputy since 1946 and one of five Cameroonian councillors to the French Union, a position he held from 1947 to 1959.[74] Kemajou succeeded his father as fo of Bazou in 1953. In December 1956, although he was the mayor of Nkongsamba, Kemajou decided to run his campaign from Bazou, in the Bamileke Region, and was reelected to the assembly as a representative of the Bangangte Subdivision. In October 1957 he was selected to be president of the assembly. Kemajou's privileged position as a wealthy French-speaking planter who inherited the chieftaincy in Bazou, his elite status, and his familiarity with both Bazou populations and Bamileke emigrant communities in the Mungo enabled him to juggle his political hats with ease. In 1957 the Bamileke deputies formed a parliamentary coalition, the Independent Peasants. Although they maintained their independence vis-à-vis the rest of the assembly, as the name of their bloc implied, their political goals included the preservation of Bamileke chieftaincies and the protection of Bamileke coffee planters' economic interests.[75]

With the continuing importance of chieftaincy throughout the Bamileke Region, combined with the cosmopolitan influence of socially and economically diverse emigrant communities in urban areas, politicians of Bamileke origin demonstrated a significant political range. As leading chiefly figureheads of the pro–French Union and the pronationalist camps, Fo Kemajou and Fo Kamdem Ninyim both straddled administrative boundaries, occupying an intermediary position between "traditional" Bamileke governance and territorial politics, and manifesting their independence from territorial political parties. While the pro–French Union chiefs established parties and formed a parliamentary bloc that symbolically underscored their autonomy vis-à-vis party politics, Kamdem Ninyim chose to demonstrate his political independence by ignoring UPC calls for a boycott. Both Kemajou and Kamdem Ninyim benefited from a familiarity with France and the inner workings of metropolitan and colonial governments; both hoped to modernize the institution of chieftaincy and expand its reach beyond its geographical borders; and both sought to preserve the chieftaincy and ensure a political role for Bamileke chiefs in Cameroon's national government. Their diametrically opposed political orientation stemmed from their differing interpretations of lepue (which historically signified political sovereignty, autonomy, and independence) and the ways in which it might best be achieved. In other words, independence-era Bamileke elites inserted their political ideals, more or less consciously, into a long-standing political debate in Grassfields chieftaincies—a debate over the meaning of lepue and whether it could best be acquired through diplomatic negotiation or through direct confrontation.[76] Although the French administration's support gave the "diplomatic" lepue seekers a political advantage in the assembly elections, the depositions of nationalist chiefs pushed a growing number of Bamileke toward the intent to acquire lepue through whatever means necessary, including through violence, from late 1956 onward.

DEPOSITIONS OF REMAINING NATIONALIST MFO

Recognizing the political salience of pro-UPC chiefs in the densely populated Bamileke Region, French administrators continued to fear them, even after Kamdem Ninyim's elimination from the political scene. Conventional scholarship presents Bamileke chiefs as part of an elite formed during colonial rule who benefited from their proximity to the French administration and supported the French administration's fight against the UPC in the 1950s. These accounts portray independence-era violence in the Bamileke Region as a civil war pitting chiefs and notables against landless peasants.[77] But in the late 1950s, Kamdem Ninyim was no anomaly in the region. Although the French supported the candidacy of the five Bamileke chiefs who were elected to the legislative assembly in late 1956, nationalist chiefs may well have outnumbered French Union supporters until the French administration, beginning with Kamdem Ninyim's deposition, eradicated them. For example, Fo Sokodjou of Bamendjou, on account of his friendship with Kamdem Ninyim and his open support of UPC nationalists, was subjected to two years of residential surveillance, then imprisoned in Bafoussam, Dschang, Bafia, Yoko, Nanga Eboko, and Yaoundé.[78] Fo Feze of Bandenkop had a warrant issued for his arrest soon after Kamdem Ninyim was imprisoned. He was sentenced, in absentia, at the same trial in Dschang, but he avoided arrest and hid in the forest around Bandenkop until he could escape to British territory, in 1959. Feze was accompanied into exile by another young upéciste, Fo Kemajou Paul of Bangou.[79] The fo of Bapa was deposed in 1958 for declaring his village's independence from Bandjoun during Fo Kamga of Bandjoun's trip to France. The fo of Bandeng was deposed and imprisoned at Dschang and replaced by Didier Tuekam of Bandjoun.[80] In every case, French administrators replaced a rebellious fo with one of their choosing, after conferring with local notables.[81] In every case, UPC militia targeted the imposter fo as a traitor to the nation (*fingung*).

The historical evidence demonstrates that, far from being a civil war launched by commoners against chiefs and notables, violence in the Bamileke Region trailed in the wake of a series of politically unthinkable depositions of chiefs and notables from their legitimate position of rule. In each chieftaincy where a deposition occurred, the replacement of the politically and spiritually legitimate ruler required the complicity of a number of notables in overseeing the succession of the imposter. Although French administrators had interfered in chieftaincy successions during the interwar period (see chapter 1), in the 1950s, that interference took on greater significance. Against the backdrop of territorial politics, Bamileke nationalists successfully reframed the depositions as the French administrators' effort to keep Bamileke chieftaincies—and hence their populations—in a state of perpetual submission or servitude to France. Those complicit in "making" and "unmaking" mfo in illegitimate ways were guilty of "selling" the "country" (*gung*).[82] The transgressions of the politicospiritual bedrock of Bamileke chieftaincies drove a wedge between the supporters of legitimate rulers and those who accepted the chiefs selected by the administration. In each of the affected chieftaincies, rifts surfaced among members of the chieftaincy nobility and the population at large, forcing people to choose sides.

The events following Fo Kamdem Ninyim's deposition in Baham illustrate the administration's strategies of deposition and replacement and their long-lasting repercussions for the Baham community. With Fo Kamdem Ninyim in prison, his half-brother Jean-Marie Teguia was selected to fill his place as chief of Baham, following the negotiations of Samuel Kamé, a Baham notable and assistant to the French chief of the Bafoussam Subdivision.[83] Kamé had sought an influential role in Baham's chieftaincy before Fo Kamwa's death,[84] but Kamdem Ninyim had distanced him on inheriting the position of fo. By using his proximity to the French administration to place Teguia on the throne, Kamé became a powerful patron of the new fo,[85] and gained access to the traditional authority he needed to complement his position in Cameroon's territorial government. Kamé knew what needed to be done to legitimize the new fo's succession. He began by seeking the support of notables who were dissatisfied with Kamdem Ninyim's short reign or those who sought positions in the French administration. Promising them greater power in the new Teguia regime, Kamé co-opted them as allies. He then advised Teguia to eradicate any Kamdem Ninyim loyalists in Baham and the emigrant communities in the Mungo, in Yaoundé, and in Douala. With his patron's assistance, Teguia orchestrated attacks on the pro–Kamdem Ninyim population of Baham and its emigrant communities.[86] He formed "cleanup crews" of French soldiers and the fo's "secret police" to round up and exile mfonte and mwabo (district chiefs)[87] who refused to recognize Teguia's legitimacy in the quarters of Kaffo, Chegne, Djemgheu, Baghom, Nka'a, Batchie, Boukue (Kamdem Ninyim's mother's native quarter), and Demgo.[88]

The elimination of the mfonte and mwabo of these districts led to the exodus of most of their inhabitants, who took refuge in the neighboring chieftaincies of Bapa, Bandenkop, Bahouan, and Bayangam while awaiting Kamdem Ninyim's restoration to power. Those loyal to Kamdem Ninyim had to make a choice: ingratiate themselves to the new imposter fo, Teguia, thus violating the politicospiritual terms of chiefly succession in gung, or flee into hiding to escape harm. Many hid in the maquis, becoming maquisards or UPC fighters almost by default.[89]

Others hid behind their words, masking the loyalties they held in their hearts. Those who claimed to be loyal to Kamdem Ninyim in some circumstances yet publicly supported Teguia in others were those the UPC militia groups later targeted most ruthlessly as mfingung—traitors, or sellers of the country.

The French administration supplied troops to protect the chief's palace and resettled Baham's population under their surveillance in the center of town. But the presence of Kamé's pro-Teguia coalition and French troops was insufficient to garner popular support for the new fo. Despite, or because of, Kamé's influence, a greater number of notables, mfonte, and émigré family chiefs supported Kamdem Ninyim, rather than Teguia, at the beginning of the "imposter's" reign. In 1958 four district chiefs—Kui Kamdem of Demgo, Sah Djoko of Batchie (today Batchie is called La'agweu), Simo Nzeudie of Djemgheu, and Kamdem Ouambo Souop of Nka'a—remained overt opponents of Teguia.[90] The night after Ninyim's arrest, compounds were burned in Kamé's quarter, Batousou'o.[91] On the night of Ninyim's trial and sentencing, attacks were carried out against the notables who supported Teguia.[92] Despite administrative protection, Teguia had to leave Baham for his own safety, and Baham was without a fo for at least two years. In each chieftaincy where a deposition took place, similar fissures split apart village and emigrant communities, and violence erupted, leaving slayings and arson in its wake. In fact, as the next chapter clarifies, the deposition of chiefs before and after the assembly elections must be understood, historically, as the single most salient factor in kindling the violent conflicts that plagued the region for nearly a decade.

POLITICAL INTERPRETATIONS OF CHIEFS' DEPOSITIONS AMONG THE BAMILEKE ELITE

Throughout 1957 the aftershocks of the elections caused a number of shifts in the political landscape. The first UPC army, the Comité national d'organisation (CNO), launched a number of attacks on the "traitors" of the nation and "lackeys" of colonialism, and committed acts of sabotage throughout the Sanaga-Maritime. The UPC, already fragmented after the 1955 proscription, continued to splinter into various ideological factions. Dr. Tagny was one of the upécistes purged from the ranks because of his public denunciation of the Kumba directors, in late 1956.[93] In particular, Tagny was against the UPC directors' decision to employ violence as a political strategy.[94] In early 1957,

Tagny was quick to join with other expelled nationalists in founding a new party, the Progressive Party of Kamerun. As Cameroon's legislative assembly went into session, Soppo Priso lost his place at the helm to Daniel Kemajou and became the leader of the legal, nationalist opposition known as the Group of Eight. And Kamdem Ninyim's deposition quickly became politicized on the territorial stage.

Since his arrest prevented his election, one can only imagine how the UPC directors' bureau might have dealt with Kamdem Ninyim had he become a member of the legislative assembly. Once imprisoned, however, he had the support of both the outlawed UPC's president, Moumié, and the leader of the legal, nationalist opposition, Soppo Priso. Both politicians publicized the story of the nationalist fo's arrest and deposition to illustrate the French administration's disdain for traditional governance. On 24 November 1956, the day of Kamden Ninyin's arrest and two days after French soldiers had stormed the Baham market, Moumié sent a telegram to the UN from Kumba, in the British Cameroons: "Whole territory militarily occupied, Chief and all notables of Baham arrested and held at Dschang prison by over a thousand soldiers. Baham and whole territory under siege. Kamdem, thirteenth chief chosen by population dethroned and replaced by chief of Bafoussam Subdivision."[95] Soppo Priso later made the Group of Eight's opposition to Kamdem Ninyim's deposition known in the pages of *La presse du Cameroun*.[96]

Thanks to the Baham affair, chieftaincy became a major issue in the nationalist politics of the late 1950s. Attitudes toward chieftaincy were collapsed into the oppositional categories of patriots and traitors in the nationalist rhetoric. Pro-French politicians (whom the upécistes labeled traitors) supported the deposition of "insubordinate" chiefs and their replacement with traditional rulers who were loyal to the French Union and supported the repression of UPC activity. From the nationalists' point of view, a chief who was enthroned by the French rather than through the usual rite of succession was a lackey of colonialism.[97] The deposition of Bamileke chiefs brought a chorus of voices into the political arena—the opinions of Bamileke populations on their chiefs' legitimacy echoed a territory-wide discussion of the validity of political representatives. Discussions of chieftaincy surfaced among Bamileke intelligentsia and in the pages of newspapers as political actors deliberately shaped rhetoric about the depositions into easily transmissible messages that could be reechoed in various discursive forums, both written and oral, thus drawing emigrant "bourgeois" as well as non-literate villagers into political discussions. An analysis of the chorus of voices speaking out about the Baham affair illustrates the ways in which popular and formal political rhetoric became mutually reinforcing modes of expression in late 1950s French Cameroon.

Following Kamdem Ninyim's deposition, notables from the Bamileke Region debated the nuances of tradition, "customary law," and the mfo's involvement in politics in the pages of *L'opinion camerounaise* and *La presse du Cameroun*. Their discussion hinged on whether Fo Kamdem Ninyim was the proper heir to the Baham chieftaincy and if so, whether or not Teguia, the fo the French administration selected to replace him, could legitimately govern. Maurice Kwamm, originally of Baham, and president of the Customary African Council for French Equatorial Africa and Cameroon, was—as his title reflects—concerned with the syncretism of tradition with late-colonial/national politics.[98] Writing for *La presse du Cameroun*, Kwamm introduced himself as "a child of Baham," and then explained the rules of succession within the chieftaincy: "tradition stipulates that the chief enthroned . . . must remain in power until his death."[99] Anyone who attempted to present himself as successor without following the normal protocol—the nine-week sequestration and the ruling of the council of nine notables—should be condemned to death.[100] He then explained that the deposition violated French administrative law and insisted that neither "Bamileke custom" nor French law permitted the enthronement of Teguia in the place of the deposed Fo Kamdem Ninyim. After referring to the territory's legal statutes, Kwamm reiterated that what truly mattered was the tradition of succession in Bamileke chieftaincies. By occupying the throne, he wrote, "[Teguia] has violated the customary laws, the laws of God. Teguia has violated tradition and the fires of custom are raging!" The only solution, Kwamm concluded, was to allow the inhabitants of Baham to study the question of traditional rule.[101]

The nationalists of the Group of Eight, none of whom were of Bamileke origin, soon added to the political commentary on the Baham affair. The Group of Eight officially declared support for Kamdem Ninyim as chief of Baham and denounced the French administration for stripping him of his title.[102] But a pro-Teguia council of Baham notables "vehemently rejected the Group of Eight's intrusion into the Baham affair . . . as [they were] incapable of knowing in depth the traditional customs of Baham."[103] Echoing Kwamm's concerns with both traditional and administrative procedure, the council stated, "Ninyim usurped the traditional title and throne and transgressed both traditional and administrative laws."[104]

What was striking was how easily the Baham elite—whether supporters of Kamdem Ninyim or of Teguia, Samuel Kamé's docile pawn—reconciled the coexistence of local traditional governance with colonial systems of law. The debate was not over whether to abolish the chieftaincy altogether, according to the French plan for its eventual metamorphosis into publicly elected office. The Bamileke elite, whatever their politics, viewed chieftaincy as compatible with a modern nation-state, and the discussion of the Baham affair reflected a general desire to "modernize" offices popularly perceived as sites of traditional power and authority.[105] But their opinions differed over two key issues: which political trend the chief should espouse, and the chieftaincy's degree of sovereignty within the framework of the burgeoning nation-state.

"Pro-French" Bamileke politicians faulted Kamdem Ninyim for becoming so engaged in politics, insisting that a fo should "delegate [political] activities to others."[106] One pro-Teguia notable, Souopdounze, who believed that Ninyim himself had succeeded the throne illegally, wrote that it was Ninyim's "fondness for politics [that] spread misery throughout Baham." Kamdem Ninyim had allegedly failed as fo of Baham for these reasons: "Instead of working with the assemblies that govern the chieftaincy, he reorganized the defunct UPC. . . . The unprotected villagers [of Baham] found themselves forced to sign up as upécistes, a movement dissolved by decree on the 13th of July 1955. . . . Anyone who did not give in . . . was branded a traitor, a sellout, a colon."[107] But the pro–French Unionists' assertion that chiefs should remain apolitical and delegate politics to others made their omission of discussions of other mfo's political activities all the more conspicuous. Six mfo had been elected to the territorial assembly on 23 December 1956, and yet none of the Bamileke intelligentsia took them to task for their participation in territorial politics.

On the other hand, Tagny, the upéciste physician from Baham expelled from the party in late 1956, spearheaded the group of Kamdem Ninyim supporters. Speaking for Bamileke nationalists, Tagny stated that the French administration had deposed Kamdem Ninyim in order to censor his nationalist activity: "A young chief was deposed. He had committed the crime of having expressed opinions other than those permitted. From now on, they [the administration] could make and unmake Bamileke chiefs, something never before seen in the memory of man in these parts."[108] The only reason Fo Kamdem Ninyim's politics had gotten him into trouble, according to Tagny, was that his "opinions" were not "those permitted." Tagny clearly thought that a fo should be allowed to adopt an anticolonial political position and make it known, and that it should not cost him the chieftaincy to do so.

In 1956 and 1957, through discussions of the chiefs' depositions, differing visions of Cameroon's future as an independent state became entangled with conflicting views on the role of chiefs in territorial governance, the place of emigrant Bamileke in chieftaincy governance, and varied understandings of lepue. Multiple loyalties and shifting allegiances surfaced in the complex intersection between a potential reinvention of chieftaincy and the political processes of decolonization and nation building. But on the surface, a clear polarization emerged between "collaborationists," who supported Cameroon's integration into the French Union, on the one hand, and nationalists, who envisaged a complete rupture from French rule, on the other. Pro-French Unionists and pro-independence nationalists both agreed that 1956 was the right year for their chiefs to be engaged in political activity. They differed over political strategy.

Those who advocated collaboration with French administrators believed that Bamileke mfo should use electoral politics—within the loi-cadre structure—to access positions in the territorial government through which they might later increase their political influence and protect the institution of chieftaincy in the Bamileke Region. On the other hand, nationalists envisioned total, immediate independence—a degree of self-determination and political sovereignty that loi-cadre did not allow. Bamileke nationalists hoped their mfo would seize the occasion offered by popular nationalist, anticolonialist sentiment to cast off foreign rule, reject the auxiliary role French administrators had assigned to them, and retrieve political sovereignty for their chieftaincies. Through their discussions of the Baham affair, Bamileke intelligentsia sought to persuade others which route Grassfielders[109] should take toward independence—the collaborationist (through which lepue status would be negotiated with the French) or the nationalist (through which lepue status would be taken back from the French by force).[110] For Bamileke nationalists in the late 1950s, lepue meant reclaiming the chieftaincy as a sovereign space, and the chief as the people's representative. It was this more dramatic form of lepue—an immediate and total rupture with foreign rule at all costs—that held greater popular appeal in late 1956 and 1957. When nationalist mfo were deposed, calls for lepue became increasingly militant, intersecting with UPC's adoption of armed rebellion. The most popular nationalist song throughout the Bamileke Region carried the refrain "If there is only one person left, he must fight for lepue even if only to throw it in the water."[111] In other words, if only one person survived the war for independence, lepue must be his to do with as he wished.

Popular Narratives of Chieftaincy and Independence

In the final years of the trusteeship, administrators in French Cameroon removed an unprecedented number of chiefs throughout the Bamileke Region from the offices to which they had legitimately succeeded. Before European rule, successions were disputed, perhaps more often than not.[112] They entailed a liminal transfer of power during which notables used ruse, speech, social networks, wife gifting, or spiritual technologies to influence the choice of the next reigning fo and to change the political identity of the chieftaincy (see chapter 1). But the widespread, synchronic depositions of chiefs by French administrators in the late 1950s were entirely different from internally disputed successions memorialized in Grassfields political history. Much of the Bamileke population perceived the 1950s depositions as an attack on both nationalist chiefs and on the institution of chieftaincy itself. In independence-era French Cameroon, the symbolic sovereignty of chieftaincy came to constitute part of a political imaginary that conceptualized freedom from foreign rule. Discussions of chieftaincy spilled over the pages of newspapers and resurfaced in popular narrative forms—in petitions to the UN and in songs performed orally. The terms and phrases used by elite Bamileke in the discussions of Kamdem Ninyim's deposition—"selling the country," "traitors," "patriots," "colons," and chieftaincy—appeared repeatedly in these popular media.[113]

Petitions from Bamileke populations to the UN often decried the French administration's "unjust" or "unlawful" depositions of chiefs, describing the violence and humiliation unleashed by a crisis in traditional governance. In protesting Kamdem Ninyim's deposition, petitioners wrote that the French had "arrest[ed] the Chief and [taken] him to Dschang, where the local authority immediately replaced him without more ado, by a chief of its own choice, contrary to the wishes and the tradition of the people of that chiefdom."[114]

Bamileke inhabitants of other villages sent complaints about chiefs acting as agents of the administration. Petitioners from Balessing, for example, described their Fo Tiogning as having "already become a French citizen,"[115] a description that can be read as a condemnation of the assimilationist ideals of loi-cadre and the French Union. The machinations of a French administration that relied on chiefly collaboration to dominate the inhabitants of the territory established what petitioners from Fonkouakem described as a rule of "French tyranny in our Territory," adding that the French appointment of a "chief over the people against our wishes" spread "dismay and panic throughout our country."[116]

While the nationalist intelligentsia portrayed chiefs placed in power by the French administration as legally and traditionally illegitimate, ordinary Grassfielders used more descriptive and demeaning metaphors for what they saw as treachery. After Kamdem Ninyim's deposition and Teguia's enthronement, songs denouncing Teguia and his supporters spread across Baham. Sung in Ghomala', the indigenous language of Baham, the verses blended contemporary political issues with memories of past histories, and framed the crisis of Baham's chieftaincy in terms of Cameroon's struggle for independence from France. The words lepue and gung recurred, as did references to Cameroon as well as references to specific actors in Kamdem Ninyim's undoing.

Using language that recalled a not-so-distant past when slaving began to penetrate the Grassfields, during the mid-nineteenth century, Grassfielders used the terms *buying*, *selling*, and *stealing* to express their opinions about their usurping rulers,[117] as in the verses of *The Song of the Night Fighters*:

> He who sells our country [gung] will pay
> If someone sells our country, he will pay and pay his whole life.
> Teguia Damgne, too bad for him who sells our country.
> He is cursed and will be cursed forever.[118]

These terms also conjured images of an invisible, spiritual realm. Throughout southern French Cameroon, rich and powerful men figure in the collective imaginary as people with the potential to harm or betray (or both) those closest to them by "selling" them to occult forces, setting them to work in *famla*, or invisible plantations.[119] Stories abound of big men who shape-shift into vampires at night to "eat" the vital parts of unsuspecting dependents. These stories reveal popular perceptions of the "doubling," or potential to betray, that accompanied opaque political power.[120] The songs from late-1950s Baham featured Teguia, Samuel Kamé, and the powerful mwala named Ta Gue Tchuentchie, one of Teguia's supporters, as untrustworthy, treacherous politicians who were "selling" gung.

> Denunciation of Antinationalists
>
> Teguia Damgne,[121] what do you have against Cameroun? [3 times]
> Ta Gue Tchuentchie, what do you have against Cameroun?
> Mwala Djyeh, what do you have against Cameroun?
> All you traitors [mfingung], what do you have against Cameroun?
>   [3 times]
> Even [Samuel] Kamé,[122] what do you have against Cameroun?
>   [3 times][123]
> Etc.[124]

Both songs used Teguia's mother's name, Damgne, as a way of underscoring his illegitimacy as fo. The use of the maternal ancestor's name distanced a child of the fo from the status of successor, whereas people used ancestors' paternal names to refer to a reigning fo. For instance, Pierre Kamdem Ninyim was the third Kamdem to reign in Baham. The appellation Teguia Damgne was thus derogatory and jeering.

Ta Gue Tchuentchie bore the high-ranking title *mwala djyeh*, which designated him as the governor of fertility, fecundity, and rain in the chieftaincy. The mwala djyeh, in an unthinkable act of the polity's betrayal, had withdrawn his support from Kamdem Ninyim as the legitimate fo at the time of his succession to advocate instead for Teguia. He was the only one of the four wala of Baham to attend Teguia's initiation as fo, and he became a commander of Teguia's campaigns launched to purge Kamdem Ninyim loyalists from the chieftaincy. On the occasion of one of these purges, on 9 July 1957, the mwala djyeh committed the unconscionable act of killing a pregnant woman, Emilienne Magwa, the wife of a UPC member, who had joined other women of the Balogo quarter to protest the tchindas' arrest of Ta Tchuenkam, a staunch Kamdem Ninyim supporter.[125] Although the French administration's report of the incident described Magwa's death as an accident, stating that Gue Tchuentchie had merely fired shots into the air to disperse the crowd of women,[126] relatives remember the incident differently.

Magwa's younger sister recalls that she was shot because she did not reveal her husband's whereabouts to the mwala.[127]

Shooting a pregnant woman, publicly, constituted without doubt the most shocking thing the official protector of the chieftaincy's fertility could have done. The event magnified pro–Kamdem Ninyim fervor and certainly encouraged villagers to support the militia when they established a base camp under the command of Paul Momo in the compound adjacent to Ta Tchuenkam's (the man arrested that day).[128] Other songs, such as the one discussed below, *Mourning after the Deposition of Fo Ninyim,* warned others to flee should they see the mwala: "If you meet the mwala djyeh on your road, disappear quickly!" Another stanza lauded Magwa as a nationalist martyr: "A pregnant woman was killed, the mwala djyeh put a pregnant woman to death, for the independence of Kamerun."[129]

In the nationalist songs, gung could be understood to refer either to the polity of Baham or to the territory of Cameroon—the term's meaning remained ambiguous, to be deciphered by those singing or hearing it. *Lepue*—the word that rendered "independence" in Ghomala'—recalled the past of an autonomous, sovereign polity such as Baham and gestured toward such a future for Cameroon, the independent nation-state. *Mourning after the Deposition,* made up of nearly twenty stanzas, illustrates the emphasis placed on the dual meaning of lepue. The song recounted the young fo's downfall, from his arrest in 1956 to his execution in 1964 (see chapter 6), and reached back into chieftaincy history as a way of accentuating Fo Kamdem Ninyim's legitimacy.

Mourning after the Deposition of Fo Ninyim

No one gives the child the breast,
No one looks after the child anymore,
For the independence of Kamerun.

The newborn does not breast-feed,
No baby breast-feeds,
For the independence of Kamerun.

Let us go to Yokadouma,
Let us go together to Yokadouma,
For the independence of Kamerun.

Ninyim is far away in the land of independence,
Ninyim is far away in the land of independence,
For the independence of Kamerun.

What is our fo's name?
What is our fo's name?
Our fo's name is Tâ Ntomdjap,
For the independence of Kamerun.

If you meet the mwala djyeh on your road,
Disappear quickly!
For the independence of Kamerun.

A pregnant woman was killed,
Mwala djyeh put a pregnant woman to death,
For the independence of Kamerun.

They killed our fo,
They killed our fo,
Our fo was hung from a post and shot,
For the independence of Kamerun.[130]

The song referred to an inconceivable neglect of children due to the troubles and mourning engendered by Fo Kamdem Ninyim's deposition and its violent aftermath. The refusal to cut or shave one's hair was a sign of mourning, especially before a fo's proper funeral celebrations had been completed. The call for a collective journey to Yokadouma, the site of Kamdem Ninyim's exile in 1958, expressed a longing for the fo's reinstitution, or perhaps a desire to be near him in his time of need to help care for him. Tâ Ntomdjap, the fo's name in the song, was a commemoration of Kamdem Nguemdjo, the fo whose name Kamdem Ninyim carried, who reigned from about 1870 to 1928. He was remembered for having distributed seeds to restore the chieftaincy's agricultural fecundity during a period of famine (Tâ Ntomdjap meant Father of the Seed Grain of Njap—a green, leafy vegetable). Kamdem II had also expanded the territory of Baham and resisted the Germans' initial attempts to occupy the chieftaincy. A mention of Kamdem II recalled an anticolonial precedent and Baham's tradition of fighting to uphold the chieftaincy's sovereign status.

By using the homonym, the song recalled Kamdem Ninyim's ancestry and suggested that he bore the same qualities as Kamdem II, Baham's greatest fo. In Grassfields culture, homonyms were said to embody the characteristics of the person for whom they were named. The description of Fo Kamdem Ninyim's execution, which came eight years after his deposition, indicated the popular recognition of him as fo until the moment of his death.

Baham inhabitants' reaction to Fo Kamdem Ninyim's deposition figured in nonnarrative performances as well, particularly during two ceremonial events held at the chief's palace compound. The first was the official funeral of the late Fo Kamwa, which took place in December 1956; the second was the *tseu* dance, traditionally performed by the notables of gung on rare occasions of celebration, which Teguia organized in August 1957. A few weeks before Fo Kamdem Ninyim's arrest, two hundred delegates from Baham communities throughout the Bamileke, the Mungo, and the Nyong and Sanaga Regions, as well as from Kumba, in British territory, met in Nkongsamba to plan Fo Kamwa's funeral ceremony. The Baham elite had scheduled the event for 9 February 1957, but following Kamdem Ninyim's arrest, the administration pushed the event forward to 12 December 1956, as if to use it to confirm Teguia's position as fo while Kamdem Ninyim was held prisoner at Dschang. French reports of the event boasted of a wide attendance of notables, émigrés, and villagers at the funeral. The French chief of the Bafoussam Subdivision attended as well, most likely with Kamé in tow.[131] But French administrators, unfamiliar with Baham, its nobility, and its quarters, misread the significance of the absence of a number of notables. The population of Baham, on the other hand, knew which of the most important notables, through their absence, demonstrated their refusal to recognize Teguia as fo. The notables who did attend Fo Kamwa's funeral celebrations were those whom nationalists would characterize as mfingung—traitors to Fo Kamdem Ninyim, to Baham, and to the nation.[132]

By tradition, the tseu dance symbolically and publicly demonstrated village notables' solidarity with the fo. Visual accoutrements—leopard skins, hats, masks, and cloth tied around the body—denoted each notable's status in the chieftaincy. The entire population participated in the dance, which originated in the compound of the fo and made one round of the market place at the top of the tsa. The people, both spectators and participants, surged and trembled, often uttering cries of joy at the "beauty" of watching their fo perform the difficult and physically demanding dance, with a servant in tow to carry his hat, as much as six feet in diameter, during his times of rest.

But the tseu dance that Teguia held at the chief's palace in August 1957, far from creating solidarity, deepened fissures in the ranks of the notables. After the tseu, French administrators, seemingly more cognizant of the notables' influence on the fo's legitimacy than they had been in late 1956, remarked that "most of the quarterheads and notables hostile to Teguia did not attend."[133] But again, they did not fully comprehend the gravity of the important notables' lack of participation in the performance of tseu. Had Teguia's legitimacy been recognized, even by a majority of Baham's notables, dissenting mfonte, wala, and mwabo could not have "opted out" of the performance.

Baham inhabitants understood the implications of the poor turnout, however, and Kamdem Ninyim's supporters challenged the notables who did perform in the tseu. During the dance, one of Teguia's supporters threw a beaded horse's tail to a notable spectator, a descendant of Fo Kamwa's maternal family who had declared he would never recognize Teguia as fo. In the moment, however, the notable accepted the tail and danced for a short time before throwing it back, as per the protocol of the dance. Immediately after the ceremony, another notable approached him and accused him of betraying Fo Kamdem Ninyim, reminding him of his pledge to support him over Teguia at all costs. The notable who had accepted the horse's tail answered, "Even if Teguia is fo, I am not pleased about it." Unable to live with the conflicting loyalties, one concealed, the other performed publicly, he was overheard muttering to himself at the inconceivability of Teguia dancing as fo in the tseu. He returned home, where he committed suicide.[134]

The conflicted notable could not have conveyed his politicospiritual message any more clearly. In terms of village political culture, the act of suicide symbolized an acute sense of shame, so great that it was unlivable. Usually acts of suicide followed a person's committing a crime he or she knew to be unpardonable. In some cases, a criminal's spouse might also take his or her own life. In this case, suicide was the only solution to the inconceivable event of the legitimate fo's deposition, followed by the imposter fo's performance of the tseu, during which this notable, loyal to Kamdem Ninyim, had inadvertently accepted the horse's tail and thus publicly signaled his acceptance of Teguia's rule. Realizing his mistake, the notable saw only one way to withdraw his public acquiescence to Teguia's reign. After his suicide, the notable's rupture with the Baham community was permanent, extending even into the spiritual world, as those who took their own lives received no burial or funeral and were thereby precluded from belonging to the ancestral community.[135]

Other members of the Baham chieftaincy took equally drastic courses of action, although it was much more common for them to join the militia groups forming throughout the region, to flee into exile across the Anglo-French boundary, to settle in the Mungo Region, or to move to the cities. Kamdem Ninyim's deposition was, as his nephew Joseph Bu Pokam Kamwa reflected forty-six years later, the event that introduced chaos into the village: "After that, people did whatever they pleased."[136]

By replacing Kamdem Ninyim with Teguia as fo of Baham, French administrators and their most loyal ally, Kamé, fueled impassioned popular support of the nationalist fo. The event synchronized locally and territorially generated narratives of independence, political legitimacy, and political representation. Perhaps the greatest strategic error on the part of the French administration in its effort to squelch UPC popularity in Bamileke communities, the depositions of chiefs begun in the Baham affair set fire to the Bamileke and northern Mungo regions. In the thinking of Bamileke populations who sought to preserve the tradition of succession and inheritance as a way of ensuring the legitimacy of the fo, those mfingung loyal to the imposter chiefs warranted revenge. As French administrators deposed other chiefs throughout the region, Bamileke populations desiring to conserve tradition became ever more closely aligned with radical nationalists. In other words, conservative traditionalists became the allies of UPC nationalists, by signing on to a movement that opposed French intrusion in chieftaincy governance. The idea that violence was the only way to combat the attack on chieftaincy began to spread, and many Bamileke men and women joined the ranks of the UPC militia throughout the Mungo and Bamileke Regions, while countless others supported them with information, money, food, and supplies.[137]

The legislative assembly of French Cameroon went into session in January 1957. On 22 February, the parliament passed the proposed Statute of Cameroon into law, officially changing the name of the territory to the State of the Cameroon.[138] For the next three years, until official independence, on 1 January 1960, the State of the Cameroon would be governed jointly by a Franco-Cameroonian administration, although legally the UN was still to act as its supervisory body. While France would continue to govern in matters of "finance, diplomatic representation, commercial law, external commerce, penal code, and external defense"—the state's most essential elements of economy, law, and international relations—the Cameroonian administration was to take control of "internal" aspects of government.[139] French high commissioner Pierre Messmer selected André-Marie Mbida, arguably the most francophobe of all Cameroonian politicians, as prime minister and, as expected, he was invested by the assembly on 4 April. Mbida declared publicly that independence could only be considered following a ten-year program of "economic, social, and political development."[140]

Sidelined nationalists petitioned the UN from their exile in British territory, and corresponded with Roger Baldwin, chairman of the International League of the Rights of Man. They continued to call for the UPC's restoration to legality and requested that the UN oversee new elections in which people might vote freely for the candidates of their choice. But the elections of 23 December 1956, the only territorial elections within which universal suffrage applied, were the last elections held before official independence. Nevertheless, although High Commissioner Pré had proscribed the UPC and its affiliate women's, youth, and labor parties, barring their members from the political field, French administrators remained powerless to dismantle the foundations that upécistes had put in place throughout most of the territory's southern half. Nationalistic ideas and a popular desire for independence from French rule spread along the channels carved out by the UPC from 1948 to 1955, and in 1956 made new inroads, via the institution of chieftaincy and the Baham affair, into the popular consciousness of Bamileke communities, both in their home chieftaincies and in urban settlements throughout the territory.

Concerns about how to situate chieftaincy vis-à-vis the territorial government in formation reflected a related struggle to better define a collective Bamileke identity against the backdrop of a Cameroonian national identity formation. As French Cameroon's political actors conceived the broad foundations of the future nation-state, politicians and intellectuals from the Bamileke Region found that a collective regional representation provided greater political capital than the historic identification with an individual chieftaincy of origin. Bamileke politicians took on the collective identity that administrative policies and discourses and host communities had thrust on them during the interwar period, and used it to represent themselves on the territorial political stage. At the same time, by making chieftaincy a matter of crucial political importance, Bamileke politicians portrayed this institution of traditional governance to be one of the essential defining elements of a collective Bamileke identity. As chiefs became involved in electoral processes and the Bamileke elite drew parallels between chieftaincy and national governance as they did in discussions of the Baham affair, national and Bamileke identity became mutually constitutive in the political imaginary of Bamileke populations. For most Bamileke political actors in 1956, the acceptance of a national identity thus became contingent on the simultaneous preservation and promotion of a Bamileke identity. Bamileke nation builders wanted to be part of the future nation only if they could belong as Bamileke. Being Bamileke meant a variety of things, but in 1956 Bamileke identity crystallized around chieftaincy; one could not be a Bamileke without a fo, without an affiliation with a home chieftaincy.

Bamileke politicians and cultural entrepreneurs seized on the opportunities provided by decolonization politics to record and document the new Bamileke identity in numerous newspaper editorials, histories, ethnographies, and doctoral theses on "Bamileke" systems of justice.[141] Bamileke intellectuals, whether nationalist or pro–French Union, emphasized parallels between the laws of chieftaincy and France's legal code, and in so doing embraced the linear narrative of Enlightenment history and nation as a community progressing from ancient times to a modern future.[142] But the histories, founding myths, and memories of the region's past formed an essential part of Bamileke perspectives on nation-state, nationalism, and nation building. Although a number of Bamileke intellectuals produced scholarship in the 1950s with a Western model of nation-state in mind, widespread Bamileke conceptions of nation and nationalism did not derive solely from European postenlightenment definitions. Ordinary Bamileke populations engaged nationalism, via chieftaincy, as a mode of expression of Grassfields history, tradition, and political culture. The reworkings of political tradition that surfaced in Bamileke communities in Cameroon's decolonization era were "'fixed' in narratives of the past,"[143] and yet contained new interpretations and emphases.[144] Nationalists used Grassfields histories of the past as well as political notions such as lepue and gung to suit their political needs in mid-1950s French Cameroon. Their engagement with territorial politics, in turn, reshaped their understandings of the past.[145]

Bamileke politicians, intellectuals, and activists on the eve of Cameroon's decolonization were doing nothing new or even especially innovative as they used the past as a political tool to legitimize their role in 1950s nation building. As elsewhere in equatorial Africa, in the Grassfields, identity and tradition have been "constantly reworked."[146] The "tradition of invention" in the region has long manifested an adaptive quality that has ensured the survival of particular ways of identifying in the face of dramatic changes over time. But in late 1950s Cameroon, the "tradition" of Bamileke identity lacked sufficient historical foundation to serve as a basis for continuity. Still relatively new and more useful outside the region than within, the collective Bamileke identity masked internal fragmentation and competition. Despite the prominence of the institution of chieftaincy, being Bamileke did not rest on a uniform identity; nor did it translate to a homogenous political position in the 1950s. And so, although Bamileke politicians and scholars attempted to define a collective identity so as to present it to the world, internally, differing ideas of how best to "be Bamileke" in the nation engendered inter- and intrachieftaincy confrontations. The numerous depositions of chiefs throughout the Bamileke Region occurred just as intellectual, political, and social debates about "being Bamileke" peaked. The depositions pushed these debates into the realm of physical and violent conflict.

Existing studies portray violence in the independence era Bamileke Region as a fight of commoners against nobility. But the historical evidence suggests rather that Bamileke chiefs, guided by their own political concerns, those of their chieftaincies, and those of their emigrant populations, understood what was at stake as they chose to side with one trend or another in the territorial political arena of 1956. Those who allied themselves with the nationalists against loi-cadre found themselves removed from the stool of power before the close of the decade. Those who collaborated with the Franco-Cameroonian administration were added to the lists of mfingung to be "isolated," "denounced," and targeted for elimination by the UPC's SDNK army.

Although there were a number of reasons why a chief might choose to become a nationalist, generational identity seems to have been the salient causal factor. With the exception of Kemajou, who was already active as a Nkongsamba politician before inheriting the chieftaincy of Bazou, the chiefs who became collaborationists were older, had been in power longer, and tended to rely mainly on the French administration as the source of their political legitimacy within the chieftaincy. On the other hand, most of the chiefs who joined the nationalist movement had recently inherited office. They were young and schooled and sought to establish their legitimacy both through new political developments and through "traditional" culture as they understood it. Political differences came to a head in 1956, when French administrators eliminated nationalist chiefs and replaced them with those who would aid in the administration's suppression of nationalist activity. The depositions of chiefs forced any still politically neutral bystanders to publicly declare their allegiance to one side or another and face the consequences. As political processes unfolded after the 1956 elections, Bamileke communities throughout the territory were polarized to a greater degree than at any time during European rule and chieftaincies perhaps more uniformly brought under French control than ever before. To many, and particularly to those who belonged to the generation of the mfo being deposed, the decolonization of chieftaincy—to render it lepue—must have seemed more essential than ever before.

PART THREE

UPC Nationalists Go Global

5 ⤳ The Maquis at Home, Exile Abroad
Grassfields Warfare Meets Revolutionary Pan-Africanism

BEGINNING IN 1957 until well into the 1960s, groups of "night fighters" set fire to dozens of chieftaincies and notables' compounds belonging to those traditional rulers whom nationalists viewed as mfingung (traitors) throughout the Bamileke Region. In the Mungo Region, groups of men, mostly field hands and wage laborers, met to attack previously agreed on targets, usually family chiefs or civil servants (or both). In the Mungo River valley's plantation towns, such as Penja, UPC fighters, whom security forces described as outlaws, or maquisards, sabotaged thousands of acres of banana and coffee trees, slaughtered livestock, and set fire to railway stations, deliberately threatening white planters' economic profits by targeting the centers of agricultural economic activity. In the area of Bafang (Bamileke Region), dozens of men and women armed with clubs, machetes, knives, and sticks stormed the Catholic missions that they perceived as sites of French dominance. Throughout the Bamileke Region, UPC militia forces created occupied zones that state security forces could not access, and civilians dug up roads and hijacked vehicles. By 1960, according to some journalistic reports, 350,000 of over 500,000 inhabitants of the Bamileke Region lived outside the administration's control.[1]

From late 1956, as violence erupted in the Sanaga-Maritime, the Mungo, the Wouri, the Mbam, and the Nkam Regions of French Cameroon, and in the Bamenda, and Kumba regions under British rule, the newly elected Cameroonian prime minister Mbida called on the French government to send troop reinforcements. His successor,

Ahmadjou Ahidjo, who became the first president of Cameroon after independence on 1 January 1960, followed suit. The number of French security forces (military, gendarmes, and public forces) increased yearly until 1960, and not until 1965 did French troops begin to withdraw from Cameroon.² As the Cameroonian government established itself as a state, it relied heavily on French military support to suppress the "UPC rebellion" throughout the territory.

From 1956 to 1964—the years before and after official independence in January 1960, between 61,300 and 76,300 civilians lost their lives in French Cameroon as a result of independence era conflicts according to official British estimates—the only official synthesis of casualties resulting from the war for independence.³ Eighty percent of those killed resided in the Bamileke Region, according to the British embassy's official report dating from 1964. Yet, calling his own numbers into question, the embassy cautioned the British Foreign Office to take them with a grain of salt. The exact number of deaths was difficult to calculate because before independence "the French army frequently burned or otherwise destroyed whole villages which were heavily infested with terrorists," resulting in "the killing of an unknown number of non-terrorist civilians." Similarly, after independence, the "Cameroon Armed Forces . . . inadvertently killed an unknown number of civilians," and throughout the conflict, "it has frequently been impossible to ascertain whether a person killed was a terrorist . . . or an innocent bystander."⁴

Today, the total number of casualties occasioned by the Cameroonian independence war remains unknown. In the 1960s while the war raged on, General Max Briand, in charge of French military operations in Cameroon, stated that some twenty thousand people had been killed in the Bamileke Region during 1960 alone.⁵ A French journalist for *Le monde*, André Blanchet, declared at a conference in 1962 that according to a reliable source the French repression of the UPC rebellion over a period of three years had caused one hundred twenty thousand casualties in the Bamileke Region.⁶ Estimates vary even more widely in recent accounts published by Cameroonian researchers, political commentators, and journalists. Based on the memoir of a late, and perhaps mythical, French helicopter pilot, Max Bardet,⁷ who wrote that "the army . . . massacred 300 to 400,000 Bamileke from 1960 to 1962," the reported number of casualties has steadily climbed over the two and a half decades. In 1995, a year after the Rwandan genocide of 1994, Jacques Kago Lele wrote that eight hundred thousand to 1 million

Cameroonians lost their lives during the independence-era conflict, from 1955 to 1965.⁸ His number eerily echoes the number of those estimated to have died during the Rwandan genocide, an event that may have prompted many of the revisionist accounts that have characterized the independence war in Cameroon as a "Bamileke genocide." In 2006, Ferdinand Chidji-Kouleu wrote that the "troubles" resulted in the deaths of some 2 million Cameroonians (or two-thirds of the population) from 1955 to 1965.⁹ Similarly fabricated and inflated estimates abound on the Internet.

The significant fluctuation in the number of casualties, and particularly the fictitious estimates of recent years, reveals that Franco-Cameroonian administrators who coordinated the suppression of the UPC revolution took care not to keep meticulous records of the number of people killed during the late 1950s and the 1960s.¹⁰ Contemporary discussions of casualties also show clearly that, although memories of the war for independence occupy a prominent place in Cameroon's collective political imaginary today, the independence war is not a part of official state history, and there are still more questions than answers.

Although estimates vary enormously when it comes to the losses caused by state forces, the number of deaths caused by UPC fighters—or maquisards, as the state labeled them—is even more ambiguous. General Briand attributed some ten thousand deaths to what he described as the Bamileke Region's "internecine battles" during 1960. In the same year, only 614 people died among the state security forces, 583 of them "African civilians."¹¹ But the numbers, as imprecise as they may be, leave no doubt that independence-era violence impacted the lives of a majority of Cameroonians, and especially those residing in the regions where UPC soldiers were active. On the brink of independence, thousands of nationalists lost their lives, fled into exile, languished in prison, or joined the maquis—the underground resistance—where they took up arms against the administration. But, during the same years just before and following official independence, thousands more Cameroonians joined the ranks of the expanding security forces—gendarmes, army, BMM, police, and armed civilian self-defense groups. Emergency law and guerilla warfare became prominent, quotidian features as the UN trust territory under French administration transitioned to an independent, postcolonial state birthed against a backdrop of violence.

This chapter and the next both evaluate the dimensions and complex layering of independence-era violence in Baham and Nkongsamba, epicenters of nationalist activity in the Bamileke and Mungo Regions. But while this chapter will explore the ways in which upécistes, beginning in late 1956, employed violence in their fight for independence from French rule and in their struggle to take power from the Cameroonian government they couched as a neocolonial puppet regime, the next will examine the violence unleashed by security forces under French command to suppress the UPC rebellion. Few, if any, scholarly accounts of independence era violence explain and analyze the convergence of global and local understandings and strategies of warfare. And yet on both the side of the state's security forces, as well as among UPC troops, soldiers were informed by local knowledge, as well as by current international trends. Cameroonian state security forces depended on the technical and tactical expertise that the French army had acquired in colonial territories elsewhere,[12] while the self-defense units affiliated with progovernment chieftaincies utilized Grassfields traditions of warfare. Likewise, UPC fighters initially drew on local cultural practices as they constituted the militia groups that launched the first attacks on civil administrators, wealthy planters, and collaborationist chiefs. But beginning in 1959, when the exiled leaders of the UPC created the Armée de libération nationale du Kamerun (ALNK), modeled on the FLN's Armée de libération nationale (ALN) and inspired by Maoist doctrine, the UPC's local militias were infused with revolutionary ideals and strategies from abroad.

THE MAQUIS IN BAMILEKE CHIEFTAINCIES: AN INTIMATE FAMILIARITY

Kamdem Ninyim's trial took place on 12 March 1957 at Dschang, the regional capital of the Bamileke Region. Over a hundred people of Baham origin attended the trial, including Kamdem Ninyim's older sister Nguemdjo, who had followed him from prison to prison since his arrest to care for him.[13] Two French Communist lawyers from Nkongsamba defended the fo but, he was found guilty on all counts and sentenced to two years in prison, five years of exile in Yokadouma, and was ordered to pay FCFA 200,000 in fines and FCFA 50,000 in damages. Subsequently, his sentence was reduced on appeal to eight months in prison and a three-year exile. Although those present remained calm upon hearing the verdict, that night, in Baham, a group of "fifty to a hundred Kamdem Ninyim supporters" attacked the "partisans of Teguia Jean-Marie" in the quarter of Batousou'o, where Samuel

Kamé resided.[14] The attackers carried hunting rifles and erected barricades of fallen trees on the roads leading into Batousou'o. The chief of the gendarmes' brigade intervened with three guards, only to be chased away by the militia, who ransacked compounds, destroyed fences, and set fire to noblemen's compounds. A company of French troops based in neighboring Bangou and a unit of gendarmes arrived on the scene, but too late to prevent the damage.[15]

Kamdem Ninyim's sentencing sparked an eruption of violence in Baham, setting off three years of arson, murders, and looting in urban and rural Baham communities throughout Cameroon. In 1957 and 1958 at least ten Baham notables were killed, most of them for being pro-Teguia. Hundreds of compounds were burned, but the most devastating fires coincided with Kamdem Ninyim's trial, in March 1957, and his preliminary release, on 30 July 1957. Kamdem Ninyim's supporters, expecting their fo's return, set fire to over one hundred huts of Teguia supporters on the night preceding his liberation, 29–30 July 1957. Teguia fled to take temporary refuge at Bamun.[16] Thirty maquisards attacked and pillaged the compound of the fo in October 1957, days after the establishment of a UPC militia camp in the Baham quarter of Nka'a under the direction of an upéciste of Baham origin, Paul Momo. The attackers broke down doors and carried off material symbols of the fo's power housed in the chief's palace. Kamdem Ninyim was exiled to Yokadouma in April 1958[17] and the fo's compound was attacked a second time in December 1958. Paul Momo and his band targeted other pro-Teguia notables and servants in the Batchie and Pumsze quarters of Baham on the night of 24–25 December 1958, leaving behind tracts and the UPC flag—the black crab on a red background.[18] By the time of independence, in 1960, over two hundred houses had been burned in Baham alone and hundreds of Baham's inhabitants displaced or killed.[19]

The Baham tsa was not the only one to be attacked. In February 1959, as the Cameroons' political future was being discussed at the UN General Assembly, Paul Momo's forces destroyed the Bandjoun tsa, governed by the steadfast French ally and ALCAM deputy Fo Kamga. During the offensive, 185 huts were burned within the fo's compound, the fo's treasury was pillaged, and three people were killed. "Dozens" of armed and masked fighters carried out the attack, and left UPC flags and tracts at the scene, addressed to "the population of Bandjoun, the colons and their lackeys" and warning them, we will kill and kill until the proclamation of Kamerun's independence.... The independence you promise to grant on the 1st of January 1960 is not the one we are demanding.... We know that Ahidjo will proclaim an independence in Kamerun that we of the maquis call "colonial independence." Independence in Kamerun without UPC support is an authorization of anticolonial war in this territory.[20]

Chieftaincies of Bafoussam, Baleng, Bayangam, Bahouan, Batcham, Balessing, Baloum, Bafou, Bandenkop, Bazou, Bamendjin, and Fomessa were ransacked and burned from 1957 through 1960.

But UPC fighters did not only target the persons in chieftaincy governance whom they defined as mfingung. They also sought to eliminate those who claimed to represent them in the nascent government of Cameroon, the "lackeys of colonialism." In the eyes of upécistes, the parliamentary deputies elected during the December 1956 loi-cadre elections were the most treacherous of politicians.[21] Those in Baham's immediate vicinity were the pro-French Fo Kamga of Bandjoun and his running mate, Samuel Wanko of Batoufam, an engineer educated in France, who was elected as deputy to ATCAM in December 1956. Although it was not until 1959 that the "night fighters" stormed the Bandjoun chieftaincy, the opportunity to attack Deputy Wanko came not quite a year after the loi-cadre elections, on 13 December 1957. A group of fifty night fighters stopped the deputy in a roadblock between Bangangté and Bafoussam as he was on his way to attend his uncle's funeral in his home chieftaincy of Batoufam. They shot him at close range with a hunting rifle and left him to bleed to death as he struggled to start his car and drive away.[22] French reports stated that the Wanko assassination was not "the result of a local initiative" but part of UPC politics to "destroy the elite that opposes its goals," comparing it to that of Dr. Charles Delangue in the Sanaga-Maritime on the eve of the 1956 loi-cadre elections.[23] Like Delangue, Wanko was killed on his home turf. The perpetrators of the violence, a band of Bamileke fighters led by Simo Pierre, called themselves *mpouogung* (children of the country, or patriots), duty bound to eliminate mfingung (sellers of the country). By participating in the elections and refusing to come to the aid of Fo Kamdem Ninyim after his deposition, Wanko had demonstrated his clear affiliation with the collaborationist efforts of other assimilated Bamileke civil servants like Samuel Kamé. Stopped at the roadblock that night, upon realizing the danger he was in, Wanko used language to emphasize his "Bamileke-ness" as a trait he shared with his assailants. He introduced himself in Ghomala' and, by some accounts, he said, "It's me, Wanko; if you don't know me [recognize me], take me to the fo."[24] But despite his use of the local language, the fighters rejected Wanko, and executed him as a fingung for his betrayal of the nation. Although French administrators portrayed it differently in their reports, the Wanko assassination was very much a local initiative as well as a nationalist one.

Pierre Bouopda Kamé, political scientist and son of Samuel Kamé, argues that the violence that erupted in the Bamileke Region in 1957 had no "nationalist or anticolonial foundation," or that it was devoid of political ideology.[25] But in Bamileke communities, chieftaincy and nationalist politics were so intertwined by 1957 that UPC militia violence became articulated with the violent reprisals carried out by traditionalists, who sought to preserve chieftaincy as an institution of governance. UPC leaders harnessed the anticolonial momentum fueled by the chiefs' depositions and encouraged attacks on mfingung. As the UPC armies took shape, regional and national political concerns converged in the maquis and spilled over into the everyday lives of Bamileke populations. The linkages between territorial and local politics surfaced in the very organization of the UPC militia in the Bamileke Region as well as in the spatial arrangement of maquis camps.[26]

On 3 December 1956, the executive committee of the UPC's youth wing (the JDC) met to discuss the organization of the underground resistance militias to be implanted before parliamentary elections scheduled for 23 December. Units of the first UPC army, the CNO, were organized in the Sanaga-Maritime, near Ruben Um Nyobé's hideout. At the same meeting, JDC leaders assigned Martin Singap, a young upéciste from Bandenkop (a chieftaincy bordering Baham to the southwest), to reorganize the Bamileke Region according to the 1956 Program in Six Points[27] and to revive UPC local committees in western Cameroon.[28] UPC leaders drew a clear distinction between the "military" nature of the CNO as opposed to the "political" purpose of the UPC.[29] A political commissioner was assigned to each of the UPC's military units to explain the army's purpose to civilian populations and to encourage support for the fighters. In turn, these liaison agents familiarized themselves with local concerns. Singap held a preliminary meeting on 29 January 1957 for delegates from throughout the Bamileke Region. At this meeting nationalists, many of whom became UPC fighters, began to draw up the list of mfo to be attacked, describing them as the "anti-UPC chiefs of the Bamileke Region."[30]

Singap disguised local committees of youth as village soccer teams. Teams from different quarters of Grassfields villages held soccer tournaments, and political discussions were undertaken during training sessions.[31] Fifteen to thirty "soldiers" were recruited from each local committee and placed under the command of a "captain." Each captain belonged to a faction of the umbrella militia in formation, the Sinistre de la défense nationale du Kamerun (SDNK). Singap held the militia's first plenary session on 10 October 1957 in the Baham quarter of Nka'a, where the first SDNK camp was based. Many village nationalists and traditionalists who sought vengeance on the imposter Teguia for violating the traditional and spiritual laws of succession attended the meeting at Nka'a. Those present selected the leaders of the SDNK the same day, with Simo Pierre as general captain, and Paul Momo, secretary.[32] The Nka'a SDNK troops operated in Baham, Bandjoun, Bandenkop, Batie, Bamendjou, and Batoufam and used two training camps, one in the Nka'a quarter of Baham, which bordered Bapa and Batie, and the other in the Chegne quarter of Baham, which bordered Bandenkop and Bangou. Upécistes called the Nka'a base camp ONU (Organisation des nations unies), underscoring the symbolic importance of the UN in the political imaginary of nationalists even as they opted for violence as a liberation strategy.[33]

In October 1957, during an assembly held in Mbouda, hundreds more soldiers voluntarily enlisted to participate in the "war." Those gathered at the Mbouda assembly listed the chieftaincies to be destroyed, reaffirming the political strategy of targeting anti-UPC mfo. Local committee leaders at the Mbouda gathering received orders to intensify the collection of the UPC "tax" that served as funding for the party and its military initiative.[34] By December 1957, in addition to the Nka'a SDNK group, a second group covered ground from Bafoussam and Dschang, including Bansoa, Bamougoum, Bameka, and Baleng. The third group, under the direction of Edouard Penlap of Baham,[35] was based in Mbouda, and extended from the Anglo-French boundary to Babete, Bamessingue, Batcham, and down to Dschang.[36] Large European plantations and livestock farms were located around Mbouda, which explains the SDNK's higher level of activity in this region, from 1957 throughout the 1960s.

As maquis camps were first established, beginning in late 1956, connections between UPC armies in the Sanaga-Maritime, Wouri, Mungo, Bamileke and Mbam Regions were initially quite strong. The Mungo Region, bordering the Bamileke Region to the northeast and British territory to the west, became a crucial crossroads and hideout for nationalist freedom fighters on the run and militia groups used the Anglo-French boundary to their advantage when retreating from French troops. Jean Sepo acted as a liaison between Sanaga-Maritime-based CNO militia that had carried out the violent boycott of the loi-cadre elections in December 1956 and the new ones in formation in the Bamileke and Mungo Regions.[37] Chrétien Dzukam, the dynamic UPC spokesman from Bandjoun, Kamdem Ninyim's friend, and école des cadres graduate,[38] continued to travel from the Bamileke Region into British territory, to the Mungo Region and to the city of Douala. He worked to keep the connections between the various resistance camps and the exiled leadership in place. But Dzukam's arrest for arms smuggling in Douala, in May 1957, eliminated him from UPC military activity, leaving Singap, his partner and friend, to continue the work of paramilitary organization in the Bamileke and Mungo Regions.[39]

Although the early organization of the underground resistance suggested the existence of an overarching nationalist army based in multiple regions, in practice the UPC directorship was unable to achieve a sustained transregional unity among the different militias. In each particular maquis, fighters' military success depended first and foremost on their intimate knowledge of specific locales. Even more than the party's nationalist ideology, UPC revolutionary violence was rooted in local context. Difficulty in communications, isolation from a centralized headquarters, a lack of supplies, weapons, and funds, as well as the prevalence of local particularities and the progressive factionalization of the UPC leadership in exile all contributed to the UPC army's inability to maintain a uniform front. Local concerns ensured fighters and civilians' commitment to armed struggle, but in part this grassroots focus prevented the emergence of a transregional, unified revolutionary purpose.

In Bamileke villages, fighters congregated in base camps that could just as easily be situated in a family compound as in uninhabited portions of land. As the UPC occupied entire zones, including inhabited chieftaincies, the maquis became the village and the village became the maquis. Settled compounds became a part of UPC maquis camps, creating a spatial and social overlap between pro-UPC chieftaincies and the "underground" resistance. This symbiosis between maquis and settled, inhabited communities rested on a high degree of complicity between fighters and the civilian population. The organization of the maquis under the command of Paul Momo, Kamdem Ninyim's age-mate and friend, UPC soldier, and secretary of the SDNK in Baham, illustrates the degree of interconnection between maquis and village.

Paul Momo, who established a base camp for the fighters under his command in his grandfather's compound in the La'agweu quarter of Baham, did not hide out in the underground. Instead, he lived in his own house within the compound and relied on the loyalty of his grandfathers' neighbors not to betray his whereabouts. He interacted with the women and children of the compound, who knew him as an uncle or a son. He resided in one of the most well built modern-style homes in Baham, on a par with Fo Ninyim's. Both homes, designed by the same architect, were built of cement bricks, painted and plastered, and contained modern, indoor plumbing. Furthermore, Momo was not destitute or land starved but owned a car. More than by a pursuit of wealth or land, Momo was motivated by a desire to restore the legitimacy of all the Bamileke *mfo*, and not only Ninyim's. His grandfather, in whose compound he based the SDNK camp, claimed to be the rightful successor to the position of fo in neighboring Bahouan.[40]

Although Paul Momo's maquis was initially linked to the UPC militia via the Bamileke Region branch of the SDNK, over time he broke away from Singap's command and no longer followed directives from higher up the chain of command.[41] Although it appears as though Momo's primary loyalties were to Kamdem Ninyim, his fo and friend, there is little, if any, evidence to substantiate claims that Momo followed the latter's orders.[42] It is likely that Momo operated autonomously, although he recruited many of his own lieutenants and soldiers among those who remained loyal to Kamdem Ninyim.[43] But although Momo's group split off from the formal UPC army in late 1958 and eschewed Singap's efforts to reorganize and unify militia groups under the command of the newly formed UPC army, the ALNK, in the Bamileke and Mungo Regions throughout 1959, the modus operandi of his maquis as well as its close interactions with civilian populations reveals the intimate familiarity with the local culture, an intimacy so characteristic of violence in the Bamileke Region during this period.

In the early stages of militia violence in the Bamileke and the Mungo Regions, UPC fighters both protected and attacked their own neighborhoods. Maquisards targeted mfingung disloyal to their cause, such as Teguia supporters in Baham, while protecting those who joined their ranks and those civilians who supported them with food, information, supplies, or lodging. Language served as primary signifier of village origin and enabled civilians to discern fighters' chieftaincy of origin, even in border zones between villages or in plantations in the Mungo. The memoirs of Grégoire Momo,[44] an assistant administrator in Dschang at the time, contain descriptions of attacks carried out on a notable's compound in Bamendjou, in which witnesses specified that the assailants spoke a "dialect incomprehensible to Bamendjous."[45] Fighters who approached isolated pedestrians on roadways or paths between homes and fields or on the way to market spoke to them to ascertain their chieftaincy of origin. Women, adolescents, and even children who acted as informants or lookouts used the vernacular to gain information. These accomplices acted as the freedom fighters' informants. On the market day after an attack on a given chieftaincy, such informants gleaned information about the population's reaction or security forces' counterinsurgency strategies and transferred it back to the maquis. The accomplices played a prominent role in the nationalist struggle. They were praised by freedom fighters, and stories about them remain an important part of oral history about the nationalist struggle in the region. For example, one such spy earned the name Hydravion (seaplane) for her speed, agility, and alleged ability to walk on water.[46]

Nationalist fighters "sang all the time, from morning until night."[47] Songs were used during training to raise troop morale. Some, such as those from Baham examined in the previous chapter, related specifically to local chieftaincy politics, convincing fighters that they fought for their own fo's legitimacy, entangling chieftaincy with nationalism on a wider scale. Others had no references to a particular chieftaincy, but they encouraged a retrieval of Grassfields political tradition and recalled an era before European occupation:

> Long ago we were free, independent/sovereign [lepue].
> When the colon came he caused the people of Cameroon to submit,

even though before they did not submit.
And in this submission, we find only suffering.
We no longer accept this submission.

Before the colons came we were not submissive,
Now the colon comes to make us submit.[48]

As a political ideal grounded in the foundations of gung and its political history, lepue guided fighters in their attacks on the chiefs and the politicians who had become mfingung, those complicit in forcing submission. As the resistance armies took root throughout the region, military operations led to soldiers' and spiritualists' reawakening of Grassfields political, material, and spiritual culture.

GRASSFIELDS SPIRITUAL TECHNOLOGY IN THE MAQUIS

In the Bamileke underground resistance, fighters' use of spiritual technologies particular to their locale linked the cause for which they fought—a refusal to submit—with the invisible, metaphysical world that they believed would help them achieve their political goals. These spiritual technologies included oath taking to ensure loyalty to the movement, vaccination rituals to protect fighters against the enemy, divining to help devise military strategy, and the magical powers associated with metalworking to forge weapons the fighters used in warfare. As a result, Grassfields spirituality constituted another local element on which UPC soldiers of Bamileke origin depended during the war for independence. Similarly, in the Sanaga-Maritime, spiritual knowledge and practice nurtured a nationalist political imaginary as the two became articulated in the space of the maquis, where the ability to interpret dreams worked in tandem with a refusal to submit to colonial domination.[49]

In the Bamileke Region, as in the Sanaga-Maritime, UPC, JDC, and UDEFEC members took oaths of loyalty to the party.[50] In the Bamileke Region these oaths resembled truth-telling ceremonies.[51] In chieftaincies like Baham, reported one UPC member, "we used the shell of the tortoise, with certain herbs. We mixed it with water. So if you committed yourself to the UPC, first you swore, and then they gave you to drink. You swore that you would serve the party, remain faithful to the party, and never betray the party or a member."[52] In the Mbouda Subdivision around the time of Fo Kamdem Ninyim's trial, hard-core

Bamileke nationalists, those who joined the militia groups in formation, renewed members' vows of loyalty to the UPC. The new oath-taking ceremony was part of the preparation for carrying out violent attacks on targets in the Bamileke and Mungo Regions.[53] First collectively, then individually,[54] each member had to swear to unquestioningly execute the will of the group leaders. With the increased fervor that accompanied the new oaths and Kamdem Ninyim's trial, UPC members began purging their ranks, ridding committees of potential mfingung, those who might "sell" (betray) their comrades. In Babete (Mbouda) in June 1957, fighters assassinated Joseph Kamgaing, a UPC member suspected of complicity with the administration.[55]

Eventually, militia leaders in Bamileke maquis camps required new recruits to take the oaths of loyalty and collaborated with a *ghèkè*—a ritual specialist who knew how to manipulate *kè* (a term usually glossed as magic or power)[56]—to prepare SDNK and ALNK troops for battle.[57] Like a truth-telling ceremony, oath-taking rituals in the maquis were often held near a body of water or in a cave, spiritually auspicious sites believed to be part of a divinely protected landscape. The use of the tortoise shell, the most potent symbol of justice in the region, underscored the oath's gravity.[58] When taking the oath, fighters promised their allegiance to the SDNK or, later, to the ALNK, and asked the gods and ancestors to curse them and their families if they betrayed the UPC cause or their companions.[59] Afterward, a ghèkè prepared the soldiers for battle through a technological process designed to shield them from danger. Ritual specialists "vaccinated" new recruits with small cuts on the neck, shoulders, hips, knees, ankles, elbows, and wrists.[60] Into the incisions, he placed "medicine" that protected the fighter from iron, making him invulnerable to any metal object or bullets. A mixture of water, kaolin, lime, *djem djem* (a pod filled with seeds), and certain barks also made fighters invincible to iron or metal. The ghèkè then used a branch of the *pfeukang* (the tree of peace)[61] to sprinkle the mixture on the fighters while invoking the gods of war, the forest, and the *mbem* (spirit protectors) of each fighter for protection, blessings, and strength.[62]

Following the vaccinations—which provided not only protection, but agility, strength, and precision to the fighters—each soldier was given a *chiamgne*, or antelope horn, to guide him or her in the forest, bark from a variety of trees, and djim djim contained in a raffia bag called a *pueh kè*.[63] Sometimes soldiers were taught that they could disappear or fly away when faced with danger, and oral histories of the independence war are rife with accounts of freedom fighters who flew away at the first sign of danger.[64] Maquis leaders also worked closely with seers who consulted the divining spider to ascertain the best moment for an attack or predict the groups' future. Jean Djonteu—aka God of Independence, operating in the forest near Penja (in the Mungo Region), a war veteran who had fought for France at Fort Lamy and who took to the maquis after Kamdem Ninyim's deposition—was one of a few maquis commanders who declared themselves to be diviners and spread a prophetic message to their troops and civilian populations throughout their years in the underground resistance.[65]

Fighters rekindled the Grassfields tradition of iron technology and created makeshift forges within which they manufactured their own weapons, including local rifles, spears, javelins, machetes, and arrows. Not only did the practice fill the immediate need for weapons in the maquis, but it also amounted to a broadly symbolic reclaiming of lepue by forgoing reliance on imported weapons to wage the struggle for independence. The forges were located throughout the Bamileke Region, although most were in the Mbouda Subdivision, which was the center of distribution of locally fabricated weapons to all UPC soldiers. The rifles were not very effective weapons, but for Bamileke nationalists, rekindling furnaces and forges that had fallen into disuse during the period of foreign administration symbolized more than the procurement of arms. It recalled the historical precedent established during eighteenth- and nineteenth-century Grassfields wars over territory during which warriors and metalworkers respected and upheld an absolute protocol toward iron.[66]

Historically, metalworking involved the ritual domestication of a dangerous substance—iron—and the skilled spiritual and artisanal abilities such a process required. Metal weapons became part of the material culture of the independence war and were one of the objects that spiritualists imbued with powerful mystical forces. The use of metal to fight battles within one's own chieftaincy or against its allies was strictly taboo, and rigid protocols harnessed the "violence" of metal. Young men interested in ironworking approached a master forger or blacksmith to request an apprenticeship. If the master artisan accepted, the two began a highly disciplined regime of instruction. An essential part of the training involved the master's instruction of self-discipline, including the avoidance of sexual relations on the eve of beginning a week-long forge session and the ability to refrain from arguing or fighting with others in the workshop. Apprentices who lacked self-control or seemed prone to violence were eliminated from further training. This highly regimented apprenticeship, supervised by both the master ironworker and the workshop's ritual specialist who decided through divination when and how to purify the workshop and which apprentices had to be filtered out, ensured the control and domestication of the dangerous substance—iron.[67]

In the nationalist era, the use of metal weapons among members of a common chieftaincy demonstrated the politics of exclusion at work, as Bamileke soldiers defined who belonged to gung and who did not. The local fabrication of weapons represented nationalists' "reactivation of the indigenous technological memory"[68] in order to access the veiled sites of transformative power, rooted in a historic material culture. In reconnecting the material and the spiritual realms, medicines, iron weapons, and antelope horns served not only to wage war but also to retrieve the concealed dimensions of politicospiritual power that remained underneath the surface during the period of European rule.[69]

The material objects of warfare worked in tandem with culturally specific traditions of fighting and both were incorporated into the independence-era maquis. Commanding officers imposed a strict regimen of training modeled on a Grassfields tradition of skilled apprenticeship and subjected new recruits to a series of tests of skill and bravery. Discipline became one of the most symbolically important elements of the militia camps in the Bamileke Region. As it had been during the period of German colonization of the Grassfields, military training and drill exercises instilled in troops a sense of belonging to a group and respecting authority.[70] In the maquis, the training of new recruits fitted into a well-established pattern of apprenticeship practiced in all occupations that required a skilled knowledge of ké and its manipulation, such as the dangerous practice of working with iron, spider divination, or even induction into secret, regulatory societies.

Fighters in the maquis faced similar training and had to prove their loyalty, their willingness to submit to their superiors, their strength and bravery, and their adhesion to rigorous moral standards. Fighters performed arduous drills to increase skill, strength, and discipline. In many cases new recruits were subjected to tests of courage, or kidnapped recruits were broken into submission through the use of *cha-cha-cha*, a practice that entailed enclosing a wayward or insubordinate fighter in a hole in the ground for hours. The officers required young cadets to execute and observe the punishment.[71] Other punishments included tying a culprit to a whipping post in the camp and beating him.[72]

THE MUNGO REGION MAQUIS

Militia groups in the Mungo Region were often made up of fighters from throughout southern Cameroon who operated together under the direction of a commander. Exchanges of mystical technologies, methods of training and discipline, and politicospiritual ideologies that occurred in the Mungo River valley maquis camps engendered a hybridization of local cosmologies and political philosophies. The Mungo Region was a melting pot for the spiritual and mystical practices of warfare, as much as it was for politics, economics, and language.[73] Because of its close proximity to the Bamileke Region, to British territory, and also due to the high percentage of Bamileke settlers there, the Mungo Region served as a pivotal crossroads for UPC armies and fighters, connecting various maquis camps throughout French and British Cameroons to the exiled UPC directors abroad. These transregional and international connections were put in place by 1959 and became stronger over the next few years. But even before the birth, in 1959, of the ALNK, the new UPC army that was to be under the central control of the UPC directors in exile, Mungo Region fighters of Bamileke origin maintained strong links to the maquis in their home chieftaincies.

Radiating outward from the chief's palace, the conflict ensuing from the deposition of Fo Kamdem Ninyim and his replacement with Teguia permeated Baham communities outside the home chieftaincy, meaning that any discussion of independence-era violence in the Bamileke Region must take into account the activities of Bamileke settlers in the Mungo Region, where they made up 90 percent of the population in some areas. UPC nationalists who joined the armed resistance primarily targeted anti-UPC leaders, whether those holding office in the territorial government of Cameroon or those who held "traditional" office. For Bamileke nationalist fighters, traitors were those who collaborated with French administrators and mfingung—anyone who betrayed either the UPC or the institution of chieftaincy by failing to uphold the traditional "laws of succession." These mfingung could certainly be found in home chieftaincies, but they were also present among the administrative officials and the family chiefs governing emigrant communities in the Mungo Region, in Yaoundé, or in Douala. Given that gung had expanded beyond its geographical boundaries throughout the period of French rule, conflicts over legitimate rule that surfaced as mfo were deposed spread into Bamileke communities throughout the territory, creating a rhizome pattern of violence that connected home chieftaincies to Bamileke emigrant communities.

Seeking the support of Baham emigrants residing in the Mungo Region and in Douala, Teguia and his entourage visited Baham communities in Douala and in the major towns in the Mungo River valley in September 1957. On 5 and 6 September, Teguia spoke before Baham communities in Nkongsamba, Mantem, and Penja, inviting those who had fled "the troubles" to return home. Teguia received a warm welcome only at Mantem, while in Nkongsamba and Penja hostile crowds rejected Teguia as fo and insulted him publicly. Jean Djonteu, a Baham resident of Penja, one of former fo Kamwa's retainers who participated in Ninyim's succession rites, called Teguia a "bandit" and a "usurper."[74] Djonteu's public insult of a fo was unthinkable in terms of Grassfields political culture, and in the past would have incurred weighty punishments, including the amputation of the culprit's ears, lifetime banishment from the chieftaincy, the removal of his title if he were a notable, and the burning of his material possessions.[75] Djonteu could not have demonstrated more clearly that, as far as he was concerned, Teguia was not the fo. Following the incident, Djonteu declared the "politics of the country" to be "bad"[76] and joined the maquis near Penja. Teguia's Mungo valley tour prompted others to make the same decision to join the armed resistance.

On 19 September 1957, two weeks after Teguia's campaign for support, a band of twenty nationalist fighters dressed in red shorts and shirts assassinated André Tchi-Tchi of Bazou and Isaac Wambo with machetes and clubs.[77] Tchi-Tchi, an assimilated Bamileke who served as both municipal councillor[78] and chief of the Bamileke of Mantem, and Isaac Wambo, Baham family chief and former chief of the Bamileke of Mantem, represented the UPC's ideal mfingung targets.[79] Wambo had belonged to the UPC local committee of Mantem and had initially supported Kamdem Ninyim but, by the time of Teguia's visit, had switched to supporting the imposter fo, making him one of the treacherous party dropouts most despised by UPC hard-liners. The band had also planned the execution of Kamdem Joseph, Teguia's brother, but, not finding him in, killed one of his servants, Ndiffo, instead.[80]

Although they downplayed the Mantem assassinations as "a tribal affair," French security reports nevertheless voiced concern over the assailants' use of discipline, uniforms, and advances and retreats coordinated by the blowing of whistles that resembled CNO operations.[81] The evidence of military discipline led French administrators to admit the link between Baham politics and UPC nationalism. Reports stated that the goal of the Mantem attackers was "to defend [Kamdem] Ninyim's interests *and* the political ideas of the UPC."[82] The attackers who carried out the Mantem assassination were all of Bamileke origin, the majority of them from Baham, although many, if not most, resided in the Mungo Region or in Douala. The group's members frequented particular bars in Douala and Nkongsamba where they could leave messages calling comrades to Baham for an assignment. Many of the fighters belonged to the New Bell (Douala) UPC local committee. Most of them held steady jobs: five or six were chauffeurs or transporters who made regular trips from Douala to Bafoussam, and at least three were butchers. The Mantem attack was conceived in a notable's home in Baham during an assembly of UPC members from Douala, Nkongsamba, Mantem, and Bafoussam. Those gathered there expressed that the "country of Baham [*gung*] was in danger, that it was the fault of certain Bahams from outside, and that they must be executed, especially those of Mantem."[83] Because the nearest large town to Mantem was Nkongsamba, the attack relied on the complicity of members of the Baham community in both Nkongsamba and Mantem.

The day before the attack, the participants arrived in Nkongsamba and regrouped in the home of Kamdem Ninyim's uncle Benoît Domtchueng, in the neighborhood of the Catholic mission. After sharing a meal, two Baham chauffeurs, Laurent Nguiffo and Bernard Kamto, transported the group to Kamto's home.[84] They ate again before Kamto and Nguiffo drove them to Mantem. Kamto, Nguiffo, and Domtchueng returned to Nkongsamba, leaving the fighters in the home of planter Maurice Kouam, where they spent the night and most of the next day. In the afternoon, a scout verified that the intended victims were at home. At 7 p.m., Kouam's neighbor brought clubs. The three butchers from Douala had meat cleavers, and one fighter had a hunting rifle he had brought from Baham. At 8 p.m., the band set out toward the homes of the intended targets. They killed Tchi-Tchi first, with the clubs and cleavers. They then continued to Kamdem's home, where they executed Ndiffo, and finally reached the home of the Baham family chief, Isaac Wambo, killing him as they had Tchi-Tchi. The group returned to Kouam's home, where they rested before leaving for Douala at 4 a.m. Kouam provided each with money for transportation. In the UPC local committee meeting of New Bell, Nouze gave an account of the Mantem operation in the home of the committee's secretary, Moïse Youmbi, formerly a member of the administration's police force.[85]

Assassinations of Bamileke chiefs of communities in the Mungo Region continued after the Mantem incident. In Penja on 1 May 1958, a band of twenty men armed with hunting rifles, clubs, and machetes killed the family chiefs of Bafoussam and Baham and wounded the Bangangte family chief. The Baham family chief, Abraham Demgang, had been a member of the UPC and a Kamdem Ninyim supporter but later showed his support for Teguia by hosting him during his 1957 campaign tour through the Mungo. Demgang also happened to fill the administration's auxiliary role of market tax collector.[86]

The Mantem assassinations conformed in many ways to the tactics of SDNK fighters operating within the Bamileke Region chieftaincies. Like Paul Momo's fighters, who moved back and forth from civilian life to the base located in Momo's compound, Wambo and Tchi-Tchi's executioners did not live in the maquis. They knew each other well, and many likely knew their victims. The attack was planned in advance in Baham but demonstrated the transregional reach of chieftaincy politics as they became articulated with the nationalist armed resistance.

A different sort of attack, bringing together fighters of different origins, reveals that UPC violence in the Mungo Region was not always related to chieftaincy politics. Although the Mantem attacks targeted traitors to the Baham chieftaincy, Mungo-based upécistes, who adopted the armed struggle, sought to eliminate "traitors" of the nation as well. In the Mungo Region, such traitors included wealthy planters and municipal councillors. The executions that were unrelated to traditional Bamileke governance were carried out by more diverse groups of fighters who, in many cases, had never met each other before the day of the attack. The attack on Daniel Ndengoue, a wealthy planter from near Njombé, which occurred only weeks after the Mantem assassinations, illuminates the differences between those operations that wielded meaning in terms of Bamileke chieftaincies politics, and those that did not.

One Sunday afternoon in October 1957, a party member informed Joseph Djileu, a twenty-nine-year-old field hand who lived near the small plantation town of Penja, of a meeting to be held in Bonandam. Djileu walked for two and a half hours to arrive at the meeting place on time. Nguengang, a resident of British territory who crossed the border for the weekly meeting, instructed the assembled group of thirty that they would kill three "whiteman's lackeys" and "traitors to the country," the municipal councillors Daniel Ndengoue, David Nguembou, and Henri Takounga. Nguengang and his companions from the British zone, two who spoke pidgin English and one who spoke Ghomala', made each member of the group of "fighters," made up of twenty Bamileke and seven Bassa men, swear that he would not be cowardly. The leaders then reviewed the troops' machetes to make sure they were sharp. Just after nightfall, seventeen fighters went to carry out the attack. One of the youngest went inside the home of planter and municipal councillor Ndengoue Daniel and lured a man, who was not even the intended victim, outside. Nguengang then ordered his group to attack. According to Djileu's account:

> Nguengang told us to strike and we mobbed that man. The Bassa holding a pistol tried, it seemed to me, to fire his weapon with its barrel pointed at the victim's head. At that moment, a second African came out of the hut. It was still not Daniel. That man grabbed the Bassa holding the pistol and tried to knock him to the ground. But he was unable to follow through, because he was also was struck with the machetes. I cannot tell you exactly who struck him with their machetes. As for myself, I struck the first victim once or twice, and struck the second one in the back, the one who was fighting with the Bassa. The last victim screamed a lot and we fled by the path we had taken to come. I immediately returned to Njoungo.[87]

The militia group operating in the vicinity of Njombé, in the Mungo River valley, was made up of Bamileke and Bassa men, who joined together for the common purpose of eliminating a wealthy planter whom upécistes had depicted as a lackey and a traitor. The leader of the attack, Nguengang, and his two companions from British territory used pidgin English as a lingua franca during the interethnic meeting. That Djileu recognized Nguengang's language to be Ghomala' suggests that he could speak Ghomala' or a closely related language. But when describing the actors in the scene, Djileu used the terms Bassa to designate those who came from the Sanaga-Maritime Region, and African when the ethnic identity remained unknown to him. Thus Djileu identified persons of Bamileke origin, not by labeling them as Bamileke, but more precisely—according to the language they spoke. His ethnic descriptions became less precise when referring to non-Bamileke who were Bassa or, if he did not know them and could not identify their language, simply African. The attack on Ndengoue showed how the Anglo-French boundary enabled UPC leaders to enter French territory to carry out an operation or conduct a meeting, only to slip back across the border once it was completed. Djileu's account also points to the mob mentality that prevailed during many of the violent attacks of those years. Because of the size of the group, Djileu was unable to know for certain who was responsible for the death of the victim. Others described a general melee or insisted that, in the confusion, they had not had a chance to strike the victims at all.[88] Even in this case, unrelated to home chieftaincy affairs, when the targets and fighters did not know one another, there was a great deal of overlap between the maquis and civilian society. It was not unusual in the Mungo Region for fighters to go about their daily lives as civilians, meet to carry out assigned assassinations of mfingung, and then return to their homes.

The attacks carried out in the Mungo Region, whether directly related to the Baham affair or not, targeted family chiefs, wealthy planters, and municipal councillors. Given Nguengang's residence in British territory, it is most likely that he acted on the orders of exiled upécistes at Kumba, one of the UPC headquarters in British territory. Upécistes were still present in British territory even though the British administration had banned the movement in June 1957 and deported all members of the directors' bureau. Yet many of the UPC militia operations in the Mungo Region, like the attack on Ndengoue, exposed the lack of weapons, training, and discipline for UPC "troops." As Djileu's account indicates, fighters in the Mungo Region had less training than those in the Bamileke Region, at least until the formation of the ALNK, in 1959.

Clearly, many of the Mungo Region's nationalist fighters lacked organization, direction, and military training. In the Bamileke Region, too, whatever uniformity had initially joined the various militias together began to unravel. The Nka'a camp, in Baham, was discovered and destroyed by French military forces in December 1957, soon after Wanko's assassination.⁸⁹ The group disbanded, and the leaders, including Captain General Simo Pierre, escaped to British territory. There, Simo organized and carried out invasions in the Mungo River valley until his arrest on 3 October 1958, two weeks after a Franco-Cameroonian military patrol killed UPC secretary-general Ruben Um Nyobé in the maquis in the Sanaga-Maritime.⁹⁰ Simo and four others became the first political prisoners sentenced to death just before independence. They faced a firing squad on a soccer field in Bafoussam on 10 July 1959, with Simo praying for Cameroon's liberation in the moments prior to his death.⁹¹ Still based in Baham, Paul Momo continued to launch attacks, but his troops sustained many losses, communication with fighters in the Mungo and British territory became ever more difficult, and the strength and unity of the SDNK was compromised. Things would change significantly once the exiled UPC leaders gained the support of Kwame Nkrumah's African Affairs Centre and the FLN, in late 1958.

EXILE: A TUNNEL FROM THE MAQUIS TO PAN-AFRICAN LIBERATION

The exile of upécistes converged with the emergence of a revolutionary, political, and anticolonial Pan-Africanism, in late 1958. The convergence led to a centralized restructuring of UPC violence within the Cameroon territories. First, the exiled UPC directors benefited from the support of heads of independent African states who subscribed in rhetoric if not always practice, to a new Spirit of Bandung—broadly conceived as anticolonialism and the emergence of a strong, nonaligned Third World—sweeping formerly colonized territories. With Ghana's independence in March 1957, Kwame Nkrumah founded the Bureau of African Affairs to aid other African colonial territories in their quest for independence.⁹² The new state's constitution pledged to recognize the sovereignty of a United States of Africa over its own, should the occasion arise. Now, during the crucial period of decolonization, Nkrumah and his supporters believed that it was up to the Black Star of Ghana to lead the way to a United States of Africa, free of European powers' economic and political control, and nonaligned with either East or West in the age of the Cold War.⁹³ For many territories in Africa still under colonial domination, Ghana's initiative came not a moment too soon. From 1958 to 1966 the African Affairs Centre, in Accra, hosted activists and exiles from Egypt, Kenya, Uganda, Malawi, the Belgian Congo, Angola, Lesotho, Zambia, and Cameroon.[94] For these African nationalists, Nkrumah's foreign policy constituted the African cornerstone of a Third World solidarity birthed at the Afro-Asian Bandung Conference, held in April 1955.[95]

In June 1957 administrators in the British Cameroons officially proscribed the UPC and its affiliated parties, placing its directors under house arrest before deporting them to Sudan, the only nation on the UPC's list of desirable hosts that opened its borders to them. Soon after their arrival, made uneasy by their radicalism and increasing visibility in the international arena, the Sudanese president encouraged them to leave.[96] Facing censorship in Sudan, Félix Moumié and other UPC leaders continued on to Cairo to establish the UPC Headquarters in exile. In December, Moumié, UPC president in exile, attended the first conference of the Afro-Asian Solidarity Organization (AASO) and was elected to serve in the organization's directors' committee along with the representatives of Ghana, Guinea, and Algeria—the nations whose leaders would become the most ardent political supporters of the UPC in the years to come.[97] The AASO's purpose was to "unify the struggle against imperialism and colonialism" by bringing together AASO national committees, political parties, labor unions, movements for peace, and youth and women's organizations.[98] In Cairo in 1957, conferencegoers addressed the Algerian war, condemned the "barbarous acts committed by Belgian colonialists against the population" of Congo, and agreed that economic sanctions and boycotts must be applied against the apartheid regime in South Africa. On the issue of Cameroon, the AASO passed a resolution painting the proscription of the UPC as "a war of renewed colonial conquest" and delegates from independent states pledged their support for Cameroon's immediate independence.[99] During press conferences, AASO spokespersons called for a withdrawal of all French and British troops from the territories of Cameroon, a cessation of American aid to the Cameroonian government, and a UN referendum on the reunification of the British and French territories.[100]

At the AASO conference in Cairo, Moumié forged connections with Ahmed Sékou Touré and Kwame Nkrumah. The leaders of Guinea and Ghana adopted the UPC as one of their revolutionary projects and helped to get the Cameroon case on the agenda of subsequent Pan-African forums. It was the sort of cause Nkrumah needed at the time. From the time of Ghana's independence, Accra became fertile ground for the cultivation of a new, political Pan-Africanism, and at the same time, a haven for the men and women in exile who struggled to attain independence for African territories still under foreign domination. Nkrumah described the freedom fighters congregated in the African Affairs Centre as the "gem of the revolution" and opened Ghana's borders to their ranks.

After the Nkrumah government agreed to host UPC, JDC, and UDEFEC leaders in Ghana, hundreds of Cameroonian nationalists fled arrest and went into exile, most ending up in Accra. Outside French territory, exiled upécistes reconstituted an explicitly extrametropolitan political movement founded on the possibilities symbolized by Nkrumah's Bureau of African Affairs, and the UPC's external support began to feed Cameroon's internal maquis rooted in indigenous, locally particular political conceptions of freedom and sovereignty.[101]

The importance of the diplomatic support Moumié and other UPC leaders had gained from independent African states during 1957 was made clear in Accra during the planning and organization of the first All-African Peoples' Conference (AAPC) throughout 1958. In April 1958 the leaders of Ghana, Ethiopia, Liberia, Libya, Morocco, Tunisia, Sudan, and Egypt (the eight independent countries in Africa) convened in Accra at the Conference of Independent African States to discuss ways to mutually "safeguard" their political and economic independence, to establish and maintain ties between independent states, and, perhaps most important, to strategize support for the liberation of the rest of Africa, still under colonial rule.[102] During the meeting, Nkrumah scribbled a note on the records suggesting that the upcoming AAPC conference, scheduled for December 1958, could "serve as a useful platform for dependent African territories to air views on matters affecting their destiny and future,"[103] and listed French Togoland, Nigeria, and the Cameroons as territories that might benefit from a conference forum.

The first AAPC conference, held in Accra, was attended by representatives from the eight independent African states, twenty-eight African territories under foreign rule, and sixty-two nationalist organizations, political parties, and trade unions.[104] The conference symbolized the new age of anti-imperial Pan-Africanism and was extremely threatening to metropolitan powers that had yet to loosen the chains on many of their colonies.[105] In the months leading up to the AAPC conference, the Franco-Cameroonian regime expressed its discordance with Ghana's official support of the UPC bureau in exile. In October 1958, upon learning of the AAPC conference plans, Cameroonian prime minister Ahidjo told the French high commissioner of Cameroon that he would not send any representatives to Accra if Moumié were invited, and he requested the intervention of the French ambassador of Ghana to prevent Moumié's participation. Furthermore, Ahidjo demanded that the French submit a strident diplomatic protest to the Ghanaian government.[106]

French colonial administrators shared Ahidjo's indignation at Ghana's official invitation of Moumié and the UPC, an "an illegal and insurrectional organization."[107] The minister of overseas France remarked that the conference "constituted a dangerous tribunal for adversaries of the Franco-African community."[108] The French high commissioner of Cameroon, Xavier Torre, attempted to ensure Moumié's exclusion from the AAPC debates and to instead "obtain permission for the veritable representatives of Cameroonian public opinion to be admitted if this conference is to be attended by representatives of French territory" in order to demonstrate the "cohesion of the *ensemble français.*"[109] But in 1958, French diplomatic influence in Africa was too weak to prevent Nkrumah and other AAPC planners from upholding the UPC's prominent position at the conference. Hence, not one delegation from the Ahidjo government attended.[110] The Pan-African foothold gave Moumié the diplomatic backing he needed to proclaim at a press conference on 12 December 1958, during the AAPC convention, that the exiled UPC directors' bureau constituted the legitimate Cameroonian government.[111]

At this first meeting, Moumié was elected to a position in the AAPC directors' committee, chaired by the Kenyan Tom Mboya. Among his colleagues were Ahmed Boumendjel, the representative of the FLN; Patrice Lumumba, future prime minister of Congo; and Kojo Botsio, minister of foreign affairs in Ghana. As planned, Moumié found himself in the thick of the newly constituted Pan-Africanist body of the AAPC and as a result he had their attention. Following the model of the Gouvernement provisoire de la République algérienne (GPRA), Moumié, head of the Cameroonian government he declared to be the legitimate one, attempted to transform the UPC's claims into a "diplomatic revolution,"[112] by compelling supportive state governments to advocate for the UPC in international forums, particularly the UN.

On 13 December 1958, the delegates attending the AAPC conference adopted a resolution on the Cameroon question. Together, the representatives of anticolonial organizations and African nations agreed

The Maquis at Home, Exile Abroad ⇔ 201

to go before the UN to request total amnesty for members of the UPC and its affiliates, the return of those exiled and deported, a referendum on the issue of reunification, and democratic elections for the Cameroonian national assembly with a UN-selected commission to organize and supervise all electoral proceedings.[113] Before the close of the AAPC, Moumié moved the official UPC headquarters from Cairo to Conakry, Guinea. With Moumié established in Conakry, UPC vice president Ernest Ouandié remained in Accra, where he drew on the resources of Ghana's Bureau of African Affairs and the African Affairs Centre. Soon after the AAPC meeting, the resolution on the Cameroon question would be echoed in the speeches of African state representatives to the UN who took the floor at the General Assembly as the political future of the Cameroons was decided in a special session devoted solely to the issue in February 1959.[114]

In addition to obtaining the diplomatic support of a majority of independent African states in late 1958, the UPC, having already begun to use arms in the fight for independence from European rule, benefited from the AAPC's discussion and definition of the legitimate use of violence to cast off colonialism. During the conference held in Accra in December 1958, African politicians, activists, and representatives debated the question of violence. Before the assembly of anticolonial political activists and intellectuals, theorist, psychiatrist, and FLN activist Frantz Fanon voiced the argument that violence was the only path to total decolonization—economic, psychological, cultural, and political.[115] After lengthy deliberation, heads of the delegations in attendance eventually reached the consensus that violence, narrowly defined, had its place in African territories' quest for liberation from colonial rule: "Recognizing that national independence can be gained by peaceful means in territories where democratic means are available, [the AAPC] guarantees its support to all forms of peaceful action. This support is pledged equally to those who, in order to meet the violent means by which they are subjected and exploited are obliged to retaliate."[116]

For the activists, politicians, and leaders behind the 1958 AAPC resolution in Accra, violence employed in wars against colonialism constituted self-defense, or a last resort to use when democratic means were made unavailable by administering authorities, as they had been in the Cameroons when the UPC had been proscribed in French, then in British territory. The 1958 AAPC resolution clearly defined the limits within which violence might be justifiably used. In the opinion of a majority of those gathered in Accra in December 1958, the use of revolutionary violence in the Cameroons in late 1958 was easily justified. After the proscription of the most popular political party in the territories, democratic means were clearly no longer available to those seeking national independence. The perspective that violence was, in the words of Aimé Césaire, "the only arm of the colonized that can be used against colonialist barbarity,"[117] justified armed struggle as the UPC's liberation strategy.

In February 1959 upécistes both within and outside the Cameroon territories, as well as a number of international sympathizers, anticipated the outcome of the UN General Assembly's decision on the Cameroon question. African delegates, most of whom had attended the AAPC two months earlier, proposed a resolution to extend complete amnesty to political prisoners, to repeal the proscription of the UPC, and to organize new, UN-supervised parliamentary elections before independence. But the American delegation "exerted every available form of pressure . . . to defeat the African resolution."[118] After heated deliberations, the assembly "voted to approve independence and to end trusteeship over the French Cameroons without requiring new parliamentary elections" and without a constitution in place. A clear sign that the UN had no intention of intervening in or supervising the decolonization process, the General Assembly's resolution stoked the fires of violence in the Cameroon territories. In 1961 independent parliamentarian Dr. Bebey-Eyidi remarked to Roger Baldwin, chairman of the International League of the Rights of Man, that those who advocated for amnesty and UN-supervised elections before independence had sought a middle road "between Ahidjo and Moumié in order to effect a general reconciliation of the different leanings of the Cameroons before independence. In not following that position, the UN opened the way for extremists who plunged our country into terror and confusion."[119] Faced with the UN decision which amounted to a political impasse eradicating the hope for a peaceful, negotiated resolution to the conflict between UPC forces and the Franco-Cameroonian administration, UPC leaders in exile drew on their Pan-African support as they moved to replace sporadic and somewhat disorganized militia violence with disciplined, centrally commanded armed forces.

THE ALNK-UPC ARMY UNDER A CENTRALIZED COMMAND

The restructuring of the UPC's armed struggle began in 1959 with the creation of a new revolutionary army, the ALNK. The ALNK was to absorb or replace all existing nationalist militias operating in the Cameroon territories. Following Simo Pierre's arrest, in October 1958, militia bands in the Bamileke and Mungo Regions increasingly fell into disunity. Momo viewed himself as Simo's obvious replacement as captain general of the SDNK, but Singap challenged his position.[120] The tensions may have been heightened because Momo's fo was in prison, while Singap's chief, Fo Feze of Bandenkop, continued to evade arrest and eventually made his way to Accra, where he obtained a scholarship to study international economic relations at Peking University.[121] Eventually Momo refused to submit to Singap's orders. Other factions emerged in the Bamileke Region, including Sop Alexandre Tagatsing's group operating from Bamendjou, which quickly gained a reputation for brutally assaulting the civilian population. Tagatsing was said to kill even pregnant women, gutting the fetus out of their bellies and leaving them on the side of the road.[122] In the Mungo Region, Jean Djonteu, a Kamdem Ninyim supporter who had taken to the maquis after Teguia's visit to Penja, seemed to be operating autonomously.[123]

The disorganization, in-fighting, and losses sustained by militia groups, some of which appeared to be unaffiliated with the UPC, prompted the directors' decision to reorganize the troops after the disappointing UN resolution on the Cameroons. Singap, whom the exiled UPC directors selected to be commander in chief of UPC fighters of the new, revolutionary ALNK, traveled to Conakry in April 1959 to meet with Moumié.[124] Singap returned to Cameroon in May 1959 to announce the creation of the ALNK and recruit loyal troops from the ranks of the dissolved SDNK in time to prepare for upcoming "independence." The ALNK's official headquarters were situated in Singap's chieftaincy of Bandenkop. The central headquarters commanded sectors and lesser districts dividing the Bamileke and the Mungo Regions into a grid. Each sector and district had its own code name, such as Accra-Ville, or Conakry: often the names recalled the faraway destinations of nationalist exiles. Each also had its graded officers and soldiers.

The UPC directors' international connections with the African Affairs Centre in Accra facilitated the revamping of the UPC army. From the time that Moumié established a base there, in late 1958, young Cameroonian nationalists were encouraged to set off on the long trek to Ghana.[125] In the late 1950s upéciste Thomas Emock, the secretary of the African Affairs Centre, communicated to the internal One Kamerun–UPC headquarters in Kumba (British Cameroons) the intent to form a revolutionary government in the Cameroons as soon as the revolutionary army was ready.[126] In response, local OK-UPC leaders began to recruit nationalist youths suitable for military training.[127] Local UPC committees and ALNK base camps in Cameroon recommended literate, intelligent, and physically fit young men in their late teens and early twenties to the overseas training program. The nominees were sent to Henri Tamo, aka Leconstant Pengoye, who served as a key liaison between UPC leaders in exile and the internal maquis.[128] As organizer and inspector of ALNK troops, Tamo sorted through applicants and provided those selected with a written mandate to take to Accra. Housed most often at the African Affairs Centre, trainees were provided with personal funds, clothing, and other supplies, and then awaited transport by air to the location of their training course.[129]

The exiles included the sons and daughters of Bamileke chiefs, or of the nascent Cameroonian bourgeoisie, urban laborers and members of labor unions, the elite cadre of late colonial intelligentsia—school teachers such as Gertrude Omog and Ernest Ouandié, the vice president of the UPC, doctors like Félix Moumié—and finally the sons of small-scale farmers and traders, many of whom had had minimal schooling.[130] In rare cases, elders accompanied the youths. Some trustworthy young men and women—such as Emmanuel Fankem, aka Fermeté, or Cécile Teck, a loyal leader of UDEFEC—were engaged as couriers to slip across borders and carry funds, arms, and correspondence from Accra to Cameroon.[131]

Moumié's father, Samuel Mekou, a permanent resident in the African Affairs Centre, became one of the key figures in Accra who oriented new arrivals and served as their liaison with the UPC director's bureau. Cameroonians on the run knew, by word of mouth, to make their way straight to the Guinean embassy upon arrival in Accra[132] where they would be put in contact with the UPC representatives in Accra. Mekou forwarded the names of prospective students or military trainees to the UPC leadership in Accra, Cairo, or later, Léopoldville (Congo), where Moumié was based in August and September 1960. At the African Affairs Centre, UPC leaders sorted out those who had excelled in school from those who had not. Scholarships were obtained for those who would some day make up the national intelligentsia.[133] The others underwent the military training that UPC leaders expected would ensure the eventual overthrow of the Franco-Cameroonian government in formation.[134]

Beginning in 1960, British police and military personnel began to discover "terrorists" who had attended training courses in China and Morocco among the UPC's ALNK soldiers whom they arrested in the southern Cameroons. They believed that similar courses were being taught in Egypt, Algeria, and the USSR, with precourse training taking place in Conakry and Accra.[135] By 1961, British administrators estimated that over a hundred "terrorists" trained overseas had managed to return to the ALNK in both French Cameroon and the British Cameroons.[136]

Chinese military officers trained the freedom fighters in China. Because training was conducted in French, the program was "equally suitable for any of the former French territories in Central Africa, for Congolese or for any Algerian, Tunisian or Moroccan youths."[137] In both China and in training camps in Morocco, military training was designed around the tactical teachings of Mao Tse-tung, and covered the use of weaponry, sabotage, and guerilla warfare. Course instructors stressed the importance of outlining a guerilla strategy based on established red zones of control from which to direct operations and in which fighters could train and congregate. After politically educating the inhabitants of secured red zones, the fighters would advance to create additional bases in the surrounding areas, or white zones.[138] Trainers familiarized students with the characteristics and handling of small firearms, hand grenades, and explosives and detonating agents, and were trained to use these charges to destroy bridges, vehicles, houses, railways, and petrol dumps.[139] In Cameroon's locally entrenched maquis, culturally specific, indigenous strategies of warfare—magical technologies, intimate knowledge of the terrain, and hunters' skills—intersected with revolutionary tactics learned abroad as internationally trained troops joined ranks with ALNK fighters who had never left.

The first training camp for ALNK soldiers within Cameroon was established in Dibombari, just north of Douala, in September 1959 and was then moved to Djoungo, in the Mungo Region, between Mbanga and Njombé. After Ouandié's return to Cameroon, in July 1961, the UPC vice president created the National Center of Training and Education at Moya, between Bangangte and Bafang.[140] There, ALNK officers instructed fighters in military tactics for revolutionary guerilla-style warfare, political ideology, and the economic perils of neocolonialism for an independent nation. In training camps the fighters underwent three-hour sessions during which they learned how to maneuver on foot and to use firearms, overseen by a World War II veteran known as Chine de Guerre.[141]

Despite Singap's, Tamo's, and Ouandié's efforts to restructure UPC fighters, ALNK troops in the Mungo and Bamileke Regions continued to have skirmishes with fighters operating under the orders of other "rebel" commanders, even as they fought against the administration's armed forces and the lackeys of colonialism. In 1960, ALNK commanding officers approached leaders of dissenting bands and attempted to negotiate their integration into the ALNK. The ALNK also began to recruit women, who would fill essential roles for the liberation army, a tactic Momo adamantly opposed.[142] Eventually, the exiled director's bureau sent Ernest Ouandié back into Cameroon, to serve as commander in chief and to further organize and discipline the troops. He arrived in Kumba in July 1961 and sneaked into the Mungo Region, accompanied by Singap's men.[143] Singap was killed in an ambush on 8 September 1961.[144] Attempting to increase troop morale the week after Singap's death, Ouandié began to hold meetings in the ALNK sectors in the Mungo and Bamileke Regions. But some rebel leaders, like Jean Djonteu, operating in the Mungo Region near Penja, categorically refused to meet with ALNK commanders, despite Ouandié's pleas for unity among troops.[145]

In spite of the persistent fissures, the combination of international and local methods of warfare completely restructured the maquis spatially, organizationally, and financially. Initially, SDNK camps in the maquis contained only forty to fifty soldiers residing in twenty or so camouflaged barracks spread out throughout the grassy hills and caves in the Bamileke Region,[146] while in the Mungo Region fighters simply congregated on the day of an attack, only to return to their homes immediately afterward. But after the formation of the ALNK, as the UPC army occupied entire zones, maquis camps became much larger. The headquarters base camp, in Bandenkop, was inhabited at times by as many as six hundred fighters.[147] In addition to the soldiers, the camps usually had cooks, lookouts who worked in shifts, and often, medical personnel, who followed either indigenous or European traditions of healing.[148] Raids on clinics to kidnap nurses and obtain pharmaceutical material became more common.

The ALNK applied the Maoist strategy of dividing the territory into red, gray, and white zones. The red zones, occupied by the ALNK, were impenetrable to state security forces and fell outside administrative control. Inhabitants of red zones did not pay taxes to the Cameroonian administration but instead paid a "national subscription" to the UPC.

Often, fighters in the Bamileke Region collected the revolutionary "tax" on market day, stopping villagers on the roads leading to the market while they had the week's ration for food in their pockets.[149] This tax, also known as *kap gung*—the money of the nation—was required of the population residing in ALNK territory, and served to distinguish *mpouogung*—patriots, from those the UPC designated as mfingung—those who "sold" the nation. In 1960 the ALNK had established a red zone of control over as many as 350,000 out of a total population of 500,000 in the Bamileke Region. Gray zones were the regions of confrontation between the ALNK and state security forces, while white zones were those areas that had yet to be penetrated by the ALNK.[150]

The operation of a full-fledged revolutionary army such as the ALNK depended on some degree of complicity with the civilian population, whether voluntary or coerced. In the Bamileke Region, mfo contributed sums to the fighters in order to "buy their peace." In the Bafang Subdivision, for example, thirteen of fifteen mfo paid off the UPC militia in 1959. Administrative reports suggested that they did so "out of fear or opportunism, not political conviction."[151] UPC militia fighters also kept watch over the family chiefs, who collected taxes for the administration, sometimes raiding their homes on the eve of their turning in the till. In February 1959 the chief of the Bafang family in Penja, Pascal Lako, told administrators that he tried to convince maquisards that he had already turned in the taxes, only to have them "discover" FCFA 350,000 when they searched the house.[152]

The most effective funding sources within the territory came from enterprises and plantations operated to generate a profit that the owners then turned over to the ALNK. In the Mungo Region, bands of outlaws traded labor for provisions, although administrators viewed the plantation owners who allowed this as complicit in the rebellion.[153] ALNK soldiers forcibly collected the "tax" from those civilians reluctant to pay it. They easily raided fields for crops by digging up tuberous roots and replanting the leaves to cover up the theft.[154] Authorities often suspected women who set off to work in the fields, ostensibly with lunch provisions for themselves, of providing home-cooked meals to "outlaws."[155]

The revolutionary army relied on links with surrounding populations for palm oil, salt, tobacco, and soap.[156] Cooking pots were difficult to come by and were a favorite commodity for looting during attacks on civilian populations.[157] Other commonly stolen goods included clothing, shoes, thread, sewing machines, and radios.[158] For over a decade, the maquisards lived in exile in their own territory, and border patrols became more effective at cutting off supply lines; many of the fighters began to prey on the civilian population to meet their needs. Often the outlaws ascribed such looting to the "national subscription," or UPC taxation, but the practice became increasingly burdensome on the civilian population as the years went by, which progressively eroded popular support for the maquisards.

As important as internal initiatives such as national subscription and the procurement of arms were, funding and weapons came from outside the Cameroon territories as well. After the UPC leaders began their Pan-African trajectory, and particularly after the formation of the ALNK, international sources for funding became more important. Repatriated black Americans in Ghana volunteered their support, but Woungly Massaga, staunchly opposed to "American imperialism," refused.[159] Moumié received a passport and funds for his 1957 trip to the UN from Cairo.[160] The Afro-Asian Solidarity Organization and the All-African Peoples' Conference provided some funding for the UPC in 1957 and 1958.[161] UPC leaders followed financial assistance and official state recognition of the UPC from place to place, but they had little specific loyalty to one source.[162] At various times throughout the 1960s, UPC soldiers in exile qualified for food rations from the governments of Guinea-Conakry, Congo-Brazzaville, and Angola.[163] During the same period, upécistes variously accepted support from the governments of these countries, as well as the USSR, Czechoslovakia, Bulgaria, China, and Cuba.

Although international sources of funding were important for the UPC bureau in exile, it was difficult for the nationalists to get funds to the UPC militia inside Cameroon. They relied on links with couriers like Emmanuel Fankem of Bandenkop, who crossed the border several times from his base in Accra from 1961 until his arrest in 1964. During those three years, he provided the ALNK with at least FCFA 2,500,000 from the Revolutionary Committee, based in Accra.[164]

Once the exiled leaders had established an international support network, the procurement of arms became somewhat easier for UPC fighters. Even before the directors left the British Cameroons, most of the firearms were smuggled across the borders with neighboring territories such as Nigeria, Equatorial Guinea, or the French Equatorial Africa territories, soon to become Gabon and Congo-Brazzaville. On 17 May 1957, French security forces in Douala intercepted a van containing over a hundred Mauser rifles, eight hundred cartridges, and fifty grenades. A subsequent police raid led to the arrest of those masterminding the importation and distribution of arms, including Chrétien Dzukam, Fo Kamdem Ninyim's friend and Singap's collaborator.[165] The event convinced administrators that nationalists had weapons and ammunition and planned to use them.[166] It also led to the administration's discovery of one of the territory's earliest arms-smuggling rings linking Diamare, in the extreme north of Cameroon, to Nigeria.[167] The border between British Cameroons and Nigeria was especially permeable and British and French administrators collaborated in an effort to curtail the trafficking, but corrupt border guards enabled a steady stream of illegal arms and munitions via Nigeria into Cameroon.[168] Arms trafficking may also have occurred along the estuaries between Cameroon and Gabon, north of Cape Lopez[169] and from Equatorial Guinea.[170]

UPC exiles who returned to Cameroon after 1957 often carried firearms. When he returned to take up the command of the ALNK, in 1960, Ernest Ouandié brought five dozen Czech MAT-49 submachine guns and MAS-36 small rifles with ammunition, provided by the Soviet Union via its embassies in Conakry and Accra.[171] Ngomba Nsame served as a liaison between ALNK militia groups in the Wouri, Mungo, and Bamileke Regions in his native region of Dibombari. Described by administrators as Ouandié's right-hand man, during the early 1960s he played a major role in arms smuggling across the Anglo-French border in Cameroon.[172]

ALNK ATTACKS FOR THE PURPOSES OF WEAPON PROCUREMENT, ECONOMIC SABOTAGE, AND PSYCHOLOGICAL INTIMIDATION

In addition to fabricating weapons in Bamileke-Region forges, ALNK fighters captured or stole arms locally from people who already owned them. UPC militiamen targeted planters, chauffeurs, transporters, and businessmen who possessed weapons, whether for their own protection or for the increasingly popular bourgeois-style hunting with rifles. Security forces, whether European or African, had plenty of firearms, which motivated attacks on remote posts and on the security guards of the concentration camps established in the Bamileke Region.[173] Freedom fighters stormed the gendarmes' camp at Mboppi, Douala, on 30–31 December 1959 and made off with an arsenal of modern weapons.[174] On 23 December 1965 rebels ambushed three civic guards with the aid of villagers in Bandenkop, Bapa, and Baham and managed to take a MAT-49 submachine gun, a MAS-36 rifle, and sixty cartridges.[175] Nationalist fighters were trained to retrieve the weapons of state military and police forces after battles whenever possible.[176] Wealthy planters in the Bamileke and Mungo Regions, whether white or Cameroonian, usually kept handguns or rifles at home and in their vehicles when traveling. In 1965 the rebels' attack on the Azziz sawmill trucks transporting logs was motivated by their desire to acquire the firearms of the self-defense guards accompanying the loads to port in Douala.[177] Priests in isolated outposts also had plenty of firepower, which may have been one reason for the frequent attacks on missions after the formation of the ALNK. Mfo and notables used rifles during chieftaincy celebrations and thus raids on chiefs' palaces presented another opportunity for fighters to collect weapons.

As the new age of UPC revolution dawned with the formation of the ALNK, in early 1959, soldiers attacked targets that more explicitly symbolized European rule, such as Catholic mission stations and gendarmeries. They also undertook deliberate campaigns of economic sabotage through the destruction of railways and Mungo and Bamileke Region farms. White planters, entrepreneurs, and transporters who traveled through the Bamileke Region toward Douala presented the easiest targets for UPC militia groups and provided them with money and firearms. The elimination of white planters and entrepreneurs fit into the UPC's revolutionary notion of total independence, which was to include economic freedom. ALNK fighters and maquisards sabotaged cash crops—bananas, coffee, oranges, and livestock—on as wide a scale as possible. In protest of neocolonial control of national agricultural resources, they targeted the vast plantations and farms still under European management, including the Nassif banana plantations at Loum and the Pastorale farms at Nkongsamba and Dschang.[178] The scale of these attacks was significant. For example, during a five-month period from July to November 1964, fifty-three head of cattle and two hundred pigs were slaughtered on Mungo Region farms; 4,500 coffee trees were uprooted in the Menoua area surrounding Dschang (Bamileke Region); 9,300 coffee trees were uprooted in the Bamboutos area, near Mbouda (Bamileke Region), and orange, kola, and banana plantations were also sabotaged there; and 2,000 coffee trees were uprooted in the Mungo valley.

Although few and far between, attacks were carried out by ALNK fighters on European settlers because they wielded a great psychological impact, especially on the white community. In late June 1959, ALNK fighters launched a series of attacks in urban areas, targeting administrative centers or European neighborhoods. On 27 June, fifty fighters stormed a Cameroonian guard and gendarmerie base camp in the Mboppi quarter of Douala. They made off with a dozen rifles, and killed a French gendarme and four Cameroonian auxiliaries. The group continued into one of Douala's European neighborhoods and attacked a cinema, a bar, and a nightclub, killing two French soldiers and wounding a dozen civilians.[179] On 4 July 1959, a Mr. Molinas, a European employee of a private factory, was killed in broad daylight near Kekem, just across the boundary between the Mungo and Bamileke Regions.[180] The next day in Yaoundé, a group of forty ALNK soldiers vandalized a police car, looted stores, and raided a number of bars and restaurants frequented almost exclusively by Europeans, killing a French bar owner and his sister. Similar attacks were carried out on the gendarmeries of Mbanga (Mungo Region) and Mbouda (Bamileke Region).[181] The attacks and killings, the first in a series of assaults on the European population, sent white settlers into a panic. The "civilian European population of Dschang" gathered in December 1959 to draft a motion to the president of the French Republic, the French prime minister, and the high commissioner of Cameroon. Signed by over forty Europeans, the motion stated that "the lives of Europeans are in imminent danger. . . . The rebel forces are ready to launch massive attacks destined to grant them control of the last points of resistance [in the area of Dschang]." The European community deemed the French armed forces insufficient and Cameroonian troops to lack training.[182]

The Dschang motion was one of many such missives. Another from Douala referred to threatening letters and the "tracts demanding our departure or promising our death" that kept the expatriate community "in complete uncertainty as to the coming of independence in a few days." The "fate of the French colons in Cameroon" had become "to risk financial ruin as an entrepreneur, to live in isolation and terror as a planter."[183] Other letters voiced fear at the number of Europeans killed and injured by those lying in wait to "take over their land, their plantations, their shops, etc." through "assassinations that the police and gendarmerie cannot control, much less prevent."[184] Already, the nearly seventeen thousand European settlers[185] wondered who would protect their interests in the face of a violent revolution, especially after political power shifted from French to Cameroonian hands. There appear to have been no more than a dozen or so Europeans assassinated in the six months before independence, but for the first time, Europeans in Cameroon had cause to recognize the thinness of the white line administering the territory.[186]

In Douala and the Mungo Region, ALNK soldiers targeted successful Cameroonian planters and burned their homes and goods. In late 1959 and early 1960, maquisards killed a "rich Bamileke transporter" in the Wouri Region, as well as Bema Moulendé a "rich planter" and his son, a municipal councillor, in Manjo.[187] Planters who walked the fine line of collaboration with the revolutionaries by allowing them to use their land for base camps, by paying wages for their labor, or by providing regular financial contributions, managed to avoid assassination. Isaac Bondja, a wealthy planter in Nkongsoung, north of Nkongsamba in the Mungo Region, provided maquisards with money and goods to dissuade them from attacking him.[188]

European members of the Catholic clergy were most vulnerable to attack during the years just before and just after official independence. From July 1959 to May 1961, there were twenty attacks on Catholic missions in the Nkongsamba Diocese alone (which included the Mungo and the Bamileke Regions) and seven clergy were killed, most of them European.[189] The Bafang Catholic mission, made up of the Ad Lucem hospital funded by Louis-Paul Aujoulat's organization,[190] a church, and a primary and secondary school, was arguably the most influential in the Bamileke Region. From September 1959 to May 1960, maquisards attacked the Bafang mission four times. During the first attack, assailants assassinated catechist Raphaël Nintcheu, and cut his body into pieces. The following week, they set fire to the quarter adjacent to the mission, and at least twenty people burned to death. The most gruesome attack came on 29 November and began as ALNK forces felled trees across the roads leading to the mission to prevent the arrival of troops and gendarmes. Hundreds then ransacked the Ad Lucem hospital, assaulting a Cameroonian nun on duty, and continued on to the presbytery. Father Héberlé, a French member of the Sacré-Cœur order, opened the door to attempt to reason with the attackers, but they shot him at close range with a hunting rifle and then cut off his head. Rebels killed Father Gilles, Father Lequeux was injured, and two unidentified bodies were burned. Friar Sarron attempted to flee, but the perpetrators pursued him and severed his head when he stumbled and fell to the ground. Other clergy managed to defend themselves, run away, or hide.[191] When state military finally arrived, the maquisards escaped into the hills, carrying the severed heads. During the raid, fighters kidnapped the nurse on duty in the dispensary. Once in the maquis, the nurse trained others to administer care to sick or wounded soldiers.[192] During the raid on the Bafang mission, attackers also captured several young women in the home economics program designed to prepare them for Christian marriage, and took them to the maquis, where they would serve as cooks and caretakers for the fighters.[193] Although competing over women went against UPC doctrine, there are both oral and written accounts revealing that UPC soldiers sometimes came to blows over female companions in the maquis. There is also evidence that some fighters in the maquis kidnapped young women to serve as "wives" or sexual companions.[194]

The attacks on missions suggested that, in the minds of ALNK soldiers, the struggle over nation had to be waged in the spiritual realm and that a European religion that had supported the administration's repression of the UPC in 1955 had to be eradicated from the territory of Cameroon. The fighters may have used the severed heads as ingredients for medicines to protect and fortify themselves.[195] In Grassfields cosmology, severing the head from the body at the time of death ensured that the dead person's spirit did not live. For Bamileke fighters, cutting off the heads of priests constituted a direct assault on the clergy's religious beliefs that the spirit would ascend to heaven after death.

THE MAQUIS "COURT"

In the years after the ALNK's formation, discipline became a greater priority for UPC leaders and the army's commanders. Eventually, the ALNK established systematic tribunals to judge and sentence transgressions.[196] Betraying the army's secrets, insubordination, loss of a weapon, stealing, and desertion each carried a death sentence. In the Mungo Region's Mount Manengouba maquis, the local ALNK unit executed Mboutchak Cathérine, aka Fidelité, in 1969 for attempting to defect.[197] Committing mystical acts of evil against other fighters resulted in a death sentence as well. In 1969 the ALNK tribunal executed Nouvelle for practicing witchcraft.[198] Raping or kidnapping women, using drugs such as hashish, embezzling funds, cowardice in battle, or power struggles constituted misdemeanors, but, depending on the severity of the transgression, could result in execution, as in the case of Nkwemo Michel, aka Nkrumah, who was executed for "embezzling revolutionary funds."[199] The ALNK court also passed judgment on civilians who refused to provide information to militia leaders, or supply food or provisions, or who denounced "patriots" (UPC nationalists and ALNK fighters).[200] Additional studies of the Cameroonian maquis are needed to discern to what degree fighters coerced the civilian population into participation in the revolution, and when and where that coercion took place. However, limited archival records—all of which exhibit a pronounced statist bias combined with the nationalist bias prevalent in most oral accounts collected today—have rendered a nuanced analysis of ALNK coercion difficult. Suffice it to say here that UPC fighters did sometimes, although certainly not always, coerce civilians and that the use of force became more prevalent as the UPC militias weakened over the years.

༄

The Cameroonian resistance originated in specific locales such as Boumnyebel (Sanaga-Maritime Region), Baham (Bamileke Region), and Penja (Mungo Region) where UPC fighters congregated in the forests and took up arms. Exiled upécistes carried their nationalist ideology from these locales and crossed territorial boundaries to Khartoum, Cairo, Accra, and Conakry. As the war between UPC soldiers and Franco-Cameroonian security forces raged on during the final years of the trusteeship period and into the first years after independence, hundreds of youths, seeking to escape arrest for upéciste activities, traveled through the Mungo Region into British territory from whence they made their way toward Accra, Ghana.[201] Many of them later returned to Cameroon's maquis sites to serve as freedom fighters, and a few made the trip back and forth across international boundaries, carrying correspondence and directives from UPC directors in exile and smuggling arms and funds into the territory. Some of the returnees had gained military training in North Africa or Peking. Aided by complicit civilians, returning exiles made their way to the underground resistance camps throughout the Mungo, Bamileke, and Mbam Regions. In 1961, UPC vice president Ernest Ouandié returned to Cameroon from Accra to serve as commander in chief of the UPC army, a position he held until his arrest in the Mungo town of Mbanga in August 1970. Ouandié's public execution, in January 1971, marked the official end to the UPC rebellion and its brutal suppression by state security forces—the violent face-off between nationalists and the postcolonial government that characterized Cameroon's first decade as an officially independent state.

Despite the vigilant command of committed revolutionaries such as Ouandié and Singap, the ALNK, plagued by difficulty in communications; lack of supplies, weapons, and funds; and the factionalization of

UPC leadership beyond Cameroon's borders, was unable to maintain a uniform front. Many of the fighters, like Djonteu of Baham, had entered the maquis for loyalty to a deposed or imprisoned fo and saw no reason to take orders from Ouandié.[202] As supplies and funds dwindled along with unity among UPC fighters, troops began to help themselves to booty in the name of the revolution, severely compromising popular support among civilians. Ouandié's caustic circulars, distributed to troops throughout the territory, deplored schisms, greed, and the overuse of guns without proper attention to political doctrine. In his directives, Ouandié cited Mao Tse-tung: "The party commands guns. It is not acceptable for guns to command the party."[203] But Ouandié's efforts proved minimally successful, and while the ALNK maintained a skeletal organizational structure in the Mungo Region, the British zone, the Bamileke Region, the Mbam Region, and the Nkam Region throughout the mid-1960s, militia groups like Djonteu's and Momo's fell outside its control. But the greatest blow to ALNK troops came not from inside but from the brutal repression of the movement, organized and orchestrated by the Cameroonian state, with the military, financial, and diplomatic assistance of the French government. The suppression of the UPC rebellion spilled over into the lives of civilians and defined the political sphere as well as the character of the postcolonial state of Cameroon after its official independence, on 1 January 1960.

As the years passed, violence in independence-era Cameroon evolved from a fight with clear objectives and adversaries (upécistes vs. state forces) into what some scholars, drawing on Primo Levy, describe as a gray zone.[204] In 1959 fighters on both sides had well-defined roles and sought to enact them. By 1965 the battlefront had disintegrated, leaving a nebulous culture of violence in its wake and instilling a new age in which it was difficult, if not impossible, for the civilian population to distinguish hero from villain, freedom fighter or gendarme from criminal. In this new postcolonial era—which slowly coalesced throughout the 1960s—the perpetrators of violence, whether revolutionaries or state security forces, wandered far from their leaders' stated political objectives and seemed to employ violence as a mode of life. During the first postcolonial decade after Cameroon achieved official independence, revolution gave way to banditry, while state protection gave way to predation.

6 ∽ "Here, God Does Not Exist"
Emergency Law and the Violence of State Building

MANY YOUNG men (and a few women) took to the maquis in the hopes of liberating Cameroon from French control, especially in those regions where the resistance army became implanted. Others joined state security forces as soldiers, gendarmes, police, security agents, members of the Cameroonian guard or the civic guard, and as members of local civil self-defense teams.[1] From 1956 to 1962 both the number of UPC militia fighters and the number of security forces increased significantly. As the UN trust territory transitioned to independence, state building had violence as its foundation. For an entire generation of Cameroonians, particularly those from regions declared to be in a state of emergency, enrollment in one of the various militia units—whether rebel or state forces—must have seemed nearly inevitable. Joining state security forces offered a way out of the maquis, and many took it. Administrators knew, too, that recruiting young men to the civic defense units was one way to keep them out of the maquis.[2] But often, young men left the maquis and rallied to the state only to return in a state-issued uniform but harboring the ambiguous loyalties of a rallied revolutionary fighter. When it became clear to ALNK commander Martin Singap in 1960 that he could not protect the thousands residing in the "red zones" of the Bamileke region, he organized assemblies to instruct people to turn themselves in to state forces. But Singap reminded people that they could rally without giving up the nationalist cause: "You will each return to your native village. . . . The enemies of our nation will think you have rallied, but you will know who you are."[3]

As the years passed, civilian populations residing in regions in a state of emergency found maquisards and civil self-defense units to be increasingly indistinguishable. Forces on both sides strayed from their stated objectives. While the ALNK's political goal was to overthrow the Franco-Cameroonian administration and rally the civil population to their cause, state forces claimed to protect civilians from terrorism and to restore peace. Although over time fighters on both sides used violence to serve immediate and individualistic goals, state forces had the support of the law, as well as French military and financial assistance to ensure that despite their excesses, they operated legally and with impunity.

Beginning with the formation of the state of Cameroon's legislative assembly, ALCAM, in 1957, nation-building mechanisms were centered on emergency legislation. Clearly inherited from the French administration that passed the first emergency laws in 1955 to proscribe the UPC, emergency legislation enabled the state's heavy-handed restriction of political and civil liberties.[4] In May 1959, as French Cameroon's assembly went into session two months after the UN General Assembly voted to end the trusteeship without holding new elections and without a constitution in place, Prime Minister Ahmadou Ahidjo proposed four bills providing him with the juridical means necessary to eradicate the UPC's underground resistance. These bills included the declaration of a state of emergency throughout the southern portion of the territory, preventative detention, press censorship, one to five years' imprisonment for "acts that constituted a threat to public order," and the establishment of criminal tribunals. They were approved in the legislative assembly by thirty-four votes to fourteen and were implemented on 16 May 1959. French troops backed Cameroonian security forces, suspects were arrested and detained without trial, and six opposition newspapers were shut down.[5]

Ahidjo followed up his initial orchestration of the state of emergency with a request that the assembly pass an even more comprehensive emergency powers bill that would assign him *pleins pouvoirs*—enabling him to govern by decree for six months. During that period, a committee made up of twenty-one assembly deputies and twenty-one government appointees would make up a consultative constitutional committee to draft Cameroon's constitution and put in place the institutions of governance.[6] The prime minister explained his proposal as a necessary measure, given the country's "exceptional situation which requires exceptional solutions."[7] In October 1959 the emergency powers bill was passed in the assembly by a vote of fifty to twelve with one abstention, despite a dynamic and impassioned protest from opposition members who took the floor to argue eloquently against it throughout the October session.[8]

The enforcement of emergency legislation in the months before the date set for official independence, 1 January 1960, depended on the rapid growth of intelligence services. Virtually nonexistent in 1956,[9] in August 1959, Cameroon's information services were restructured by French general Louis Le Puloch under a Central Coordination Committee, modeled on the Paris-based Service de documentation extérieure et de contre-espionnage (SDECE), which gathered intelligence from a number of different branches, including the Bureau de documentation du haut commissariat (BEDOC), as well as the police, gendarmerie, and military.[10] By 1962 the Service des études de la documentation (SEDOC, the postcolonial heir to BEDOC) was linked directly to the presidency and centralized all information and documents related to the interior and exterior security of the state. SEDOC headquarters received reports and information from the army, the gendarmerie, the national security forces, and the ministries of state and synthesized these reports for President Ahidjo (whom the national assembly voted in as president of the newly independent Republic of Cameroon on 5 May 1960). An institution of incarceration, interrogation, and torture for political prisoners, the Brigade mixte mobile de recherche et d'exploitation opérationnelles (BMM) served as SEDOC's primary source of intelligence, and the two institutions collaborated closely. All of SEDOC's information about political subversion was sent to the BMM for immediate investigation. In turn, the BMM informed security forces of information uncovered during interrogations in order to ensure the rapid success of "antiterrorist" operations.[11]

The state of emergency decrees continued to be renewed throughout Ahidjo's presidency as the regime applied them in order to suppress the ongoing UPC rebellion. Emergency legislation allowed President Ahidjo's continuing reliance on the French army, set in motion the recruitment of youths to the growing ranks of state security forces, and facilitated the rapid expansion of national intelligence agencies. But more important, emergency legislation culminated in the broad Law on Repression of Subversion, passed in March 1962, which defined a political subversive as "anyone who propagates false information, news, or rumors or who engages in tendentious commentary on news, when the information, news, rumors, or commentary may endanger public authorities."[12] For the rulers of postcolonial Cameroon, the urgent circumstances of the war on terror required the law against subversion. Antisubversion legislation, in turn, served to justify press censorship, the eradication of any political opposition, and, after only five years of tightly controlled multipartyism, enabled the establishment of the single-party state government that would remain in place, legally, until December 1990.[13]

More diffuse than *maquisard, outlaw,* or *rebel,* the label *political subversive* could be applied to anyone who did not actively promote the maintenance of the Ahidjo regime. To uphold the law against subversion, state administrators relied on the extensive and intrusive national intelligence agency, SEDOC. Its prime source of intelligence came from civilian informants who used the purveyance or withholding of information as a survival strategy and sometimes as an instrument to advance their own financial or political agendas. The postindependence generation was one collectively shaped by a proximity to violence and the widespread accusations and suspicious it bred among civilians. The indiscriminate brutality of militia and security forces, torturous interrogations, and public executions constituted the physical violence of warfare, while emergency legislation culminating in the antisubversion law of 1962 fueled the symbolic violence of the postcolonial age. Broad enough to apply to anyone, the antisubversion law justified the imprisonment and execution not just of maquisards but also of popularly elected members of the opposition in Cameroon's assembly, civil servants, clergy, Jehovah's Witnesses, and rank-and-file members of Ahidjo's political party, the Union camerounaise (UC).

Like those of UPC soldiers, the tactics of state security forces quickly metamorphosed from a controlled fight against the rebels into disorganized, undisciplined and often criminal attacks on civilians, thus contributing to a culture of violence in postcolonial Cameroon.[14] By 1970, a boxcar load of political prisoners dispatched from Douala to Yaoundé had suffocated to death, military officers had set fire to an entire Nkongsamba neighborhood over a pretty girl, and a deputy in Cameroon's assembly had hired former maquisards to slaughter a missionary family in Bangangte in order to seal a business deal. As the violence spread, stoked by maquisards and state forces alike, the regions that bore the brunt of it underwent a collective transformation. The population became attuned to survival tactics that included silence, mutual distrust and suspicion, a disavowal of the political, and camouflaged political loyalties.

STATE OF EMERGENCY—THE EXCEPTION BECOMES THE RULE

As in a number of other colonial territories, late-colonial emergency legislation continued after official independence, comprising the foundation of postcolonial governance.[15] The state of emergency, first declared under French administration in 1955, led to the rapid increase in security forces, the establishment of protected resettlement villages in areas adjacent to the ALNK's red zones (particularly in the Bamileke and Sanaga-Maritime regions), and the creation of a surveillance grid enabling security forces to identify and control the movement of populations in the affected zones. The implementation of these measures depended heavily on gathering intelligence through the use of spies and torturous interrogations carried out in the various BMM prisons throughout the territory. The emergency measures carried over from the late trusteeship period and became more rigorous under the Ahidjo regime, culminating in the creation of military tribunals to judge those accused of subversion, and in the purging of political oppositionists from the ranks of the national assembly. By 1966, the Federal Republic of Cameroon was officially and legally a single-party state, and every elected official as well as those nominated by the government adhered to the political party of which President Ahidjo was chairman—the UNC. Although emergency legislation had been passed to eradicate the upéciste rebellion, it soon became a permanent, rather than exceptional, measure instrumental to Ahidjo's one-party nation-building plan, which rested on a concept he called "ethic of unity." State agents made use of emergency laws, particularly the antisubversion law, to impose the ethic of unity at every level of government, from the national to the local.

In 1956, military forces in Cameroon consisted of one Battalion of the Tirailleurs of Cameroon (BTC) made up of four companies, each with three sections. The other security forces—the gendarmerie, the Cameroonian guard, the national security forces, and the police—totaled just over two thousand.[16] Just as the French administration used the May 1955 uprisings to justify their legal dissolution of the UPC and its affiliates, the Franco-Cameroonian government cited the assassination by "night fighters" of Deputy Wanko on 13 December 1957 (see chapter 5) to deny amnesty to political detainees and apply full-throttle military suppression of UPC activity in the Bamileke and Mungo Regions. The Wanko assassination coincided eerily with the revocation of amnesty that had been under discussion in the French national assembly and Cameroon's assembly since 1956.[17] The deputy's murder also came a month after the arrival of Lieutenant Colonel Jean Lamberton as commanding officer of troops in the Bamileke Region.

The security forces' actions in the days after the Wanko assassination set the standard for subsequent military repression of the rebellion. Lacking the troops to place the entire territory under martial law, the administration employed security forces composed of the army, the air force, the marines, various intelligence organizations, gendarmes, police forces, the Cameroonian guard, the civic guard, and, wherever possible, armed civilians structured as self-defense units. The search for those involved in the Wanko assassination introduced new military tactics in the Bamileke Region, including systematic searches, control points, curfews, and efforts to place the entire population of a given region under a surveillance grid. Under Lamberton's command, security forces eventually took fifteen hundred people "suspected" of participating in the crime into custody at Dschang. The security forces' collective response to the Wanko assassination marked the initial coordination between military troops and civilian defense teams and led to the enactment of the official agreements reached in early 1957 about France's contributions to the formation of a Cameroonian army.[18]

The military in the Bamileke Region had Koutaba, just across the Noun River, in Bamum territory, as their base.[19] In November 1957, a month before the Wanko assassination, troops were deployed throughout the Bamileke Region, with two sections of troops each in Bamendjou, Batie, and Bayangam, and one in Bangou (each of these villages bordered Baham).[20] Bafang and Bafoussam hosted one section each of the Cameroonian guard. More troops were stationed near Mbouda, at the Anglo-French border, to create a "zone of insecurity for the rebels."[21] Other troops were brought in as needed, and reinforcements sent from French Equatorial Africa enabled the installation of sections at Bapa, Bangam, Fotouni, Bafoussam, Bansoa, Bameka, and Baham.[22] In the Mungo Region, troops were stationed in small settlements from south of Loum to Nkongsamba.[23] The greatest difficulty security forces faced when putting down the rebellion in the Bamileke Region was the dispersal of inhabitants in compounds far away from the chieftaincy centers and the lack of roads to reach them. Because of militia fighters' familiarity with geography and the layout of compounds in their own locales, SDNK and ALNK forces managed to create red zones, to which security forces did not have access.[24] By 1960, a majority of the Bamileke region's population—seven out of ten people, by some estimates—resided in these red zones. Only the Bafoussam Subdivision had some "eight to ten chieftaincies that remained loyal"[25] to the Ahidjo government. To break the UPC army's hold on the region, French and Cameroonian administrators needed additional troops, a centralized intelligence agency with informants in every locale, stronger regional administrations in constant communication with the state administration, loyal civil defense units, and resettlement camps to replace chieftaincies as a mode of governance.

In December 1959, on the eve of official independence, two more battalions of French troops, including parachutists, were brought in "to reinforce the military forces attempting to restore order in Bamileke country and in the portion of the Sanaga-Maritime that anarchy has overtaken."[26] By 1960 there were three BTCs and a total of 2,800 troops in the army; the gendarmerie boasted 2,600 men; and the public and auxiliary forces were 4,700 strong.[27] In the four years leading up to independence, the number of security forces went from under 2,800 to over 10,000. The withdrawal of French troops in Cameroon did not begin to take place until 1965.[28]

Although French military presence continued after independence, the French Ministry of Foreign Affairs placed the new Cameroonian government at the forefront of command, whether in the management of security forces or of intelligence. On 12 December 1959, the French prime minister informed the high commissioners in Yaoundé and Brazzaville that the French government had decided to provide the Cameroonian government with the aid necessary to restore calm to the Bamileke Region, but that "the government of Cameroon must take full responsibility for its actions."[29] At the same time, the French prime minister asked the high commissioners to use "every means at your disposal . . . to reinforce army and gendarme troops," and to "urgently suggest to me the supplementary means you deem necessary, including the organization and arming of militias and self-defense. Furthermore, I ask you to invite the Cameroonian government to prepare with our support the training of personnel necessary to administer the Bamileke Region."[30] In 1960 the French government "placed [General Max Briand] at the Cameroonian government's disposal" to command the security forces in collaboration with the Ahidjo administration.[31]

In 1961 the Ahidjo regime created the Ministry of the Armed Forces to coordinate the actions of security forces. Sadou Daoudou, minister of the armed forces, worked closely with Jean Fochivé, the director of SEDOC. Both were assisted by Samuel Kamé, the notable of Baham origin who had played an instrumental role in Fo Kamdem Ninyim's deposition in late 1956. By 1961, Kamé wore several administrative and political hats. He was secretary general of the armed forces, counselor to the prime minister, and inspector of administrative affairs for SEDOC.[32] Kamé also held prominent positions in the president's party, the UC, which became the Union nationale camerounaise (UNC) in 1966, as policy adviser. He consistently promoted the curtailment of political and civil liberties as a necessary step toward national consolidation—in fact, French observers, even those favorable to an emerging Françafrique, remarked that Kamé tended toward fascism.[33] A friend and supporter of Ahidjo's from the days Kamé attended the École nationale de la France d'outre-mer, the latter held shadow positions that linked him directly to the presidency but kept him out of the public eye. This allowed him a great deal of influence in the most important realms of government throughout the first postcolonial decade.[34] Experienced in both patterns of Bamileke traditional governance and state administration, Kamé acted on the assumption that power was not always located in the most prominent positions but could be accessed in less visible ways. He knew that the more "secret associations" he belonged to, the more power he wielded.[35]

In 1962, convinced that the UPC militias' stronghold on the Bamileke region was due to underadministration, ALCAM divided the province into five departments, each with its own departmental administration and federal inspector,[36] while the Federal Republic of Cameroon was divided into six administrative regions, each governed by an appointed prefect. Administrative federal inspectors, representatives of the federal government in all matters of "social life and justice," were placed in each region to "ensure the execution of laws" and answered only to the federal authorities.[37] As general federal inspector, Kamé oversaw the regional federal inspectors.

Security forces needed recruits who knew the landscape as well as UPC militiamen. Mfo who continued to collaborate with the administration, such as Fo Kamga of Bandjoun, helped to funnel young men into self-defense and civic guard units that worked with the Franco-Cameroonian military, gendarmerie, and police force.[38] Throughout the region, these young civilians operating in concert with security forces became known as commandos. The civic guard attracted former UPC militiamen into its ranks, some of whom maintained their loyalty to the revolutionary forces and used their new positions to gain information and obtain uniforms or arms.[39] The recycling of former maquisards into the civic guard incurred the multiple loyalties of those playing both sides in the postindependence era and blurred the line between the two sides. Today, Bamileke survivors of the independence war speak of French military officers who armed "both the self-defense units and the maquisards."[40]

The administration's interest in assembling a civic guard was twofold. These young men with a thorough knowledge of the locale helped orient troops and intelligence agents from outside the Bamileke region. More important, the formation of civic-guard and self-defense units served to "occupy two thousand young men who would be in the maquis if they were not a part" of the self-defense teams,[41] thus serving as a state-building strategy to recruit and train thousands of young men in the practice of government loyalty. When Ahidjo began to tour the Bamileke region, in 1959, Cameroonian and French officials made much of his review of self-defense troops, particularly in those regions plagued by UPC militia activity. For example, in Mbouda, a stronghold of armed resistance to the state, thousands of young self-defense volunteers, armed with machetes, congregated from surrounding villages and paraded before Ahidjo during his September 1959 visit.[42] Collaborating with the armed forces to eradicate the maquis, the self-defense troops became instrumental in policing and informing on the populations gathered in the protected resettlement villages that the administration put in place in the Bamileke region.

Protected Resettlements

In the areas that state security forces occupied in the Bamileke region, administrative policy was to regroup inhabitants into a common area, known as a *regroupement* (protected villages or resettlement camps).[43] Civic guards patrolled the settlements to keep refugees safe from rebel attacks, but the system was not just about civilian safety—it served, too, as a surveillance strategy and was one more way for the French administration to dismantle "archaic" and "problematic" traditional chieftaincies in the Bamileke region. By 1962 the French ambassador to Cameroon, Jean-Pierre Bénard, informed Jacques Foccart, the French president's chief of staff for African and Malagasy matters from 1960 to 1974, that eighty camps had replaced chieftaincies in the five newly named Bamileke departments.[44] These new habitats, which French administrators believed provided a more equitable access to land, depended on the "liquidation of the chieftaincy . . . and its abuses, especially in matters of land."[45] French administrators believed that the camps would "ameliorate the social condition of the masses" and "cut the roots of terrorism."[46] Ambassador Bénard wrote of the importance of getting the population's complete and sincere support of "their new habitat." He listed security and bringing an end to the "waste of land caused by the formula of dispersed familial compounds" as the advantages that would be sure to convince the population to settle in the camps. Bénard also wrote of the necessity of creating schools, dispensaries, and water reservoirs near the camps.

But even those metropolitan-educated Bamileke elites collaborating with the new state government, such as Samuel Kamé, did not view the regroupement plan as a permanent, realistic solution to violence and land shortages in the Bamileke region, and the resettlement camp system was completely alien to Bamileke villagers. Jeanette Noubi, a child at the time of her residence in one of the camps, recalls the day the "commandos" arrived in October 1959 and forced the people of Bandenkop into exile in a makeshift refugee camp in Bangou. They left in a "caravan," without time to pack, grabbing only what they could on the way out. "All the villagers who wanted to survive were obliged to make the exodus to the refugee camp in Bangou," Noubi recounted.[47] The "camp" was rudimentary, consisting of small huts built of raffia palms, without walls or roofs, on an unsheltered hillside. In the rainy season, people had to sit in the mud, there were few cooking pots to be had, and refugees avoided lighting fires or lanterns, so they simply slept at sundown. Leaving the camp, even to work in the fields, jeopardized the survival of refugees who could be "slaughtered, either by maquisards or by commandos."[48] Commandos, whom survivors of the period describe as from "the north," dark skinned, and tall with facial scarifications, had no knowledge of village vernacular and did not distinguish civilians from maquisards.[49] "They killed first, before asking any questions," severed the heads of their victims, and set them around the periphery of the camp.[50]

At least some people from villages torn apart by the violence of the independence era stayed in the resettlement camps until as late as 1975.⁵¹ Gradually, shelters built hastily out of raffia palm branches became huts constructed of brick. Some camps became new village centers, and those refugees who feared returning to their chieftaincies of origin for whatever reason settled there permanently.⁵² Other groups of villagers, like those of Baham, resisted the concentration camp system throughout the "period of troubles." Rounded up by force and sent into exile to the camp at Bangou during the day, many inhabitants of Baham returned to their compounds by nightfall.⁵³ Still other "refugees" used the planting cycle as their reason for returning "home" during periods of harvest. These planters built "field shacks" as "temporary" shelters. Eventually, these became their newly built homes in the compounds that they had left behind. A covert exodus from the camps began almost at the inception of the system and grew, as people felt it was safe for them to return home. The system envisioned by French administrators as a way to bring about agrarian reform that would "ameliorate the social condition" ultimately lost out to the restoration of gung—the traditional chieftaincy. The regroupement system ultimately failed, much as the resettlement project of the Noun's left bank had failed in the 1930s.⁵⁴ The administration had greater success controlling the movements of populations residing in the towns and cities by requiring identification cards, imposing a curfew, and setting up control points and nighttime inspections of entire neighborhoods.

Curfews, ID Cards, Control Points, and Expulsion

Beginning in the late 1950s, administrators and security forces in French Cameroon searched, identified, surveilled, and situated civilians and tried to control their movements.⁵⁵ While the territory was still under French rule, administrators and military officers created and imposed an administrative grid throughout the territory, inventorying neighborhoods and houses, counting the number of people in each, and penalizing those who lacked proper documentation.⁵⁶ Although a decree requiring the registration of births had been passed in 1935, it was not enforced until the mid-1950s, when administrators and security forces began arresting hundreds who had not made an official record of their children's birth and those without official identification cards. The government also created the new administrative positions of neighborhood chief and block chief. Neighborhood chiefs and block chiefs represented the national government at the lowest level and were accountable for the "subversive acts committed within their blocks" and neighborhoods.[57]

Beginning on the eve of independence, security forces executed midnight roundups of entire neighborhoods to flush out any "irregulars" who lacked jobs, fixed residence, or proper identification. These "drifters" were then either arrested on subversion charges or "expelled" to their region of origin. A census of problem areas officially inventoried the number of villages, quarters, huts, men, women, boys, and girls in a given town, neighborhood, or rural community. The official record of the number of inhabitants per home served as the legal basis for the systematic expulsions.[58] Administrators used expulsion to deal with suspects that they could not sentence to prison for lack of evidence.[59] Security forces rounded up sometimes over twenty or more candidates for expulsion per day[60] and placed them in prison to be processed, often without telling them why or for how long they were being kept in custody. A group of prisoners awaiting expulsion to the Bamileke region in the Nkongsamba prison wrote:

> At present, we don't know if we are *refoulés* [expelled] or not, but we are already in agony in these conditions. There are ninety of us divided into two small rooms measuring five square meters. . . . We stay, eat, piss, and shit in the same room. Considering that we are refoulés, we prefer to be sent directly to our native land rather than being kept locked up here.[61]

After Cameroon's independence, the Ahidjo regime continued to use the emergency legislation that French administrators had passed.[62] Using the powers granted him by the constitution adopted via popular referendum on 21 February 1960,[63] Ahidjo passed a "presidential decree" on 8 May 1960 declaring a state of emergency in the departments of Wouri, Bamileke, Nyong-et-Sanaga, Mungo, Mbam, Sanaga-Maritime, Nyong-et-Kellé, Ntem, Nkam, and Dja-et-Lobo. Exceptional legislation in the form of presidential decrees continued for many of these areas throughout the 1960s.[64] Residents of these provinces needed a number of documents in order to move about without risking arrest or expulsion or both. The pass (*laissez-passer*) required for transporters and other travelers had the bearer's name, photograph, place of origin, point of departure, length of and reason for journey, and identity number.[65]

Prefects, subprefects, district chiefs and security forces could inspect the laissez-passer on demand,[66] and did so, especially in the Mungo region. Throughout the Mungo region, anyone arriving from another province had to present himself to the closest administrative authorities or security post to state his presence and obtain a visa authorizing his stay.[67] From seven in the evening to five in the morning throughout the Mungo region, the circulation of public transport was forbidden,[68] and a general curfew was applied to the entire province from eight in the evening to five in the morning.[69] In the Bamileke region, no vehicles were allowed to circulate without prior administrative authorization,[70] and no vehicles could travel at night in the Bafoussam and Mbouda Subdivisions and in portions of the Dschang Subdivision.[71]

To enforce the emergency laws, security forces inspected and searched entire neighborhoods in the middle of the night in sealing off operations (*opérations de bouclage*), or police raids. The purpose of these police roundups was to "create a climate of insecurity for suspects who try to implant themselves in urban areas."[72] Before beginning the operation, security forces surrounded and sealed off the neighborhood to be inspected and set up a control point. Soldiers or police then began knocking on doors, forcing everyone outside to be inspected. The raids usually began at one or two in the morning and lasted for up to twelve hours. In Nkongsamba, Mbanga, and Loum, over two thousand people could be inspected at once.[73] Nearly 10 percent of those "inspected" were detained and taken to the police station for an "in-depth examination of the situation."

During the raids, security forces relied on the information provided by *indiques*, or civilian informants. Wearing a hood and standing at the control point, the informant nodded when he recognized a known "outlaw" or someone who supported the maquisards. The informant's nod sufficed to send a suspect directly to the BMM for interrogation. In Nkongsamba, the bar owner Romain Kouam, originally from Baham, worked as an informant during the midnight roundups. The hooded Kouam "sold" the people whom he heard about in his bar during the day and not a few of his personal enemies. Eventually, security forces learned that Kouam used his position to orchestrate individually motivated purges of the Baham community and they sent him to prison. While in custody, Kouam was killed with a hunting rifle.[74]

The raids became increasingly brutal and, as the years passed, had as much to do with collecting money and looting for material goods as catching "political subversives." In Nkongsamba, the police commissioner's reports indicated that "taxes" of nearly FCFA 400,000 were raised during a single operation.[75] In Loum, people described the roundups as "torturous," "barbaric acts." They complained of being beaten as they left their homes to present themselves at the checkpoint and accused gendarmes and police of raping young girls.[76] Intelligence agents who learned of the complaints replied that the intimidation tactics were "beneficial" and that a "psychological campaign" would restore the population's "confidence" in the authorities.

Less disruptive than the nightly police raids, the police checkpoints in Nkongsamba served to verify official documents and carry out systematic searches.[77] The controls took place after setting up *bouchons hermétiques* (hermetic stoppers) in different parts of town to funnel people into the checkpoint where "suspects" were identified and taken directly to the police station. If police forces lacked evidence for a suspect's "crime," they placed him or her under "discreet" state surveillance until they could gather "proof."[78] Often the procurement of proof was achieved through the use of spies (indiques) or as the result of interrogation techniques, including torture, carried out in the internment centers known as the BMM.

Truths, Countertruths, Secrets, and Lies

The administration's use of spies increased as people negotiated for their freedom, their physical well-being, or their lives in exchange for information.[79] In the Mungo region, even low-level administrators were encouraged by their superiors to use indiques to serve as their eyes and ears in the most intimate spaces. The French administration had begun using spies to combat SDNK activity as early as 1958. Upon discovering that Philippe Layou from Bafoussam provided the administration with information on SDNK strategies in early June, fighters followed Layou from the Anglo-French border and assassinated him near Nkongsamba.[80] In the late 1950s the French prefect in Nkongsamba actively recruited indiques. One of those informants was the orphaned son of an Mbo father and a Bamileke mother.[81] Recognizing the young man's interethnic background as an asset, the prefect trained him as an informant and eventually placed him among laborers at the Niabang plantation near Nkongsamba. The young man used his language skills and familiarity with both Bamileke and Mbo cultural practices to forge ties with plantation workers, many of whom aided the maquisards. He continued working for the administration, even after independence.

Indiques became so numerous throughout the first postcolonial decade that they seemed to hear and see everything, even in the most private spaces of people's homes. In 1970 in Manjo, four wives of François Tchoupe, all originally from the Bamileke chieftaincy of Bamougoum, were returning from the fields when they crossed paths with three maquisards.[82] The fighters spoke to the women in their language and asked them to greet their husband. Upon reaching their home, two of the women told their husband about the encounter, and he asked them not to say anything more about it. One of their co-wives, Pauline Mayounga, overheard the discussion from her bedroom and spoke of it to her sister, who worked as an informant for the neighborhood chief, Ismanou Mougnol. Chief Mougnol sent for Tchoupe, who claimed that his wives had not told him of a meeting with maquisards. The neighborhood chief then sent his secretary to go with Tchoupe to get his wives. Upon interrogation at the Manjo gendarmerie, the wives gave an account of their encounter with the maquisards but claimed they had not spoken of the incident to anyone, even their husband, upon returning home. When questioned about dress and weapons of the "outlaws," the women were deliberately ambiguous. One said, "They wore uniforms like self-defense troops, that's why I didn't say anything."

The neighborhood chief surmised that when Tchoupe went to fetch his wives, he told them not to admit to having recounted the incident because his secretary did "not understand Bafoussam." Police interrogating Tchoupe and his wives were convinced that the "outlaws must certainly be attached to this family," due to their common use of language and their greeting to Tchoupe through his wives.[83] The authorities in Manjo decided to transfer the women and Tchoupe to the Nkongsamba BMM and insisted that "their exploitation by the BMM be carried out in depth."[84]

The prevalence of indiques in everyday life in the Mungo and Bamileke regions shaped discursive practices, fostering heightened levels of concealment and coded language. People from the same locale sometimes managed to protect themselves by communicating in their own language when dealing with assailants, indiques, or security forces who did not understand it. Guards in prisons and BMMs usually forbade suspects from speaking in their mother tongue, but remarks exchanged between suspects in the vernacular, however brief, could serve as survival strategies. Security forces often read the use of a common language as a sign of civilians' collaboration with maquisards. Realizing this, Tchoupe's wives switched to speaking pidgin once they were in custody in the police station. Speaking in one's mother tongue did not always preclude betrayal by an indique, however. Although Tchoupe's wives spoke to him in their shared vernacular in his own bedroom, their secret made its way to the neighborhood chief, carried by someone close to their household.

The management of secrets and lies became an ominous part of the culture of violence when a morsel of information, or a name dropped in the right ear, could lead to someone's arrest, interrogation, and perhaps death. Some people used the collection and distribution of information to eliminate an enemy by accusing him of collusion with the rebellion, to destroy the political reputation of an administrator or party official, or to carry out personal vendettas of revenge. Perhaps jealousy of her co-wives motivated Pauline Mayounga's account of the incident to her sister, whom she may well have known was an informant to the neighborhood chief.

Those known to have participated in UPC activity in the past proved especially easy targets. Ignace Néguin Djoko had been active as an upéciste in the late 1950s, smuggling nationalists and documents across the Anglo-French boundary in his pickup truck and dropping them off at the UPC headquarters in British territory. In 1959, he was arrested for smuggling cigarettes (which he carried as a decoy to lure administrators' attention away from the fugitives he transported) and following his release from the Buea prison in 1961, he struggled to regain a normal life as a taxi driver in Yaoundé. He married and settled with his wife in the Madagascar quarter of Yaoundé. One day in 1968, while driving his taxi, he picked up Kamto Bernard,[85] a former UPC comrade from Baham, and drove him to his destination. A year or so later, Djoko was arrested by security forces and accused of conspiring with Kamto to bring weapons to Yaoundé for an impending coup d'état (allegedly masterminded by ALNK commander in chief Ouandié in the maquis and the Catholic bishop of Bamileke origin, Msgr. Albert Ndongmo).[86] Djoko later discovered that another former UPC comrade living in Madagascar told security forces that he had met and conspired with Kamto on more than one occasion. Speculating about the informant's motives in 2002, Djoko insisted that the only logical explanation for the betrayal was that one day his accuser had asked him for tobacco and Djoko replied that he had none. Djoko spent seventy-five months in the Yaoundé branch of the BMM for his alleged involvement in the Ndongmo coup attempt. Djoko's reason for telling the story of his 1970 arrest was to illustrate how much had changed since the days of the tight-knit loyalty that prevailed among upécistes in 1957.[87] By 1970, after the long, arduous years of repression and the UPC's factionalization, many former upécistes felt bitterness, hatred, and jealousy in the place of solidarity and became willing to sell out those to whom they had once entrusted their lives.

Ordinary people without any specific motive to manipulate intelligence for their personal gain shared information with both security and UPC militia forces, as a survival strategy. Subjected to torturous interrogations in the BMM, former upécistes often succumbed to the role of informant. Other comrades recognized this, especially when they observed that someone had been released from the BMM without signs of crippling or scarring. Those who refused to inform during their interrogations bore their physical markings of torture as a symbol of loyalty. In Baham, to avoid accusations of complicity with the rebellion or of loyalty to the deposed fo, Kamdem Ninyim, civilians strove for neutrality by becoming two faced, using half-truths and half-lies as a survival strategy. In the Nka'a quarter of Baham, a wealthy notable, Tocpa Ta'akouo, explained that when the maquisards came, he had to "speak wisely, lies and truths. They came as though they wanted to kill me, but I told them truths and countertruths. When we finished talking, they went behind the compound and stole my hog. But if I had not had the hog, I wouldn't be here today."[88]

The BMM Interrogations and Incarceration: "Here, God Does Not Exist"

The torture of suspects made up an essential component of the state's repression of the rebellion, beginning under French administration, during the trusteeship period.[89] The BMM's full name, Brigade mixte mobile de recherche et d'exploitation opérationnelles (Mobile mixed brigade for operational research and exploitation), clearly conveys its use. As a branch of the national and regional intelligence bureaus that the French reorganized and centralized in August 1959, the BMM coordinated the efforts of police, military, and gendarmes in their search for "political subversives."[90] The BMM stations, located in Yaoundé, Douala, Nkongsamba, and other smaller towns, became extensions of SEDOC used to gather intelligence about the rebellion or other forms of political subversion. After tips from indiques or denunciations by civilians, security forces sent suspects to the BMM for "exploitation" or "in-depth interrogation." Maquisards who were arrested or who turned themselves in were interrogated for days about activities they had carried out while in the maquis, the names of their band of troops and commanding officers, and the names of civilians who had provided them with provisions or information.[91]

Archival documents contain no reference to the conditions of the BMM or the methods used during interrogations. At most, a chilling phrase occasionally stated that "so and so succumbed after his interrogation," or that the hardened rebel who refused to provide the names of his accomplices would have to undergo a particularly arduous "exploitation." Oral informants, too, hesitate to speak of their experience in the BMM, other than to say that it was widely known as the place no one could survive. Many survivors' accounts of the BMM refer to the ominous phrase written on the walls or repeated by the guards: "Here, God does not exist." Prisoners were exposed to rooms with blood on the walls, and pictures of severed heads sometimes covered the walls. In the torture room, known as the chapel, guards hung suspects by their knees and elbows on a large swing. They remained bound, sometimes for hours at a time, to a bar that could be raised or lowered, swung back and forth, or dunked into a tub of water below.[92] Prisoners who survived this experience usually did so by "selling" their accomplices. Today, it is not unusual to meet people bearing the physical markers of their BMM experience. Souop Kamogne of Banka, Baham, who spent eleven days on the swing, with periods of respite in between, suffered so much damage to the tendons in his legs that he uses crutches to walk. Souop Cuichoue, of Pumsze, Baham, carries a crisscross pattern of deep scars on his back from the whippings he received. The scars are a source of pride for former UPC comrades who bear them because they demonstrate that, despite the torture they withstood, they refused to betray their comrades. The BMM prisons at Yoko, Mantem, and Tchollire were connected to work camps and housed prisoners who received sentences of forced labor. Neither the prisoners nor their families knew how long the sentence would last, and very often suspects were detained without trial.[93]

The BMM loomed large in the imaginary of political activists and the population at large. The state's powers of command—intelligence and security forces—converged in this one space. It was a place where no one knew or could venture to care what happened to prisoners, where innocent people could be betrayed by coerced confessions, or deliberately "sold" by suspects who, when arrested, decided to "take others with me,"[94] a place stripped of any familiarity or point of reference. The BMM housed those state administrators deemed political subversives, whether they were former upécistes who did not carry the "UNC party card," Jehovah's Witnesses who refused to vote, or priests who spoke out against the state's excessive repression. It was a place, too, where prisoners were deliberately stripped of their political agency: "In fact, you could only leave once you had been sufficiently 'washed' and had renounced any interest in political questions."[95] The BMM interrogations and prisons became the most extreme methods of the state's psychological campaign waged against political subversives.

As in the Sanaga-Maritime, the French administration and their Cameroonian successors referred to psychological campaigns as the way to dismantle popular support of UPC revolutionaries.[96] Fear became a tool, wielded by the state, both to "create insecurity" and to "gain popular confidence." The state acknowledged its competition with maquisards for popular support, which depended on the population not fearing or respecting "the malefactors more than us. Their entire interest and intelligence must be to collaborate with us to systematically condemn and combat terrorism."[97] Through "diverse psychological campaigns undertaken by administering authorities and political leaders throughout the department," civilians were "invited" to "regularly and objectively inform the security forces."[98] Despite nearly two decades of such "sensitivity and mobilization campaigns,"[99] as late as 1973 authorities in Nkongsamba complained that "no change has occurred in the popular mentality, most of the population continues to observe a great silence."[100] Before independence, French administrators had complained of silence in the Bamileke and Mungo Regions as well.[101] For state administrators, the "questionable" collective "silence" and "passivity," signaled popular support of the rebellion, and administrators began to perceive it as a defining characteristic of Bamileke populations.[102] For the population at large, however, silence had become a survival strategy as an atmosphere of fear and dread settled across the country.[103]

STATE ACTION AGAINST THE OPPOSITION IN CAMEROON'S ASSEMBLY

In the climate of Ahidjo's reign, it became increasingly difficult for politicians to speak out against the president's dictatorial use of emergency legislation lest they be accused of subversion for siding with the rebellion.[104] Yet a few members of the assembly continually tried to galvanize both internal and international opposition to the Ahidjo regime. These vocal oppositionists were muted through arrest and imprisonment following show trials, as in the case of Dr. Marcel Bebey-Eyidi, one of only three independent candidates to have been elected to Cameroon's assembly in December 1956. In late 1959 and again in 1960, Bebey-Eyidi and other oppositionists called for Cameroonian political leaders to participate in a roundtable discussion of a national program that would serve to reconcile radical nationalists and more conservative forces.[105] The advocates of the roundtable, including Soppo Priso of MACNA and André-Marie Mbida, who had lost his position to Ahidjo in 1957, believed that the UN had failed as a supervisory body in March 1959, when the general assembly voted to end the trusteeship in French Cameroon. Although they were clearly in the minority in the pro-Ahidjo assembly, a handful of moderate nationalist deputies had hoped that the UN would implement measures—such as amnesty of upécistes, the lifting of the ban on the nationalist party, and UN-supervised elections—to mediate between "Ahidjo and Moumié in order to effect a general reconciliation of the different leanings of the Cameroons before independence."[106] When the UN did nothing to arbitrate the political crisis on the eve independence thus allowing the trust territory to acquire independence without holding new elections and without a constitution in place, those opposed to Ahidjo's UC policies understood that the sole responsibility to legally effect political change fell to them. Although attempts to organize a political roundtable proved unsuccessful, Bebey-Eyidi, a World War II veteran who had fought in the first division of the Forces françaises libres and completed his medical training in Paris after the war, continued to publicly denounce Ahidjo's united national party, the UC. In his correspondence with Roger Baldwin, chairman of the ILRM, an NGO based in New York, Bebey-Eyidi enumerated Ahidjo's "fascist and dictatorial tendencies," including military tribunals set up "to judge the innocent," the suppression of opposition newspapers including *L'opinion au Cameroun*, of which he was editor, the censorship of mail, and the state surveillance of members of legal political parties.[107]

On 28 June 1962, Bebey-Eyidi and three of his fellow deputies[108] were arrested for writing, signing, and sending an open letter to President Ahidjo in which they critiqued the state's authoritarian suppression of civil and political liberties in the name of squelching the ongoing rebellion.¹⁰⁹ The four deputies were stripped of their parliamentary immunity, were tried under the antisubversion law in what Baldwin described in an ILRM press release as "the first political action taken against the organized opposition in the Cameroon parliament," and were sentenced to thirty months in prison and a fine of FCFA 300,000.¹¹⁰ Writing to Baldwin from Yoko prison a year after his trial, Bebey-Eyidi surmised that by arresting and imprisoning him and his colleagues, the Ahidjo regime had rid itself of troublesome adversaries and at the same time had made an example of them to deter other would-be oppositionists.¹¹¹ The state's public executions of "subversives" served as an even more compelling deterrent.

PUBLIC EXECUTIONS

The postcolonial age of intelligence gathering, surveillance, denunciation, interrogation, and torture culminated in dramatic public executions and public display of the bodies or severed heads of "outlaws" and "subversives." Following the precedent set by French administrators, postcolonial administrators transformed the elimination of political opposition leaders into public events that would "have the most significant repercussions for the fight against the rebellion."¹¹² While the territory was still under French rule, the 1958 assassination of Ruben Um Nyobé and his comrade Jean Albert Basso by a military patrol in the forest of the Sanaga-Maritime was followed by a display of the bullet-riddled bodies in Boumnyebel (Sanaga-Maritime). The bodies were buried in the Presbyterian mission's cemetery, after being encased in concrete to prevent the retrieval of the corpses or body parts. According to administrative reports, Um Nyobé's death led to the rallying of "thousands" of people in the Sanaga-Maritime Region.¹¹³ But after the execution, the showcasing of the corpses, and the burial, administrators, not wanting Um to be depicted as a national hero who was cowardly assassinated by the French colonialists, immediately set about effacing the event. Although agents of the territorial information bureau took photographs during the ad hoc wake at Boumnyebel, they were not made available to the national press.¹¹⁴ On 18 and 19 September 1958, the high commissioner seized and censored eight metropolitan and Cameroonian newspapers reporting Um Nyobé's death.¹¹⁵ A journalist for *L'effort camerounais* remarked that the administration's censorship was "a curious manner of understanding the exigencies of journalism. In another country, a press conference would have been organized immediately."¹¹⁶

In July 1959 the French administration executed Pierre Simo, the captain general of SDNK forces in the Bamileke Region until his arrest in 1958, and four other freedom fighters by firing squad on the Bafoussam soccer field.[117] In 1958, during the Wanko assassination trial of ninety-seven persons accused of the crime, although only seventy-two defendants were present at the trial, a total of seventeen were sentenced to death (ten of them in absentia).[118] According to French administrators and military commanders, public executions in the Bamileke Region were the only thing that might lead to a "détente," after the area's "psychological putrefaction" made manifest by the failure of the population and traditional chiefs to cooperate with security forces.[119] Although UPC president Moumié's assassination, in late October 1960, carried out in a covert, undercover operation in Geneva, was far from public, the elimination of the nationalist leader was designed to deal a final blow to the UPC's unity and international support.[120] Death sentences abounded in the year leading up to official independence,[121] and the postcolonial administration continued to stage public executions, which they required civilians to attend in order to maximize their "psychological" impact on unwilling spectators. Postcolonial-era violence shifted to the realm of the symbolic as state administrators displayed severed heads and used public executions as part of their "psychological campaign" to combat "putrefaction." Far from being isolated events, public executions became a part of daily life in the Mungo and the Bamileke regions during the first postcolonial decade. In the matter-of-fact tone of an administrative report, J. B. Ndoumou, chief of the Nkongsamba BMM, wrote in 1970, "An outlaw, Nokingune Gabriel, alias Tergal, condemned to death a few months ago, was publicly executed at Loum on 15 July, while, as usual, the military authorities publicly exposed the heads of rebels who were victims of the operations related above."[122] The public execution of Pierre Kamdem Ninyim, the former fo of Baham who became a member of the national assembly in the 1960 elections, became another grim chapter in the political history of the chieftaincy against the backdrop of Cameroonian state building.

The Execution of Deputy Pierre Kamdem Ninyim

As though recognizing the continuing repercussions of Kamdem Ninyim's deposition in the Bamileke region, President Ahidjo pardoned the former fo and released him from exile in Yokadouma in time for the constitutional referendum of 21 February 1960.[123] When elections were held in April 1960, Kamdem Ninyim gained a seat in the national assembly as a member of the newly formed Bamileke party, the Popular Front for Unity and Peace (FPUP), that took eighteen seats out of a hundred. Shortly thereafter, Ahidjo named Kamdem Ninyim minister of public health, making him the youngest minister to serve in Cameroon to date. In May 1960 the state extended the promise of amnesty to "outlaws" and former SDNK captain general Paul Momo of Baham joined the administration, traveling throughout the Bamileke region with Kamdem Ninyim to speak on the importance of détente.[124] But after only a month, Momo rejoined the maquis, where he was killed on 17 November 1960.

During his short tenure as minister of public health, Kamdem Ninyim contributed to Baham's development by ensuring the establishment of administrative buildings and a hospital. In Baham, the population began to recount the history of succession in a way that favored Kamdem Ninyim over Teguia, saying that Kamdem Ninyim was divinely chosen to be the ruler of Baham, but at the national level, rather than within the chieftaincy. Following Kamdem Ninyim's pardon, in 1960, Teguia left Baham and took refuge in the Baham community on the left bank of the Noun, leaving the chieftaincy to Kamdem Ninyim for a brief period.[125] Kamdem Ninyim's political resilience and popularity proved threatening to President Ahidjo, and perhaps even more so to one of his closest advisors, Samuel Kamé. In 1961, Kamdem Ninyim's position as minister was not renewed, although he remained a representative in the Cameroon assembly.

On 30 August 1963, Kamdem Ninyim's fellow FPUP deputy in the assembly, Noé Mopen, was traveling from Bafoussam to Bangangte. In an eerie reenactment of the Wanko assassination, Mopen's car was stopped in an ambush, and he was robbed and killed. Initial news reports described Mopen's "accidental death" while on his way to his village,[126] but within days, the official newspaper, *La presse du Cameroun*, revised the story to read that Mopen had been "assassinated" by maquisards.[127] On 12 September, Kamdem Ninyim was accused of orchestrating the crime and was stripped of parliamentary immunity, arrested, and imprisoned in Yaoundé, where he awaited trial before the military tribunal. He managed to escape, only to be found a few hours later. Kamdem Ninyim's trial for the Mopen assassination coincided with that of Théodore Makanda Pouth, a CNO commander active in the Sanaga-Maritime maquis since 1956. The state newspaper published their names side by side in the headlines, lauding the "complete liquidation of terrorism in Cameroon" that their arrests supposedly heralded.[128]

Kamdem Ninyim's trial, scheduled for 21 October 1963, was pushed back, perhaps to give the state time to promulgate the Law on Repression of Subversion (which had been passed in March 1962 and modified on 23 October 1963) stipulating that the decisions of the military tribunal could no longer be appealed.[129] On 30 October 1963, Ninyim was tried with seventeen others for Mopen's assassination and condemned to death at his sentencing hearing, presided by the *commissaire du gouvernement*, André Fouman-Nti. Kamdem Ninyim was charged on counts of assassination, acting as an accomplice to assassination, posing a threat to the state's interior security, belonging to a criminal association, failure to denounce a crime, and illegal possession of arms and munitions.[130] During the trial, the state alleged that Deputy Mopen had recently denounced Kamdem Ninyim's collusion with maquis forces in the Bamileke region and that Kamdem Ninyim had arranged for the deputy's elimination in order to cover up his subversive activity. Kamdem Ninyim's defense attorneys, Maîtres Benjamin Matip, Léon Fouletier, and Roger Gourgon, declared that the witnesses' testimony had been coerced.[131]

On 3 January 1964, Pierre Kamdem Ninyim, the former chief of Baham, minister of public health, and parliamentary deputy, was publicly executed by firing squad in Bafoussam.[132] The administration summoned the population of Baham to Bafoussam, without telling them why. Military personnel led Kamdem Ninyim to the execution post before a crowd of forty thousand people, eight times the number assembled for the execution of the four maquisards in Douala that took place at the same time.[133]

The firing squad shot Kamdem Ninyim before an assembly of his shocked and disbelieving former subjects who were being closely watched by security forces. Ignace Neguin Djoko recalled, "They watched our faces to see if anyone was sad. After his death it was complete suspicion among Bahams, they did not even want you to speak his name."[134] The population of Baham left the scene as quickly as possible, many of them not knowing where or how their fo would be buried. But the body was buried in a communal cemetery in Bafoussam, where "they dug a deep grave and filled it over with concrete," to prevent the retrieval of the skull. Normally, a fo's funereal celebration took place in the chief's palace compound, but since "they had already placed someone there who was against him, who would have been the one to organize it, it was impossible."[135] It was in his maternal family that they carried out "the customs for Ninyim's death."[136]

In Baham, versions of Kamdem Ninyim's execution categorically accuse Kamé of having orchestrated it in a second attempt to usurp power in gung (his first attempt being his involvement in the young fo's deposition, in 1956). Oral informants often blur Kamdem Ninyim's two arrests, failing to situate them before or after independence. Many say that Kamdem Ninyim was "torn from the chief's palace twice." However, in both events, Kamé figures as the antagonist who used his proximity to the administration to negotiate his own position of power within gung.[137] "The Baham notables could do nothing to help Kamdem Ninyim because Kamé already had his fate in hand. All Bahams knew that Kamé was Ahidjo's right-hand man; when he told Ahidjo, 'Do this,' he did it."[138] Several narrators insisted that Ahidjo was absent on the day that Kamdem Ninyim was put to death and, upon learning that the execution was to take place, the president sent a telegram to Bafoussam ordering a stay. But Kamé precipitated the execution, and the telegram arrived too late to save Kamdem Ninyim. Most informants insisted that Mopen was Kamdem Ninyim's mentor in the assembly, one of his closest friends, making Kamdem Ninyim's involvement in his murder "unthinkable." Those who insist that Kamdem Ninyim was framed accuse one of his closest assistants, Joseph Kamguie, who had access to his seal (cachet), of fabricating a letter ordering Mopen's murder on which he forged Kamdem Ninyim's signature. Kamdem Ninyim's public execution resulted in his final and permanent exile from the chieftaincy, a process through which the legitimate fo of Baham was uprooted and cut off from the spiritual landscape of gung following his death and improper burial.[139]

Following Kamdem Ninyim's execution, "Baham was beaten down, destroyed. Notables died of the weight of their anguish."[140] A collective resignation to Kamdem Ninyim's execution and Teguia's reign as fo was communally performed in a "reconciliation" ceremony, or *gouo'o*, held at the chieftaincy's sacred site (feuveuck) in 1967.[141] But, for many, "Baham will never recover [from the Kamdem Ninyim execution]. They killed him like that."[142] Kamdem Ninyim's life, reign as fo, political activity, and execution can be read as a metaphor for Baham's ambivalent political relationship with the Cameroonian state. The relationship between church and state also became fraught with tension in the early postcolonial period, as the Catholic Church emerged as an ardent and vocal critic of government practices.

The Critical Church

Although the executions enabled governing officials to publicly perform the state's monopolization of political power, many of the state's most brutal acts of repression against unknown "subversives" occurred out of the public eye. On 1 February 1962 fifty-two political prisoners were loaded into a boxcar with no windows or doors to be transferred from Douala to Yaoundé. At the first stations along the way, the gendarme escorting the prisoners opened the train car's doors and provided water. The prisoners protested so loudly at each stop that the escort feared their cries would instigate riots among bystanders in the station. He decided to leave the car closed during the rest of the journey, which took place in the heat of the day. When the train arrived in the Yaoundé station, twenty-five of the prisoners, including eight women and a child, had died. President Ahidjo, who was hosting Liberian president William Tubman for dinner when he got word of the event, instructed the prefect to deal with the matter "discreetly." The prefect of Yaoundé, a Mr. Ngoh, enlisted a corvée of prisoners to bury the corpses in a gully near the train station in the middle of the night.[143]

The grave-digging prisoners and surviving passengers spread the word about the fatal train ride during family visits before being sent to their final destination, Yoko prison.[144] Soon, Monsignor Zoa, the bishop of Yaoundé became aware of the event and pressured state officials to make it public. The next day the government circulated a memorandum explaining that "certain detainees died in a train car while being transported and an official investigation of the affair is being carried out." Zoa deemed the government's announcement insufficient and planned a requiem mass for the unnamed victims to be held on 22 February 1962. The minister of the interior and the prefect of Yaoundé pulled *L'effort camerounais* from the newsstands, deported the editor in chief, Father Fertin, and threatened Bishop Zoa with deportation. Bishop Zoa held the requiem mass as planned and printed the administrative decrees censoring the paper and deporting Fertin in the 25 February 1962 edition of *L'effort camerounais*.

Bishop Zoa's position provided a foretaste of the antagonistic relationship between the postcolonial state and the Catholic Church, which began to be seen as a protective barrier against the regime's brutality. Bishop Albert Ndongmo of the Nkongsamba Diocese went even further in defining the church's role as a protective one, and would be charged, in 1970, with having mounted a coup attempt in 1968.[145] The disintegration of the state-church alliance in the first postcolonial decade signaled an important change from the trusteeship and mandate eras, as a now mostly African clergy advocated the protection of civil and political liberties in lieu of political repression.

THE GRAY ZONE: ORDERED VIOLENCE OR CRIMINAL ACTIVITY?

If the violence of the late 1950s could fit a Fanonian revolutionary and counterrevolutionary pattern, by 1960 a Levian gray zone had begun to emerge.[146] UPC freedom fighters, unaffiliated maquisards, commandos, and civic guards became indistinguishable in the eyes of the civilian population. When interrogated by police or gendarmes, the civilian population often claimed not to have known that a maquisard seen in the area was not a member of the civic guard. For example, in Loum, a man in a combat uniform, armed with a .12 caliber rifle, crossed the center of town and hired a taxi "without any reaction on the part of the population, who say that their quarter chief said it was a civic guard from Njombé."[147] Yet, security forces found that no civic guards had traveled from Loum that day.[148] Women who came across maquisards on their way home from the fields insisted upon interrogation that they wore "uniforms that resembled those of the commandos."[149] Near Manjo, a fifteen-year-old girl who was nearly kidnapped by maquisards on her way home from the fields, said, "When I noticed the individuals before the attack, I thought we were dealing with civic guards, but what led me to think they might be rebels was the attitude and appearance of some who were dressed as villagers and armed with machetes."[150] Jean-Marie Kwakep, who had seen maquisards lying in wait by the side of the road before the attempted kidnapping, described them as "being in military uniform. . . . The one closest to the path asked me, 'Papa, are you returning from the fields?'" Further down the path, Kwakep stopped to draw water, and another planter, who had also confused the maquisards with security forces, remarked, "If it were still in the day when soldiers shot at people in plantations without reason, they would shoot at you where you came to draw water." For civilians, maquisards and commandos were equally dangerous. Security forces were said to shoot "without reason," and the maquisards were known to seek money, young recruits, or revenge on those they believed to have betrayed them. Those who came in contact with the men in uniform did not seek to know who they were or what they were doing, but simply passed them, exchanged greetings, and then alerted each other to their presence. Survival in the postindependence era required just such a disinterest on the part of everyday people.

Like the ranks of the UPC militia, which used violence to settle their own internal disputes, security forces also profited from the atmosphere of rebellion to "get even" with one another and blame the maquisards. In 1963 in Nkongsamba's Third Ward (the neighborhood that hosted the diocesan headquarters), soldiers fought over a beautiful woman, Julienne, who was to marry Corporal-Chief Pokam. As Pokam drank in the Ewondo Bar, one of his colleagues who had been drinking in the nearby Tergal Bar shot him as a way to get Julienne for himself. Upon hearing the news, soldiers in the nearby military base still under French command spread the news that "they killed a soldier in the Third Ward!" Without taking the time to identify the perpetrators to which the ambiguous "they" referred, soldiers rampaged through the neighborhood, armed with matches and kerosene, setting fire to everything in sight. The military officers restored order only after the neighborhood had been devastated, hundreds of people burned, and countless others rendered homeless.[151] After the fires, the soldiers claimed that maquisards had killed the corporal-chief in the Third Ward, which was notorious for its support of the rebels due to neighborhood residents having often hosted traveling upécistes, including Ernest Ouandié.

As the culture of violence permeated the Mungo and Bamileke regions, a new duplicitous relationship between state politicians, businessmen, and maquisards emerged. By the middle of the 1960s, some maquisards, many of whom had tired of the life of outlaws and were increasingly devoid of political aspirations, hired themselves out to big men in the communities. An example from Bangangte (the Nde Department of the Bamileke region) suffices here to illustrate the opportunistic ways some politicians and entrepreneurs used outlaws for hire to advance their own political or economic agendas.

On the rainy night of 21 August 1965, a band of assassins stormed the home of a Swiss Protestant missionary family, the Markoffs.[152] The intruders shot and killed Mrs. Markoff, director of the mission school, and Mr. Valdvogel, a guest, who had just arrived in Cameroon three days earlier. According to the state's investigations, the criminals were all "former maquisards" who had turned themselves in and returned to legality during the amnesty grace period of May 1960. They had then formed an association of "killers for hire" disguised as a UC youth committee. One of the young men, François Yitna, had obtained a scholarship from the Protestant mission to study in France at the École normale d'Auch. In 1965 he returned to Cameroon a certified teacher and expected to be named one of the administrative directors of the school.

Deputy Thadée Nya Nana, representative of the Nde Department in the assembly, owned a bookshop in Bangangte, and had allegedly reached an agreement with Yitna that, if he became director of the school, all the students would purchase their books from Nana's bookstore. Together, they plotted Mrs. Markoff's murder in order to vacate the position of director. Nana supplied the weapons, put Yitna in touch with their accomplices, and promised them FCFA 100,000 to eliminate Mrs. Markoff. Nana, Yitna, and two others were condemned to death for the crime in the trial held on 29 October 1965. The remaining Protestant missionaries left the region, leaving "ten thousand young Cameroonians without schooling."[153]

Although some accounts suggest that rivals within the UC party framed Thadée Nya Nana for a crime he did not commit,[154] the murder of the missionaries in Bangangte shows the complexity of the "rebellion" and the ways in which it permeated everyday political and business rivalries. Many of the actors in the mission attack had once had or still had personal ties to the UPC or to outlaws, or both. Deputy Nana orchestrated the crime and used his ties to former maquisards turned card-carrying members of the UC. The plurality of motives, the number of actors, and the population's refusal to provide any information to investigating security forces illustrated the ambiguous collusion between outlaws and card-carrying members of Ahidjo's party. Regardless of their true perpetrators, violent acts such as the attack on Mrs. Markoff could easily be blamed on maquisards, and a number of opportunists counted on a collective fear of terrorist outlaws to get away with serious crimes.

A gruesome attack on a health clinic in the Mungo region town of Loum illustrates the complete degradation of discipline and political purpose among militia still in the maquis ten years after Cameroon's official independence and reveals that a degree of collaboration persisted between maquisards and civilians. On 9 July 1970 in Loum, a month before the arrest of ALNK commander in chief Ernest Ouandié in nearby

Mbanga, a band of ten outlaws attacked Dr. Happi's clinic, killed two teenage student nurses with machetes, and kidnapped a woman.[155] The investigation slowly revealed that the attack had taken place with the help of at least one of the clinic nurses, Pierre Wedji, who provided the "rebels" with the keys to the clinic's pharmacy. Wedji, whose late father had served as the president of the UPC committee in the town of Tombel, was not at the clinic on the day of the attack, but stopped in the late afternoon to pick up the day's till. He arrived on the scene to discover the student nurses, hands bound with wire, lying in pools of blood. The seventeen-year-old nurse, Joseph Tchome, who died at the scene, was the son of the committee's vice president. Wedji smeared himself in the blood of the victims, and when security forces questioned his behavior, he said simply that it was because he felt remorse.

The woman who was kidnapped, Nyah Magdalene, was in the clinic keeping watch over her sick co-wife. But she was also the mistress of a rebel who trafficked pharmaceutical products between Loum and Melong. Dr. Happi, originally from the Bamileke town of Bafang, entrusted the management of the clinic to the head nurse, Abel Youmbi, originally from the Nde Department of the Bamileke region, where he had worked at the Protestant mission hospital of Bangwa. Although Youmbi had been accused of supporting maquisards while in Bangwa, Happi considered him to be a good and trustworthy worker and refused to remove him from his leadership position in the clinic. The Bafang community of Loum had been pressuring Happi to replace Youmbi with Joseph Nkopipje, also from Bafang. When Happi turned down their requests, Bafang elites formed an association to collect funds for the foundation of a new clinic to compete with Dr. Happi's.

Intelligence reports after the Loum clinic attack pointed to the involvement of everyone from Bishop Ndongmo to maquisard Jean Djonteu, aka God of Independence), who was believed to be profiting from his outlaw status to conduct business affairs. The reports' authors theorized a number of possible motives for the attack, including the kidnapping of Nyah Magdalene, bad blood between maquisards, "tribal fights" between the Bafang and Bangwa communities of Loum, and even the "tense political atmosphere of Loum," where divisions blocked the UNC political party, which had "not yet been implanted in the locale." In the aftermath of the attack on the clinic, security forces increased surveillance and police raids, but their efforts met with "total silence, and a unprecedented passivity, never before seen in the history of the Mungo rebellion."[156] The clinic closed, leaving the twenty thousand inhabitants of Loum without health care. The case of the Happi clinic attack was never solved, although two of the maquisards who carried it out were arrested and two more killed by security forces before the end of July.

Like the murder of the missionaries in Bangangte, the Loum clinic attack shows that by the 1970s violence had little to do with political ideology but instead was wielded to influence small-scale, localized, and everyday financial or political rivalries. Many of the actors in the mission attack and both victims and perpetrators in the clinic raid had once had or still maintained personal ties to the UPC and maquis fighters. Both the "outlaw" perpetrators of the crime and the elite of Loum had motives for raiding and sabotaging the clinic, while in Bangangte, Deputy Nana allegedly orchestrated Markoff's murder by using his ties to former maquisards turned members of the UC. In the case of Loum, the plurality of motives and the number of leads proved too difficult for state administrators to unravel.

In August 1970, ALNK commander in chief Ouandié's arrest in Mbanga, followed by that of Monseigneur Ndongmo of the Nkongsamba Diocese, whom President Ahidjo had selected to negotiate with the ALNK only to later accuse him of plotting a coup, closed the chapter on the rebellion. Yet the official closure marked by the trial and sentencing of Ouandié, Ndongmo, and those accused as their accomplices did nothing to alleviate the tensions, suspicions, and atmosphere of mistrust that reigned in the Mungo and Bamileke regions. After a dramatic public trial during which were issued a total of 104 convictions for conspiracy against the state or attempted coups (or both), Ouandié was publicly executed by firing squad on 15 January 1971. Ndongmo, who had also been condemned to death, eventually had his sentence commuted to permanent exile after the Vatican intervened on his behalf. Maquisards continued to operate in the Mungo region throughout the early 1970s, and security forces continued to scour them out, round them up, and publicly execute them. In Nkongsamba, executions of "rebels" took place in public squares as late as 1975.[157]

In the aftermath of the Ouandié-Ndongmo trial, no one was above suspicion. Even members of the state party, the UNC, who exhibited the greatest enthusiasm and initiative were denounced as supporters of the rebellion by envious colleagues.[158] Jehovah's Witnesses took center stage as "political subversives" for their refusal to vote.[159] Failure to salute the flag as it was being raised in Loum earned Barthélemy Kamgue a stay in solitary confinement.[160] A collective suspicion eroded sociopolitical interactions, in UNC party meetings, in marketplaces, in churches, and in rural villages. People knew that it was in these familiar, intimate spaces that they ran the greatest risk of being accused or denounced by those who claimed to know them best.

During the first postcolonial decade, the momentum of violence emboldened people — whether soldiers, "outlaws," or civilians — to commit acts of murder, arson, and looting. People seeking vengeance in private matters, whether over questions of debt, women, political power, or mystical wrongdoing, disguised their attacks on neighbors, friends, enemies, or in-laws as terrorist attacks. The most insidious attacks involved the hire of maquisards to carry out tasks of brutality assigned by wealthy and ambitious men in the community who had turned to killing as a way to further their political or financial goals. On the other hand, agents of the state settled personal scores and claimed that their actions were to suppress terrorism and combat political subversion. As assaults and surveillance carried out by security forces increased, they became less justifiable as the repression of political subversives, and instead overlapped with criminal activity, as UPC militia and state forces became increasingly indistinguishable to the population at large. Yet, in the eye of the Cameroonian state, a crucial distinguishing factor separated the entangled categories of state agent and subversive: the rule of law.

Security forces carried out campaigns of repression and psychological "purification" and operated with impunity under the protection afforded by law, even when their actions were criminal. The laws that undermined the civil and political liberties of every Cameroonian, most significantly the law against subversion, were justified as exceptional emergency measures necessary to combat the ongoing rebellion against the state government. These laws were rooted in emergency legislation passed in the late 1950s and extended and enhanced under the postcolonial Ahidjo regime. In the first few years following French Cameroon's official independence, the state of emergency became permanent in the regions where the UPC was most active, and the exceptional measures taken to uproot the maquis soon became a part of "ordinary" legislation.[161] When emergency legislation metamorphoses into everyday rule of law, it is useful to ask, what is it that the law permits emergency measures to accomplish?[162] In Cameroon, as in a number of other postcolonial African states, laws derived from late-colonial states of emergency permitted political leaders to exercise violence legally on a daily basis. In turn these laws enabled the "refashioning of order" into a one-party state.[163] And had not the late-colonial era thoroughly confirmed that the state of exception (emergency and martial law) was the not-so-hidden secret of modern power, and emergency legislation part and parcel of the normal mode of governing?[164]

CONCLUSION

"After the War, We Stop Counting the Dead"
Reconciliation and Public Confession

IN 1967 a reconciliation ceremony brought the entire population of Baham, including those residing outside the chieftaincy, to the chieftaincy's sacred site, feuveuck. The purpose of the gathering was to make an expiatory sacrifice for purification that was performed when it seemed evil had taken over the entire chieftaincy. A sacrifice carried out on a chieftaincy's sacred site to promote collective healing usually coincided, as it did in 1967, with public confession, or gou'o. During the 1967 ceremony at feuveuck, the people of Baham listed the crimes and misdeeds they had committed during the decade of war following Fo Kamdem Ninyim's deposition. They appealed to the gods and to the community of the living for forgiveness and promised never to begin again. The public confession at feuveuck was also a truth-telling ceremony. Lying, concealing the truth, or failure to participate would have incurred the wrath and punishment of the gods and led to continuing "troubles."

The public confession at feuveuck brought together chieftaincy notables—the fo, district chiefs, and family chiefs representing the fo in communities outside Baham—as well as Baham ritual specialists and guardians of the site. Msgr. Ndongmo, the bishop of Bamileke origin presiding over the Nkongsamba Diocese, as well as local state officials, including the mayor and subprefect, also attended the ceremony at feuveuck as though it served not only to reconcile the people of Baham with each other but also to reconcile Baham's traditional authorities with church and state authorities in postcolonial Cameroon.

The Baham reconciliation ceremony of 1967 fit a governmental trend to integrate localized spiritual elements into centralizing political practices of the state. It marked an ambivalent collaboration between "traditional" and state governance, at least for the immediate goal of establishing peace in Baham. Outsiders had never before participated in a public confession, reconciliation, and healing ceremony on a Grassfields chieftaincy's communal sacred site. Although the public confession at feuveuck took place in the presence of outsiders to the chieftaincy, it carried the greatest significance for the inhabitants of Baham. For them the public confession at feuveuck symbolized a renewal of the spiritual alliance tying together the living inhabitants of gung, the spirits, the land, and the institutions of governance. It was the moment of truth and marked the end of the era of the dangerous truths and countertruths that had been the cause of so much suspicion and betrayal. During the public confession, many villagers were shocked to discover that in some cases the perpetrators of violence were members of their own family or people they had believed to be their intimate friends. Reconciliation could not be achieved in one event, however. Even today, families of those who disappeared during the period of troubles continue to search for and symbolically bury their dead (following the instructions of healers and diviners), and relations between the living have proven equally difficult to mend.

In Nkongsamba and the rest of the Mungo Province during the late 1960s and early 1970s, reconciliation ceremonies conceived by state administrators seemed artificial and contrived in comparison to the public confession held at feuveuck. Jean-Jacques Ngolle and other Nkongsamba-based politicians conceived of a ritual they called the oath of the black dog. In towns throughout the Mungo, subprefects worked with neighborhood and block chiefs to gather the inhabitants, ward by ward and block by block, for a public confession. After purchasing "oathing cards," people lined up before the subprefect, neighborhood chief, and a black dog on a designated day. Each person stepped up to the dog and confessed to crimes committed during the period of troubles, professed loyalty to the government, promised not to participate in or support the rebellion in any way, and, after this public declaration, beat the dog with a stick. After every person in the neighborhood had confessed, the dog was buried. In Nkongsamba the black dogs were thrown in a special burial site next to the UNC party headquarters.

The black-dog oathing ceremony held less credence for Mungo populations than the public confession on the communal chuep'si did in Baham. Some Mungo-based Catholics—following the lead of Bishop Ndongmo, who compared the black dog ceremonies to the practice of witchcraft—refused to beat the dog. Authorities eventually allowed devout Catholics to swear on the Bible during the ceremonies as an alternative to beating the dog. But people did not believe that lying when taking the black-dog oath would lead to serious spiritual consequences. People who remember those years sometimes remark, "I never saw anyone die after they lied and hit the dog." Nevertheless, the black-dog ceremony had to be completed by every inhabitant of the Mungo towns in which it was carried out. Carrying the oathing card was as important as carrying the UNC party card, the national identity card, or the proof of the payment of taxes.

Even after the public confessions, the residual effects of the violent repression of the UPC rebellion continued to shape everyday life in postcolonial Cameroon. For Bamileke populations, tensions between state and chieftaincy remained unresolved. As prime minister on the eve of independence, Ahidjo spoke of the role of traditional chiefs, especially from the Bamileke Region, in state governance:

> The public authorities must understand the necessity of harmonizing traditional society with modern democracy. The public authorities must contribute to the evolution of *commandement* and traditional chieftaincies, [making them] compatible with municipal institutions. We must respect the original foundations of our society, and chieftaincies play a vital and decisive role in our country, now and for a long time to come.[1]

The promise of working to harmonize "traditional society with modern democracy" was soon forgotten during the regime's transition to a policy that Ahidjo dubbed the "ethic of unity." By 1962 the UC purposely eschewed "tribalism," or reliance on traditional structures in recruiting adherents,[2] and in the years after Ahidjo's speech about the importance of chieftaincies, the state party leadership replaced "traditional chiefs" in postcolonial governance, as illustrated by the story of Kamdem Ninyim and his powerful nemesis, Samuel Kamé. At the First National Council of the UC, held in Yaoundé in April 1963, Kamé insisted that the "regime appears as the means, the instrument of public action of the party,"³ and advocated "mobilizing the masses," especially the youth, into cadres of Cameroon's single party.⁴ The UNC combatted tribalism even more systematically, and the Law of 12 June 1967 banned "any associations exhibiting an exclusively tribal or clan character" that the party considered to be "contrary to national unity."⁵

Despite Baham's history as one of the most fervently nationalist of Bamileke chieftaincies during the war for independence, its most visible representative in the postcolonial state became Kamé, administrator and UC party leader. But many people of Baham refused to recognize Kamé's right to speak on their behalf. For some, the relationship between Teguia and his patron signified the invasion of Baham by *keu-keu*, the ambiguous, complex, and dangerous sphere of the political. This Ghomala word for politics, *keu-keu*, carries singularly negative connotations. *Keu-keu* literally means a massive tangle of wire or string with no beginning or end, and therefore impossible to unravel. Notables who survived the deposition of Kamdem Ninyim and the independence war in Baham minimized, insofar as possible, the state's intrusion into the internal matters of Baham's governance, including succession, and sought instead to protect the chieftaincy by distancing it from state politics. For many, the journey toward reconciliation in Baham could only truly begin once the relationship between chieftaincy and state, embodied in Kamé's relationship with Teguia, had been severed.

Upon Teguia's death, in 1986, chieftaincy notables and commoners alike began heated debates about who should succeed him. It was as though the fo's genealogical history had to be scrutinized for the moment at which succession had gone awry, and the will of the governing ancestors had been disobeyed. One group insisted that the fo's lineage should be traced as far back as the reign of Kamdem II, Tâ Ntomdjap.⁶ In the end, kamveu's consensus was that "Baham has suffered too much for this ordeal," and the notables' council decreed that Teguia's son, Pouokam II, would succeed his father as fo. The kamveu notables poured raffia wine on the ground at the conclusion of their meeting in a binding alliance, such that not one of them would go back on his word. Recalling the succession events in 2003, Jean-Bernard Pogo *dit* Defotimsa recounted how a Yaoundé-based state administrator, attempting to propose a different successor than the one the notables' association had agreed on, convened a meeting with the kamveu at the Baham sub-prefect's office. Word of the meeting spread through the marketplace and "all the elite of Baham got in their cars," drove to the subprefect's office, and began milling around outside. The kamveu notables had already explained that to change their decision would rekindle animosity in the village. State officials, upon seeing the melee outside, adjourned the meeting and allowed the kamveu's decision to stand.

The memory of the "time of troubles," the eventual execution of Fo Kamdem Ninyim, the burning of compounds, huts, and sacred sites, the arrests and expulsions in Mungo Province towns, all rendered many people of Baham at best, distrustful, and at worst, fearful, of the postcolonial state that came into being. Rather than participate in state political practices, much of the Bamileke population residing in regions most decimated by the independence war tended, like the notables of Baham, to turn inward, toward the foundations of Grassfields political culture that had resurfaced during the nationalist era. This entailed a renewal of the spiritual alliance and a partial retrieval of autonomy (lepue) as an alternative to political involvement in the postcolonial state.

One of this book's historical perspectives on Cameroon's decolonization is the Bamileke chieftaincy of Baham. The history of Cameroon's independence struggle is remembered and recounted today as a part of Baham's local history. But the repercussions of the UPC nationalist movement and its repression spread beyond the boundaries of Bamileke chieftaincies such as Baham and their emigrant communities in areas like the Mungo River valley. Its history reaches throughout Cameroon and beyond its borders to Accra, Conakry, Algiers, Paris, and Beijing and must be told from many vantage points: the history of UPC nationalism is both a local and an international history. By moving from a local, to a territorial (or national), to a transregional lens, this history of UPC nationalism examines grassroots political cultures' articulation with the politics of decolonization, as well the intersection between Third World anticolonial revolution and Pan-Africanism.

In Ghana, the Nkrumah regime that supported upécistes and other African anticolonialists in exile toppled in 1966, just as a hundred or so UPC fighters trained in Accra, Algiers, or Beijing gathered in the forest swamps of northern Congo-Brazzaville and attempted (unsuccessfully) to invade Cameroon from the southeast to join Ouandié's soldiers in the maquis.[7] But there are several important reasons to explore the "failed" project of continental unity through the lens of a "failed" nationalist movement and vice versa. Doing so enables an empirical as well as a conceptual understanding of the vision of Pan-African federation that took shape in Accra from 1957 to 1966, and suggests the ways in which the creation of that political vision set a precedent for later liberation movements in southern and lusophone Africa. It also allows a postcolonial Cold War worldview from which to assess the ways in which anticolonial nationalism navigated an East-West geopolitical fault line.

PAN-AFRICAN FEDERATION—PIPEDREAM OR PRECEDENT?

This history of the Pan-African trajectory of UPC nationalists takes seriously the projects of African federation that transcended metropolitan boundaries, languages, and alliances. In recent years, historians of empire, human rights, and Africa's decolonization have minimized the importance of Pan-Africanism in the independence era.[8] Jan Eckel, for example, writes that in "the bewildering mélange of ideas" that characterized the thinking of Asian and African activists after the Second World War, "there was hardly anything on which leaders of the anticolonial struggle did not disagree," including "future intra-African relations as articulated in 'Pan-Africanism.'"[9] But in stressing ideological differences across so vast an area (Asian and African territories in their ensemble), scholars such as Eckel turn a blind eye to the patterned ideological and political commonalities that *did* surface within a heterogeneous world on the verge of independence. Historians of empire, such as Frederick Cooper, have emphasized patterns and allegiances stemming from a sense of belonging to a common imperial community. Focusing on French West Africa, Cooper suggests that "older forms of pan-Africanism" had withered by the mid-1950s and argues that interterritorial federation centered on a common metropole was the preferred supranational option for former colonial territories.[10] But Cooper and others who view decolonization through a metropolitan or imperial lens have overlooked visions of African federation that existed in competition with what Gary Wilder describes as those "built on the imperial history that bound metropolitan" and colonial populations "together within an interdependent entity."[11]

Even historians and political scientists of French Africa's decolonization who have worked on the UPC, the Parti Démocratique Guinéen (PDG), or the Sawaba independence movement in Niger—all movements that eschewed inclusion in a greater France and looked instead toward Accra and Algiers—have emphasized the radicalism or exceptionalism of these movements.[12] But as postcolonial theorist Patrick Williams has argued, "the portrayal of opposition as isolated, therefore insignificant, unrepresentative, and irrelevant is very much a colonialist strategy."[13] When the historical perspective of decolonization is centered in Accra, Conakry, or Algiers, rather than in Paris, these anomalous, "radical" nationalist movements can no longer be seen as unique, stand-alone movements. Instead, the links actively forged among Ghanaian, Guinean, Algerian, Congolese, Cameroonian, and other nationalists, anticolonialists, and political activists suggest that they were part of a pattern emerging beyond the scope of the French community or the British Commonwealth—a pattern arising from what Christopher J. Lee has described as "a realm of community politics situated between the nation-state as such and outsized global political entities, namely the United Nations."[14] But because most of the nationalist movements in colonial territories that referenced Accra or Algiers rather than London or Paris failed to achieve political power in their home states, historians have mostly overlooked the larger, transregional pattern they created. As scholars continue to examine the implications of these Third World transregional networks, understandings of decolonization will most likely evolve to consider their importance more deeply, but despite important syntheses published in recent years,[15] in-depth transregional studies of anticolonial African nationalist movements for the postwar period have yet to be done.

For many African nationalists, former French subjects and évolués among them, Afro-Asian solidarity, nonalignment, and political, cultural, and economic rupture with colonial powers made up the very foundation of anticolonial nationalism *and* opened new routes to Pan-African federation. As historian Vijay Prashad insists, in the wake of Bandung, the Third World "represented a coalition of new nations that possessed the autonomy to enact a novel world order committed to human rights, self-determination, and world peace as outlined by the Bandung communiqué."[16] Those political actors who, in discourse and practice, pledged allegiance to the sovereignty of a United States of Africa viewed territorial independence not as an obstacle to, but as a prerequisite to, or—in the case of UPC nationalists—an anticipated benefit of inclusion in a larger Pan-African framework. The case of the UPC shows the ways through which the new political tradition of a complementary symbiosis between Pan-Africanism and African nationalism was conceived. As long as visions of Pan-Africanism shored up Africa's anticolonialist struggles, the external UPC remained linked to the internal resistance, the exile of nationalists continued to bolster the movement within their territory's boundaries, and the international credibility and visibility of the UPC increased.

Discussions of transregional political organization, revolutionary Pan-Africanism, and the support that independent African states provided to liberation movements in southern and lusophone Africa do figure in the scholarly literature of Africa's later decolonization, although these trends are usually depicted as novel and innovative, rather than as political configurations and practices arising out of an earlier era of decolonization.[17] Yet these later transregional alliances built, in many ways, on the political and diplomatic practices established through the continent's armed anticolonial liberation movements of the 1950s, as exemplified by the FLN's and the UPC's shared inspiration and collaboration—a relationship that the Touré and Nkrumah regimes sought to facilitate and to sustain.[18]

For nearly a decade, the FLN and the UPC appeared to be operating almost in tandem when it came to the organization and design of their respective anticolonial revolutions. Although the reasons for this striking parallel have not been explored in the scholarly literature, concurrent events and linkages can be mentioned here by way of illustrating the connection that began to be set in place soon after the Second World War. In 1948, while still under the direction of Messali Hadj, founder of the Mouvement pour la triomphe des libertés démocratiques (MTLD), future leader of the FLN's external delegation Aït Ahmed defined the practice of revolutionary international diplomacy as a need to integrate "the people's war" in the international context and to use as the movement's "vital force . . . the historic movement which leads the peoples of Asia and Africa to fight for their liberation. . . . They will follow our example as we follow the example of other peoples who liberated themselves by force of arms or who are fighting still."[19] In the early 1950s, Ruben Um Nyobé met Hadj's Tunisian representative, spokesperson for the movement to liberate North Africa, at the UN in New York.[20] In late 1954 the young founders of the FLN declared the "internationalization of the Algerian problem"—by defeating France's portrayal of it as an internal affair and taking the FLN's case to the UN—to be as important as the struggle's internal, military dimension.[21] As FLN leaders succeeded, in late 1954, in persuading Saudi Arabia to petition the UN Security Council on the movement's behalf, thus alerting international public opinion to the existence of an Algerian question, the UPC leaders continued tirelessly to bring the question of the Cameroons' independence and reunification to the attention of the Fourth Committee, Trusteeship Council, and General Assembly. The FLN's participation in the Bandung Conference of Asian and African states in April 1955 as part of a united North African delegation culminated in the resolution recognizing that all had a right to independence.[22] In May, immediately after the resolution, the number of FLN attacks escalated in Algeria,[23] while in French Cameroon, upécistes orchestrated violent uprisings in the major cities and towns for the first time.[24] But perhaps nothing communicated the kind of political community being envisioned in the late 1950s as clearly as the FLN and UPC leaderships' declarations, in September and December 1958, respectively, of provisional governments for which they sought diplomatic recognition.[25] These declarations occurred around the same time that the heads of state in Guinea and Ghana announced their supranational federation in November, the month before the AAPC meeting in Accra. Surely these spontaneous declarations of government and federation should be seen as the boldest expression of the imagined possibilities and alternative political communities to which Lee and other scholars refer when historicizing the Bandung "moment and its political afterlives."[26]

As the Spirit of Bandung waned, in the early 1960s, the territorial concerns of new postcolonial states began to take precedence over the idea of supranational unity, and visions of Pan-African federation faded away. For many heads of newly independent African states, Accra-based freedom fighters represented a threat to state power more than the embodiment of Pan-African liberation. The positions of African heads of state on the "Cameroon crisis" in the late 1950s and early 1960s revealed their various perspectives on the broader question of African unity among newly independent states. Throughout the 1960s, alternative schemes of Pan-African federation emerged in competition with the vision centered in Accra. The latter became known as that of the "Casablanca group" and advocated a Pan-African assembly as well as political and economic committees, and a high command of chiefs of staff to aid and assist nationalist forces. The African governments in the Casablanca group promised support for the UPC. The Brazzaville group, made up of future member states of the Organisation Commune Africaine et Malagache, all former French territories, conceived of a federation based on a continued alliance with France, prioritized the suppression of the ongoing revolutionary movements in Côte d'Ivoire, Niger, Upper Volta, and Cameroon, and forged diplomatic relations to achieve that goal. The Monrovia group took issue with political subversion and pledged "non-interference in the internal affairs of states," placing national sovereignty above supranational alliance.[27] By the mid-1960s all but a minority of African heads of states agreed that the Organization of African Unity, formed in 1963, must have as its purpose both continued cooperation with metropolitan governments and the safeguarding of member states' national sovereignty. Dreams of a supranational Pan-African federation gave way to a mutual desire to protect and uphold national sovereignty, and African nations' support for the UPC dwindled as it became a diplomatic liability for the states that had supported it. The UPC would prove unable to achieve its revolutionary goals without the transregional assistance it had relied on in the late 1950s and early 1960s.

By the mid-1960s postcolonial African states showed signs of the "Africanized colonialism" that Fanon had predicted as it became clear that colonial structures—particularly the political excesses of the state and continued economic and diplomatic control wielded by former metropolitan powers (and especially France over its former African territories)—had survived decolonization.[28] But the history of the UPC's international dimensions illustrates the lasting effects of the political alternatives that nationalists envisioned during the first wave of Africa's decolonization. Patterns of political liberation conceived in Accra and embodied in the freedom fighters arriving by the hundreds from territories under colonial rule fed into a black transnationalist imaginary. Accra seemed, for a few years, to represent the time, the place, and the strategy through which century-old aspirations and longings of Pan-Africanist thinkers would be fulfilled. It was also one of the many sites through which these ideas spread and took root in the lives and imaginations of ordinary Africans. Although the UPC and the United States of Africa failed together, the symbiosis between nationalist movements and Pan-Africanism built on a historic and diasporic ideological precedent and in turn established a new precedent for the Pan-African support of exiled freedom fighters that characterized later African liberation movements.

THE COLD WAR FROM A POSTCOLONIAL VANTAGE POINT

The UPC's struggle for the Cameroons' independence took place on a transnational scale and against the backdrop of the Cold War. Accordingly, the case of the UPC allows us to rethink the ways in which

African anticolonial nationalisms intersected with Cold War geopolitics by offering a new vantage point—beyond that of the United States, the Soviet Union, or China—from which to witness the emergence of a polarized world.[29] Until recently, Cold War scholars have privileged the perspective of one or the other superpower competitors, evaluating peripheral political actors such as anticolonial revolutionaries as pawns situated somewhere along the East-West axis.[30] But since the late 1990s some scholars have sought to evaluate the ways in which anticolonial nationalists navigated the challenges posed by Cold War politics and diplomacy in the formulation of their nationalist agendas and particularly their foreign policies.[31] A similar scholarly initiative surfaced concurrently among Americanists who began to trace the linkages between civil rights activism in the United States and an expanding global anti-imperialism articulated in anti-racist terms.[32] These recent revisionist histories illustrate that, while the Cold War influenced local political processes, including anticolonial nationalisms and civil and human rights movements, Cold War dynamics were rarely the primary concern of the actors engaged in postwar liberation politics and activism. Instead, politicians, revolutionaries, and activists tried to use superpower rivalry to their advantage, for instance, by threatening to accept—or by accepting—Soviet or Chinese support.[33]

Upécistes were adept practitioners of these tactics. They drew on communist bases of support, beginning with the French Communist Party, and expanding into ever-greater international circles. It is undeniable that a number of upécistes, both within the Cameroon territories and abroad, adhered to communist ideology, particularly those aspects emphasizing economic autonomy and liberation from imperial rule. But not all upécistes embraced communist theory or practice, nor did communism figure as the dominant international ideology in the movement's political or rhetorical toolbox. Significantly, a greater number of Cameroonian students committed to the nationalist cause were on scholarship in France than were in the Eastern Bloc.[34] Determined that their movement not become a Cold War battlefront, UPC leaders sought support from unaligned religious and humanitarian organizations as well as some with socialist or communist leanings, while attempting to benefit from opportunities afforded by Cold War–era superpower rivalry.[35] By 1957, UPC leaders had forged connections with an emerging network of anti-imperialist human rights activists in the United States, Great Britain, and, eventually, France. Among the human-rights NGOs that supported upécistes in their quest for the implementation and protection of UN-sanctioned political and civil liberties was the New York–based ILRM, the earliest such organization to obtain consultative status with the UN and which was chaired by the civil libertarian and founder of the American Civil Liberties Union, Roger Baldwin. In the UK, upécistes found supportive networks in the Movement for Colonial Freedom, conceived by Fenner Brockway, British pacifist and Labor MP, as well as the Africa Bureau (AB), an organization based in London, for which the Anglican bishop and antiapartheid activist Reverend Michael Scott served as ubiquitous spokesperson and figurehead.[36] In France, a consistent humanitarian supporter of upécistes was Father Alexandre Glasberg, a Second World War resister who founded the organization L'Amitié Chrétienne in 1942 to provide aid and support to Jews and other victims of Nazism, and who, after the end of the war, founded the NGO Centre d'Orientation Sociale des Étrangers (COSE).[37]

Even this brief inventory of the movement's international supporters reveals clearly that upécistes turned with as much enthusiasm to liberal humanitarian organizations, such as the ILRM, and Christian associations, such as the AB, as they did to Beijing or Moscow. Yet, overlooking this broad base of support, Western powers insisted on viewing the UPC through a Cold War lens. French administrators categorized the UPC as a communist organization and generated media spin depicting the movement as one controlled from Moscow or Beijing. Major American newspapers, if they covered the independence war in Cameroon at all, sometimes portrayed the UPC as communist in nature. However, perhaps discerning that the Cameroons did not pose an extreme Cold War threat to global democracy, they were more likely to describe UPC paramilitary soldiers as fighting some ill-defined cause for a particular "tribe," using primitive and superstitious ritual warfare.[38]

It is worth considering why a strategy that proved successful for the FLN and its provisional government did not ultimately lead to the same kind of success for the UPC. The Cameroons were of lesser economic, strategic, and geopolitical importance to superpowers, and, although upéciste leaders attempted to construct and amplify an international support network similar to Algeria's and to use media to sway world opinion, they never achieved the same degree of internationalization as did the FLN. While the FLN's GPRA gained official recognition from thirteen states within ten days of its creation,[39] the UPC government that President-in-exile Moumié proclaimed in late 1958 went unrecognized. The FLN had 177 GPRA officials in thirty-eight countries,[40] while the UPC had no more than two dozen exiles capable of minimal diplomatic influence and in fewer countries. The French elimination of UPC leaders—particularly the assassination by poisoning, on 3 November 1960, of Moumié, who had pursued and maintained the greatest number of transnational ties—dealt the movement's international network a considerable blow, whereas in the ranks of the FLN, replacements for leaders could more easily be found. With the UPC lacking the support of Arab countries and unable even to maintain the support of a majority of independent African states after official independence,[41] the French as well as the Americans surely found the movement's reliance on Chinese support for its post-1960 paramilitary force relatively unthreatening. By granting official independence after the UPC's proscription (which ensured that upécistes could not participate in elections as candidates or voters) and with a postcolonial government loyal to the former metropole in place, France shed a diplomatic liability. At the same time, France continued to offer military strength to the Ahidjo regime to quell the continuing UPC rebellion, according to bilateral agreements in matters of military assistance, national defense, strategic mineral resources, and diplomacy.[42] Despite its Cold War frame, Cameroon's decolonization was a violent process dominated by local and regional issues.

Notes

Unless otherwise indicated, all interviews were conducted by the author and all translations are mine.

ABBREVIATIONS IN NOTES

AGEFOM	Agence économique
ANY	Archives nationales Yaoundé
APD	Archives préfecturales de Dschang
APN	Archives préfecturales de Nkongsamba
CAOM	Centre des archives d'outre-mer
CHAN	Centre historique des archives nationales
CHETOM	Centre d'histoire et des troupes d'outre-mer
CO	Colonial Office, Kew
CUT	Comité de l'unité togolaise
FO	Foreign Office, Kew
ILRM	International League of the Rights of Man
NA	National Archives, Kew
NYPL	New York Public Library
SEDOC	Service de documentation extérieure et de contre-espionnage
SHAT	Service historique de l'armée de terre
UCU	Usambara Citizens Union
UNGA	United Nations General Assembly
UNTC	United Nations Trusteeship Council

INTRODUCTION: LAYERING NATIONALISM FROM LOCAL TO GLOBAL

1. I use the term Grassfields to refer to the region stretching west to east from the Cross River to the Mbam, and from the Katsina Ala River in the north to the Manenguba mountain range in the south. The Grassfields thus comprised the present-day anglophone North West Region, and the Bamileke and Bamun Regions, which together make up the francophone West Region. See Jean-Pierre Warnier, *Echanges, développement, et hiérarchies dans le Bamenda pré-colonial (Cameroun)* (Stuttgart: Franz Steiner Verlag, 1985); Lorenz Homberger, ed.,

Cameroon: Art and Kings (Zurich: Museum Rietberg, 2008). The Bamileke Region was a French administrative division designating the portion of the Grassfields under French rule, according to the French administration's classification. French administrators divided French Cameroon into regions, each of which was further divided into subdivisions; these administrative units became provinces and departments, respectively, at the time of official independence in 1960. On 12 November 2008, President Paul Biya issued a decree changing the provinces to regions. Thus, the Bamileke Region became the Western Province in the 1960s and is now the West Region. Throughout this volume, "region" is not capitalized when it refers to the geographical area: e.g., the eastern portion of the Grassfields. However, when it refers to a specific political division under French rule, "region" is capitalized: e.g., the Bamileke Region.

2. Since the Portuguese named the present-day Wouri River the Rio dos Camarões for the abundance of crustaceans therein in 1472, Cameroon has had various spellings. From 1884 to 1916, the period of German occupation, the name of the territory was spelled Kamerun. At the signing of the Treaty of Versailles, the eastern portion of the former German colony became Cameroun (or French Cameroon, in English), while the British called the western portion the Cameroons (meaning the Northern and Southern Territories). Throughout this book, the plural is used when the British and French territories are referred to together, while the French territory is usually referred to as French Cameroon. After independence, the independent nation-state is referred to as Cameroon.

3. National Archives (NA), Kew Gardens, Foreign Office (FO), 371/176876, 22 July 1964, Goodfellow, British Embassy, Yaoundé, to Mellon, West and Central Africa Department.

4. Other historians have emphasized the extrametropolitan dimensions of anticolonial movements in former French territories. See, for example, Klaas van Walraven, "From Tamanrasset: The Struggle of Sawaba and the Algerian Connection, 1957–1966," *Journal of North African Studies* 10, nos. 3–4 (2005): 507–27; Matthew Connelly, *A Diplomatic Revolution: Algeria's Fight for Independence and the Origins of the Post–Cold War Era* (Oxford: Oxford University Press, 2002); Elizabeth Schmidt, *Cold War and Decolonization in Guinea, 1946–1958* (Athens: Ohio University Press, 2007), which historicizes Guinea's shift toward what I describe as an extrametropolitan political practice. For an account of an extrametropolitan alternative available to Muslim Africans under French rule on the eve of decolonization, see Gregory Mann and Baz Lecocq, "Between Empire, *Umma*, and the Muslim Third World: The French Union and African Pilgrims to Mecca, 1946–1958," *Comparative Studies of South Asia, Africa and the Middle East* 27, no. 2 (2007): 361–83.

5. On the role of African anticolonialists in the global nuclear disarmament movement, see Jean Allman, "Nuclear Imperialism and the Pan-African Struggle for Peace and Freedom, Ghana, 1959–1962," *Souls: A Critical Journal of Black Politics, Culture, and Society* 10, no. 2 (2008): 83–102.

6. The growing historiography of postwar human rights is currently polarized between those who argue that African and Asian anticolonial activists rarely, if

ever, invoked human rights as part of their political platforms and those who argue that a commitment to human rights characterized Third World politics beginning in the 1950s. Those in the first group tend to be Europeanists. See Samuel Moyn, *The Last Utopia: Human Rights in History* (Cambridge, MA: Harvard University Press, 2010), esp. chap. 3, "Why Anticolonialism Wasn't a Human Rights Movement"; Jan Eckel, "Human Rights and Decolonization: New Perspectives and Open Questions," *Humanity: An International Journal of Human Rights, Humanitarianism, and Development* 1, no. 1 (2010): 111–35. Those on the other side of the debate are mostly historians of Africa and Asia's decolonization or historians of US civil rights movements. See Vijay Prashad, *The Darker Nations: A People's History of the Third World* (New York: New Press, 2007), 45–46; Roland Burke, *Decolonization and the Evolution of International Human Rights* (Philadelphia: University of Pennsylvania Press, 2010); Fabian Klose, *Menschenrechte im Schatten kolonialer Gewalt: Die Dekolonisierungskriege in Kenia und Algerien, 1945–1962* (Munich: R. Oldenbourg Verlag, 2009); Carol Anderson, "International Conscience, the Cold War, and Apartheid: The NAACP's Alliance with the Reverend Michael Scott for South West Africa's Liberation, 1946–1951," *Journal of World History* 19, no. 3 (2008): 297–325. My own research reveals that as inhabitants of UN Trust Territories, Cameroonian nationalists (leaders as well as rank-and-file members) invoked human rights talk throughout the anticolonial period. See Meredith Terretta, "'We Had Been Fooled into Thinking That the UN Watches over the Entire World': Human Rights, UN Trust Territories, and Africa's Decolonization," *Human Rights Quarterly* 34, no. 2 (2012): 329–60.

7. For the conventional literature on Cameroon's decolonization and the UPC, which relies primarily on French and UN sources, see David Gardinier, *Cameroon: United Nations Challenge to French Policy* (Oxford: Oxford University Press, 1963); Willard R. Johnson, *The Cameroon Federation: Political Integration in a Fragmentary Society* (Princeton: Princeton University Press, 1970); Victor T. Le Vine, *The Cameroons from Mandate to Independence* (Berkeley: University of California Press, 1964); Richard Joseph, *Radical Nationalism in Cameroun: Social Origins of the UPC Rebellion* (Oxford: Oxford University Press, 1977); for a perspective that discusses the UPC as part of the indigenization of post–Second World War political processes, see Janvier Onana, *Le sacre des indigènes évolués: Essai sur la professionalisation politique (l'exemple du Cameroun)* (Paris: Dianoïa, 2004).

8. For a discussion of the political possibilities occasioned by decolonization, see Frederick Cooper, "Possibility and Constraint: African Independence in Historical Perspective," *Journal of African History* 49, no. 2 (2008): 167–96.

9. The studies mentioned in note 7, above, rely almost entirely on French and UN sources. A recent journalistic work by Thomas Deltombe, Manuel Domergue, and Jacob Tatsitsa includes oral testimony, but focuses primarily on French and Cameroonian sources. Deltombe, Domergue, and Tatsitsa, *Kamerun! Une guerre cachée aux origines de la Françafrique, 1948–1971* (Paris: La Découverte, 2011).

10. J.-A. Mbembe, introduction to *Le problème national kamerunais*, by Ruben Um Nyobé (Paris: L'Harmattan, 1984), 18–25.

11. Joey Power suggests that one result of a weakened central coordination is the increased importance of local politics and institutions through which to mobilize. Power, *Political Culture and Nationalism in Malawi: Building Kwacha* (Rochester: University of Rochester Press, 2009), 75.

12. I use *disappearings* in the Argentinean sense. See Marguerite Feitlowitz, *A Lexicon of Terror: Argentina and the Legacies of Torture* (New York: Oxford University Press, 1998). On the repressive tactics implemented by the Ahidjo regime, see Jean-François Bayart, *L'état au Cameroun*, 2nd ed. (Paris: Presses de la fondation nationale des sciences politiques, 1985); Peter Geschiere, "Hegemonic Regimes and Popular Protest: Bayart, Gramsci, and the State in Cameroon," in *State and Local Community in Africa*, eds. Wim van Binsbergen and G. Hesseling (Brussels: Centre d'étude et de documentation africaine, 1986); Michael Schatzberg, "The Metaphors of Father and Family," in *The Political Economy of Cameroon*, ed. Schatzberg and William Zartman (New York: Praeger, 1986). For an assessment of postcolonial Cameroon's political, economic, and sociocultural ties to France see Richard Joseph, ed., *Gaullist Africa: Cameroon under Ahmadu Ahidjo* (1978; repr., Enugu, Nigeria: Fourth Dimension, 2002). See also Nicodemus F. Awasom, "Politics and Constitution-Making in Francophone Cameroon, 1959–1960," *Africa Today* 49, no. 4 (2002): 3–30.

13. For a portrayal of Accra as "the center of gravity for Black internationalism" from 1957 to 1966, see Allman, "Nuclear Imperialism," 85–86. For an account of upécistes' interactions with other nationalists and Pan-Africanists in Accra from 1957 to 1966, see Meredith Terretta, "Cameroonian Nationalists Go Global: From Forest *Maquis* to a Pan-African Accra," *Journal of African History* 51, no. 2 (2010): 189–212.

14. *Glocal* refers to the simultaneity of globalizing and localizing forces in a given setting. See Roland Robertson, "Glocalization: Time-Space and Homogeneity-Heterogeneity," in *Global Modernities*, ed. Mike Featherstone, Scott Lash, and Robertson (Thousand Oaks, CA: Sage, 1995), 25–44.

15. Terretta, "Cameroonian Nationalists."

16. Michelle Ann Stephens, *Black Empire: The Masculine Global Imaginary of Caribbean Intellectuals in the United States, 1914–1962* (Durham: Duke University Press, 2005), intro., chaps. 4, 7.

17. Brent Hayes Edwards, *The Practice of Diaspora: Literature, Translation, and the Rise of Black Internationalism* (Cambridge, MA: Harvard University Press, 2003); Allman, "Nuclear Imperialism."

18. See, for example, Prashad, *Darker Nations*; Christopher J. Lee, ed., *Making a World after Empire: The Bandung Moment and Its Political Afterlives* (Athens: Ohio University Press, 2010); Allman, "Nuclear Imperialism."

19. For a discussion of petitions sent by Cameroonian women nationalists, see Meredith Terretta, "A Miscarriage of Revolution: Cameroonian Women and Nationalism," *Stichproben: Wiener Zeitschrift für kritische Afrikastudien* 12 (2007): 61–90. For a discussion of the methodological and theoretical considerations involved in using petitions as a historical source, see Terretta, *Petitioning for Our Rights*,

Fighting for Our Nation: The History of the Democratic Union of Cameroonian Women, 1949–1960 (Buea: Langaa, RPCIG, 2013).

20. United Nations Trusteeship Council (hereafter UNTC), petition from Mr. Pierre Fayep, 26 November 1956, T/PET.5/998, protesting the arrest of the Chief of Baham on 22 November 1956. See also UNTC, petition from Jeunesse démocratique camerounaise, Local Branch of the Haoussa Quarter, Kimba, 26 November 1956, T/PET.5/991, protesting the arrest of Pierre Nyoum [sic], Chief of Baham, for refusing to "vote in favour of the Loi-Cadre"; UNTC, T/PET.5/1054, petition from Mrs. Gertrude Nguemdjo, Babete-Mbouda, c/o the Central Council of UDEFEC, Kumba, 9 December 1956.

21. UNTC, T/PET.5/1109, petition from Mrs. Passa Tchaffi, Chair of the UDEFEC Committee at Bafang, and Mrs. Agathé Matene, received 20 February 1957.

22. UNTC, T/PET.5/112, petition from Mrs. Chrestine Emachoua concerning the Cameroons under French Administration, Baboucha, 13 December 1956.

23. UNTC, T/PET.5/400, Lydia Dopo to the High Commissioner of the French Republic in the Cameroons, 28 February 1954.

24. In their highlighting of local issues in local terms, the petitions from Cameroon seem to differ from those sent from Tanganyika, at least as portrayed and analyzed by Steven Feierman, who surmises that petitioners affiliated with the Usambara Citizens Union (UCU) omitted issues—such as rainmaking and chiefly authority—from petitions addressed to the Trusteeship Council because they knew that "it was inappropriate and counterproductive to write to London or New York about healing the land," even though this was an issue that Shambaa peasant intellectuals believed to be at the crux of their moral and political economy. Feierman, *Peasant Intellectuals: Anthropology and History in Tanzania* (Madison: Wisconsin University Press, 1990), 210, chap. 8. Another important distinction is that while many petitions from Tanganyika were written in kiSwahili, the petitions from the Cameroons were written in French or English. As such, the words of Cameroonian petitioners who did not speak French or English were translated, most likely by a scribe writing the petition. When reading the petitions for their local content, I have relied heavily on the oral source material gathered over a period of two years in the Bamileke Region, which includes extensive interviews on etymology of certain terms that recurred in UPC or Grassfields political rhetoric (or both) and the historical meaning of these terms. Questions of translation, whether literal or not, are analyzed in further depth in chapter 4 of the present volume.

25. On the notion of political repertoire, or "speech genre," which emerges as the "product of the interaction between interlocutors," see Tzvetan Todorov, *Mikhaïl Bakhtine: Le principe dialogique, suivi de Écrits du cercle de Bakhtine* (Paris: Seuil, 1981), as quoted in Jean-François Bayart, *The Illusion of Cultural Identity*, trans. Steven Rendall et al. (Chicago: University of Chicago Press, 2005), 112.

26. Vernacularization entails the reception and conversion of outside discourses into indigenous language and worldview. It is the process through which the content of outside discourses is reinterpreted and transformed. For a relevant discussion

of vernacularization, see Pier Larson, "'Capacities and Modes of Thinking': Intellectual Engagements and Subaltern Hegemony in the Early History of Malagasy Christianity," *American Historical Review* 102, no. 4 (1997): 970–71, 997–1002.

27. On this point, it is useful to compare the expressions of Cameroonian nationalism with those prevalent among Kikuyu populations in late-colonial Kenya. See Derek Peterson, *Creative Writing: Translation, Bookkeeping, and the Work of Imagination in Colonial Kenya* (Portsmouth, NH: Heinemann, 2004).

28. On the UPC's varied international networks of support, see Terretta, "Human Rights"; Terretta, "Cameroonian Nationalists."

29. Connelly, *Diplomatic Revolution*, 4. Connelly describes "human rights reports, press conferences . . . youth congresses, and fighting over world opinion and international law" as weapons of greater importance for Algerian nationalists than conventional military arms.

30. For accounts of Um Nyobé's time in the underground resistance and the effect his presence had on the populations of the Sanaga-Maritime, see Achille Mbembe, *La naissance du maquis dans le Sud-Cameroun (1920–1960)* (Paris: Karthala, 1996) ; Mbembe, "Domaines de la nuit et autorité onirique dans les maquis du Sud-Cameroun, 1955–1958," *Journal of African History* 31, no. 1 (1991): 89–121. On the underground resistance in the Bamileke and Mungo Regions, see Meredith Terretta, "'God of Peace, God of Independence': Village Nationalism in the *Maquis* of Cameroon, 1957–1971," *Journal of African History* 46, no. 1 (2005): 75–101; Deltombe, Domergue, and Tatsitsa, *Kamerun!* Although existing scholarship has mostly failed to reflect this, UPC militia camps were based on both sides of the Anglo-French boundary. See Joseph Takougang, "The Union des populations du Cameroun and Its Southern Cameroons Connection," *Revue française d'histoire d'outre-mer* 83, no. 319 (1996): 8–24; Terretta, "Cameroonian Nationalists," 199–200.

31. As upécistes called underground resistance militia camps—surely a reference to the French resistance during the Second World War. Algerian revolutionaries also used the term *maquis*.

32. A useful comparison of the blend of local and international discourses and practices used by militias is Mariane C. Ferme and Danny Hoffman, "Hunter Militias and the International Human Rights Discourse in Sierra Leone and Beyond," *Africa Today* 50, no. 4 (2004): 73–95.

33. Prashad, *Darker Nations*, 45–46. See also Christopher J. Lee, "At the Rendezvous of Decolonization: The Final Communiqué of the Asian-African Conference, Bandung, Indonesia, 18–24 April 1955," *Interventions* 11, no. 1 (2009): 81–93, 87.

34. Ralph Austen and Jonathan Derrick, *Middlemen of the Cameroons Rivers: The Duala and Their Hinterland, c. 1600–c. 1960* (Cambridge: Cambridge University Press 1999).

35. Peter J. Yearwood, "'In a Casual Way with a Blue Pencil': British Policy and the Partition of Kamerun, 1914–1919," *Canadian Journal of African Studies* 27, no. 2 (1993): 218–44.

36. See Michael D. Callahan, *Mandates and Empire: The League of Nations and Africa, 1914–1931* (East Sussex: Sussex Academic Press, 1998); Callahan, A

Sacred Trust: The League of Nations and Africa, 1929–1946 (East Sussex: Sussex Academic Press, 2004).

37. On loi-cadre as French imperial reform and on its implementation in French Africa, see Schmidt, *Cold War*, 97–98, 112–14.

38. See Onana, *Sacre*, 172–74, 179–86.

39. Janvier Onana, citing *New Commonwealth*, 30 April 1956, writes that upécistes sent forty-five thousand petitions in 1956 alone. Onana, *Sacre*, 228. This number is confirmed by records of discussions among Trusteeship Council members and personnel of the NGO with consultative status with the UN, the International League of the Rights of Man. See, for example, New York Public Library (hereafter NYPL), International League of the Rights of Man (hereafter ILRM), box 9, file: UN-TC (1954–1956), Frances R. Grant, ILRM Secretary to Dr. Benjamin Cohen, Under-Secretary, UN Trusteeship Council, 10 February 1956.

40. See Meredith Terretta, "Chiefs, Traitors, and Representatives: The Construction of a Political Repertoire in Independence-Era Cameroun," *International Journal of African Historical Studies* 43, no. 2 (2010): 227–58.

41. Petition to UNTC, Marthe Penda, Secretary of the Babimbi branch of UDEFEC, Ngambe, 13 December 1954.

42. Thomas Spear, "Neo-Traditionalism and the Limits of Invention in British Colonial Africa," *Journal of African History* 44, no. 1 (2003): 3–27.

43. Power, *Nationalism in Malawi*; Elizabeth Schmidt, "Top Down or Bottom Up? Nationalist Mobilization Reconsidered, with Special Reference to Guinea (French West Africa)," *American Historical Review* 110, no. 4 (2005): 975–1014.

44. Feierman, *Peasant Intellectuals*, chap. 8; Carol Anderson, "International Conscience, the Cold War, and Apartheid: The NAACP's Alliance with the Reverend Michael Scott for South West Africa's Liberation, 1946–1951," *Journal of World History* 19, no. 3 (2008): 297–325. For more on the Tanganyikan petitions, see Ullrich Lohrmann, *Voices from Tanganyika: Great Britain, the United Nations and the Decolonization of a Trust Territory, 1946–1961* (Berlin: Lit Verlag, 2007).

45. On this point, see David E. Apter, "Ghana's Independence: Triumph and Paradox," *Transition* 98 (2008): 6–23.

46. Chieftaincies varied in population from two hundred to sixty thousand inhabitants (at the beginning of German rule). Ian Fowler and David Zeitlyn, introduction to *African Crossroads: Intersections between History and Anthropology in Cameroon*, eds. Ian Fowler and David Zeitlyn, vol. 2 of *Cameroon Studies*, ed. Shirley Ardener, E. M. Chilver, and Ian Fowler (Providence, Rhode Island: Berghahn Books, 1996), 3.

47. Warnier, *Échanges*; Jean-Pierre Warnier and Paul Nkwi, *Elements for a History of the Western Grassfields* (Yaoundé: Department of Sociology, University of Yaoundé, 1982); Nicolas Argenti, *The Intestines of the State: Youth, Violence, and Belated Histories in the Cameroon Grassfields* (Chicago: University of Chicago Press, 2007).

48. This shared consciousness is one of the criteria of ethnic identity, according to Crawford Young, "Nation, Ethnicity, and Citizenship: Dilemmas of Democracy and Civil Order in Africa," in *Making Nations, Creating Strangers: States*

and Citizenship in Africa, ed. Sara Dorman, Daniel Hammett, and Paul Nugent (Boston: Brill, 2007), 241–64.

49. On the linguistic diversity of the region, see Warnier and Nkwi, *Elements*, 34–35.

50. Dominique Malaquais, *Architecture, pouvoir et dissidence au Cameroun* (Paris: Karthala, 2002), 23–24. See also Jean-Louis Dongmo, *La maîtrise de l'espace agraire*, vol. 1 of *Le dynamisme Bamiléké (Cameroun)* (Yaoundé: Centre d'édition et de production pour l'enseignement et la recherche, University of Yaoundé, 1981), 10. The official French spelling included acute accents: Bamiléké.

51. On the importance of a "long time-span" that includes precolonial history in Africa, see Steven Feierman, "Colonizers, Scholars, and the Creation of Invisible Histories," in *Beyond the Cultural Turn: New Directions in the Study of Society and Culture*, ed. Victoria B. Bonnell and Lynn Hunt (Berkeley: University of California Press, 1999), 182–215; Feierman, "Africa in History: The End of Universal Narratives," in *After Colonialism: Imperial Histories and Postcolonial Displacements*, ed. Gyan Prakash (Princeton: Princeton University Press, 1995), 40–65.

52. Although located in equatorial Africa, Grassfields traditional governance and religious practice more closely resemble structured systems of the early West African forest region states to the west (Yoruba, Benin, Dahomey) than the stateless, segmentary lineage societies (Duala, Beti, Fang) of Cameroon's Equatorial forest region. For an in-depth discussion of Grassfields governance and political culture and history in the late nineteenth century, on the eve of colonial occupation, see chapter 1 of the present volume.

53. Although the message of which Lamin Sanneh historicizes the "translation" is Christianity, his explanation of the ways in which Christianity was "indigenized" is conceptually useful here. Sanneh, *Translating the Message: The Missionary Impact on Culture* (Maryknoll, NY: Orbis, 1989).

54. For the story of one maquisard's journey from the Mungo Region to Baham in order to carry out spiritual sacrifices on the sacred sites of the chieftaincy and of his lineage compound, see Terretta, "'God of Peace.'"

55. This is the other side of the coin in the study of nationalism for Prasenjit Duara, who presents a "'bifurcated' conception of history as an alternative to linear History. . . . Bifurcation points to the process whereby, in transmitting the past, historical narratives and language appropriate dispersed histories according to present needs, thus revealing how the present shapes the past." Duara, *Rescuing History from the Nation: Questioning Narratives of Modern China* (Chicago: University of Chicago Press, 1995), 3.

56. Jane Guyer, "Traditions of Invention in Equatorial Africa," *African Studies Review* 39, no. 3 (1996): 1–28; Spear, "Neo-Traditionalism," 3–27.

57. Ian Fowler and David Zeitlyn, preface to Fowler and Zeitlyn, *African Crossroads*, xviii.

58. Ibid.; Guyer, "Traditions of Invention"; Spear, "Neo-Traditionalism." But see also Argenti, who argues that Grassfields traditions are "interpretations that coexist and struggle for dominance without any one of them necessarily being more correct or legitimate than any other." Argenti, *Intestines of the State*, chap. 2, and cf. 269.

59. Dongmo, *Espace agraire*; Andreas Eckert, "African Rural Entrepreneurs, and Labor in the Cameroon Littoral," *Journal of African History* 40, no. 1 (1999): 109–26.

60. Centre des archives d'outre-mer (hereafter CAOM), Affaires politiques 3335/1, Propagande et action psychologique des groupements extrémistes au Cameroun, n.d. (apparently 1955).

61. On this polarity and the political discourse that emerged surrounding it in Bamileke communities in the late 1950s, see Terretta, "Chiefs, Traitors."

62. The three-legged stool is the symbolic and physical seat of power for Grassfields chiefs and notables.

63. Oral tradition bears evidence of this polarity of negotiation versus confrontation. The founding myths of some chieftaincies, such as Baham, premise "ruse" as the strategy the early founders employed to ensure Baham's sovereignty. See Jean-Marie Tchegho, *L'enracinement culturel en Afrique: Une nécessité pour un développement durable: Le cas des Bamiléké du Cameroun* (Yaoundé: Éditions CLÉ, 2001). Others, such as those from Bandenkop, reference a series of wars. See Daniel Mepin, "Je mourrai face au soleil: Epopée tragique en 15 tableaux" (Bonn: self-published, 1983). Still others, like those of Bandjoun, highlight negotiations between the chieftaincy's founders and the autochthonous populations that preceded the newcomers. See Malaquais, *Architecture*, 78–91.

64. Terretta, "Cameroonian Nationalists." On the "Spirit of Bandung" see Lee, "Asian-African Conference," 87. Lee writes, "One momentous result of the conference was the *feeling* of political possibility presented through this public occasion of 'Third World' solidarity, what eventually was referred to as 'the Spirit of Bandung.'"

65. Ras T. Makonnen, *Pan-Africanism from Within*, ed. Kenneth King (Nairobi: Oxford University Press, 1973), 214–15.

66. Emmanuel Hansen, "Frantz Fanon: Portrait of a Revolutionary Intellectual," *Transition* 46 (1974): 25–36; Frantz Fanon, *Toward the African Revolution: Political Essays*, trans. Haakon Chevalier (1967; repr., New York: Grove Press, 1988), 154–55.

67. Centre historique des archives nationales (CHAN), Section du XXe siècle, Foccart papers, Fonds publics 2092, Ministère des affaires étrangères, Directeur d'Afrique-Levant, 15 December 1958.

68. Frantz Fanon, *The Wretched of the Earth*, trans. Richard Philcox (New York: Grove Press, 2004), 198.

69. National Archives (hereafter NA), Colonial Office (hereafter CO) 554/2367, Governor General of Nigeria to the Secretary of State for the Colonies, 30 September 1960.

70. Terence Ranger, "Nationalist Historiography, Patriotic History, and the History of Nation: the Struggle over the Past in Zimbabwe," *Journal of Southern African Studies* 30, no. 2 (2004): 215–34, 217.

71. Ibid.

72. Ibid.

73. See Jean-Paul Bayémi, *L'effort camerounais, ou, la tentation d'une presse libre* (Paris: L'Harmattan, 1989), 9–10; Richard Bjornson, *The African Quest for Freedom*

and Identity: Cameroonian Writing and the National Experience (Bloomington: Indiana University Press, 1991), 136–37, 154–55, chap. 17; on the exile of Abel Eyinga and the banning of books by Mongo Beti, see CHAN, Section du XXe siècle, Foccart papers, Fonds privés 153 et 318. See also Abel Eyinga, "Tortures au Cameroun," *Le monde*, 13 June 1972; his exchanges with Fernand Oyono, *Le monde*, 27 May 1972.

74. See Achille Mbembe, "Ecrire l'Afrique à partir d'une faille," *Politique africaine* 51 (1993): 69–97.

75. Mbembe, *Naissance* ; Mbembe, "Pouvoir des morts, language des vivants," in Bayart, Mbembe, and Toulabor, *Politique par le bas*, 183–229; Mbembe, "Domaines"; Elizabeth Schmidt, "Anticolonial Nationalism in French West Africa: What Made Guinea Unique?" *African Studies Review* 52, no. 2 (2009): 1–34; Klaas van Walraven, "Decolonization by Referendum: The Anomaly of Niger and the Fall of Sawaba, 1958–1959," *Journal of African History* 50, no. 2 (2009): 269–92; Walraven, "From Tamanrasset"; David Lan, *Guns and Rain: Guerillas and Spirit Mediums in Zimbabwe* (Berkeley: University of California Press, 1985); Feierman, *Peasant Intellectuals*; Bruce Berman and John Lonsdale, *Unhappy Valley: Conflict in Kenya and Africa*, 2 vols. (Athens: Ohio University Press, 1992); Peterson, *Creative Writing*.

76. This approach draws on revisionist histories of the civil rights movement that present the movement as being composed of locally entrenched battles that nevertheless were a part of a growing black internationalist thought, rather than a national movement. See Brenda Gayle Plummer, *Rising Wind: Black Americans and US Foreign Affairs, 1935–1960* (Chapel Hill: University of North Carolina Press, 1996); Penny Von Eschen, *Race against Empire: Black Americans and Anticolonialism* (Ithaca: Cornell University Press, 1997); Carol Anderson, *Eyes Off the Prize: The United Nations and the African American Struggle for Human Rights, 1944–1955* (Cambridge: Cambridge University Press, 2003); Kevin K. Gaines, *American Africans in Ghana: Black Expatriates and the Civil Rights Era* (Chapel Hill: University of North Carolina Press, 2006).

77. In recent years, a few histories of African nationalism and decolonization have straddled the colonial-postcolonial divide. See, for example, Power, *Nationalism in Malawi*.

78. Luc Sindjoun, "L'opposition au Cameroun, un nouveau jeu politique parlementaire," introduction to *Comment peut-on être opposant au Cameroun? Politique parlementaire et politique autoritaire*, ed. Sindjoun (Dakar: Codesria, 2004), 4.

79. My approach to field research resembles the "ethnographic immersion" method described in Michael G. Schatzberg, "Seeing the Invisible, Hearing Silence, Thinking the Unthinkable: The Advantages of Ethnographic Immersion" (paper presented at the 104th Annual Meeting of the American Political Science Association, Boston, August 28–31, 2008).

80. On this point, see Ann Stoler, *Along the Archival Grain: Epistemic Anxieties and Colonial Common Sense* (Princeton: Princeton University Press, 2009).

81. Many former upécistes or their offspring have preserved caches of UPC records, some of which have been released in published form. The first of these was of course the collection of Ruben Um Nyobé's writings edited and prefaced by J. A. Mbembe in 1984: Um Nyobé, *Problème national*. But see also Abraham Sighoko Fossi, *Discours*

politiques (Paris: L'Harmattan, 2007); Sighoko Fossi, *Papa s'appelait Fossi Jacob: Itinéraire d'un martyr de l'indépendance du Cameroun* (Paris: L'Harmattan, 2011).

82. See, for example, François Fotso, *La lutte nationaliste au Cameroun, 1940–1971* (Paris: L'Harmattan, 2010).

CHAPTER 1: GOD, LAND, JUSTICE, AND POLITICAL SOVEREIGNTY IN GRASSFIELDS GOVERNANCE

1. I am grateful to Jean-Bernard Pogo and other elder members of the Association of Baham Elites in Nkongsamba for their explanations of the term *gung*.

2. "District" is not an official administrative designation, but here refers to the ways in which chieftaincies were divided into smaller subunits, historically, even prior to colonization.

3. Michael Schatzberg, *Political Legitimacy in Middle Africa: Father, Family, Food* (Bloomington: Indiana University Press, 2001), 1.

4. The myths of origin in Grassfields polities "cannot be seen as constituting an oral history or an oral tradition in any straightforward sense." See Nicolas Argenti, *The Intestines of the State: Youth, Violence, and Belated Histories in the Cameroon Grassfields* (Chicago: University of Chicago Press, 2007), 34.

5. Ibid., 45; Ralph A. Austen and Jonathan Derrick, *Middlemen of the Cameroon Rivers: The Duala and Their Hinterland, c. 1600–1960* (Cambridge: Cambridge University Press, 1999), 23–25.

6. Jean-Pierre Warnier, "The Grassfields of Cameroon: Ancient Center or Recent Periphery?" *Africa Today* 58, no. 3 (2012): 58–72. To compare with Warnier's previous theory of Grassfields settlement, see Warnier, "Histoire du peuplement et genèse des paysages dans l'ouest camerounais," *Journal of African History* 25, no. 4 (1984): 395–410.

7. Argenti makes this estimate, which is much higher than any previous study. Argenti, *Intestines*, 55. But the literature on Grassfields involvement in the slave trades is scant and warrants further exploration. See also Austen and Derrick, *Middlemen*; Elizabeth M. Chilver, "Nineteenth-Century Trade in the Bamenda Grassfields," *Afrika und Übersee* 45, no. 4 (1961): 233–58; Bongfen Chem-Langhëë, "Slavery and Slave Marketing in Nso' in the Nineteenth Century," *Paideuma* 41 (1995): 177–90; Jean-Pierre Warnier, "Slave-Trading without Slave-Raiding in Cameroon," *Paideuma* 41 (1995): 251–72.

8. Argenti, *Intestines*, chap. 2.

9. Ibid., 45.

10. Joseph Kiegaing, "Les sites sacrés chez les Baham (Ouest-Cameroun)" (master's thesis, University of Yaoundé I, 2002), 40.

11. See Argenti, *Intestines*, chap. 2.

12. Crawford Young, "Nation, Ethnicity, and Citizenship: Dilemmas of Democracy and Civil Order in Africa," in *Making Nations, Creating Strangers: States and Citizenship in Africa*, ed. Sara Dorman, Daniel Hammett, and Paul Nugent (Boston: Brill, 2007), 241–64.

13. On the term Bamileke as a German soldier's mispronunciation of the phrase "Mba Lékéo" (lit., people of the valley), see Dominique Malaquais, *Architecture*,

pouvoir et dissidence au Cameroun (Paris: Karthala, 2002), 23–24. See also Jean-Louis Dongmo, *La maîtrise de l'espace agraire*, vol. 1 of *Le dynamisme Bamiléké (Cameroun)* (Yaoundé: Centre d'édition et de production pour l'enseignement et la recherche, University of Yaoundé, 1981), 10.

14. I use the term *mystical technologies* because it is the term of choice of Bamileke French speakers to describe both the fo's engagement with the unseen world and evildoers' acts, such as poisoning, night flying, and vampirism. Francophone Bamileke also speak of "barks" and "medicines" when discussing ways in which people manipulate the mystical. The term *witchcraft* (*sorcellerie*) is rarely, if ever, used.

15. This account is from Louis Tissot Nguiffo *dit* Wafeu Kam Tameu, *Contributions à l'histoire du royaume Baham* (Yaoundé: Éditions Traditions Vivantes, 1995).

16. I am grateful to Jean-Bernard Pogo and other elder members of the Association of Baham Elites of Nkongsamba for their explanations of the term *lepue*.

17. Elizabeth M. Chilver, "Paramountcy and Protection in the Cameroons: The Bali and the Germans, 1889–1913," in *Britain and Germany in Africa: Imperial Rivalry and Colonial Rule*, ed. Prosser Gifford and Wm. Roger Louis (New Haven: Yale University Press, 1967), 479–511; Eugen Zintgraff, *Nord-Kamerun. Schilderung der im Auftrage des Auswärtigen Amtes zur Erschliessung des nördlichen Hinterlandes von Kamerun während der Jahre 1886–1892 unternommenen Reisen* (Berlin: Gebrüder Paetel, 1895).

18. Enock Katté Kwayeb, *Les institutions de droit public du pays Bamiléké, Cameroun* (Paris: Librairie générale de droit et de jurisprudence, 1960), 16.

19. Jean-Joseph Chendjou, "Les Bamiléké de l'Ouest Cameroun; Pouvoirs, économie et société: 1850–1916: La situation avant et après l'accentuation des influences européennes" (doctoral thesis, University of Paris I, 1986).

20. Jean-Bernard Pogo, *dit* Defotimsa, pers. comm.

21. Today, the initiation period lasts only nine weeks. For a monograph on contemporary succession and the initiation rites of Grassfields mfo, see Jean Tatsimo, *La place du "la'kem" chez les Bamiléké: Le cas des Nda'a* (Douala: Éditions Saint-François, 1993). For a historical perspective, see Chendjou, "Bamiléké," 115–31; for Bandjoun and Batie, see Jean Hurault, *La structure sociale des Bamiléké* (Paris: Mouton, 1962): 59–70. For a firsthand account by a fo's wife in Bangangte, see Claude Njiké-Bergeret, *Ma passion africaine* (Paris: Éditions Jean-Claude Lattès, 1997). Missionary accounts from the 1920s and 1930s are available in the series *Récits missionnaires illustrés*, Société des missions évangéliques de Paris (SMEP) (Paris, 1921–35). See accounts by Franck Christol, Josette Debarge, Alice and Henri Nicod, and others.

22. Chendjou, "Bamiléké," 106–25, 200–204. For the contemporary composition of kamveu in Baham, see Nguiffo, *Contributions*, 57–58.

23. Kam Toukam, intrvw., Medjo, Baham, 23 August 2002.

24. Te Dzusonke, intrvw., Hiala, Baham, April 2003.

25. Te Dzusonke, intrvw.; Fo Feze Ngandjong Marcel, intrvw., Bandenkop, November 2002.

26. Argenti, *Intestines*, chap. 2.

27. Malaquais, *Architecture*, 64–67.

28. Ibid.

29. The fo granted the wabo title in cases of exceptional social success after years (sometimes generations) of loyal service. In return for the title, the wabo presented seven wives to the fo. Hurault, *Structure sociale*, 72, 75.

30. *Fonte* literally means a fo that pledges loyalty to another, therefore, a lesser fo. Chendjou, "Bamiléké," 57.

31. Mékeu Tchuenden, intrvw., Ngougoua, Baham, 12 November 2002.

32. For political scientist Michael Schatzberg, "political thinkability" defines the moral matrix of legitimate governance in a polity. Schatzberg, *Political Legitimacy in Middle Africa: Father, Family, Food* (Bloomington: Indiana University Press, 2001), chap. 1.

33. Hurault, *Structure sociale*, 121; Malaquais, *Architecture*, 86–89.

34. Chendjou, "Bamiléké," 202.

35. See Michael Rowlands and Jean-Pierre Warnier, "Magical Iron Technology in the Cameroon Grassfields," in *African Material Culture*, ed. Mary Jo Arnoldi, Christraud Geary, and Kris Hardin (Bloomington: Indiana University Press, 1996), 51–72; Malaquais, *Architecture*, 86–89; Louis Perrois and Jean-Paul Notué, *Rois et sculpteurs de l'ouest Cameroun: La panthère et la mygale* (Paris: Karthala, 1997), 73.

36. Rowlands and Warnier, "Magical Iron Technology."

37. Pamela Feldman-Savelsberg, *Plundered Kitchens, Empty Wombs: Threatened Reproduction and Identity in the Cameroon Grassfields* (Ann Arbor: University of Michigan Press, 1999). Spider divination—using a spider's tracks to divine the future—is a spiritual technology common throughout the Grassfields region. See David Zeitlyn, "Spiders in and out of Court, or, 'The Long Legs of the Law: Styles of Spider Divination in Their Sociological Contexts," *Africa: Journal of the International African Institute* 63, no. 2 (1993): 219-40.

38. Perrois and Notué, *Rois et sculpteurs*, 104–10; Malaquais, *Architecture*, 89–91.

39. Fo Marcel Feze, intrvw., Bandenkop, November 2002; emphasis in original.

40. On this point, see Kwayeb, *Institutions*, 25–26.

41. Kiegaing, "Sites sacrés," 62. See also the play narrating the settlement of Bandenkop authored by Daniel Mepin, *Je mourrai face au soleil* (unpublished manuscript, 1983).

42. Kwayeb, *Institutions*, 82–84.

43. Kiegaing, "Sites sacrés," 95.

44. See conclusion to this volume.

45. For descriptions of various trials, see Chendjou, "Bamiléké," 150–52; Kwayeb, *Institutions*, 81–83.

46. Kwayeb, *Institutions*, 81. Today, the tortoise truth-telling ceremony is no longer used, since, according to my informant, people began using magic to influence the tortoise. Te Dzusonke, intrvw., Hiala, Baham, April 2003.

47. Chendjou, "Bamiléké," 147–49.

48. Ibid., 147.

49. Chendjou, "Bamiléké," 74–77.
50. Te Dzusonke, intrvw., Hiala, Baham, April 2003; Chendjou, "Bamiléké," 77.
51. Malaquais, *Architecture*, 55–61; Kiegaing, "Sites sacrés," 72, 75, 82.
52. The yam tree also designates the borders and limits of compounds granted by the fo or the notable. The first thing the new owner did upon receiving his grant, was to plant the yam on each side of his property. Interview with Te Dzusonke, intrvw., Hiala, Baham, April 2003.
53. Chendjou, "Bamiléké," 77–78, 228.
54. For a useful explanation of the matrilocal spatial arrangement in the polygynous household of a Bamileke notable, see Pamela Feldman-Savelsberg, "Cooking Inside: Kinship and Gender in Bangangté Idioms of Marriage and Procreation," *American Ethnologist* 22, no. 3 (1995): 483–501.
55. Chendjou, "Bamiléké," 147.
56. See chapter 5 of this volume.
57. Kiegaing, "Sites sacrés," 67.
58. Ibid., 65.
59. Ibid., 67.
60. Ibid.
61. Meredith Terretta, "'God of Peace, God of Independence': Village Nationalism in the *Maquis* of Cameroon, 1957–1971," *Journal of African History* 46, no. 1 (2005): 75–101.
62. Sandra Greene provides a history of the ways in which sacred sites and burial sites used by the Anlo changed from the nineteenth to the twentieth centuries. Greene, *Sacred Sites and the Colonial Encounter: A History of Meaning and Memory in Ghana* (Bloomington: Indiana University Press, 2002), 9.
63. Chilver, "Paramountcy"; Zintgraff, *Nord-Kamerun*.
64. Marc Michel, "Les plantations allemandes du Mont Cameroun, 1885–1914," *Revue française d'histoire d'outre-mer* 57 (1970): 183–213; Andreas Eckert, "African Rural Entrepreneurs, and Labor in the Cameroon Littoral," *Journal of African History* 40, no. 1 (1999): 109–26.
65. Peter J. Yearwood, "'In a Casual Way with a Blue Pencil': British Policy and the Partition of Kamerun, 1914–1919," *Canadian Journal of African Studies* 27, no. 2 (1993): 218–44.
66. As opposed to the "indirect rule" theorized and applied by Sir Frederick Lugard in the northern British territory of the Cameroons. Lugard, *The Dual Mandate in British Tropical Africa* (Edinburgh: W. Blackwood and Sons, 1922). For Governor General Van Vollenhoven's circular, see "Circulaire du gouverneur général Van Vollenhoven, 15 août 1917," *JO AOF*, 1917, 467, as quoted in Jacques Lombard, *Autorités traditionnelles et pouvoirs européens en Afrique noire: Le déclin d'une aristocratie sous le régime colonial* (Paris: Librairie Armand Colin, 1967), 128.
67. This document, filed in CAOM, Agefom 956/3199, is entitled "À travers la forêt-vierge et la brousse des Camerouns." The document is translated from a 1914 German account of the entire German period, dealing with the forest and the interior (Yaoundé), Duala, Bakweris, Bakokos, Bassas, anthropophages, evil spirits, and fetishes. The translation is written out in manuscript, but unfortunately the

translation is not dated. It appears to be quite early in the mandate period, probably not after 1920.

68. Ibid.

69. Argenti, *Intestines*, 98.

70. CAOM, série géographique, carton 30/260, "Cameroun: La situation politique en 1920." This report was undoubtedly addressed to the League of Nations.

71. France, *Rapport au Ministère des Colonies sur l'Administration des Territoires occupés du Cameroun pendant l'année 1927* (Paris: Imprimerie générale LaHure, 1928), 24.

72. Janvier Onana, *Le sacre des indigènes évolués: Essai sur la professionalisation politique (l'exemple du Cameroun)* (Paris: Dianoïa, 2004), 42.

73. Oral informants suggest that Pouokam I attacked Bayangam to thwart a plot mounted against him by members of his own family who had their sights on the position of fo. Kouomou, intrvw., Batousou'o, Baham, 14 April 2003. Kouomou is a descendant of Pouokam I's dynasty.

74. Olivier Tavernier, "Histoire de la chefferie Baham de ses origines à nos jours" (master's thesis, University of Aix-en-Provence, 1995), 31–34.

75. Ibid. Tavernier suggests that the French favored Kamwa for the position of fo. A majority of my informants in Baham in 2002 and 2003 stated that Kamwa was not the legitimate successor of Pouokam I and furthermore that Kamwa orchestrated Pouokam's imprisonment and used his proximity to the French administration to become fo. If this were the case, both of Kamwa's sons, who occupied the position of fo in the 1950s, would have been illegitimate as rulers by default. One of the opinions on succession held by Baham populations today is that to reestablish legitimacy in gung, the line should be retraced to Pouokam I. Interviews with Kam Tou Kam, Medjo, Baham, 23 August 2002; Jean-Bernard Pogo *dit* Defotimsa (Nkongsamba); André Tchuenkam, La'agweu, Baham, 12 November 2002.

76. The treasury of the tsa was quite wealthy during the German period. In response to the chief of Bali's request for tribute to protect Bangwa from the "beasts with red skin that eat people everywhere they go," Nono Tchoutouo sent gunpowder and a total of 230 girls, 84 tusks of ivory, 800 goats, 9 bolts of indigo-dyed woven cloth, and 24 beaded necklaces. In 1931, realizing that the chief of Bali had duped him, since the white people had come and had not eaten anyone, Tchoutouo asked for these things back. Debarge, "Mission médicale."

77. Ibid.

78. Ibid.

79. Ibid.

80. Ibid.

81. CAOM, Agence économique (hereafter AGEFOM) 956/3199, "Coutumes rituelles," n.d., apparently around 1920.

82. Ibid.

83. See, for example, France, Ministère des Colonies, *Rapport annuel du Cameroun 1931* (Paris: Imprimerie générale LaHure, 1932), 72. The Bamileke Region is described as "a fetishistic region."

84. Circulaires de M. le gouverneur général J. Brévié sur la politique et l'administration indigène en AOF, Gorée, 1935 (Circulaires des 27 et 28 September 1932), as quoted in Lombard, *Autorités traditionnelles*, 130–31.

85. France, Ministère des Colonies, *Rapport annuel du Cameroun 1932* (Paris: Imprimerie générale LaHure, 1933), 9.

86. France: Ministère des Colonies, *Rapport annuel du Cameroun, 1933* (Paris: Imprimerie générale LaHure, 1934), Arrêté fixant le statut des chefs indigènes, 4 February 1933, 147. See also Onana, *Sacre*, 41–53.

87. Marc-Olivier Laurent, "Pouvoir et société dans le pays Bamiléké: La chefferie traditionnelle face au changement social dans la région de Banka-Bafang" (doctoral thesis, University of Paris V, René Descartes, 1981), 115.

88. *Rapport annuel du Cameroun 1933*, 155–56, Arrêté portant organization au Cameroun d'Écoles de préparation des futurs chefs.

89. *Rapport annuel du Cameroun, 1932*, 72. See also Onana, *Sacre*, 52.

90. This strategy was officially suggested for the Grassfields in 1934: "It has come to me . . . that it is more and more desirable to partially relieve the chiefs of tax collection. . . . It is therefore useful to use the notables and quarterheads as auxiliaries to facilitate the chief's collection of taxes." Archives préfecturales de Dschang (hereafter APD), Chef de la Région, Dschang, to Messieurs les Chefs de subdivision de Dschang, Bafang, Bafoussam, Foumban, Banganté, Dschang, Lettre-circulaire, 24 November 1934, unfiled document.

91. CAOM, Agefom 912/2728, rapport de tournée, 9–25 October 1934, M. Gentil Robert, Adjoint de 2ᵉ classe des services civiles, Chef de subdivision de Bafoussam.

92. See introduction to this volume.

93. Rapport de tournée, 9–25 October 1934, M. Gentil Robert.

94. Ibid.

95. CAOM, AGEFOM 912/2728, rapport de tournée de M. Henry Geli, Adjoint des services civils, Adjoint au chef de subdivision de Bafoussam, 9–18 March 1935; rapport de tournée de M. Raynaud, 8–17 May 1935, Dschang.

96. CAOM, AGEFOM 912/2728, rapport de tournée de M. Henry Geli, Adjoint des services civils, Adjoint au chef de subdivision de Bafoussam, 9–18 March 1935; rapport de tournée de M. Raynaud, 8–17 May 1935, Dschang. Settlers would either return to their villages of origin or move on to the right bank. In 1934 some fifty people of Baham II went to live on the right bank, and Gentil had to ask Fo Kamwa to get them to move back to the left bank.

97. It peaked at 3,740 migrants in 1935 and tapered off to 1,671 by 1957. See Dongmo, *Espace agraire*, 357.

98. Rapport de tournée, 9–25 October 1934, M. Gentil Robert.

99. Forty out of 70 Baham families had fled from Baham II by 1940. In Bayangam II, only 35 men remained out of 100 families settled there in 1935. By 1940, 28 families had left Bamendjou II, 100 families had left Batoufam II, and 155 from Bamougoum II had either left or died of malaria. This constituted about 50 percent of the population in these areas in 1934 and 1935. For a more in-depth analysis of the Noun settlement project, see E. Rohde, "'Projet Rive Gauche du Noun': The Miscarriage of Bamiléké Settlement Projects under French Administration in

Bamoun (Cameroon)," in *Land Law and Land Ownership in Africa: Case Studies from Colonial and Contemporary Cameroon and Tanzania*, ed. Robert Debusmann and Stefan Arnold (Bayreuth: Bayreuth African Studies, 1996), 203–21.

100. As suggested by Laurent, "Pouvoir et société," 107. Laurent's thesis is that the French administration's involvement in chieftaincy government merely accelerated modifications already underway within Bamileke society by reinforcing the chief's tendency toward autocracy. Laurent thus reads the struggle for independence in the Bamileke Region in the 1950s as a popular rejection of chiefly despotism expressed as conflicts over land ownership and galvanized by the economic rise and fall of a coffee economy. His position mirrors the progressive French administrative view of the 1950s, as expressed in the monthly newspaper *Le Bamiléké*.

101. Circulaire Eboué, as quoted in Laurent, "Pouvoir et société," 114–15.

102. Félix Eboué, *La nouvelle politique indigène pour l'AEF* (Paris: La France des cinq parties du monde, 1945), 15, as quoted in Lombard, *Autorités traditionnelles*, 133.

103. Eboué seems to have been aware of this issue as early as 1918, when he wrote a French-Sango-Banda-Baya-Mandjia dictionary based on eight years of research in Oubangui-Chari. In it he gives two Sango words for the French word *chef*: *bia* and *makũdji*. *Bia*, or *gbia* as it has been transcribed in other dictionaries, refers to a precolonial form of leadership that was less centralized and less geographically focused, while *makũdji*, *mokonji*, or *mokonzi* is a word that was taken from Lingala and used specifically to describe leaders imposed by the French. See Luc Bouquiaux et al., *Dictionnaire sango-français* (Paris: Société d'études linguistiques et anthropologiques de France, 1978), 216; Félix Eboué, *Langues sango, banda, baya, mandjia: Notes grammaticales, mots groupés d'après le sens, phrase usualles, vocabulaire* (Paris: Larose, 1918), 72. I am grateful to Philip Janzen for bringing these translations to my attention.

104. Laurent, "Pouvoir et société," 116.

105. APD, 3e partie, Code Pénal Coutumier, Bafang, 30 Avril 1937, Chef de subdivision, André Raynaud. Unfortunately, I recovered only the third part of the document.

106. R. P. Albert, SCJ, Supérieur de la maison du Sacré-Coeur, Montréal, *Au Cameroun français: Bandjoun* (Montréal: Les éditions de l'arbre, 1943), 74.

107. On this point, see similar arguments made for French Equatorial Africa in Florence Bernault, "Body, Power and Sacrifice in Equatorial Africa," *Journal of African History* 47, no. 2 (2006): 207–39.

108. Argenti, *Intestines*, chap. 4.

109. Jean-Pierre Warnier, *L'esprit d'entreprise au Cameroun* (Paris: Karthala, 1993), 203.

110. Argenti, *Intestines*, chap. 6; Warnier, *Esprit d'entreprise*, 197–221.

111. Argenti, *Intestines*, 46–50; Malaquais, "Building in the Name of God: Architecture, Resistance and the Christian Faith in the Bamileke Highlands of Western Cameroon," *African Studies Review* 42, no. 1 (1999): 48–78. Christian missionization in the Grassfields region did not have a standardizing or homogenizing effect on Grassfields identity comparable to that seen elsewhere in nineteenth- and early-twentieth-century sub-Saharan Africa. See, for example, J. D. Y. Peel, *Religious*

Encounter and the Making of the Yoruba (Bloomington: Indiana University Press, 2000, esp. chap. 10). For one thing, the Basel Mission, the only Christian mission established in the Grassfields during the German period, withdrew during the First World War, and all mission schools had closed by 1915. Not until 1918 did the SMEP move into the region to begin missionization almost from scratch. Although the Germans, and later the British and French, relied on those educated in mission schools as interpreters in the Grassfields region, these literate Grassfielders were exceptional. Furthermore, regional linguistic diversity was such that European missionaries did not work in indigenous languages in the Grassfields. The Basel Mission's short-lived attempt to use the Bali language to spread Protestant teachings met with resistance on the part of Grassfields chiefs. Malaquais, "Building," 56. Grassfields chiefs, insofar as they accepted mission schools and churches at all, did so with the same spirit of autonomy as they governed their chieftaincies. In other words, Christianity cannot be viewed as instigator of a Grassfields or Bamileke "cultural nationalism," nor was missionization uniform or sustained enough to play a foundational role in ethnogenesis.

112. France, Rapport au ministère des colonies sur l'administration des territoires occupés du Cameroun pendant l'année 1921; *Rapport annuel du Cameroun, 1931,* 2; Onana, *Sacre,* 67.

113. Malaquais, "Building." In stark contrast to dwindling missions in the Bamileke Region, during the interwar period in the rest of southern French Cameroon, particularly the Sanaga-Maritime and around Yaoundé, enrollment in mission schools expanded dramatically, from 3,000 students in 1921 to 92,491 in 1938. Richard Bjornson, *The African Quest for Freedom and Identity: Cameroonian Writing and the National Experience* (Bloomington: Indiana University Press, 1991), 25.

114. Malaquais, "Building," 69.

115. Ibid., 62.

116. See, for example, Philippe Laburthe-Tolra, *Les seigneurs de la forêt: Essai sur le passé historique, l'organisation sociale et les normes éthiques des anciens Béti du Cameroun* (Paris: Publications de la Sorbonne, 1981); Jan Vansina, *Paths in the Rainforests: Toward a History of Political Tradition in Equatorial Africa* (Madison: University of Wisconsin Press, 1990).

117. On this point, see Onana, *Sacre,* 42.

CHAPTER 2: "BAMILEKE STRANGERS" MAKE THE MUNGO RIVER VALLEY THEIR HOME

1. Richard Joseph, *Radical Nationalism in Cameroun: Social Origins of the UPC Rebellion* (Oxford: Clarendon Press, 1977), 8; Andreas Eckert, "African Rural Entrepreneurs and Labor in the Cameroon Littoral," *Journal of African History* 40, no. 1 (1999): 109–26.

2. Joseph, *Radical Nationalism,* 142.

3. Ibid., 147.

4. For a list of the populations indigenous to the Mungo, their oral histories, and sociopolitical organization, see also Jean-Philippe Guiffo, *Nkongsamba: Mon beau village* (Yaoundé: Éditions de l'Essoah, 2001), 10–18.

5. Jean-Louis Dongmo, *La maîtrise de l'espace agraire*, vol. 1 of *Le dynamisme Bamiléké (Cameroun)* (Yaoundé: Centre d'édition et de production pour l'enseignement et la recherche, University of Yaoundé, 1981), 231.

6. Ibid., 118.

7. These discriminatory policies adversely affected African planters' commercial banana exports, as discussed below. Joseph, *Radical Nationalism*, 120–21.

8. Ibid., 142, 144, 120–21.

9. Ibid., 53.

10. See, for example, Jean-Claude Barbier, Jacques Champaud, and Francis Gendreau, *Migrations et développement: La région du Moungo au Cameroun* (Paris: ORSTOM, 1983).

11. Joseph, *Radical Nationalism*, 145.

12. Ibid., 145.

13. Ibid., 51–52. Article 4 of the League of Nations Mandate agreement for French Cameroon forbade all forced labor except for "essential public works and services." On French implementation and abuses of the *prestation* system, which was essentially a labor tax that could be paid in labor or in currency contra the terms of the League of Nations Mandate, see Léon Kaptué, *Cameroun: Travail et main-d'oeuvre au Cameroun sous régime français, 1916–1952* (Paris: L'Harmattan, 1986), 161–65. On conscripted labor and the French administration's justification thereof, see ibid., 166–74.

14. Joseph, *Radical Nationalism*, 50, 123.

15. Ibid., 123.

16. Ibid., 51–52.

17. Ibid., 122, 145.

18. Ibid., 145.

19. See Janvier Onana, *Le sacre des indigènes évolués: Essai sur la professionalisation politique (l'exemple du Cameroun)* (Paris: Dianoïa, 2004), 298.

20. Throughout the German period, the Mungo Region hosted vast commercial plantations. The greatest initial challenge in land administration faced by the French was the redistribution of the large concessionary plots abandoned by German companies after the conquest of Cameroon by the Anglo-French forces in the First World War. These sequestered German lands were not dealt with definitively until 1927. See Marc Michel, "Les plantations allemandes du mont Cameroun," *Revue française d'histoire d'outre-mer* 57 (1970): 183–213; CAOM, AGEFOM 970/3322, 1927.

21. Dongmo, *Espace agraire*, 116–29.

22. Joseph, *Radical Nationalism*, 51.

23. Ibid.

24. Ibid.

25. François Nkankeu, "Occupation du sol et conflits fonciers sur les cendres volcaniques du Moungo (Cameroun)," *Canadian Journal of Regional Science* 31, no. 2 (2008): 307–24, 313. See also Joseph, *Radical Nationalism*, 123, 143; Jacques Binet, "Droit foncier coutumier au Cameroun," *Monde non-chrétien*, no. 18 (1951).

26. Bamileke immigrants to the Mungo seemed to be reenacting the practice of settlement archived in the founding myths of many Grassfields chieftaincies, which recounted how founding hunters provided meat to autochthons inhabiting the lands they settled. See Dongmo, *Espace agraire*, 58–63; Nkankeu, "Occupation du sol," 313–14. Today, oral accounts of Bamileke settlement emphasize the early migrants' cleverness and ruse. Mercedes Yougaing, intrvw., Nkongsamba, 13 March 2002.

27. Ralph A. Austen, "The Metamorphoses of Middlemen: The Duala, Europeans, and the Cameroon Hinterland, ca. 1800–ca. 1960," *International Journal of African Historical Studies* 16, no. 1 (1983): 1–24.

28. Nkankeu, "Occupation du sol," 313.

29. Thomas Fokoueng, intrvw., Nkongsamba, 2002.

30. Despite an abundance of oral and performative material in the region, there is little or no scholarly literature pertaining to Mungo spiritual technologies. For one of the only studies in the academic tradition, see A. Lam, "Plaidoyer pour une culture en déclin: Le cas du peuple Ngoh/Ngoe dans la région des monts Manengouba, Koupé, et Nlonako, Cameroun" (unpublished manuscript, 1995).

31. See the previous chapter.

32. The parallels with new settlement patterns and socioeconomic patterns introduced by the colonial economy in Yoruba communities are striking. See Sara Berry, *Fathers Work for Their Sons: Accumulation, Mobility, and Class Formation in an Extended Yorùbá Community* (Berkeley: University of California Press, 1985). Similarly, parallels may be drawn between Bamileke settlement of the Mungo Region and Yoruba settlement of various parts of Nigeria, particularly the Western Province, during a similar period. Like Bamileke emigrants, Yoruba railway workers preserved what Lisa A. Lindsay describes as "hometown connections" in place, ensuring continued links with extended family and participation in home chieftaincies. Lindsay, *Working with Gender: Wage Labor and Social Change in Southwestern Nigeria* (Portsmouth, NH: Heinemann, 2003), esp. chap. 6.

33. Bernard Nkuissi, "Nkongsamba. Les années obscures de la fondation de 1898 à 1923. Essai de monographie urbaine" (DES memoir, University of Lille, 1967).

34. Dongmo, *Espace agraire*, 231.

35. Hermine Nicole Jombe Essome, "Le Mungo et l'agitation syndicalo-politique, 1944–1958" (master's thesis, École normale supérieure, Yaoundé, 1989), 53.

36. CAOM, AGEFOM, 970/3318, le Commissaire de la République to M. le Directeur de l'Agence économique des territoires africains sous mandat, 2 May 1928.

37. France, Ministère des Colonies, *Rapport annuel du Cameroun, 1933* (Paris: Imprimerie générale LaHure, 1934), 108–9.

38. Ibid.

39. Ibid.

40. CAOM, AGEFOM 970/3316, Ministre des colonies, Directeur des affaires economiques, Paris, 17 October 1928.

41. CAOM, AGEFOM 913/2729, Fourth term report 1928. In the fourth term of 1928 the reporting administrator indicated that eight thousand laborers were needed to meet labor demands in the Mungo Region.

42. Ibid.

43. CAOM, AGEFOM 913/2729, Fourth term report 1928.

44. Odile Chatap-Ekindi, "Changements et ruptures dans le Mungo de 1911 à 1950" (doctoral thesis, University of Provence, Aix-en-Provence, 1992), 129–31.

45. Ibid., 113–15.

46. Ibid., 114–19.

47. Ibid.

48. CAOM, AGEFOM 970/3315, Marchand to Chef de circonscription de Nkongsamba, 5 August 1930.

49. Ibid.

50. The definitive theory of mise en valeur is elaborated in the minister of colonies Albert Sarraut's tome *Mise en valeur des colonies françaises* (Paris: Payot, 1923).

51. As per decree recorded in CAOM, AGEFOM 913/2735, *Journal officiel du Cameroun*, 1 April 1925.

52. See also Chatap-Ekindi, 168–70.

53. CAOM, AGEFOM, 970/3316, Administration générale à M. le Chef de circonscription de Nkongsamba, 28 May 1933.

54. CAOM, AGEFOM, 970/3316, Affaires économiques à M. le Chef de circonscription de Nkongsamba, 3 June 1929. The Pastoral Company's request for an additional 3,000 hectares was denied.

55. CAOM, AGEFOM, 970/3316, Administration générale à M. le Chef de circonscription de Nkongsamba, 28 May 1933.

56. CAOM, AGEFOM 913/2737, Agriculture au Cameroun.

57. From 1930 to 1950 there were very few new requests for large plantations. Chatap-Ekindi, "Changements et ruptures," 199–203.

58. Moulendé and his son would be killed by UPC militia in 1959. Bondja and Tchoua, who refused positions in the administration, survived independence-era violence.

59. Andreas Eckert, "Rural Entrepreneurs."

60. Dongmo, *Espace agraire*, 277–81. See also Joseph, *Radical Nationalism*, 146. Joseph writes that Bamileke planters recruited relatives as laborers from their home chieftaincies "in ways that can reasonably be called impressment."

61. On the Bamileke work ethic motivating migration to the Mungo Region, see Jean-Pierre Warnier, *L'esprit d'entreprise au Cameroun* (Paris: Karthala, 1993), chap. 2.

62. Chatap-Ekindi, "Changements et ruptures," 140, 155; Nkankeu, "Occupation du sol," 314; Joseph, *Radical Nationalism*, 123, 143.

63. An earlier version was passed on 20 August 1927, but because of a lack of land surveyors, it was not enforced. France, Ministère des colonies, *Rapport annuel du Cameroun, 1932* (Paris: Imprimerie générale LaHure, 1933), 22.

64. Chatap-Ekindi, "Changements et ruptures," 162.

65. In the interwar period, professional anthropology began to reinforce "technologies of administration" throughout France and West Africa, according to Gary Wilder, "Colonial Ethnology and Political Rationality in French West Africa," in *Ordering Africa: Anthropology, European Imperialism, and the Politics of Knowledge*, ed. Helen Tilley and Robert J. Gordon (Manchester: Manchester University Press, 2007): 336–75, 337. French administrators' ethnic categorization of Bamileke in the Mungo in the 1930s fit this broader trend. On the distinction, in French colonial administrators minds, between autochthon groups and migrant populations, see Peter Geschiere, *The Perils of Belonging: Autochthony, Citizenship, and Exclusion in Africa and Europe* (Chicago: University of Chicago Press, 2009), 13–16.

66. CAOM, AGEFOM, 970/3321, Bleu to Marchand, 24 November 1931.

67. The Mungo was not the only region in which the label *stranger* was applied to Bamileke migrants. Lynn Schler refers to the formation of a "stranger" identity in New Bell, the African neighborhood in colonial Douala. Schler, *The Strangers of New Bell: Immigration, Public Space and Community in Colonial Douala, Cameroon, 1914–1960* (Pretoria: University of South Africa Press, 2008), 11–12.

68. On this point, Richard Joseph says, "What eventually emerged among these heterogeneous populations was their re-identification along supra-ethnic—or place of origin—lines." Joseph, *Radical Nationalism*, 147.

69. Conseil des notables de la région du Mungo, 21 juin 1937, as quoted in Chatap-Ekindi, "Changements et ruptures," 162.

70. Archives nationales Yaoundé (hereafter ANY), Rapport de tournée, October 1933 dans la région Abo-Sud, APA 11798/k, as cited in Guiffo, *Nkongsamba*, 21.

71. Ibid.

72. Chatap-Ekindi, "Changements et ruptures," 152.

73. Nkankeu, "Occupation du sol," 311–12. There is little statistical information, either in official records or in the scholarship, on the distribution of the remaining Mungo Region land. The commercial banana, rubber, and palm oil plantations in the southern half of the region, stretching from Loum to Douala, doubtless made up the bulk of the remaining surface area, as well as smaller plots owned by African planters for which there are only sparse and sporadic records dating to the French period.

74. Chatap-Ekindi, "Changements et ruptures," 207.

75. Ibid., 208–9. In the Bamileke Region, the restrictions on coffee growing were made official by a decree of 10 May 1937, which stated that in the densely populated Bamileke Region, coffee growing had minimized the production of food crops, and the coffee plantations outnumbered French capacities to inspect them. From 1937, no new plantation could be created without authorization from the chief of the region.

76. Joseph, *Radical Nationalism*, 146.

77. Thomas Fokoueng, intrvw., Nkongsamba, 2002. This leverage increased over the years. See below in this chapter for a discussion of Bamileke labor in the 1950s.

78. Barbier, Champaud, and Gendreau, *Migrations et développement*, 34–41.

79. CAOM, AGEFOM, 989/3430, Chef du Bureau de l'administration générale et des affaires economiques à M. le Commissaire de la République française, Yaoundé, 19 September 1932.

80. Parallels can be drawn between French policies toward stranger populations in the Mungo Region and in the African neighborhood of New Bell, in Douala. See Lynn Schler, "Ambiguous Spaces: The Struggle over African Identities and Urban Communities in Colonial Douala, 1914–45," *Journal of African History* 44, no. 1 (2003): 51–72.

81. Guiffo, *Nkongsamba*, 235.

82. Agar Ndenmen, daughter of Isaac Bondja, intrvw., Melong, 3 August 2002.

83. My emphasis. CAOM, AGEFOM 989/3421, Circular from Bonnecarrère, 28 November 1933.

84. Ibid., my emphasis.

85. The quotas were: one representative each for Manehas, Baken, Mouamenam, Bareko, Abo-Nord, Bakoko, Ndokpenda, Elong, Balondo, Bongkeng-Penja; two representatives each for Mbo, Balong, Baneka, Bakaka, Abo-Sud, Pongo, and Babong. All the above were cantons in the Mungo Region. One representative each for Bamileke, Yaoundé, and "*étrangers.*" Circulaire from Bonnecarrère, 28 November 1933.

86. Data are from Fabien Fohom, "L'usine à café dans le Moungo de 1935 à 1986: Une analyse historique" (master's thesis, University of Yaoundé I, 1988), 16–17. This number seems high. Dongmo estimates Bamileke to have made up roughly 36 percent (11,327 out of 31,681 inhabitants) of the Nkongsamba Subdivision and 33 percent of the Mungo Region in 1947 (22, 266 out of 68,092). Dongmo, *Espace agraire*, 231.

87. Schler suggests that colonial-appointed chiefs in New Bell (Douala) purchased their political authority, and argues that through bribery for access to positions, "the power of money" replaced "local criteria determining access to positions of political power." Schler, *Strangers of New Bell*, 62. Similarly, the "chiefs" that French administrators put in place in Mungo-region towns were salaried and were more often perceived as functionaries or civil servants of the administration than as traditional authorities. On the French administration's remuneration of chiefs see Onana, *Sacre*, 45–49.

88. Youmbi Njako at Njombé, Djujeb Tafo at Penja, and Fongang-Tokam at Loum-Chantiers.

89. CAOM, AGEFOM 912/2728, Rapport de M. Henry, Adjoint principal à Mbanga, Recensement des Bamiléké habitant le Chemin de Fer Nord entre Nyombé et Loum, 24 June 1935.

90. On Nkappa, see Chatap-Ekindi, "Changements et ruptures," chap. 7 and 187–90.

91. French administrators encountered similar difficulties when seeking to administer immigrant populations in the New Bell district of Douala. They attempted to appoint chiefs to represent specific ethnic groups in New Bell in the early 1920s. However, "these colonial-appointed chiefs were generally not regarded as legitimate representatives or leaders of the immigrant population." Schler, *Strangers of New Bell*, 42.

92. See chapter 1 of this volume.

93. Interview with Bomda Daniel, of Bandenkop, residing in the Fifth Ward, Nkongsamba, 29 March 2003. The "family chief" of Bandenkop was named Tchedjou Fabwe and governed the Bandenkop population in Nkongsamba before Daniel's arrival in 1953.

94. Usually, a dynamic individual with strong ties to the chieftaincy of origin who showed promise in the new region would be nominated in a village meeting. Abundant applause clenched the nomination. It is only in the last few years that many village communities have begun to have elections in which individual votes for a family chief are counted. Jean-Bernard Pogo, Jean Joseph Mkam, and others, pers. comm., Nkongsamba, 2001–3.

95. See, for example, Warnier, *Esprit d'entreprise*, chap. 8.

96. Nicolas Argenti, *The Intestines of the State: Youth, Violence, and Belated Histories in the Cameroon Grassfields* (Chicago: University of Chicago Press, 2007), 163. On tapenta as a category of subversive "cadets" in the Grassfields, see also Michael Rowlands, "Inconsistent Temporalities in a Nation-Space," in *Worlds Apart: Modernity through the Prism of the Local*, ed. Daniel Miller (New York: Routledge, 1995): 23–42; Jaap van Slageren, *Les origines de l'église évangélique du Cameroun: Missions européennes et christianisme autochtone* (Leiden: Brill, 1972), 84; Jean-Pierre Warnier, "Rebellion, Defection, and the Position of Male Cadets: A Neglected Category," in *African Crossroads: Intersections between History and Anthropology in Cameroon*, eds. Ian Fowler and David Zeitlyn (Oxford: Berghahn Books, 1996): 115–23.

97. Argenti, *Intestines*, 164.

98. Ibid., 164–65.

99. Eckert, "Rural Entrepreneurs," 123.

100. On the nature of the spiritual alliance underwriting Grassfields governance and emigrants' adherence to that alliance, see Meredith Terretta, "'God of Peace, God of Independence': Village Nationalism in the *Maquis* of Cameroon, 1957–1971," *Journal of African History* 46, no. 1 (2005): 75–101.

101. On precolonial Grassfields settlement patterns see Jean-Pierre Warnier, "Histoire du peuplement et genèse des paysages dans l'ouest camerounais," *Journal of African History* 25, no. 4 (1984): 395–410.

102. Soils at lower altitudes, like those near raffia groves and rivers or creeks, were darker and more fertile. For a geographer's analysis, see Dongmo, *Espace agraire*, chap. 1.

103. CAOM, AGEFOM 912/2728, Rapport de M. Henry, Adjoint principal à Mbanga, recensement des Bamiléké habitant le Chemin de Fer Nord entre Nyombé et Loum, 24 June 1935. Dongmo concurs with these findings, although he relies on the data of another colonial administrator, I. Dugast. By 1943, there were 5,615 men as opposed to 1,575 women, and 1,704 boys for 736 girls from the Bamileke Region in the Mbanga Subdivision. Dongmo, *Espace agraire*, 230.

104. Warnier argues that from 1916 onward, Bamileke elders and cadets competed to appropriate the resources introduced under colonialism and to exclude their competitors from them. Warnier, *Esprit de l'entreprise*, 211. This competition

could have indeed facilitated young emigrants' ability to leverage their social standing in their home chieftaincies, but, by the late 1930s, overt competition had given way to a working alliance between elder nobility and younger, successful "cadets."

105. Chatap-Ekindi, "Changements et ruptures," 137; Agar Ndenmen, daughter of Isaac Bondja, intrvw., Melong, 3 August 2002.

106. Chatap-Ekindi, "Changements et ruptures," 115.

107. Agar Ndenmen, intrvw., Melong, 3 August 2002.

108. Ibid.

109. The Potasse d'Alsace–sponsored signs are still visible on both plantations today.

110. See, for example, Warnier, *Esprit d'entreprise*, chap. 8; Argenti, *Intestines*, chap. 6; Malaquais, *Architecture*, chap. 5.

111. Archives préfecturales de Nkongsamba (hereafter APN), Assemblée générale, 29 April 1950, a/s des modifications à apporter de reconnaissance des droits fonciers indigènes, unfiled document.

112. Ibid.

113. Joseph, *Radical Nationalism*, 146.

114. ANY, 2 AC 7776, A. Viossat to High Commissioner, Cameroon, 25 June 1952, as quoted in Chatap-Ekindi, "Changements et ruptures," 237–38.

115. ANY, 2 AC 7776, Mungo, Main-d'Oeuvre Bamiléké, 1952, Marchand, Chef de région du Mungo à M. le Haut-Commissaire de la République, 12 July 1952, as quoted in Chatap-Ekindi, 239.

116. Dongmo, *Espace agraire*, 231.

117. On Ngondo, see Joseph, *Radical Nationalism*, 78–79; Onana, *Sacre*, 190–200.

118. For a discussion of tontines as used by Bamileke and Grassfields communities in Cameroon today, see Warnier, *Esprit d'entreprise*, 69–86. For a historical perspective on Grassfields savings networks prior to European colonization, see J.-P. Warnier, *Échanges, développement, et hiérachies dans le Bamenda pré-colonial (Cameroun)* (Stuttgart: F. Steiner, 1985), 87–96.

119. Essome, "Mungo et l'agitation," 54.

120. Gaston Donnat, *Afin que nul n'oublie: L'itinéraire d'un anti-colonialiste: Algérie, Cameroun, Afrique* (Paris: L'Harmattan, 1986).

121. Essome, "Mungo et l'agitation," 51.

122. Ibid., 54–55.

123. Ibid., 60–65; Joseph, *Radical Nationalism*, 145.

124. Chatap-Ekindi, "Changements et ruptures," 215–34.

125. Essome, "Mungo et l'agitation," 56–57.

126. Chatap-Ekindi, "Changements et ruptures," 244. For an overview of French banana plantation owners' management policies in the Mungo, see Barbara J. Heinzen, "The United Fruit Company in the 1950s: Trusteeships of the Cameroons," *African Economic History* 12 (1983): 141–56.

127. Essome, "Mungo et l'agitation," 57, 63.

128. For Donnat's role and collaboration with Ernest Fines, Communist Councillor to the Union Française, see CAOM, Affaires politiques 3306/1, Casimir

(Yaoundé) à M. le Ministre de la France d'outre-mer, Telegram, no. 204–5, 23 December 1949; CAOM, Affaires politiques 3335/1, "Synthèse sur l'implantation de l'UPC au Cameroun," no. 905/PS-2, M. le Haut Commissaire de la République du Cameroun, Dir. des affaires politiques, 3ᵉ bureau, à M. le Ministre de la France d'outre-mer, 29 April 1955. Fines would later serve as one of the primary organizers of the labor movement. He was eventually imprisoned by the French administration and deported back to France.

129. "Ces races [qui] arrivent à peupler un pays qui ne leur appartient pas." CAOM, Affaires politiques 3306/1, Voeux exprimés par Pandong Fritz, Chef supérieur des Mbos, Subdivision de Nkongsamba, Région du Mungo, Cameroun in Haut-Commissaire à M. le Ministre des affaires étrangères, 4 August 1951.

130. Ibid.

131. See chapter 4 of this volume.

132. Onana, *Sacre*, 298.

CHAPTER 3: TROUBLESOME, REBELLIOUS, OUTLAWED

1. Paul Nugent, *Africa since Independence* (New York: Palgrave MacMillan, 2004), 42.

2. Mr. Um Nyobé to the Trusteeship Council, 17 December 1952, New York, United Nations General Assembly (hereafter UNGA), 7th sess., 4th committee, 309th meeting, Report of the Trusteeship Council, A/2150; add. 1, p. 426.

3. Ibid., add. 1, 425.

4. CAOM, Affaires politiques 3335/1, "Synthèse sur l'implantation de l'UPC au Cameroun," 29 April 1955. For very useful political statistics from postwar French Cameroun, see Janvier Onana, *Le sacre des indigènes évolués: Essai sur la professionalisation politique (l'exemple du Cameroun)* (Paris: Dianoïa, 2004), 293–308.

5. On the political parties sponsored by the French administration and their lack of popularity, see Richard Joseph, *Radical Nationalism in Cameroun: Social Origins of the UPC Rebellion* (Oxford: Oxford University Press, 1977), chap. 6; Onana, *Sacre*, chap. 5.

6. On MACNA, see chapter 4 of this volume.

7. For the story of its founding, see Joseph, "National Politics in Postwar Cameroun: The Difficult Birth of the UPC," *Journal of African Studies* 2, no. 2 (1975): 201–29.

8. Cameroonian representatives included Ruben Um Nyobé, an active trade unionist at the time; Mathias Djoumessi, the ruler of the Grassfields chieftaincy of Foreke-Dschang; and Celestin Takala, a Bamileke merchant based in Douala. See Edward Mortimer, *France and the Africans, 1944–1960: A Political History* (London: Faber and Faber, 1969), chap. 5.

9. Youba Pouamoun, "Félix-Roland Moumié, 1925–1960: L'itinéraire d'un nationaliste intransigeant" (master's thesis, École normale supérieure de Yaoundé, 1997), 18.

10. Elizabeth Schmidt, "Cold War in Guinea: The Rassemblement Démocratique Africain and the Struggle Over Communism, 1950–1958," *Journal of African*

History 48, no. 1 (2007): 95–121, offers the most nuanced account of the various RDA branches' positions vis-à-vis the PCF from 1950 to 1958, and examines closely grassroots' anticolonial activists' disenchantment with the RDA's accommodation of the French government from 1950 on. See also Elizabeth Schmidt, *Cold War and Decolonization in Guinea, 1946–1958* (Athens: Ohio University Press, 2007), chap. 2; Joseph, *Radical Nationalism*, 171–72. For a brief history of the UPC's alliance with the RDA and the PCF, see Simon Nken, *L'UPC: De la solidarité idéologique à la division stratégique, 1948–1962* (Paris: Éditions Anibwe, 2010), 113–22.

11. Schmidt, "Cold War in Guinea," 96–97.

12. Thomas Deltombe, Manuel Domergue, and Jacob Tatsitsa write that during the UPC's early years, Um Nyobé insisted that independence should not completely sever cultural and economic ties with metropolitan France. Deltombe, Domergue, and Tatsitsa, *Kamerun! Une guerre cachée aux origines de la Françafrique, 1948–1971* (Paris: La Découverte, 2011), 82.

13. On this point, see Joseph, *Radical Nationalism*, 171.

14. Much of the recent scholarship on French empire and decolonization has shed new light on the postwar project of a greater France. For an overview, see Alice L. Conklin, Sarah Fishman, and Robert Zaretsky, *France and Its Empire since 1870* (Oxford: Oxford University Press, 2011), chap. 10. Gary Wilder argues that imperial history bound metropolitan and colonial populations "together within an interdependent entity." Gary Wilder, "Untimely Vision: Aimé Césaire, Decolonization, Utopia," *Public Culture* 21, no. 1 (2009): 101–40.

15. Deltombe, Domergue, and Tatsitsa, *Kamerun!* 201–4.

16. In the UN trust territory of French Togo, the nationalist parties in favor of reunification with British Togoland—namely the Comité de l'unité togolaise (CUT), Sylvanus Olympio's party; and Juvento, the Togolese youth movement—also emphasized trust territory status to argue against the application of loi-cadre. The nationalists boycotted territorial assembly elections held in 1955 because voters were not given the opportunity to choose between the reunification of Togoland and continued association with the French Union. As a result of the boycott, the thirty seats were won by the representatives of parties supporting the continued adherence of French Togoland to the French Union. The Parti togolais du progrès took fifteen seats in the south, while the Union des chefs et populations du Nord took fifteen seats in the north. Due to the boycott, the territorial assembly favorable to association with the French Union was in place in time for loi-cadre to be applied in 1956 without the French having to proscribe the CUT. "Elections in French Togoland," *Africa Digest* 3, no. 2 (July–August 1955): 26. Perhaps due to pressure from the British, who closely observed political processes in British Togoland (of particular concern was the question of whether British Togoland would be incorporated into the Gold Coast), the UN followed the political events of the Togo territories more closely than they did in the Cameroons. UN scrutiny of the political situation in French and British Togoland was sufficient to ensure UN supervision of the 1956 plebiscite held in British Togoland to determine whether Togolanders preferred incorporation into the independent Gold Coast over remaining under

British trusteeship. "British Togoland: Plebiscite in Favour of Integration," *Africa Digest* 3, no. 8 (May–June 1956): 7. The UN also supervised elections held in French Togo on 27 April 1958. Despite UN supervision, the elections were widely fraudulent, and plural voting rampant. Olympio's party, a coalition of the CUT and Juvento, nonetheless carried thirty-three seats out of forty-six. "The Togo Elections," *Africa Today* 5, no. 4 (1958): 6–12. See also the account of a Mr. Dorsinville, commissioner for the supervision of the elections in Togoland under French administration, in UNGA, A/C.4/464, 14 December 1960, made by the representative of Haiti at the 1086th meeting of the 4th Committee (Dorsinville).

17. Africans under French rule who "assimilated" French cultural practices, primarily through education, were deemed to be évolués. This status afforded them greater privileges than most colonial subjects. For histories of the assimilation process in French West Africa, see Alice Conklin, *A Mission to Civilize: The Republican Idea of Empire in France and West Africa, 1895–1930* (Stanford: Stanford University Press, 1997); Tony Chafer, "Teaching Africans to Be French? France's 'Civilising Mission' and the Establishment of a Public Education System in French West Africa, 1903–30," *Africa* 56, no. 2 (2001): 190–209; Chafer, "Education and Political Socialisation of A National-Colonial Political Elite in French West Africa, 1936–1947," *Journal of Imperial and Commonwealth History* 35, no. 3 (2007): 437–58. There is comparatively less scholarship on assimilation and the évolué status in French Equatorial Africa and the League of Nations mandate territories. But see Florence Bernault, *Démocraties ambigües en Afrique centrale: Congo-Brazzaville, Gabon, 1940–1965* (Paris: Karthala, 1996); Phyllis Martin, *Leisure and Society in Colonial Brazzaville* (Cambridge: Cambridge University Press, 1995). David Gardinier has discussed assimilation policies in French Cameroon during the mandate and trusteeship periods. Gardinier, *Cameroon: United Nations Challenge to French Policy* (Oxford: Oxford University Press, 1963).

18. The representatives of political parties, such as ESOCAM, put in place by French administrators to stanch the UPC's popularity, often referred to the UPC as the "party of inferiors" or a movement of the "lower class." Deltombe, Domergue, and Tatsitsa, *Kamerun!* 89, 139.

19. The variances and nuances of the separation of colonial populations into citizens, subjects, évolués, and indigènes were complex and shifted over time. For a precise, detailed analysis of the theory and practice of these distinctions, see Catherine Coquery-Vidrovitch, "Nationalité et citoyenneté en Afrique occidentale français: Originaires et citoyens dans le Sénégal colonial," *Journal of African History* 42, no. 2 (2001): 285–305.

20. On a positively viewed Third World, see Vijay Prashad, *The Darker Nations: A People's History of the Third World* (New York: New Press, 2007), 45–46.

21. Benedict Anderson, *Imagined Communities: Reflections on the Origins and Spread of Nationalism* (1983; repr., London: Verso, 2001), 53–54. For a biographical sketch of Ruben Um Nyobé, see J.-A. Mbembe, introduction to *Le problème national kamerunais*, by Ruben Um Nyobé, ed. J.-A. Mbembe (Paris: L'Harmattan, 1984), 18–25. See also Deltombe, Domergue, and Tatsitsa, *Kamerun!* 79–83. On Moumié's life and biography, see Pouamoun, "Moumié"; Nken, *L'UPC*, 92–96.

22. See chapter 5 of this volume.

23. Um Nyobé, *Problème national*, 100–107.

24. Ibid., 307–8.

25. Meredith Terretta, "A Miscarriage of Revolution: Cameroonian Women and Nationalism," *Stichproben: Wiener Zeitschrift für kritische Afrikastudien* 12 (2007): 61–90.

26. Um Nyobé's speeches before the UN's Fourth Committee can be found in their entirety in Um Nyobé, *Problème national*, chap. 3.

27. CAOM, Affaires politiques 3335/1, Lassalle, Bureau de documentation de l'AEF-Cameroun, Brazzaville, n.d. [mid-1955?].

28. Pouamoun, "Moumié," 58.

29. Overall, more integrationist than anticolonial before the Second World War, a marked shift toward liberation from colonial rule surfaced in Pan-Africanist thought beginning with the Fifth Pan-African Congress, held in Manchester in 1945. Aimé Césaire articulated this anticolonial, Pan-Africanist perspective in his impassioned *Discours sur le colonialisme*, published in 1955, and Frantz Fanon strengthened the articulation between revolutionary anticolonialism, political independence, and African unity even more in his 1961 work *Les damnés de la terre (The Wretched of the Earth)*.

30. Historians of Africa's decolonization have emphasized these important aspects of popular nationalist movements. See especially Susan Geiger, *TANU Women: Gender and Culture in the Making of Tanganyikan Nationalism, 1955–1965* (Portsmouth, NH: Heinemann, 1997); Elizabeth Schmidt, *Mobilizing the Masses: Gender, Ethnicity, and Class in the Nationalist Movement in Guinea, 1939–1958* (Portsmouth, NH: Heinemann, 2005), 133–36; Joey Power, *Political Culture and Nationalism in Malawi: Building Kwacha* (Rochester: University of Rochester Press, 2010); Jay Straker, *Youth, Nationalism, and the Guinean Revolution* (Bloomington: Indiana University Press, 2009).

31. Ruben Um Nyobé, "Recommandation no. 1," in *La pensée de Um Nyobé* (Yaoundé: Bureau national provisoire de l'UPC, 1961), 32, as quoted in Joseph, *Radical Nationalism*, 230.

32. On the structure of the PCF and the RDA, see Schmidt, *Cold War and Decolonization*, chap. 1; Nken, *L'UPC*, 109–22.

33. "Voici les responsables de l'agitation au Cameroun," *Paris-presse, L'intransigeant* 1 (June 1955): 12, as quoted in Joseph, *Radical Nationalism*, 230.

34. On the notion of cosmopolitan nationalists as figures both rooted in a particular locale and familiar with a world beyond, see Kwame Appiah, "Cosmopolitan Patriots," *Critical Inquiry* 23, no. 3 (1997): 617–39.

35. See Mbembe, introduction to Um Nyobé, 18–25.

36. Pouamoun, "Moumié," 18.

37. For a description of the intellectual milieu in which Moumié was trained as a doctor, see Chafer, "Teaching Africans."

38. Pouamoun, "Moumié," 15–30.

39. Josette Debarge, *La mission médicale au Cameroun*, Récits missionnaires illustrés, 35 (Paris: SMEP, 1934); "Mission Meeting Number," *Drum Call*, January 1955.

40. Mélanie Boutchoueng, "Ernest Ouandié (1924–1971): L'homme et son action politique" (master's thesis, University of Yaoundé I, 1994), 21.

41. On the history and character of New Bell as an "African neighborhood," in Douala, see Lynn Schler, *The Strangers of New Bell: Immigration, Public Space and Community in Colonial Douala, Cameroon, 1914–1960* (Pretoria: University of South Africa Press, 2008).

42. Boutchoueng, "Ernest Ouandié," 18–40.

43. Marie-Irène Ngapeth-Biyong, intrvw., Yaoundé, July 1999. Ngapeth-Biyong died in November 2002. See also Ngapeth-Biyong, *Cameroun: Combats pour l'indépendance* (Paris: L'Harmattan, 2010).

44. For a discussion of the mobility of RDA activists from Senegal, Côte d'Ivoire, Guinea, and Mali, see Ruth Morgenthau, *Political Parties in French-Speaking West Africa* (Oxford: Clarendon Press, 1964), esp. chaps. 4–7.

45. Only 11,456 Cameroonians (out of a population of roughly three million) were employed as salaried workers by the administration as of 1955. Joseph, *Radical Nationalism*, 152–53. For an account of patterns of schooling and literacy during the interwar period, see Richard Bjornson, *The African Quest for Freedom and Identity: Cameroonian Writing and the National Experience* (Bloomington: Indiana University Press, 1991), chap. 2.

46. James C. Scott, *Domination and the Arts of Resistance: Hidden Transcripts* (New Haven: Yale University Press, 1990), 124. Scott describes the instigators of a dissident subculture within a society largely dominated by repressive rule. He suggests that leaders of hidden dissidence are *of* but not wholly *in* their sociocultural milieu. They are therefore socially marginal, even if respected. Because of their degree of mobility, they capitalize on the "autonomous social sites" discovered in their journeys. In the case of Cameroonian nationalist leaders, these autonomous social sites included members' homes, transport cars, or even entire neighborhoods (e.g., the New Bell quarter of Douala).

47. On Bamileke migrants' economic activities, see chapter 2 of this volume, as well as Joseph, *Radical Nationalism*, 141–48; Andreas Eckert, "African Rural Entrepreneurs and Labor in the Cameroon Littoral," *Journal of African History* 40, no. 1 (1999): 109–26; Schler, *Strangers of New Bell*.

48. Paul Tchedim, intrvw., Demgo, Baham, 3 September 2002.

49. Ignace Djoko Néguin, Bernard Kamto, Thérèse Mewa, and Djoko Domguia, intrvws. Baham, 2002. James C. Scott posits a link between discursive space and social place. Scott, *Domination*, 122–23.

50. The approximate translation of *école des cadres* in the context of French Cameroon's decolonization is "administrators' school."

51. CAOM, Affaires politiques, 3335/1, École des cadres, Douala, New Bell, Note de renseignements, 10 May 1955.

52. Ibid.

53. For Dzukam's alliance with Kamdem Ninyim and his role in diffusing UPC ideology throughout the Bamileke Region, see chapter 4 of this volume.

54. Nken, *L'UPC*, 140–47.

55. See Tzvetan Todorov, *Mikhaïl Bakhtine: Le principe dialogique, suivi de Écrits du cercle de Bakhtine* (Paris: Seuil, 1981), 128, as quoted in Jean-François

Bayart, *The Illusion of Cultural Identity*, trans. Steven Rendall et al. (Chicago: University of Chicago Press, 2005), 111.

56. Bayart urges scholars to "draw up a list of the 'essential genres' of politics coexisting in a given society by locating their origin (autochthonous or imported), the historical conditions under which they crystallized and their possible hybridization." Bayart, *Illusion*, 111.

57. The USCC trade union and the UPC party did evolve out of the study circles put in place by French Communists such as Gaston Donnat and Ernest Fines after the Second World War. But the party remained self-sufficient, and even the French director of the Sûreté in Cameroon, Pierre Divol, characterized the UPC as unambiguously nationalist, writing in his confidential report that the UPC "has never been an African communist party." ANY, 2 AC 8341, Pierre Divol, "Synthèse de l'implantation de l'UPC," 26 March 1955, as quoted in Deltombe, Domergue, and Tatsitsa, *Kamerun!* 79.

58. For a discussion of Roland Pré's place in France's anticommunist colonial politics, see Deltombe, Domergue, and Tatsitsa, *Kamerun!* 150–56. After their defeat at Diên Biên Phù, in 1954, French military officers began to underscore the importance of the conquest of hearts and minds in combatting the "communist indoctrination" of the population that led to the loss of French Indochina. The primary weapon in this new type of warfare was psychological. Applying this new style of combat, Pré used "counterpropaganda" in an attempt to separate "the masses" from the UPC.

59. Frederick Cooper notes a similar inversion and appropriation of "assimilationist and universalist rhetoric" among African trade unions in the 1950s. Cooper, *Decolonization and African Society: The Labor Question in French and British Africa* (New York: Cambridge University Press, 1996), 292.

60. CAOM, Affaires politiques, 3335/1, Ministre de la France d'outre-mer à M. le Haut-Commissaire de la République au Cameroun, "Campagne d'agitation déclenchée par l'UPC," 14 January 1955, Direction des affaires politiques, 3e bureau. The 10 January 1936 decree was the one the Pré administration would use to justify the prescription of the UPC and its affiliates (the JDC, UDEFEC, and USCC) later that year. See below.

61. For references to anticolonial activists' use of French law and history to claim their rights, see, among others, Cooper, *Decolonization*; Myron Echenberg, *Colonial Conscripts: The Tirailleurs Sénégalais in French West Africa, 1857–1960* (Portsmouth, NH: Heinemann, 1991); Schmidt, *Mobilizing the Masses*.

62. UNGA, 9th sess., 4th comm., 292–93.

63. See Terretta, "Miscarriage of Revolution." For a comparative analysis of political processes in Congo-Brazzaville and Gabon that referred to De Gaulle's dependence on francophone Africa in the Second World War, see Bernault, *Démocraties ambigües*.

64. On this point, see also Bjornson, *African Quest*, chap. 3.

65. APN, Bordereau à M. le Chef de la région, Nkongsamba, Rapport politique, 1er Trimestre, 25 July 1955 (unfiled).

66. Marie-Irène Ngapeth, "Les obsèques de l'UPC et de ses satellites," distributed by the UDEFEC; Louis Marie Pouka, *dit* Sosso Ekongolo, "Invocation mystique:

Pastiche d'un poème" and "L'arrivée de la mission de visite"; Félix Moumié, "A mes frères emprisonnés pour que vive le Cameroun"; Um Nyobé, "Signification historique du drapeau kamerounais" and "Le filet est jeté sur les colonialistes"; Prosper Djeté and Kougoum Joseph, "Avis à la population camerounaise," "Le frétillement colonial," "Les colonialistes en soutane," "L'heure est venue pour l'indépendance et l'unification immédiate," and "Les envoyés des Nations unies sont arrivés à Yaoundé." Many of these tracts were actually written by Samuel Tagne Djoko, who was arrested on 27 October 1955 in Nkongsamba. Pro-UPC students in France penned such titles as "Au public camerounais" and "Contre le tribalisme," which urged Cameroonians to form delegations to be heard by the UN.

67. Derek Peterson, *Creative Writing: Translation, Bookkeeping, and the Work of Imagination in Colonial Kenya* (Portsmouth, NH: Heinemann, 2004); Matthew Connelly, *A Diplomatic Revolution: Algeria's Fight for Independence and the Origins of the Post–Cold War Era* (Oxford: Oxford University Press, 2002); Terence Ranger, foreword to Josephine Nhongo-Simbanegavi, *For Better or For Worse? Women and ZANLA in Zimbabwe's Liberation Struggle* (Harare: Weaver Press, 2000), v.

68. On gossip, hearsay, and rumor as transfer of oral information, see Jan Vansina, *Oral Tradition as History* (Madison: University of Wisconsin Press, 1985).

69. APN, "The new articles of faith for the *upéciste* ideology," Bordereau à M. le Chef de la region, Nkongsamba, Rapport Politique, 1er Trimestre, 25 July 1955 (unfiled).

70. CAOM, Affaires politiques 3335/1, À tous les Comités central et de base de l'UPC, "Organisation rationelle de la pétition populaire pour l'envoi au Cameroun d'une mission d'enquête parlémentaire et de l'ONU," annex no. 5, Section des renseignements généraux, no. 1282/S/PS2, Yaoundé, 12 May 1955.

71. Luise White, *Speaking with Vampires: Rumor and History in Colonial Africa* (Berkeley: University of California Press, 1999), 33.

72. Ibid., 33: "It is through talking that people learn about cause and intention."

73. "The Right to Petition," *Africa Today* 5, no. 1 (January–February 1958): 10–14, 13.

74. Ibid.

75. Carol Anderson, "International Conscience, the Cold War, and Apartheid: The NAACP's Alliance with the Reverend Michael Scott for South West Africa's Liberation, 1946–1951," *Journal of World History* 19, no. 3 (2008): 311, 315–22; Roger S. Clark, "The International League for Human Rights and South West Africa, 1947–1957: The Human Rights NGO as Catalyst in the International Legal Process." *Human Rights Quarterly* 3, no. 4 (1981): 109–10.

76. C. Anderson, "International Conscience," 314–16, 321–22.

77. Janvier Onana writes that nationalists sent forty-five thousand petitions in 1956 alone. Onana, *Sacre*, 228, citing *New Commonwealth*, 30 April 1956. See also NYPL, Manuscripts and Rare Books Division, ILRM, box 9, file: UN-TC (1954–56), Frances R. Grant, ILRM Secretary to Dr. Benjamin Cohen, Undersecretary, UN Trusteeship Council, 10 February 1956; NYPL, ILRM, box 9, file: UN-TC (1954–1956), Dr. Benjamin Cohen to Frances R. Grant, 20 February 1956; UNTC, T/PV.663/33, Examination of Petitions—Statement by the Undersecretary, 1956.

78. Um Nyobé, *Problème national*, 173–74.

79. UNTC, T/PET.4/32, Petition from the comite féminin de l'UPC, 20 November 1949.

80. UNGA, A/C.4/SR.393, Report of the Trusteeship Council, 5 December 1953, Fourth Committee, 393rd Meeting, 8th Session, Official Records.

81. Um Nyobé, *Le problème national*, 174.

82. See, for example, ANY, Réunion d'UDEFEC, 7 December 1956, and La Grande Conference d'UDEFEC, Section de Babimbi, 4 December 1956, 1 AC71; UNGA, A/C.4/SR.393, 8th sess., Official Records, Report of the Trusteeship Council, 5 December 1953, Fourth Committee, 393rd meeting.

83. The petitions from Cameroon differ with those from other trust territories in Africa in that they address political issues relevant to specific locales and polities and include women petitioners. In contrast, see Steven Feierman, *Peasant Intellectuals: Anthropology and History in Tanzania* (Madison: University of Wisconsin Press, 1990), chap. 8; Ullrich Lohrmann, *Voices from Tanganyika: Great Britain, the United Nations and the Decolonization of a Trust Territory, 1946–1961* (Berlin: Lit Verlag, 2007).

84. For example, Feierman discusses petitions from the Usambara Citizens Union in Tanganyika. Feierman's analysis of the UCU's use of petitions sheds light on the party's differentiation between written and spoken ideology. In Feierman's analysis, the UCU deliberately omitted commonly discussed issues — such as rainmaking and chiefly authority — from petitions addressed to the Trusteeship Council. Feierman surmises that UCU leaders probably knew that "it was inappropriate and counterproductive to write to London or New York about healing the land," even though this was an issue that Shambaa peasant intellectuals believed to be at the crux of their moral and political economy. Feierman, *Peasant Intellectuals*, 210, chap. 8.

85. Luise White challenges the separation of oral and written narratives in the historiography. White, *Speaking with Vampires*, chap. 8.

86. Deltombe, Domergue, and Tatsitsa, *Kamerun!* 165; Um Nyobé, *Problème national*, 306–17.

87. Um Nyobé, *Ecrits sous maquis*, 103.

88. Ibid.

89. CAOM, Affaires politiques 3335/1, "Synthèse sur l'implantation de l'UPC au Cameroun," Haut-Commissaire, Directeur des Affaires politiques à M. le Ministre de la France d'outre-mer, 29 April 1955. For very useful political statistics from postwar French Cameroun, see Onana, *Sacre*, 293–308.

90. CAOM, Affaires politiques 3335/1, "Synthèse sur l'implantation de l'UPC au Cameroun," Haut-Commissaire, Directeur des Affaires politiques à M. le Ministre de la France d'outre-mer, 29 April 1955.

91. For a discussion of veterans' political organization in French West Africa, see Echenberg, *Colonial Conscripts*.

92. CAOM, Affaires politiques, 3335/1, Direction de Sûreté, Section des renseignements généraux, Yaoundé, 12 May 1955.

93. As quoted in ibid.

94. Deltombe, Domergue, and Tatsitsa, *Kamerun!* 169.

95. Bayart, *Illusion*, 110.

96. Tejumola Olaniyan, "Cartooning Nigerian Anticolonial Nationalism," in *Images and Empires: Visuality in Colonial and Postcolonial Africa*, ed. Paul S. Landau and Deborah D. Kaspin (Berkeley: University of California Press, 2002), 125. Olaniyan describes this practice as a paradox since, even as it contributed to a critique of European cultural imperialism, it also engendered "imperialism's consolidation by the repeated broadcast of its visual codes." I see such practices as political cartooning, the creation of anticolonial newspapers, the act of petitioning the United Nations, or the use of photographs to depict French repression of UPC nationalists as an inversion of colonial practices—a deliberate turning inside-out of colonialism to contribute to its undoing.

97. For a discussion of the number of political representatives that French administrators put forward as spokespersons (or *interlocuteurs valables*) in the late 1940s and the 1950s, see Deltombe, Domergue, and Tatsitsa, *Kamerun!* 129–46. See also Meredith Terretta, "Chiefs, Traitors, and Representatives: The Construction of a Political Repertoire in Independence-Era Cameroun," *International Journal of African Historical Studies* 43, no. 2 (2010): 227–58. For counterpropaganda measures articulated via the Catholic Church and various media, see Deltombe, Domergue, and Tatsitsa, *Kamerun!* 158, 159.

98. Ann Laura Stoler, *Along the Archival Grain: Epistemic Anxieties and Colonial Common Sense* (Princeton: Princeton University Press, 2009), 57: "Students of the colonial consistently have argued that the authority to designate what would count as reason and reasonable was colonialism's most insidious and effective technology of rule, one that, in turn, would profoundly affect the style and strategies of anticolonial, nationalist politics." Stoler critiques this perspective by painstakingly demonstrating the random self-contradictions and irrationalities of colonial rule in the Dutch Indies.

99. For Achille Mbembe, African insubordination to colonial rule consisted of a radical reshaping of thinking that took place in the "imaginary" order composed of symbols, language, and narrative expression—the invisible sphere of the supernatural, night, and dreaming. See Mbembe, "Domaines de la nuit et autorité onirique dans les maquis du Sud-Cameroun, 1955–1958," *Journal of African History* 31, no. 1 (1991): 89–121; Mbembe, "Pouvoir des morts, language des vivants: Les errances de la mémoire nationaliste au Cameroun," in Bayart, Mbembe, and Toulabor, *Politique par le bas*, 183–229; Mbembe, *La naissance du maquis dans le Sud-Cameroun (1920–1960): Histoire des usages de la raison en colonie* (Paris: Karthala, 1996), chaps. 11, 12.

100. Mbembe, *Naissance*; Mbembe, "Pouvoir des morts."

101. See chapter 2 of this volume. On the relationship between the CGT and the formation of trade unions in French Africa, see Schmidt, "Cold War in Guinea"; Cooper, *Decolonization*, chaps. 7, 11.

102. Composed of Marcus Mouaha, president; Joseph Moussio Njoh, secretary general; Etienne Tchegue, assistant secretary general; Maurcie Ngambo, treasurer; David Nsongue, assistant treasurer; and the following members: Charles

Ngoume, Alfred Elong, Daniel Ntouba, Daniel Nkondje, Jacques Matike, Eugène Emadion, Zacharie Tchatchouang, Alexandre Mangoua, Japhet Ngassa, Arouna Njoya, René Ebongue.

103. Jean-Philippe Guiffo, *Nkongsamba: Mon beau village* (Yaoundé: Éditions de l'Essoah, 2001), 84–85.

104. Esaïe Wagoue, "L'impact du mouvement nationliste UPC à Banyangam, 1955–1965" (master's thesis, École normale supérieure de Yaoundé, 1993), 77.

105. Ibid.

106. Ibid., 78.

107. "Recommandation no. 1," *Pensée de Um Nyobé*, 32, as quoted in Joseph, *Radical Nationalism*, 230.

108. Wagoue, "Mouvement nationliste UPC," 78.

109. Jean-François Bayart used this phrase in his analysis of postcolonial Cameroon to describe social juniors (persons lacking wealth or traditional or administrative titles—in short, the nonelite.) Bayart, *L'état au Cameroun*, 2nd ed. (Paris: Presses de la fondation nationale des sciences politiques, 1985). For the portrayal of Bamileke upécistes as social cadets, see, among others, Jean-Pierre Warnier, *L'esprit d'entreprise au Cameroun* (Paris: Karthala, 1993), chap. 8; Dominique Malaquais, *Architecture, pouvoir et dissidence au Cameroun* (Paris: Karthala, 2002), chap. 4 ; Nicolas Argenti, *The Intestines of the State: Youth, Violence, and Belated Histories in the Cameroon Grassfields* (Chicago: University of Chicago Press, 2007), chap. 6.

110. Wagoue, "Mouvement nationliste UPC," 78.

111. Ignace Néguin Djoko, intrvw., Baham, March 2002.

112. CAOM, Affaires politiques 3335/1, Propagande et action psychologique des groupements extremists au Cameroun, n.d. [1955?]. See also Nken, *L'UPC*, 128.

113. CAOM, Affaires politiques 3335/1, Propagande et action psychologique des groupements extremists au Cameroun, n.d. [1955?] and CAOM, Affaires politiques 3309/1, Note de synthèse sur les activités politiques et sociales du mois de janvier 1955.

114. CAOM, Affaires politiques 3335/1, Propagande et action psychologique des groupements extrémistes au Cameroun, n.d. [1955?].

115. In light of the UN's international surveillance, it was better policy for the French to portray traditional chiefs in the Bamileke Region as pro-French. Communist and non-Western members of the Trusteeship Council focused on indigenous government and viewed it as an expression of popular political aspirations. The reference to the number of pro-UPC traditional chiefs in a written administrative report was rare enough to be anomalous. CAOM, Affaires politiques 3335/1, Propagande et action psychologique des groupements extrémistes au Cameroun, n.d. [1955?].

116. Ibid.

117. CAOM, Affaires politiques 3335/1, Extrait rapport politique mensuel, Région Bamileke, September 1954.

118. CAOM, Affaires politiques 3335/1, Note sur les difficultés de l'UPC en région Bamileke, Direction des Affaires politiques et administrative, n.d. [1955?].

119. CAOM, Affaires politiques 3335/1, Propagande et action psychologique des groupements extrémistes au Cameroun, n.d. [1955?].

120. Bonnecarrère, Commissaire de la République aux Messieurs les Chefs de circonscription, circulaire, Yaoundé, 28 October 1932; *Rapport annuel adressé par le gouvernement français au conseil de la société des nations conformément à l'article 22 du pacte sur l'administration sous mandat du territoire du Cameroun pour l'année 1932* (Paris: Imprimerie générale LaHure, 1933), 198.

121. *Rapport annuel adressé par le gouvernement français au conseil de la société des nations conformément à l'article 22 du pacte sur l'administration sous mandat du territoire du Cameroun pour l'année 1933* (Paris: Imprimerie générale LaHure, 1934), 9.

122. *Rapport annuel adressé par le gouvernement français au conseil de la société des nations conformément à l'article 22 du pacte sur l'administration sous mandat du territoire du Cameroun pour l'année 1931* (Paris: Imprimerie générale LaHure, 1932), 6: "Several dynastic chiefs no longer view their rights as deriving from their lineage, but believe that their powers come from the investiture bestowed upon them by the mandate administration."

123. Citing Djoumessi as the pioneer of a new generation of chiefs draws on Malaquais's depiction of Djoumessi as responding to the formation of a new and modern Bamileke bourgeoisie. Malaquais, *Architecture*, 309–15. However, I contend that, far from being the only chief to respond to the social and economic innovations of his population, as Malaquais suggests, he was the first of a wider trend.

124. For more on these mfo's participation in nationalism, see chapter 4 of this volume.

125. CAOM, Affaires politiques 3335/1, petition from Central Committee, UPC, Bafang, 12 April 1955.

126. For the emergence of these family chiefs as Bamileke village communities' self-initiated political organization in their host communities, see chapter 2 of this volume.

127. Guiffo, *Nkongsamba*, 239.

128. See chapter 2.

129. The Evolution sociale du Cameroun was formed in June 1949 in the Bassa region, with considerable assistance by the French administration. The party's purpose was "to establish anti-UPC committees, based upon the clanic sub-divisions of the Bassa people." Joseph, *Radical Nationalism*, 176. See also Onana, *Sacre*, 172–74. ESOCAM never gained popular support, although the French administration sponsored a representative of the party to speak before the UN General Assembly in 1952.

130. On the BDC and Dr. Aujoulat, see Deltombe, Domergue, and Tatsitsa, *Kamerun!* 158–61; Onana, *Sacre*, 179–86; Simon Nken, "Louis-Paul Aujoulat: Figure controversée de la vie politique camerounaise, 1935–1956," *Canadian Journal of African Studies* 49, no. 2 (2010): 256–82.

131. Deltombe, Domergue, and Tatsitsa, *Kamerun!* 163.

132. CAOM, Affaires politiques 3335/1, Note sur les difficultés de l'UPC en région Bamileke, Direction des affaires politiques et administrative, n.d. [1955?].

133. Wabo Souop Kam Toukam, Medjo, Baham, 23 August 2002, intrvw. conducted in Ghomálà, Joseph Kiegaing present as interpreter.

134. CAOM, Affaires politiques 3325, Directeur de la Sûreté, Note de renseignements, 11–18 February 1956.

135. Nken, "Aujoulat"; Onana, *Sacre*, 179–87. For Frederick Cooper, Aujoulat and the BDC exemplified French social Catholicism—social justice and harmony, family stability and workers' rights—as applied by lay Catholics in the colonies. See Cooper, *Decolonization*, 291.

136. On Daniel Kemajou's political career, see Bayart, *L'état*, 57; Deltombe, Domergue, and Tatsitsa, *Kamerun!* 237; Guiffo, *Nkongsamba*, 210–15; and Onana, *Sacre*, 209.

137. See chapter 2.

138. On this point, see chapter 4.

139. The stipulated details defining the contract were: *Constitution du terrain, État du terrain, Durée, Remise en valeur en, Terrain planté de, Articles divers demandés, Valeurs partiels, Valeurs totales terrain.*

140. The matter caught the attention of the minister of overseas France, who cautioned the high commissioner that allowing the UPC to intervene in a land distribution case would amount to "allowing a political organization to mediate between the government and its constituents, which would set a dangerous precedent." CAOM, Affaires politiques 3335/1, Ministre de la France d'outre-mer à M. le Haut-Commissaire, 20 April 1955.

141. See chapter 2. These customary contracts enabled Bamileke settlers, in some cases, to obtain definitive legal deeds to the land they had come to occupy by agreement with their autochthonous hosts. In 1956 the autochthonous population decided to deny the validity of these customary contracts.

142. Accounts of the May 1955 uprisings can be found in Joseph, *Radical Nationalism*, chap. 9; Mbembe, *Naissance*, chap. 10; Deltombe, Domergue, and Tatsitsa, *Kamerun!* chap. 9. My purpose here is not to provide of definitive account of the May uprisings and their suppression throughout the territory but to focus on the events in the Mungo Region.

143. CAOM, Affaires politiques 3335/1, Section des renseignements généraux, Direction de Sûreté, Yaoundé, 12 May 1955.

144. Ibid.

145. Deltombe, Domergue, and Tatsitsa, *Kamerun!* 170.

146. As quoted in Guiffo, *Nkongsamba*, 90.

147. CAOM, Affaires politiques 3337, Chronologique des évenements survenus à Nkongsamba, 22–30 May 1955, Délégation du haut-commissariat.

148. Ibid.

149. Deltombe, Domergue, and Tatsitsa, *Kamerun!* 171.

150. As quoted in Guiffo, *Nkongsamba*, 90–91. The statement was most likely issued by the chiefs of the region in all problem areas of the territory. A verbatim statement was distributed by the chief of the Dja-et-Lobo Department, M. Huber, on 30 May 1955, according to *France-observateur*, 23 June 1955. A sign posted at the entry to Isaac Bondja's plantation (see chapter 2) in Nkongsoung, just north of Melong, bears the same inscription, even today.

151. Guiffo, *Nkongsamba*, 90–91; Abel Eyinga, *L'UPC: Une révolution manquée?* (Paris: Éditions Chaka, 1991). For the practice of justice and the use of exile as a punishment, see chapter 2.

152. Roger Baldwin, "Report from the UN," *Africa Today* 3, no. 3 (1956): 10.

153. CAOM, Affaires politiques 3335/1, UPC à M. le Procureur au Cameroun, M. le haut-commissaire, M. le Président du Conseil national français, M. le Secrétaire-Général des Nations unies, M. le Juge d'instructions, n.d. [1955?].

154. Um Nyobé, *Problème national*, 306–7.

155. Schmidt, "Cold War in Guinea," 102.

156. CAOM, Affaires politiques 3335/1, Teitgen to Roland Pré, draft, 10 March 1955.

157. On this point, see Meredith Terretta, "'We Had Been Fooled into Thinking That the UN Watches over the Entire World': Human Rights, UN Trust Territories, and Africa's Decolonization," *Human Rights Quarterly* 34, no. 2 (2012): 329–60; C. Anderson, "International Conscience"; Clark, "International League."

158. Frederick Cooper, "Possibility and Constraint: African Independence in Historical Perspective," *Journal of African History* 49, no. 2 (2008): 167–96.

159. See, for example, Elizabeth Schmidt, "Anticolonial Nationalism in French West Africa: What Made Guinea Unique?" *African Studies Review* 52, no. 2 (2009): 1–34; Klaas van Walraven, "Decolonization by Referendum: The Anomaly of Niger and the Fall of Sawaba, 1958–1959," *Journal of African History* 50, no. 2 (2009): 269–92.

160. Schmidt, "Anticolonial Nationalism."

161. Tony Chafer, *The End of Empire in French West Africa: France's Successful Decolonization?* (Oxford: Berg, 2002).

162. For an overview of these tactics, see Deltombe, Domergue, and Tatsitsa, *Kamerun!* 153–67.

CHAPTER 4: NATIONALISTS OR TRAITORS?

1. French Cameroon's assembly was constituted in 1946 as the Assemblée représentative du Cameroun (ARCAM), with forty seats; in 1952 the territorial body became the Assemblée territoriale du Cameroun (ATCAM), with fifty seats; and in 1956, the Assemblée législative du Cameroun (ALCAM), with seventy seats.

2. On the spiritual alliance inscribed in the landscape and embodied in the fo, see chapter 1 of this volume.

3. See chapter 1.

4. Janvier Onana, *Le sacre des indigènes évolués: Essai sur la professionalisation politique (l'exemple du Cameroun)* (Paris: Dianoïa, 2004), 209–21.

5. Karen Fields, *Revival and Rebellion in Colonial Central Africa* (Princeton: Princeton University Press, 1985); Joey Power, *Political Culture and Nationalism in Malawi: Building Kwacha* (Rochester: University of Rochester Press, 2010); Mahmood Mamdani, *Citizen and Subject: Contemporary Africa and the Legacy of Late Colonialism* (Princeton: Princeton University Press, 1996); Olufemi Vaughan, *Nigerian Chiefs: Traditional Power in Modern Politics, 1890s–1990s* (Rochester: University of Rochester Press, 2006); Lynn M. Thomas, *Politics of*

the Womb: Women, Reproduction, and the State in Kenya (Berkeley: University of California Press, 2003).

6. Achille Mbembe, *La naissance du maquis dans le Sud-Cameroun (1920–1960): Histoire des usages de la raison en colonie* (Paris: Karthala, 1996), chap. 1.

7. On lamidates in northern Cameroon, see Quentin Gausset, "Historical Account or Discourse on Identity? A Reexamination of Fulbe Hegemony and Autochthonous Submission in Banyo," *History in Africa* 25 (1998): 93–110. On chieftaincy in the Bamileke Region, see chapter 1 of this volume.

8. Ralph Austen and Johnathan Derrick, *Middlemen of the Cameroons Rivers: The Duala and Their Hinterland, c. 1600–c. 1960* (Cambridge: Cambridge University Press, 1999); Jane I. Guyer, *Family and Farm in Southern Cameroon* (Boston: Boston University Press, 1984); Philippe Laburthe-Tolra, *Les seigneurs de la forêt: Essai sur le passé historique, l'organisation sociale et les norms éthiques des anciens Béti du Cameroun* (Paris: Publications de la Sorbonne, 1981).

9. Peter Geschiere, "Chiefs and Colonial Rule in Cameroon: Inventing Chieftaincy, French and British Style," *Africa: Journal of the International African Institute* 63, no. 2 (1993): 151–75.

10. See CHAN, Fonds publics 466, Foccart papers, French Ambassador to Cameroon, M. Benard to Jacques Foccart, Yaoundé, 7 February 1962.

11. *Le Bamiléké: Organe mensuel des chefferies de la région Bamiléké et des Bamilékés de l'extérieur*, May–July 1955.

12. Geschiere, "Chiefs and Colonial Rule," 156.

13. See chapter 1.

14. Ruben Um Nyobé, *Écrits sous maquis*, ed. J.-A. Mbembe (Paris: L'Harmattan, 1989), 140.

15. Ibid.

16. Richard A. Joseph, *Radical Nationalism in Cameroun: Social Origins of the UPC Rebellion* (Oxford: Oxford University Press, 1977), 41–42. For a nuanced analysis of JEUCAFRA's political action and organizational identity, see Onana, *Sacre*, 81–99.

17. UPC meetings in the Wouri Region (Douala) had supported Soppo Priso's candidacy in a rerun of the 1952 elections of parliamentarians to ATCAM. Joseph, *Radical Nationalism*, 184–85.

18. For Soppo Priso's position, see Joseph, *Radical Nationalism*, 312–13; *La presse du Cameroun*, 28 March 1956, 1, 5. On loi-cadre, see Tony Chafer, *The End of Empire in French West Africa: France's Successful Decolonization?* (Oxford: Berg, 2002): 163–92; Ruth Schachter Morgenthau, *Political Parties in French-Speaking West Africa* (Oxford: Clarendon Press, 1967), 65; David Gardinier, *Cameroon: United Nations Challenge to French Policy* (Oxford: Oxford University Press, 1963), 77.

19. Joseph, *Radical Nationalism*, 184–86.

20. *La presse du Cameroun* reported seven thousand people in attendance at Soppo Priso's assembly in Nkongsamba on 24 June 1956. *La presse du Cameroun*, 26 June 1956. The French administration reported fifteen hundred to eighteen hundred. CAOM, Affaires politiques 3323/2, "Synthèse des événements qui se

sont produits au Cameroun au cours du mois de Juin 1956," Rapport politique, Yaoundé, 28 July 1956.

21. CAOM, Affaires politiques 3323/2, "Synthèse des évenements qui se sont produits au Cameroun au cours du mois de Juin 1956," Rapport politique, Yaoundé, 28 July 1956.

22. Jean-François Bayart refers to this position as the "liberal left" but accentuates Soppo Priso's MACNA as its source, drawing too sharp a distinction between National Union members and upécistes. In fact, the UPC and National Union overlapped significantly in 1956, with National Union drawing on UPC political ideology and popularity. See Bayart, *L'état au Cameroun*, 2nd ed. (Paris: Presses de la fondation nationale des sciences politiques, 1985), 35–36.

23. See "Le sang coule au Cameroun," *Afrique nouvelle*, 8 January 1957.

24. See chapter 1 of this volume.

25. Dr. Aujoulat may have been the one to provide funding for the education of Kamdem Ninyim, the fo of Baham's heir. See Joseph, *Radical Nationalism*, 177–78. By February 1955, however, Aujoulat seemed to have become aware of "communist infiltration . . . thanks to Cameroonians who were offered private tuition in the communist 'seminaries' in France . . . with the aim of learning methods of agitation and revolution which have succeeded elsewhere." Aujoulat, quoted in Joseph, *Radical Nationalism*, 258. See also Simon Nken, "Louis-Paul Aujoulat: Figure controversée de la vie politique camerounaise, 1935–1956," *Canadian Journal of African Studies* 44, no. 2 (2010): 256–82.

26. Four categories of narratives of Kamwa's succession remain in Baham today. One refers back to Kamwa's succession of Pouokam, and cites *it* as illegitimate, therefore making both Kamdem Ninyim's and Teguia's reigns illegitimate. Another indicates that Kamdem Ninyim was the true successor. Another depicts Teguia as the true successor. Finally, the conciliators intentionally refuse any engagement with the question of legitimacy, and remind the Baham community that they have suffered too much over the succession issue. This final and prevailing version blankets the tensions that fester between the different camps and seeks to convince all inhabitants and emigrants of Baham to resign themselves to supporting the fo in power. These differing accounts appear in published historical studies, including, for example, the clearly biased account written by Samuel Kamé's son, Pierre Bouopda Kamé, *De la Rébellion dans le Bamiléké* (Paris: L'Harmattan, 2008). See also François Fotso, *La lutte nationaliste au Cameroun, 1940–1971* (Paris: L'Harmattan, 2010).

27. Michel Debonnaire Kamguia, intrvw., Chiala, Baham, 23 August 2002.

28. Kamdem Ninyim had a close relationship with Domtchueng, his uncle in Nkongsamba, but it is difficult to know whether the relationship was developed before Ninyim's departure to study in France. At Ninyim's initiation as fo, Domtchueng may have served as his *tabue* (religious specialist who cleared the way for all other participants in the la'akam rites and signals when the initiate wishes to speak) during his nine weeks of seclusion. See Nguiffo *dit* Wafeu Kam Tameu, *Contributions à l'histoire du royaume Baham* (Yaoundé: Editions Traditions Vivantes, 1995), 49–52. Nguiffo lists "Domtchueng" as Ninyim's tabue but does not list his first name.

29. Sons of the fo were not allowed access to sacred sites in the tsa, and had to rely on the services of one of the official sacrificers.

30. M. Ritz, intrvw., Lycée Pascal, Paris, 22 May 2003.

31. See "L'ordre et la paix doivent être rétablis à Baham," *L'opinion au cameroun*, 17 October 1957. According to this article, written by a Baham notable, Michel Sou'opduonze, after Kamdem Ninyim's deposition, all governing institutions of the chieftaincy considered Kamdem Ninyim to be an intellectual at the time of his succession.

32. See chapter 3 of this volume.

33. Kamé, *Rébellion*, 32.

34. CAOM, Affaires politiques 3325, Note de renseigements, 24–31 March 1956, 31 March–7 April 1956.

35. Ibid.

36. The French used the term *tchinda* generically to refer to the mfo's security forces, although there were a variety of such "guardians," each with a specific purpose. For Fongang's arrest, see CAOM, Affaires politiques 3323/2, Rapport politique, Yaoundé, 28 July 1956.

37. T. A. Ndefo Noubissi, intrvw., Bamougoum, 23 November 2000, as quoted in Thomas A. Ndefo Noubissi, "La police et la question nationale au Cameroun sous administration française (1945–1960)" (master's thesis, University of Yaoundé I, 2001).

38. CAOM, Affaires politiques 3325, Rapport hebdomadaire de sûreté, 2–10 November 1956.

39. See chapters 5 and 6 of this volume.

40. See also Meredith Terretta, "Chiefs, Traitors, and Representatives: The Construction of a Political Repertoire in Independence-Era Cameroun," *International Journal of African Historical Studies* 43, no. 2 (2010): 227–58.

41. The unprecedented investment in French Africa via FIDES was financed mostly by increased taxation in France's African colonies. Patrick Manning, *Francophone Sub-Saharan Africa, 1880–1995*, 2nd ed. (Cambridge: Cambridge University Press, 1998), 123–27.

42. UNTC, petition sent to the United Nations from Emachoua Chrestine, Babucha, 13 December 1956. The petitions from Cameroon record the petitioners' last name first in accordance with the petitioner's way of signing his/her name. In Cameroon, as in much of French-speaking equatorial Africa, it was customary throughout the colonial period for the surname to precede the Christian name in formal settings.

43. CAOM, Affaires politiques 3325, Rapport hebdomadaire de sûreté, 12–19 May 1956.

44. Ibid.

45. Ibid.

46. See CAOM, Affaires politiques 3347/2, Rapport de Sûreté, 4–25 May; CAOM, Affaires politiques 3348/1, Rapport de Sûreté, 26 June–10 July 1958.

47. A compelling speaker in the vernacular in and around Baham, Dzukam viewed market days throughout the region as occasions to recruit villagers to the

nationalist movement, using anecdotes and parables as if "spreading the gospel." Ignace Néguin Djoko and Tchedim, intrvws., Baham, 2002.

48. CAOM, Affaires politiques 3325, Rapport hebdomadaire de sûrete, 9–16 July 1956.

49. CAOM, Affaires politiques 3325, Rapport hebdomadaire de sûreté, 14–21 August 1956.

50. Detainees were not prisoners. No arrest warrant was required to hold a political detainee in prison indefinitely. Michel Debonnaire Kamguia (himself a political detainee), intrvw. following Kamdem Ninyim's deposition and arrest, 23 August 2002, Chiala, Baham.

51. See chapter 5 in this volume.

52. CAOM, Affaires politiques 3325, Note de renseignements, 5–13 September 1956.

53. Ibid.

54. Deltombe, Domergue, and Tatsitsa, *Kamerun!* 223–24, 227.

55. Joseph, *Radical Nationalism*, 185.

56. CAOM, Affaires politiques 3325, Rapport hebdomadaire de sûreté, 9–16 June 1956. On Ekwabi's win over the UPC candidate, Abel Kingue, in the Mungo, see Joseph, *Radical Nationalism*, 184.

57. CAOM, Affaires politiques 3325, Rapport hebdomadaire de sûreté, 2–9 July 1956.

58. Massing was inarguably a UPC supporter, but after the party's proscription joined the National Union. CAOM, Affaires politiques 3325, Rapport hebdomadaire de sûreté, 16–25 June 1956. Massing was one of Fo Kamdem Ninyim's dependable Nkongsamba supporters.

59. On Tagny, see CAOM, Affaires politiques 3325, Rapport hebdomadaire de sûreté, Note de renseignements, 5–13 September 1956, 14 September 1956.

60. CAOM, Affaires politiques 3325, Rapport hebdomadaire de sûreté, 2–9 July 1956.

61. CAOM, Affaires politiques 3325, Rapport hebdomadaire de sûreté, 19–26 November 1956.

62. CAOM, Affaires politiques 3325, Rapport hebdomadaire de sûreté, 12 December 1956–2 January 1957.

63. Ruben Um Nyobé, "En guise de résponse de Tagny Mathieu, 18 mai 1957," in Abraham Sighoko Fossi, *Discours politiques* (Paris: L'Harmattan, 2007), 381.

64. With only 19.75 percent of the population registered to vote, the Sanaga-Maritime Region had the lowest ratio of registered voters to general population in all of French Cameroon. Onana, *Sacre*, 299.

65. CAOM, Affaires politiques 3347, Rapport de Sûreté, 12 December 1956–2 January 1957 ; Onana, *Sacre*, 299, 303. In 1956 there were 1,736,449 registered voters in French Cameroon out of a population of 3,213,347. The population of the Bamileke and Mungo Regions was 464,355 and 103,056, respectively.

66. CAOM, Affaires politiques 3325, Rapport hebdomadaire de sûreté, Note de renseignements, 26 November–4 December 1956, Yaoundé, 6 December 1956.

67. CAOM, Affaires politiques 3325, Rapport hebdomadaire de sûreté, 19–26 November 1956, Yaoundé, 30 November 1956.

68. Kamdem Ninyim was born before the enforcement of the *état civil* decree requiring all children's births to be registered with the administration. On 23 February 1951, the chief of the Bafoussam Subdivision, Bernard Rousseau, presided over the registration of Kamdem Ninyim's birth and recorded it as having occurred in 1936 at the Baham chief's compound. Realizing in 1956 that he did not meet the minimum age requirement for representatives in the assembly, Kamdem Ninyim petitioned for a new birth certificate that declared his year of birth to be 1933. The actual year of Kamdem Ninyim's birth remains a matter of debate. See Kamé, *Rébellion*, 58–59.

69. Bayart, *État au Cameroun*, 36.

70. Data on the ratio of traditional chiefs to civil servants elected to ALCAM are derived from Onana, *Sacre*, 209–10.

71. *Le Bamiléké*, issue 6 (October 1955).

72. CAOM, Affaires politiques 3336, Direction des affaires politiques et administratives, 1er bureau, Election à l'Assemblée Territoriale, 22 January 1957.

73. Ibid.

74. See chapter 3 of this volume.

75. On the Independent Peasants (Paysans Indépendants), see Bayart, *État au Cameroun*, 34.

76. Oral tradition bears evidence of the negotiation-versus-confrontation divide. The founding myths of some chieftaincies, such as Baham, premise "ruse" as the strategy the early founders employed to ensure Baham's sovereignty. See Jean-Marie Tchegho, *L'enracinement culturel en Afrique: Le cas de Bamiléké du Cameroun* (Yaoundé: Éditions CLÉ, 2002). Others, such as those from Bandenkop, reference a series of wars fought. See Daniel Mepin, *Je mourrai face au soleil: Epopée tragique en 15 tableaux* (Bonn: unpublished manuscript, 1983). Still others, like Bandjoun, highlight negotiations between the chieftaincy's founders and the autochthonous populations that preceded the newcomers. See Malaquais, *Architecture*, 78–91.

77. See, for example, Bayart, *État au Cameroun*, 40–42; Malaquais, *Architecture*, 321–24. Both works cite Kamdem Ninyim as an exception and overlook the number of other mfo who fought against French rule.

78. Fo Sokodjou, intrvw., Bamendjou, 2002; Tekù Joseph Kamdem (who was imprisoned with him at Dschang in 1959), Nkongsamba, pers. comm.

79. Fo Marcel Ngandjong Feze, intrvw., Bandenkop, November 2002.

80. NYPL, Rare Books and Manuscripts Division, ILPM, box 12, file: Printed Matter: Cameroons, One Kamerun, National Secretariat, PO box 49, Kumba, S. Kamerun, Communiqué de Presse, J.I. Kamsi, n.d. [late 1958?].

81. CAOM, Affaires politiques 3301, Note sur la situation politique au Cameroun, 1–31 May 1958.

82. See, for example, Mathieu Tagny, "Pour que la paix revienne en pays Bamileke," *Presse Camerounaise*, 14 May 1959.

83. See Kamé's curriculum vitae in *Le Bamiléké*, issue 5 (September 1955).

84. Kamé allegedly tried to trick Fo Kamwa into naming him prince by telling him that he needed a certification of royal blood in order to gain admission to a special "princes' school" in France. In Baham oral tradition, the school to which he sought admission was the one Kamdem Ninyim eventually attended, widely believed in the village to grant admission only to princes. Kam Toukam, intrvw., Medjo, Baham, 23 August 2002; Etienne Tamwa, intrvw., Djemgheu, Baham, 1 September 2002.

85. Toukam intrvw.; Tamwa intrvw.

86. On Teguia's cleanup strategies, see Meredith Terretta, "'God of Peace, God of Independence': Village Nationalism in the *Maquis* of Cameroon, 1957–1971," *Journal of African History* 46, no. 1 (2005): 75–101.

87. Mfonte were not the only district chiefs. Fonte (lit., underling chief) was the title designating quarterheads submissive to the fo. Conversely, district chiefs, who were mwabo or woumbe (high-ranking notables), were the fo's collaborators or, more likely, successors of notables who had been. See chapter 1 of this volume.

88. A. B. Sonke, "La chefferie de Baham de 1945 à 1960: Ses rapports avec la puissance coloniale et les nationalistes" (master's thesis, University of Yaoundé I, 1993–95), 72.

89. Michel Debonnaire Kamguia, intrvw., Chiala, Baham, 23 August 2002. Kamguia explained that all Kamdem Ninyim supporters became refugees or exiles after his arrest. See also Terretta, "'God of Peace.'"

90. CAOM, Affaires politiques 3327/1, Rapport de Sûreté, 1–22 January 1958, Yaoundé, 23 January 1958.

91. CAOM, Affaires politiques 3325, Rapport hebdomadaire de sûreté, 19–26 November 1956.

92. CAOM, Affaires politiques 3347/2, Rapport de Sûreté, Yaoundé, 8–24 March 1957.

93. Sighoko Fossi, *Discours politiques*, 379–83.

94. A detailed account of the various schisms in the UPC after the proscription can be found in Nken, *L'UPC*, chap. 4. On Tagny, see pp. 273–81. See also Mbembe, *Naissance*, 341–48.

95. UNTC, T/PET.5/974, petition from Félix Moumié, president of the UPC, 24 November 1956.

96. "La deuxième motion du groupe d'action nationale du Cameroun concernant l'affaire de Baham," *La presse du Cameroun*, no. 2187, 27–28 August 1957.

97. For an in-depth interpretation of *valet* as used by upécistes from the Bassa region, see Mbembe, *Naissance*, 304–6.

98. Kwamm's council was created in 1951 to study African culture and juridical rules. See Bernault, *Démocraties ambigües*, 247.

99. *La presse du Cameroun*, 11 July 1957.

100. On succession in Grassfields chieftaincy, see Jean Tatsimo, *La place du "la'kem" chez les Bamiléké: Le cas des Nda'a* (Douala: Éditions Saint-François, 1993); Jean-Joseph Chendjou, "Les Bamilékés de l'Ouest Cameroun: Pouvoirs, économie et société: 1850–1916. La situation avant et après l'accentuation des

influences européennes" (doctoral thesis, University of Paris I, 1986), 115–31; Jean Hurault, *La structure sociale des Bamiléké* (Paris: Mouton, 1962), 59–70.

101. Kwamm used the word *commandement*, which I have translated here as traditional rule. *La presse du Cameroun*, 11 July 1957.

102. *La presse du Cameroun*, 27–28 August 1957. On MACNA as a nationalist front, see Joseph, *Radical Nationalism*, 313–16.

103. *La presse du Cameroun*, 17 September 1957.

104. Ibid.

105. This is a variation on Geschiere's study of chiefs and administrators who undertook efforts to "traditionalize" offices that were essentially "modern" positions of power. Geschiere, "Chiefs and Colonial Rule," 152.

106. *La presse du Cameroun*, 11 July 1957.

107. *Opinion camerounaise*, 17 October 1957.

108. Tagny, "Pour que la paix revienne en pays Bamileke."

109. At the high-water mark of nationalist sentiment among populations of Grassfields origins, it makes sense to refer to Grassfielder rather than Bamileke nationalists. Transborder ties increased significantly in the late 1950s as exiled UPC nationalists regrouped in the British Cameroons. Ndeh Ntumazah's adherence to the party in the Mankon region of Bamenda and the ensuing formation of One Kamerun ensured increased levels of anglophone Grassfielder membership in the nationalist movement. Of course, nationalists envisaged an eventual reunification of the Cameroon territories, a goal that held particular significance for Grassfielders and Mungo inhabitants along the Anglo-French boundary. The ties between francophone and anglophone Grassfielders during the era of decolonization remain underresearched, but see Meredith Terretta, "Cameroonian Nationalists Go Global: From Forest *Maquis* to a Pan-African Accra," *Journal of African History* 51, no. 2 (2010): 189–212. See also Thomas Sharp, "Binaries of Nations: The 'Anglophone Problem' in Cameroon and the Presentation of Historical Narratives on the Internet" (master's thesis, University of Manchester, 2008).

110. See chapter 1.

111. Pierre Tagieutseu, of Djemgheu, Baham, shared this song wth me.

112. Jean-Pierre Warnier, "Chefs de l'ouest et formation de l'état au Cameroun," in *Le retour des rois: Les autorités traditionnelles et l'état en Afrique contemporaine*, ed. Claude-Hélène Perrot and François-Xavier Fauvelle-Aymar (Paris: Karthala, 1999), 315–22.

113. The vernacularization of nationalist discourse occurred in other regions of Cameroun as well. For an account of upécistes' use of *colon* in the Bassa region, see Mbembe, *Naissance*, 303–4.

114. UNTC, T/PET.5/998, petition from Mr. Pierre Fayep, 26 November 1956, protesting the arrest of the chief of Baham on 22 November 1956. See also UNTC, T/PET.5/991, petition from Jeunesse Démocratique Camerounaise, Local Branch of the Haoussa Quarter, Kimba [sic], 26 November 1956, protesting the arrest of Pierre Nyoum [sic], Chief of Baham, for refusing to "vote in favour of the loi-cadre"; UNTC, T/PET.5/1054, petition from Mrs. Gertrude Nguemdjo, Babete-Mbouda, c/o the Central Council of UDEFEC, Kumba, 9 December 1956.

115. UNTC, T/PET.5/1084, petition from the people of Balessing, 24 January 1957.

116. UNTC, T/PET.5/512, petition from the UDEFEC Branch of Fonkouakem, 22 November 1954. In this case, two French officials had supported the takeover of Mbafam village by Mbonda Elie, who had no legitimate claim to rule.

117. See Nicolas Argenti, *The Intestines of the State: Youth, Violence, and Belated Histories in the Cameroon Grassfields* (Chicago: University of Chicago Press, 2007), chap. 2; Jean-Pierre Warnier, "Slave-Trading without Slave-Raiding in Cameroon," in "Slavery and Slave Dealing in Cameroon in the Nineteenth and Twentieth Centuries," ed. Bongfen Chem-Langhéé, special issue, *Paideuma* 41 (1995): 251–72

118. This song was performed by Magne Colette, of Baham, and transcribed and translated by André Gabiapsi. On the method of collection, translation, and transcription of oral material, see the introduction.

119. Jan H. B. den Ouden, "In Search of Personal Mobility: Changing Interpersonal Relations in Two Bamiléké Chiefdoms," *Africa: Journal of the International African Institute* 57, no. 1 (1987), 3–27; Peter Geschiere, *The Modernity of Witchcraft: Politics and the Occult in Postcolonial Africa* (Charlottesville: University Press of Virginia, 1997); Philippe Laburthe-Tolra, *Initiations et sociétés secrètes au Cameroun: Essai sur la religion Béti* (Paris: Karthala, 1985). For an analysis of political power as a secret consumption, a metaphoric "eating" of the powerless in postcolonial Africa, see Jean-François Bayart, *L'état en Afrique: La politique du ventre* (Paris: Karthala, 1989); Michael G. Schatzberg, *Political Legitimacy in Middle Africa: Father, Family, Food* (Bloomington: Indiana University Press, 2001).

120. Geschiere, *Modernity of Witchcraft*.

121. Damgne was the name of Teguia's mother. By adding it to the name Teguia, singers essentially underscored that Teguia was not the true heir to his father.

122. In the song, Samuel Kamé is called Kame Kamdem, but this name refers to Samuel Kamé, the Baham notable and administrator discussed above.

123. This song was performed in Ghomala', the indigenous language of Baham, by Magne Colette in Baham, September 2002, and transcribed and translated by André Gabiapsi.

124. This song was performed by Magne Colette in Baham, and transcribed and translated by André Gabiapsi. Other versions of this song exist throughout chieftaincies in the area, and Robert Fankem, of Bandja, also brought it to my attention. He knew only the refrain and was thus unable to verify whether other villages inserted the names of political actors specific to their own chieftaincy politics.

125. In late-colonial Guinea, the killing of the pregnant PDG activist M'Balia Camara took on a similar stature for nationalists. See Elizabeth Schmidt, *Cold War and Decolonization in Guinea, 1946–1958* (Athens: Ohio University Press, 2007), 86–87.

126. CAOM, Affaires politiques 3320, Rapport de Sûreté, 6–18 July 1957.

127. Magne Colette, intrvw., Nkongsamba, 24 June 2002.

128. The event occurred in the present-day La'agweu quarter of Baham. Tchuenkam was imprisoned for five years, first in Bafoussam, then at the Mantoum labor camp. Tchuenkam, intrvw., La'agweu, Baham, March 2003.

129. Those who remembered the songs indicated that Cameroon should be spelled Kamerun, following the nationalists' spelling of the period.

130. This song was performed by Mékeu Tchuenden, Ngoungoua, Baham, 12 November 2002, and transcribed and translated by André Gabiapsi.

131. CAOM, Affaires politiques 3325, Rapport hebdomadaire, 2–10 November 1956 and 4–11 December 1956.

132. See chapter 5 of this volume.

133. CAOM, Affaires politiques 3320, Rapport de Sûreté, 3–25 August 1957.

134. Communication with various informants. Due to the highly sensitive nature of this particular event, I am preserving the anonymity of those involved and those who recounted the story.

135. Communication with Thérèse Mewa, Baham, and Raymond Kamdem, Nkongsamba, 2002.

136. Interview with Kamdem Ninyim's sister, Mafo Elisabeth Nguemdjo, and her son, Bu Pokam Kamwa Joseph, Hiala, Baham, 23 August 2002.

137. See chapters 5 and 6.

138. Victor T. Le Vine, *The Cameroons from Mandate to Independence* (Berkeley: University of California Press, 1964), 162.

139. Ibid.

140. Ibid., 163.

141. See, for example, Enock Katté Kwayeb, *Les institutions de droit public au pays Bamiléké, Cameroun: Evolution et régime actuel* (Paris: Librarie générale de droit et de jurisprudence, 1960); André Tchi-Tchi, in *Le Bamiléké*, issue 22 (February 1957).

142. On this point, see Prasenjit Duara, *Rescuing History from the Nation: Questioning Narratives of Modern China* (Chicago: University of Chicago Press, 1995), 5.

143. Ian Fowler and David Zeitlyn, preface to *African Crossroads: Intersections between History and Anthropology in Cameroon*, ed. Fowler and Zeitlyn, vol. 2 of *Cameroon Studies*, ed. Shirley Ardener, E. M. Chilver, and Ian Fowler (Providence, Rhode Island: Berghahn Books, 1996), xviii; Jane Guyer, "Traditions of Invention in Equatorial Africa," *African Studies Review* 39, no. 3 (1996): 1–28; Thomas Spear, "Neo-Traditionalism and the Limits of Invention in British Colonial Africa," *Journal of African History* 44, no. 1 (2003): 3–27.

144. Nicolas Argenti argues that Grassfields traditions are "interpretations that coexist and struggle for dominance without any one of them necessarily being more correct or legitimate than any other." Argenti, *Intestines*, chap. 2. This narrative plurality enabled the flexibility and variability that Bamileke intellectuals and politicians found most useful in the age of decolonization.

145. This is the other side of the coin in the study of nationalism for Duara, who presents a "'bifurcated' conception of history as an alternative to linear History. . . . Bifurcation points to the process whereby, in transmitting the past, Historical narratives and language appropriate dispersed histories according to present needs, thus revealing how the present shapes the past." Duara, *Rescuing History*, 3.

146. Fowler and Zeitlyn, preface, xviii.

CHAPTER 5: THE MAQUIS AT HOME, EXILE ABROAD

1. Roland Defresnes, "Voyage au pays de la peur: Dans les maquis Bamiléké." *Afrique nouvelle*, no. 659, 30 March 1960 in CAOM, Agence économique de la France d'outre-mer 1007/3571.

2. CAOM, AGEFOM 1007/3570, AFP spécial outre-mer, no. 4055, 13 January 1960; Centre d'histoire et des troupes d'outre-mer (hereafter CHETOM), Archives territoriales de campagne du Cameroun, 15H52, dossier 3; CHAN, Foccart papers, Fonds publics 2000, 1965.

3. NA, Foreign Office (hereafter FO), 371/176876, British Embassy, Yaoundé to Mellon, West and Central Africa Dept., 22 July 1964.

4. Ibid.

5. Service historique de l'armée de terre (hereafter SHAT), 6H240, General Max Briand, Rapport sur les opérations militaires au Cameroun en 1960, 7 April 1961, as quoted in Thomas Deltombe, Manuel Domergue, and Jacob Tatsitsa, *Kamerun! Une guerre cachée aux origines de la Françafrique (1948–1971)* (Paris: La Découverte, 2011), 24.

6. André Blanchet, "Le Cameroun 1962: Pacification et réunification," conférence devant le Groupe d'études des problèmes africains, Centre d'étude de politique étrangère, 26 October 1962, 7–8, as quoted in Deltombe, Domergue, and Tatsitsa, *Kamerun!* 24–25.

7. Deltombe, Domergue, and Tatsitsa call Bardet's existence into question by hypothesizing that his "memoir" was fabricated by Constantin Melnik, who had been chief of security and information services at Matignon between 1960 and 1962 and who became editor in chief of Éditions Grasset, the publisher of Bardet's account, *O.K. Cargo!*, during the 1980s. Deltombe, Domergue, and Tatsitsa, *Kamerun!* 18–19.

8. Jacques Kago Lele, *Tribalisme et exclusions au Cameroun: Le cas des Bamiléké* (Yaoundé: Éditions du Crac, 1995).

9. Ferdinand Chindji-Kouleu, *Histoire cachée du Cameroun* (Yaoundé: Éditions Saagraph, 2006).

10. Undoubtedly, the Cameroons' files in the Britain's Foreign and Commonwealth Office and Predecessors, Records of Former Colonial Administrations, also known as the Migrated Archives, contain additional official numbers.

11. Max Briand, "Rapport sur les opérations militaires au Cameroun en 1960," 7 April 1961, 9, SHAT 6H240, as quoted in Deltombe, Domergue, and Tatsitsa, *Kamerun!* 432.

12. In *Kamerun!* Deltombe, Domergue, and Tatsitsa foreground the imperial trajectories of French administrators and military officers.

13. Mafo Nguemdjo Elisabeth and Bu Pokam Kamwa Joseph (Kamdem Ninyim's sister and nephew), intrvws., Chiala, Baham, 23 August 2002.

14. CAOM, Affaires politiques 3347/2, Rapport de Sûreté, 8–24 March 1957.

15. Ibid.

16. Michel Débonaire Kamguia, intrvw., Chiala, Baham, 23 August 2002.

17. CAOM, Affaires politiques 3301, Note sur la situation politique au Cameroun, 13 March–30 April 1958.

18. CAOM, Affaires politiques 3301, Note sur la situation politique au Cameroun, 1–31 December 1958.

19. CAOM, Affaires politiques 3347/2, Rapport de Sûreté, 8–24 March 1957, Yaoundé. See also Meredith Terretta, "'God of Peace, God of Independence': Village Nationalism in the *Maquis* of Cameroun, 1957–1971," *Journal of African History* 46, no. 1 (2005): 75–101.

20. CAOM, Affaires politiques 3327/2, Note sur la situation politique au Cameroun, 1–28 February 1959.

21. Stella Mbatchou, "Contribution à la connaissance de l'histoire de l'Armée de libération nationale kamerunaise (ALNK), 1959–1971" (master's thesis, University of Yaoundé I, 2003), 18. See also CAOM, Affaires politiques 3301, Rapport de Sûreté, 26 September–25 October 1958.

22. CAOM, Affaires politiques 3301, Rapport de Sûreté, 26 September–25 October 1958; CAOM, Affaires politiques 3301, Note sur la situation politique au Cameroun, 15 November–15 December 1957, annex 5; CAOM, Affaires politiques 3320, Rapport de Sûreté, Note de renseignements, 12–31 December 1957.

23. CAOM, Affaires politiques 3301, Note sur la situation politique au Cameroun, 15 November–15 December 1957, annex 5.

24. As quoted in Esaïe Wagoue, "L'impact du mouvement nationliste UPC à Banyangam: 1955–1965" (master's thesis, École normale supérieure de Yaoundé, 1993), 96.

25. Pierre Bouopda Kamé, *De la rébellion dans le Bamiléké* (Paris: L'Harmattan, 2008).

26. Although a comparative history of armed struggles for independence from colonial rule in Africa is beyond the scope of this work, the organization of the maquis in Cameroon resembled anticolonial resistance movements elsewhere, particularly in Kenya, Zimbabwe, and Algeria. Norma Kriger, *Zimbabwe's Guerilla War: Peasant Voices* (Cambridge: Cambridge University Press, 1992); Daniel Branch, *Defeating Mau Mau, Creating Kenya: Counterinsurgency, Civil War, and Decolonisation* (Cambridge University Press 2009); David Lan, *Guns and Rain: Guerrillas and Spirit Mediums in Zimbabwe* (Berkeley: University of California Press, 1985).

27. See chapter 4 of this volume.

28. CAOM, Affaires politiques 3320, Note de renseignements, 13–25 November 1957.

29. M. Boutchoueng, "Ernest Ouandié (1924–1971): L'homme et son action politique" (master's thesis, University of Yaoundé I, 1994), 52.

30. CAOM, Affaires politiques 3320, Note de renseignements, 13–25 November 1957.

31. Mbatchou, "Armée de libération," 18.

32. Boutchoueng, "Ouandié," 62–63.

33. Ignace Néguin Djoko, intrvw., Baham, March 2002.

34. Mbatchou, "Armée de libération," 23.

35. Jean-Pierre Penlap, intrvw., Dschang, March 2003.

36. CAOM, Affaires politiques 3301, Note sur la situation politique au Cameroun, 15–31 December 1957.

37. Ibid. The CNO in the Sanaga-Maritime faced the heavy repression of the French-led military operation known as Zone de Pacification (ZOPAC). UPC militia groups that formed in the Bamileke and Mungo Regions picked up the CNO's momentum. For a detailed account of the ZOPAC operation, see Marc Michel, "Une décolonisation confisquée? Perspectives sur la décolonisation du Cameroun sous tutelle de la France, 1955–1960." *Revue française d'histoire d'outre-mer* 86 (1999): 229–58; Deltombe, Domergue, and Tatsitsa, *Kamerun!* chaps. 14, 15, 16.

38. See chapters 3 and 4.

39. Singap was also an école des cadres graduate and formerly the editor in chief of the UPC periodical, *Lumière*. He had close ties to Bamileke communities throughout the Mungo Region and, as a "son" of Bandenkop, supported the pro-UPC Fo Feze of Bandenkop, Kamdem Ninyim's friend and collaborator in nationalist campaigning throughout 1956. See chapter 4.

40. Jean-Pierre Penlap, intrvw., Dschang, March 2003. The following account of Momo's life and family is taken from this interview.

41. Deltombe, Domergue, and Tatsitsa, *Kamerun!* 339–40.

42. Dominique Malaquais writes that Kamdem Ninyim "commanded" Momo's militia. Malaquais, *Architecture, pouvoir et dissidence au Cameroun* (Paris: Karthala, 2002), 323. Fotso writes that "thanks to the chief of Baham, Pierre Ninyim Kamdem," Momo "created his headquarters at Nka." Fotso, *La lutte nationaliste au Cameroun, 1940–1971* (Paris: L'Harmattan, 2010), 278.

43. This account appears in Deltombe, Domergue, and Tatsitsa and is the only one based on cited oral and written evidence to discuss Momo's operations after Pierre Simo's arrest. See Deltombe, Domergue, and Tatsitsa, *Kamerun!* 343–44.

44. Momo is a common name in the region and last names are not necessarily family names in Bamileke culture—the children of the same father bear different last names. There is no evidence suggesting that Grégoire Momo was related to Paul Momo.

45. Grégoire Momo, *Informations sur le terrorisme en Pays Bamileke: Ses causes et effets* (unpublished manuscript, 1986), 17.

46. Mbatchou, "Armée de libération," chap. 5. This could have been Madiesse Thérèse, alias Avion de Terre de Bafang. See APN, Note de renseignements, Sûreté Loum, 18 December 1966.

47. Again, for comparison with village populations' use of song during the nationalist period in the Sanaga-Maritime, see Achille Mbembe, "La palabre de l'indépendance au Cameroun," in Bayart, Mbembe, and Toulabor, *Politique par le bas*, 161. Pierre Tagieutseu, pers. comm., Djemgheu, Baham, 2002.

48. Jean-Pierre Penlap sang the portions of these two songs for me. He sang in Ghomala' and translated into French on the spot, but I was unable obtain the written Ghomala' form. Penlap, intrvw., Dschang, March 2003.

49. Achille Mbembe, "Domaines de la nuit et autorité onirique dans les maquis du Sud-Cameroun (1955–1958)," *Journal of African History*, 31, no. 1 (1991): 89–121, 90.

50. The most well known case of oathing during Africa's decolonization is undoubtedly that of Mau Mau among Kikuyu in Kenya. The Mau Mau oaths

were more widespread, elaborate, and systematically applied than the ones taken in the Bamileke or the Sanaga-Maritime Regions in Cameroon. The Mau Mau oaths completed and enhanced Kikuyu initiation rites undergone by young men and women upon their entry into adulthood. See John Lonsdale, "The Moral Economy of Mau Mau: Wealth, Poverty, and Civic Virtue in Kikuyu Political Thought," in Bruce Berman and John Lonsdale, *Unhappy Valley: Conflict in Kenya and Africa*, 2 vols. (Athens: Ohio University Press, 1992), 429–30, 439. In the Bamileke Region, where there was no ritualized initiation into adulthood linked with chronological age groups, oath taking occurred in specific circumstances, such as truth-telling ceremonies, "tying up" a contract, or during induction into secret associations.

51. See chapter 1 of this volume.

52. Ignace Néguin Djoko, intrvw., Baham, March 2002. The oaths led many Bamileke *upécistes* to refuse to give the names of their comrades during torturous interrogations once in the custody of security forces.

53. Interviews. Due to the sensitive nature of this information, informants requested anonymity in this instance.

54. Ignace Néguin Djoko, intrvw., Baham, March 2002. The oath taking took place in Babete, Mbouda, which hosted a significant Baham community.

55. Interviews. Due to the sensitive nature of this information, informants requested anonymity in this instance.

56. Jean Hurault, *La structure sociale des Bamiléké* (Paris: Mouton, 1962), 121; Malaquais, *Architecture*, 86–91. On *kè*, see chapter 1 of the present volume.

57. French administrative reports described the induction into the SDNK as "a witchcraft ceremony during which oath taking takes place." CAOM, Affaires politiques 3301, Note sur la situation politique au Cameroun, 15–31 December 1957. Mbatchou refers to this ritual specialist as *ngaakà*, which is the word used in the Nde region by Medumba speakers. She translates the term as "witch of the maquis," as per her informants. Mbatchou, "Armée de libération."

58. See chapter 1.

59. Mbatchou, "Armée de libération," 27.

60. Ibid., 26. This information is based on Mbatchou's interview with Feuh Ndouh, an ALNK ngaakà of Bazou.

61. For a description of the symbolic meaning of *pfeukang* and *djim djim* as used during transactions with the spirits, see chapter 1.

62. Jean Djonteu, intrvw., Baham, November 2002; Mbatchou, "Armée de libération," chap. 5. Mbatchou uses the term *tserenkie* for the god who guided fighters in the forest, and *ngondu* and *kienkung* for the gods of war.

63. Jean-Paul Notué and Louis Perrois describe the pueh kè as a raffia bag containing products linked to the practice of kè, including the chiamgne. Perrois and Notué, *Rois et sculpteurs de l'ouest Cameroun: La panthère et la mygale* (Paris: Karthala, 1997), 374.

64. Jean Djonteu, intrvw., Baham, November 2002; Jean-Pierre Penlap, intrvw., Dschang, March 2003; François Tchuenkam, intrvw., Baham, September 2002.

65. Terretta, "God of Peace."

66. See Michael Rowlands and Jean-Pierre Warnier, "Magical Iron Technology in the Cameroon Grassfields," in *African Material Culture*, ed. Mary Jo Arnoldi, Christraud Geary, and Kris Hardin (Bloomington: Indiana University Press, 1996), 51–72.

67. On these points, see Jean-Pierre Warnier, "Métallurgie ancienne, identifications et domestication de la violence au Cameroun," in *Matière à politique: Le pouvoir, les corps et les choses*, ed. Jean-François Bayart and Warnier (Paris: Karthala, 2004), 181–93.

68. Achille Mbembe, "Pouvoir des morts, language des vivants: Les errances de la mémoire nationaliste au Cameroun," in Bayart, Mbembe, and Toulabor, *Politique par le bas*, 183–229, 215.

69. On this point, see Mariane Ferme, who describes the material objects in Mende culture that "signal the presence of secrecy in everyday life." Ferme, introduction to *The Underneath of Things: Violence, History, and the Everyday in Sierra Leone* (Berkeley: University of California Press, 2001).

70. Nicolas Argenti, *The Intestines of the State: Youth, Violence, and Belated Histories in the Cameroon Grassfields* (Chicago: University of Chicago Press, 2007), 161–63.

71. The cha-cha-cha recalled the punishments that mfo applied to criminals before European occupation. Extreme transgressions of village law warranted live burial in trenches dug for that purpose. See Jean-Joseph Chendjou, "Les Bamilékés de l'ouest Cameroun: Pouvoirs, économie et société: 1850–1916: La situation avant et après l'accentuation des influences européennes" (doctoral thesis, University of Paris I, 1986), 159. On this practice in UPC militias, see Mbatchou, "Armée de libération," 25–26.

72. Public whipping was a punishment used for thieves in the Grassfields before European occupation. Chendjou, "Pouvoir, économie," 160.

73. See chapter 2 of this volume.

74. CAOM, Affaires politiques 3320, Rapport de Sûreté, 13–27 September 1957.

75. According to a project carried out by French administrators in 1937 to translate "customary" crime and punishment into a French penal code. APD, partial document, 3e partie, Code Pénal Coutumier, Sanctions Coutumières (see Article 57), Report prepared by André Raynaud, Chef de subdivision, Bafang, 30 April 1937.

76. APN, Atteinte à la sûreté intérieure de l'état: Affaire Chedjui Jean. Djonteu was not a French speaker, and so it can be assumed that this was a translation from Ghomala'. Most likely he would have used the term *gung* to express "nation," once again allowing for the term's inherent ambiguity in Grassfields languages.

77. For an account of the assassination, see CAOM, Affaires politiques 3320, Rapport de Sûreté, 13–27 September 1957. For the trial of the assailants, see CAOM, Affaires politiques 3348/1, Rapport de Sûreté, 11–25 August 1958.

78. *Le Bamiléké*, issue 7 (November 1955): 3; issue 31 (November 1957): 3.

79. Tchi-Tchi had received a nobility title from Fo Kemajou of Bazou (see chapter 4), and the event had been featured in *Le Bamiléké*, as had his election to the position of municipal councillor. He occasionally contributed articles on Bamileke culture and history to *Le Bamiléké*.

80. CAOM, Affaires politiques 3320, Rapport de Sûreté, no. 1889, 13–27 September 1957.

81. Ibid.

82. CAOM, Affaires politiques 3320, Rapport de Sûreté, 28 September–11 October 1957.

83. Ibid.

84. CAOM, Affaires politiques 3348/1, Direction de Sûreté, 11–25 August 1958; Bernard Kamto, Djoko Domguia, intrvws., Baham, November 2002.

85. Ibid.

86. CAOM, Affaires politiques 3348/1, Rapport de Sûreté, 22 April–14 May 1958.

87. CAOM, Affaires politiques 3301, Rapport sur les activités criminelles au Cameroun français (Mungo) des membres de l'UPC refugiés au Cameroun sous tutelle Britannique, 16 June 1958, Procès verbal, interrogation Djileu Joseph, 29 years old, 28 November 1957, Gendarmerie de Loum.

88. Ibid., account given by Song Emmanuel, twenty-three years old, 28 November 1957, Gendarmerie de Loum, ibid.

89. CAOM, Affaires politiques 3301, Note sur la situation politique au Cameroun, 15 November–15 December 1957, annex 5.

90. For a biographical sketch of Ruben Um Nyobé and an account of his execution, see J.-A. Mbembe, introduction to Ruben Um Nyobé, *Le problème national kamerunais*, ed. J.-A. Mbembe (Paris: L'Harmattan, 1984), 18–25.

91. UNTC, petition from Rachel Ndambouen, T Pet. 4&5/47. Ndambouen described Simo and the others as "children of Kamerun." For French discussion of the death sentence for SDNK fighters in the Bamileke Region, see CAOM, Affaires politiques 3327/2, Note sur la situation politique au Cameroun, 1–28 February 1959, Haut-Commissaire, Bureau de documentation.

92. The bureau was constituted informally from the date of Ghana's independence, and given a legal status in 1959, after Padmore's death. Kwesi Armah, *Peace without Power: Ghana's Foreign Policy, 1957–1966* (Accra: Ghana University Press, 2004), 27. I am grateful to Akosua Darkwah for providing me with a copy of this publication.

93. On this point, see David E. Apter, 'Ghana's Independence: Triumph and Paradox,' *Transition* 98 (2008), 6–22.

94. Ras T. Makonnen, *Pan-Africanism from Within*, ed. Kenneth King (Nairobi: Oxford University Press, 1973), 214–15.

95. The Conference of Bandung signaled an anti-imperial shift in the global political economy and engendered the nonaligned movement and the emergence of a Third World. See Antoinette Burton, Augusto Espiritu, and Fanon Che Wilkins, "The Fate of Nationalisms in the Age of Bandung," *Radical History Review*, no. 95 (2006): 145–48, 147; Christopher J. Lee, ed., *Making a World after Empire: The Bandung Moment and Its Political Afterlives* (Athens: Ohio University Press, 2010); Jane Burbank and Frederick Cooper, *Empires in World History: Power and Politics of Difference* (Princeton: Princeton University Press, 2010), 427.

96. CHAN, Foccart papers, Fonds privés 149, Service de documentation extérieure et de contre-espionage (SDECE), "Soudan-Cameroun (UPC)," 30 September 1958.

97. All information on the AASO is taken from CHAN, Foccart papers, Fonds publics 2092, Note d'information, "La conférence de solidarité Afro-Asiatique de Conakry (11–16 Avril 1960)," Ministère des Affaires Etrangères, Dir. de l'Afrique-Levant.

98. The AASO's director's committee was composed of twenty-seven members, each one representing a particular nation: Algeria, Cameroon (UPC), Peoples' Republic of China, Belgian Congo, North Korea, Ghana, Guinea, India, Indonesia, Iraq, Iran, Japan, Kenya, Lebanon, Liberia, Morocco, Mongolia, Uganda, Pakistan, UAR, Southern Rhodesia, Somalia, South-West Africa, Tunisia, the Soviet Union, North Vietnam, Yemen. The organization's permanent secretariat made up of twelve members chosen by the directors' committee: UAR, China, India, Indonesia, Iraq, Japan, USSR, Cameroon (UPC), Uganda, Algeria (FLN), Guinea, Congo. The UPC held seats in both the director's committee and the permanent secretariat. Ibid.

99. CHAN, Foccart papers, Fonds publics 2092, Note d'information, "La conférence de solidarité Afro-Asiatique de Conakry (11–16 Avril 1960)," Ministère des affaires étrangères, Dir. de l'Afrique-Levant.

100. Ibid.

101. For the vernacularization of the UPC's nationalist ideology in the region of the Sanaga-Maritime, see Mbembe, "Domaines de la nuit"; Mbembe, *La naissance du maquis dans le Sud-Cameroun (1920–1960)* (Paris: Karthala, 1996).

102. Ghana National Archives, SC/BAA/136, Conference of Independent African States, 15 April 1958.

103. Ibid.

104. Makonnen, *Pan-Africanism*, 58.

105. Jane Burbank and Frederick Cooper write that "older forms of pan-Africanism" had withered by the mid-1950s and that, by that time, "already the devolution of power to territorial structures was underway." See Burbank and Cooper, *Empires*, 425. Yet the AAPC of 1958 and the AASO Conference of 1957 symbolized the growth of a new form of Pan-Africanism that premised interterritorial cooperation over territorial sovereignty.

106. CHAN, Foccart papers, Fonds publics, Directeur des affaires politiques, 3e bureau, Ministre de la France d'outre-mer à M. le Ministre des affaires étrangères, 31 October 1958.

107. CHAN, Foccart papers, Fonds publics, Torre à Ministre de la France d'outre-mer, Directeur du cabinet, Directeur des affaires politiques, Paris, 18 July 1958.

108. CHAN, Foccart papers, Fonds publics, Ministre de la France d'outre-mer au Ministre des affaires étrangères, Direction des affaires politiques, 3e bureau, 15 July 1958.

109. CHAN, Foccart papers, Fonds publics, Torre à Ministre de la France d'outre-mer, Directeur du cabinet, Directeur des affaires politiques, Paris, 18 July 1958.

110. CHAN, Foccart papers, Fonds publics, télégramme du Directeur des affaires politiques, M. Pignon et Chef du 3e bureau, Rostain, à M. le Haut-Commissaire, Cameroun, 19 December 1958.

111. CHAN, Foccart papers, Fonds publics 2092, Ministère des affaires étrangères, Directeur d'Afrique-Levant, 15 December 1958.

112. See Matthew Connelly, *A Diplomatic Revolution: Algeria's Fight for Independence and the Origins of the Post–Cold War Era* (Oxford: Oxford University Press, 2002), intro., 3–13.

113. CHAN, Foccart papers, Fonds publics 2092, Spécial outre-mer, Bulletin Sud-Sahara, 11 December 1958.

114. "Talking Drums: Commentary on African Affairs," *Africa Today* 6, no. 2 (1959): 3–6, 21.

115. Emmanuel Hansen, "Frantz Fanon: Portrait of a Revolutionary Intellectual," *Transition* 46 (1974): 25–36; Frantz Fanon, *Toward the African Revolution: Political Essays*, trans. Haakon Chevalier (1967; repr., New York: Grove Press, 1988), 154–55. For a discussion of Nkrumah's ambivalent reaction to Fanon's direct challenge to the principle of nonviolent "Positive Action," see Jeffrey S. Ahlman, "The Algerian Question in Nkrumah's Ghana, 1958–1960: Debating 'Violence' and 'Nonviolence' in African Decolonization" *Africa Today* 57, no. 2 (2010): 66–84.

116. Patrick Duncan, "Non-Violence at Accra," *Africa Today* 6, no. 1 (1959): 30–32.

117. Hansen, "Fanon," 86.

118. "Talking Drums: Commentary on African Affairs," *Africa Today* 6, no. 2 (1959): 3–6, 21.

119. NYPL, Rare Books and Manuscripts Division, ILRM, box 14, file: General Correspondence, Cameroon, Bebey-Eyidi to Roger Baldwin, 24 October 1961.

120. On this argument, see Mbatchou, "Armée de libération," 31–35.

121. Fo Marcel Ngandjong Feze, intrvws., Bandenkop, 1999, 2001, 2002, 2003.

122. Djuidje, intrvw., Baham, 27 August 2002. The particular ways in which independence-era violence affected pregnant women recurs in oral and written accounts. Pamela Feldman-Savelsberg, Flavien Ndonko, and Song Yang argue that Bamileke women perceive political crises in terms of the threats they pose to reproductive fertility. See Feldman-Savelsberg, Flavien T. Ndonko, and Song Yang, "Remembering 'The Troubles': Reproductive Insecurity and the Management of Memory in Cameroon," *Africa* 75, no. 1 (2005): 10–29.

123. Terretta, "God of Peace."

124. The name echoed the FLN, which Ouandié, Moumié, and Kingue had become connected with in Algeria. Boutchoueng, "Ouandié." On Singap as commanding officer, see Mbatchou, "Armée de libération," 34–35. Mbatchou bases this information on her interviews with Woungly Massaga, carried out in Yaoundé in 2002, and his private collection of UPC archives.

125. Makonnen, *Pan-Africanism*, 215. Those housed at the African Affairs Centre included Patrice Lumumba, from the Belgian Congo; Felix Moumié and Ernest Ouandié, of Cameroon; Holden Roberto, of Angola; Egyptian president Nasser's representative, Dr. Gallal, Rabaroca; Hastings Banda and Kenneth Kaunda of southern central Africa, Mbiyu Koinange and Jaramogi Oginga Odinga of Kenya.

126. NA, Colonial Office (hereafter CO) 554/2367, extract from South Cameroons Intelligence Report for September 1960, pt. 2. Upécistes in British territory

established a base in the thickly forested area on the British side of the Anglo-French border near the town of Kumba. Young men showing military promise were recruited through this base.

127. Ibid.

128. Deltombe, Domergue, and Tatsitsa, *Kamerun!* 344.

129. NA, Foreign Office (hereafter FO) 371/155341, annex A to Periodic Intelligence Report (hereafter PERINTREP) no. 8/61.

130. Intrvws. with Job Njapa, Nkongsamba, 2002, 2003, 2004, 2008; Ignace Néguin Djoko, Baham, 2002, 2003, 2004; Fo Marcel Ngandjong Feze, Bandenkop, 1999, 2001, 2002, 2003; Marie-Irène Ngapeth-Biyong, Yaoundé, 1999; Jacqueline Kemayou, New Bell, Douala, 2005.

131. NA, CO 554/2367, Governor-General of Nigeria to Secretary of State for the Colonies, 30 September 1960.

132. Intrvws. with Job Ngoule Njapa, Jacqueline Kemayou, Woungly Massaga, Yaoundé, 2003, 2005. See also NA, CO 554/2367, B. A. Flack to R. C. Cox, Esq., Commonwealth Relations Office, London, 26 February 1960, re Petition to High Commissioner (22 February 1960) from four persons, political refugees from Cameroon.

133. Ibid.

134. Ibid.

135. NA, FO 371/155341, annex A to PERINTREP no. 8/61.

136. NA, FO 371/155341. See "Peking Training Young Africans in Terrorism: Disruption Planned," *Sunday Telegraph*, 23 July 1961; "Overseas Training of ALNK Terrorists," Undersecretary of State for War, 16 June 1961.

137. "Peking Training Young Africans in Terrorism: Disruption Planned," *Sunday Telegraph*, 23 July 1961.

138. NA, FO 371/155341, "Overseas Training of ALNK Terrorists," Undersecretary of State for War, 16 June 1961.

139. NA, FO 371/155341, annex A to PERINTREP no. 8/61.

140. Mbatchou, "Armée de libération," 66.

141. Ibid., chap. 5. The training camp directed by Jean Chine de Guerre, elsewhere referred to as Jean Chine Pouvoir du Peuple was located in the Bakoua Tongo region. APN, Bulletin de renseignements, Service de documentation extérieure et de contre-espionnage (hereafter SEDOC), 17–29 August 1964.

142. Mbatchou, "Armée de libération," 35.

143. Boutchoueng, "Ouandié," 66.

144. For an account of the mysterious circumstances of Singap's death, see Deltombe, Domergue, and Tatsitsa, *Kamerun!* 531–32.

145. Jean Djonteu, intrvw., Baham, November 2002.

146. CAOM, Affaires politiques 3301, Note sur la situation politique au Cameroun, 1–31 May 1958.

147. See a description of the ALNK's general headquarters in *La nouvelle expression*, édition spéciale, 24 January 2002.

148. APN, Rapports hebdomadaires; interviews.

149. Momo, *Informations sur le terrorisme*.

150. Archives du Professeur A. Owona, "L'UPC; Le terrorisme au Cameroun," as cited in Boutchoueng, "Ouandié," 65.

151. CAOM, Affaires politiques 3327/2, Note sur la situation politique au Cameroun, 1–28 February 1959.

152. This serendipitous timing suggests a degree of complicity between UPC fighters and tax collectors, whether voluntary or coerced. CAOM, Affaires politiques 3327/2, Note sur la situation politique au Cameroun, 1–28 February 1959.

153. See, for example, the case of Jean Yankam, allegedly given funds by the UPC to operate his business for their profit. APN, Note de renseignements, Sûreté Loum, 2 February 1967. The wealthy Bandenkop baker in Nkongsamba, Timothé Yimo, was also believed to be funding the ALNK in this way. Communication with informants; APN reports.

154. Djonteu, intrvw., Baham, 4 September 2002.

155. APN reports.

156. See, for example, APN, Fiche d'interrogatoire, Gendarmerie nationale, Région du Littoral, compagnie de Nkongsamba, Brigade de Loum, no. 8/4, account of Ekobe Ngo Michelin, alias Conscience, 19 January 1971.

157. Intrvw. with anonymous person, who told me that raiding maquisards stole even the cooking pot on the fire, after dumping its contents out on the ground.

158. APN, Rapports hébdomadaires and Bulletins de renseignements, 1962–1970.

159. CHAN, Foccart papers, Fonds publics 1999, Ambassadeur Bernard à M. Couve de Murville, Ministre des Affaires étrangères, Yaoundé, 14 March 1964.

160. CAOM, Affaires politiques 3301, Note sur la situation politique au Cameroun, 15 November–15 December 1957.

161. For a history of the UPC's involvement with these two organizations, and African member states' position vis-à-vis the UPC, tempered by the widening Sino-Soviet split, see CHAN, Foccart papers, Fonds publics 2092, Note d'information, 6e Session du Conseil de Solidarité Afro-Asiatique, Algiers, March 1964.

162. On the external organization of the UPC, see Dieudonné Pouhe Pouhe, "Les liaisons extérieures de l'UPC, 1948–1960" (master's thesis, University of Yaoundé I, 1999).

163. Job Njapa, intrvws., Nkongsamba, 2002–3, 2005.

164. CHAN, Foccart papers, Fonds publics 1999, Ambassadeur Bernard à M. Couve de Murville, Ministre des Affaires étrangères, Yaoundé, 14 March 1964. The UPC Revolutionary Committee formed in Accra in 1962. See Bureau du comité directeur de l'UPC, "La vérité sur le comité révolutionnaire," Accra, 19 December 1963, personal collection of UPC archives, Thierry Wendjel, Nkongsamba.

165. CAOM, Affaires politiques 3347/2, Rapport de Sûreté, 4–25 May 1957.

166. Ibid.

167. Ibid.

168. APN, Directeur de la sûreté fédérale, J. Evina à M. le Préfet du Mungo, "Pour Information," Procès verbal de la réunion du comité des responsables du maintien de l'ordre, 25 January 1962, Buea.

169. CAOM, Affaires politiques 3301, Note sur la situation politique au Cameroun, 1–31 May 1958.

170. CAOM, Affaires politiques 3347/2, Rapport de Sûreté, 4–21 April 1957.

171. Mbatchou, "Armée de libération," chap. 4. According to his interview with Stella Mbatchou, Woungly Massaga was to receive and reassemble the disassembled weapons. By 1966, most of these weapons had fallen into the hands of law enforcement, and there were no more shipments from Ghana.

172. APN, Procès verbal de passation de service, Arrondissement de Dibombari, Département du Mungo, 5 February 1964.

173. Mr. and Mrs. Noubi, assisted by Wache Jules, intrvw., Rue des manguiers, Yaoundé, January 2002.

174. Mbatchou, "Armée de libération," chap. 4.

175. APN, Bulletin de renseignements, SEDOC, 12 December 1965–6 January 1966.

176. Intrvws. with Job Njapa, Nkongsamba, 2002, 2003, 2004, 2008, Nkongsamba.

177. APN, Bulletin de renseignements hébdomadaire, SEDOC, 20 December 1964–2 January 1965; Bulletin de renseignements hébdomadaire, SEDOC, 2–16 August 1964.

178. All these were carried out in operations attributed to maquisards. APN reports.

179. Deltombe, Domergue, and Tatsitsa, *Kamerun!* 345.

180. Goustan Le Bayon, *Les prêtres du Sacré-Coeur et la naissance de l'église au Cameroun* (Paris: Procure des missions SCJ, 1986), 116.

181. Deltombe, Domergue, and Tatsitsa, *Kamerun!* 345.

182. CHAN, Foccart papers, Fonds privés 151, Motion à M. le Président de la République française, M. le Premier Ministre, Chef du gouvernement français, M. le Haut-Commissaire de la République française au Cameroun, 11 December 1959. Many of those signing the motion were clergy.

183. CHAN, Foccart papers, Fonds privés 151, to M. le Président de la République française, 16 December 1959.

184. CHAN, Foccart papers, Fonds privés 151, G. Navez, Douala, à M. Delbecque, 20 July 1959.

185. Richard Joseph, *Radical Nationalism in Cameroun: Social Origins of the UPC Rebellion* (Oxford: Oxford University Press, 1977), 170–71.

186. See A. H. M. Kirk-Greene, "The Thin White Line: The Size of the British Colonial Service in Africa," *African Affairs* 79, no. 314 (1980): 25–44.

187. Moulendé was one of the first Cameroonian planters to obtain a registered deed for a large European-style plantation in the Mungo. He was the only such planter indigenous to the area. The other two, Bondja and Tchoua, were Bamileke immigrants to the region. See chapter 2 of this volume.

188. Agar Ndenmen, intrvw., Melong, 3 August 2002. On Bondja, see chapter 2.

189. Gabriel Djiomo, "L'église catholique et l'Union des Populations du Cameroun (UPC) à l'Ouest: 1948–1970" (master's thesis, University of Yaoundé I, 1999), 60–61.

190. On Aujoulat, see chapter 3.

191. This account is taken from one of the Sacré-Cœur priests who was in the Nkongsamba Diocese at the time, Le Bayon, *Sacré-Coeur*, 118–19.

192. APN, Note de renseignements, Sûreté Loum, 18 December 1966.

193. Mbatchou, "Armée de libération," 58.

194. See, for example, APN, Renseignements judiciaires, Procès verbal, no. 1144, Brigade de Manjo, 7 December 1970. Unfortunately, few women who were a part of the maquis have come forward to date to talk about their experiences. The absence of the voice of Cameroonian women revolutionaries can be read as their much smaller number relative to men and perhaps, too, as a greater ambivalence, on the part of women, toward their role in the maquis.

195. Father Siou, intrvw., Nkongsamba, February 2002.

196. I first learned of the existence of the ALNK tribunal through an interview with Father Siou, Nkongsamba, February 2002.

197. APN, Forces armées nationales, Secteur militaire du Littoral, Quartier de Nkongsamba, Synthèse mensuelle de renseignements, 27 June–31 July 1970.

198. Nouvelle was a fighter in the ALNK District of Manengouba, condemned to death by the Tribunal Criminel Spécial Sous-maquis. APN, Forces armées nationales, Secteur militaire du Littoral, Quartier de Nkongsamba, Synthèse mensuelle de renseignements, 27 June–31 July 1970.

199. Nkwemo was from Bangou, and was a fighter in the ALNK, District of Manengouba, condemned to death by the Tribunal criminel spécial sous-maquis. APN, Forces armées nationales, Secteur militaire du littoral, Quartier de Nkongsamba, Synthèse mensuelle de renseignements, 27 June–31 July 1970.

200. Mbatchou, "L'Armée de libération nationale kamerunaise," chap. 5.

201. Meredith Terretta, "Cameroonian Nationalists Go Global: From Forest *Maquis* to a Pan-African Accra," *Journal of African History* 51, no. 2 (2010): 189–212.

202. Deltombe, Domergue, and Tatsitsa, *Kamerun!* 529–37.

203. CHAN, Foccart papers, Fonds publics 466, Bureau du comité directeur sous-maquis, Circulaire a tous les organismes reguliers de l'UPC, 31 January 1962, in April 1962, Affaires intérieures.

204. Javier Auyero, *Routine Politics and Violence in Argentina: The Gray Zone of State Power* (Cambridge: Cambridge University Press, 2007).

CHAPTER 6: "HERE, GOD DOES NOT EXIST"

1. CAOM, AGEFOM 1007/3571, AFP Spec OM, 3958.

2. Roland Desfresnes, "Voyage au pays de la peur. Dans les maquis Bamiléké," *Afrique nouvelle*, no. 659 (30 March 1960).

3. ANY, 1AA158, Bulletin de renseignement hebdomadaire du GTN du 12 au 18 octobre 1960, 2, Procès verbal de la séance de l'assemblée des combattants, upécistes et Udefec, tenue à Maingui le 5 septembre 1960, as quoted in Thomas Deltombe, Manuel Domergue, and Jacob Tatsitsa, *Kamerun! Une guerre cachée aux origines de la Françafrique (1948–1971)* (Paris: La Découverte, 2011), 429.

4. Fabian Klose has argued convincingly that colonial administrators passed emergency laws to justify the systematic human rights violations that accompanied their suppression of anticolonial uprisings. Klose, "'Source of Embarrassment': Human Rights, State of Emergency, and the Wars of Decolonization," in *Human Rights in the Twentieth Century*, ed. Stefan-Ludwig Hoffman (Cambridge:

Cambridge University Press, 2011): 237–57. While I agree with Klose's argument, I go a step further here to demonstrate that postcolonial governments such as Cameroon's built on the emergency legislation passed by departing European administrators to construct single-party state regimes within which civil and political liberties were curtailed. See also Nasser Hussain, *The Jurisprudence of Emergency: Colonialism and the Rule of Law* (Ann Arbor: University of Michigan Press, 2003).

5. Nicodemus F. Awasom, "Politics and Constitution-Making in Francophone Cameroon, 1959–1960," *Africa Today* 49, no. 4 (2002): 3–30.

6. Ibid., 11–14. See also Victor Le Vine, *The Cameroons from Mandate to Independence* (Berkeley: University of California Press, 1964), 186–88.

7. As quoted in Awasom, "Politics," 11.

8. Ibid., 14; LeVine, *Cameroons*, 188.

9. Or at least not very effective, according to the report by CAOM, Affaires politiques 3321, Mr. Massa, Inspecteur, concernant le renseignement au Cameroun, Yaoundé, 13 August 1956, à M. le Ministre de la France d'outre-mer.

10. Deltombe, Domergue, and Tatsitsa, *Kamerun!* 371–72.

11. APN, Procès verbal de la réunion du comité des responsables du maintien de l'ordre, 25 January 1962, Buea, Soit transmis à M. le Préfet du Mungo. Present at the meeting: Sadou Daoudou, minister of the armed forces, M. Fochivé, Directeur du service de la sécurité auprès de la présidence fédérale, Lt.-Col. Aurousseau, Gendarmerie.

12. Marie-Emmanuelle Pommerolle, "A quoi servent les droits de l'homme? Action collective et changement politique au Cameroun et au Kenya" (doctoral thesis, Université Montesquieu-Bordeaux IV, 2005), 137.

13. And it would remain in place practically as well, until the present, since Ahidjo's former prime minister Paul Biya, who succeeded him as president in 1982 is still in power as of 2013. On the legal shift to multipartyism, in late 1990, see Joseph Takougang and Milton Krieger, *African State and Society in the 1990s: Cameroon's Political Crossroads* (Boulder: Westview, 1998), 107–9.

14. The purpose here is not to recount a conventional military or political history of state formation, nor to inventory postindependence Franco-Cameroonian conventions and agreements. These conventional histories have been written by other scholars. For a classic approach focused mostly on "formal" politics, see Le Vine, *Cameroons*. Revisionist histories include Janvier Onana, *Le sacre des indigènes évolués: Essai sur la professionalisation politique (l'exemple du Cameroun)* (Paris: Dianoïa, 2004). The most extensive military history to date can be found in Deltombe, Domergue, and Tatsitsa, *Kamerun!*

15. Emergency law was implemented in the late-colonial era in, for example, Kenya and Algeria. See Klose, "'Source of Embarrassment'" and, more generally, Hussain, *Jurisprudence of Emergency*. On the continued use of late-colonial-era counterinsurgency politics in postcolonial governance see Daniel Branch, "Loyalists, Mau Mau and Elections in Kenya: The First Triumph of the System, 1957–1958," *Africa Today* 53, no. 2 (2006): 27–50. For the case of Nyasaland and postcolonial Malawi, see Joey Power, *Political Culture and Nationalism in Malawi: Building Kwacha* (Rochester: University of Rochester Press, 2009).

16. CAOM, Affaires politiques 3321, Mission d'inspection, Rapport d'ensemble no. 35/E, Les Services militaires et de sécurité au Cameroun, Inspecteur général de la France d'outre-mer Monguillot à M. le Ministre de la France d'outre-mer, Yaoundé, 25 September 1956.

17. On the amnesty issue, see CAOM, Affaires politiques 3302/1, Spénale, Directeur du cabinet du ministre de la France d'outre-mer to the Ministre de la France d'outre-mer, 1 March 1956 and the response from Haut-Commissaire Messmer, Yaoundé, 29 May, 9 October 1956. For the position of pro-amnesty PCF members (Jean Llante and Henri Bourbon) in the French national assembly, see *Libération*, 16 December 1956. For the position of the minister of overseas France in late 1957, see CAOM, Affaires politiques 3302/1, Bulletin d'information de la France d'outre-mer, no. 2773, 27 November 1957, no. 2792, 30 November 1957. The national assembly had decided to pass the amnesty law. In a telegram to the high commissioner, the minister of overseas France stated that Cameroonian approval of the law was "legally unnecessary but politically necessary." At the same time the minister applauded then prime minister André-Marie Mbida, who stated on 27 November 1957 that amnesty should not be granted to political prisoners in the case of an increase of violence. Less than a month later, Deputy Wanko was assassinated. Three days after his death, on 16 December 1957, Cameroon's asssembly unanimously voted against amnesty. Soppo Priso later protested, stating that the vote had been passed while the assembly was still in a state of shock over Wanko's death. A partial amnesty measure was granted to political prisoners by the law of 17 February 1958, but only for the least severe crimes. CAOM, Affaires politiques 3320, Rapport de Sûreté, Note de renseignements, 12–31 December 1957. Full amnesty would not be extended to UPC members and fighters until May of 1960.

18. CAOM, Affaires politiques 3347/2, Rapport de Sûreté, 4–11 February 1957.

19. The camp was established in 1955 as a training base. From 1958 to 1963 new buildings were constructed. From 1959 to 1961 the Seventeenth Battalion of the Marine Infantry was installed at Koutaba to help the BTCs with "maintenance of order" in the Bamileke Region. On 3 October 1964, the French turned the camp over to the Cameroonian army. CHETOM, Fréjus, 15H52, dossier 3.

20. One section numbered between sixty and one hundred troops.

21. CAOM, Affaires politiques 3301, Troupes AEF/Cameroun, État-Major, 2e bureau, Compte-rendu mensuel de renseignements, 1–30 June 1958, Colonel du Crest de Villeneuve.

22. CAOM, Affaires politiques 3327/2, Note sur la situation politique au Cameroun, 1–31 October 1958.

23. CAOM, Affaires politiques 3301, Bulletin sur la situation militaire au Cameroun, 1–31 December 1958, Général de corps d'armée Le Puloch, Commandant supérieur des forces armées de la zone de défense de l'AEF/Cameroun, État-major, 2e bureau, no. 23/2/S, Brazzaville, 8 January 1959.

24. Archives du Pr A. Owona (now allegedly in the possession of Professor Daniel Abwa, Chair of the Department of History at Yaoundé I), "L'UPC, le terrorisme au Cameroun," cited in M. Boutchoueng, "Ernest Ouandié (1924–1971): L'homme et son action politique," (master's thesis, University of Yaoundé I, 1994).

25. Roland Defresnes, "Voyage au pays de la peur."
26. CAOM, AGEFOM 1007/3570, AFP spécial outre-mer, no. 4055, 13 January 1960.
27. CHETOM, Archives territoriales de campagne du Cameroun, 15H52, dossier 3.
28. CHAN, Foccart papers, Fonds publics 2000, 1965.
29. CHAN, Foccart papers, Fonds privés 148, Premier Ministre to Haut-Commissaire Cameroun, Haut-Commissaire Brazzaville, telegram HAUSAIRGAL DAKAR, Presicom Paris, 12 December 1959.
30. Ibid.
31. CAOM, AGEFOM 1007/3571, AFP Spécial outre-mer, no. 3958. On Briand, see chapter 5 of this volume.
32. Kamé was the administrator responsible for Fo Kamdem Ninyim's replacement by with Teguia after his deposition. On Kamé's career, see chapter 4.
33. CHAN, Foccart papers, Fonds publics 466, Claude Rostain to Président de la République, Président de la Communauté, "Evolution de la politique intérieure camerounaise," 2–8 March 1962.
34. See chapter 3.
35. See chapter 1: the more powerful village notable had the greatest number of meetings to attend during the week.
36. CAOM, Agefom 1007/3570, AFP no. 4305, 6 November 1960.
37. CHAN, Foccart papers, Fonds publics 466, AFP 60, n.d. [1962?], Cameroun, Affaires intérieures, 1962.
38. Max Olivier-Lacamp, *Le figaro*, 24 March 1960.
39. CAOM, AGEFOM 1007/3571, AFP no. 4116, 24 March 1960.
40. Mary Louise Graham, pers. comm., January 2004.
41. Desfresnes, "Voyage au pays de la peur."
42. CAOM, AGEFOM 1007/3571, AFP Spec. OM, no. 3958.
43. On resettlement camps, forced villagization, and other forms of spatial arrangement as a system of governance in colonial and postcolonial Africa, see the useful overview in Achim von Oppen, "The Village as Territory: Enclosing Locality in Northwest Zambia, 1950s to 1990s," *Journal of African History* 47, no. 1 (2006): 57–75. On forced resettlement as a "rehabilitation" strategy employed by the colonial government, see Caroline Elkins, "The Struggle for Mau Mau Rehabilitation in Late Colonial Kenya," *International Journal of African Historical Studies* 33, no. 1 (2000): 25–57.
44. Known as Monsieur Afrique, Foccart oversaw French policy toward its former African territories from 1960 to 1974. An extensive account of his activities during this time can be found in Jacques Foccart and Philippe Gaillard, *Foccart parle: Entretiens avec Philippe Gaillard*, 2 vols. (Paris: Fayard/Jeune Afrique, 1995–97). From 1960 to 1965, Bénard, who was a personal friend of General Briand, briefed Foccart on the minute details of the inner workings of Cameroon's government and the Franco-Cameroonian military campaign to suppress the rebellion. See Deltombe, Domergue, and Tatsitsa, *Kamerun!*, 399, 400.
45. CHAN, Foccart papers, Fonds publics 466, Bénard to the Ministre des Affaires Etrangères, Au sujet du pays Bamiléké, 30 April–3 May, Yaoundé, 8 May 1962.

46. Ibid.
47. Jeannette Noubi, intrvw., Yaoundé, 16 February 2002.
48. Ibid.
49. Ibid. See also CAOM, AGEFOM 1007/3570, AFP SP outre-mer, no. 3900, 10 July 1959, which described reinforcements from Chad and "Oubangui," including gendarmes and armed police forces, placed throughout the southern portion of the country.
50. Jeannette Noubi intrvw.
51. Fo Sokodjou, intrvw., Bamendjou, March 2002.
52. For an enlightening analysis of the changes produced in Bamileke society by the spatial rearrangement of chieftaincies during the period of "troubles," see Dominique Malaquais, *Architecture, pouvoir et dissidence au Cameroun* (Paris: Karthala, 2002).
53. Thérèse Mewa, intrvw., Baham, 6 September 2002.
54. See chapter 1.
55. For examples of these sorts of operations carried out before independence, see CAOM, Affaires politiques 3301, Note sur la situation politique au Cameroun, 1–31 May 1958; Note sur la situation politique au Cameroun, 1–31 July 1958. In Nkongsamba in July 1958, fifteen hundred individuals were "controlled," leading to the expulsion of seventy-five people of Bamileke origin and fifteen arrests. "The population is satisfied with the purge of criminal elements from the town," claimed the report.
56. The grid strategy was first conceived by the directeur de sûreté in Cameroon. See APN, Direction de la Sûreté, Note à l'attention de M. le Premier Ministre, Yaoundé, 21 September 1959. Ahidjo then placed the orders to the appropriate prefects to put surveillance grids in place. APN, Directeur du cabinet, M. Godefroy, pour le Premier Ministre to M. le Préfet du Moungo, Nkongsamba, Yaoundé, 2 October 1959, "Contrôle des Centres urbains." Variations on the grid strategy and control of movement were widely applied throughout colonial Africa and particularly apartheid South Africa. See, for example Mustapha K. Pasha and John D. Rusk, "Africa Rights Monitor: South Africa: Terror and Resistance," *Africa Today* 33, no. 1 (1986): 69–79; Philip Frankel, "The Politics of Passes: Control and Change in South Africa," *Journal of Modern African Studies* 17, no. 2 (1979): 199–217.
57. CAOM, Agefom 1007/3570, AFP no. 4249, 1 September 1960. The block chief system was first implanted in problematic neighborhood of New Bell, Douala, but soon spread to Yaoundé, Nkongsamba, and other towns in the Mungo and the Bamileke regions.
58. APN, Communication du Maire, Commune mixte rurale, Melong, "Recensement," 15 September 1961.
59. APN, Chef de la BMM de Douala, 12 December 1960.
60. APN, Direction de la Sûreté, Police urbaine de Nkongsamba, Rapport journalier, Activité de la police urbaine de Nkongsamba au cours de la journée du 2 Novembre 1960, Chef de détachement, J. Epanlo.
61. APN, Les refoulés du Wouri et du Moungo, Prison de Nkongsamba à M. le Commissaire, 24 November 1960.

62. Article 25 of Ordonnance no. 58-1375, 30 December 1958: "In case of troubles caused by armed forces, or of signals that such troubles will occur, the High-Commissioner and Prime Minister may pass a joint decree proclaiming the state of emergency." Loi no. 59–33 of 27 May 1959 added the *état de mise en garde* and the *état d'alerte* to the options available for exceptional legislation. See Luc Sindjoun, *L'état ailleurs: Entre noyau dur et case vide* (Paris: Economica, 2002), 261.

63. For a detailed account of the political discussions and maneuvering behind the drafting of the constitution and its adoption via popular referendum, see Awasom, "Politics and Constitution-Making."

64. APN, Décret présidentiel no. 60/124, 8 May 1960, nos. 61– 62, 24 April 1961, etc.

65. Although there is a difference of scale, the parallels with the pass laws and influx control of apartheid South Africa are remarkable. See Michael Savage, "The Imposition of Pass Laws on the African Population in South Africa, 1916–1984," *African Affairs* 85, no. 339 (1986): 181–205.

66. APN, Njoya Arouna, Ministre d'état chargé de l'intérieur, on laissez-passer in Nkongsamba and Bafang, 7 October 1961. The laissez-passer was put in place by French administrators in Douala and Nkongsamba. See APN, Circulaire d'application de la décision laissez-passer, no. 554/DR/RMU, "Vise à entraver les possibilités de déplacement des terroristes," 15 July 1959, Chef de région, Mungo, L. Domissy. The laissez-passer was applied in the Wouri, the Mungo, and the Bamileke Regions.

67. APN, Arrêté préfectoral 1/303/A.DMU, 12 July 1960.

68. Ibid.

69. Ibid.

70. APD, Décision no. 290/DR/RBK, Dschang, 2 July 1959, Chef de région Ter Sarkissof.

71. CAOM, Affaires politiques 3348/1, Rapport de Sûreté, 26 September 1958.

72. APN, Directeur du Cabinet, M. Godefroy, pour le Premier Ministre à M. le Préfet du Moungo, Nkongsamba, Yaoundé, 2 October 1959, "Contrôle des Centres urbains."

73. APN, Délégataion générale à la Sûreté nationale, le commissaire de police de la ville de Nkongsamba à M. le Préfet du Moungo à Nkongsamba, 13 February 1970.

74. To catch Kouam in the act of a false identification, security forces sent some of their own personnel, whom they knew to be innocent, through the control point. Security forces killed Kouam during what he had been told would be a hunting expedition. Joseph Mkam, Victor Djimi and others, pers. comm.

75. APN, Délégataion générale à la Sûreté nationale, le commissaire de police de la ville de Nkongsamba à M. le Préfet du Moungo à Nkongsamba, 13 February 1970.

76. APN, Document et informateur du service, 24 July 1970, Opérations de police menées dans le Mungo.

77. APN, Commissariat de police de Nkongsamba, Note de service, Objet: Contrôle de police, Nkongsamba, 21 December 1960, Moukoko, Commissaire de police.

78. See, for example, APN, Note de renseignements, Sûreté Loum, 19 December 1967, which recommended that Anne Nkamga be placed under "discreet surveillance" because she had accused the local self-defense unit of working badly.

79. The work of Luise White probes the importance of the timing of secret hoarding and lie telling in discursive practices in colonial and postcolonial Africa. She argues that secrets and lies can serve to negotiate power and status and to shape the way that history is narrated. White, "Telling More: Lies, Secrets, and History," *History and Theory* 39, no. 4 (2000): 11–22; White, *The Assassination of Herbert Chitepo: Texts and Politics in Zimbabwe* (Bloomington: Indiana University Press, 2003). Mariane Ferme posits a correlation between a culture of violence and elevated degrees of concealment. Ferme, *The Underneath of Things: Violence, History, and the Everyday in Sierra Leone* (Berkeley: University of California Press, 2001), intro.

80. CAOM, Affaires politiques 3301, Troupes AEF/Cameroun, État-Major, 2e bureau, Compte-rendu mensuel de renseignements, 1–30 June 1958.

81. This informant asked me not to reveal his identity.

82. The details of the story of Tchoupe's wives' encounter with maquisards appears in APN, Fiche d'interrogatoire, Manjo, 30 July 1970, Gendarmerie, Région du Littoral, Compagnie de Nkongsamba, Brigade de Manjo; APN, Bulletin de renseignements, Objet: Non dénonciation des malfaiteurs, 30 July 1970, Brigade de gendarmerie de Manjo.

83. Ibid.

84. APN, Fiche d'interrogatoire, Manjo, 30 July 1970, Gendarmerie, Région du Littoral, Compagnie de Nkongsamba, Brigade de Manjo.

85. On Kamto's activities as a upéciste in Nkongsamba, see chapter 5 of this volume.

86. The Ndongmo affair is discussed in greater detail below in this chapter.

87. See chapter 5.

88. Tocpa Ta'akouo, intrvw., Banka, Baham, 1 September 2002.

89. A study on the police forces in Cameroon during the Trusteeship period addresses security forces' use of torture during interrogations. See Thomas A. Ndefo Noubissi, "La police et la question nationale au Cameroun sous-administration française (1945–1960)" (master's thesis, University of Yaoundé I, 2001).

90. Deltombe, Domergue, and Tatsitsa, *Kamerun!* 371–72.

91. See, for example, APN, Atteinte à la sûreté intérieure de l'état: Affaire Chedjui Jean, Commissaire de police, Chef de la Brigade mixte mobile de Nkongsamba à M. le Préfet du Département du Moungo, Nkongsamba, 7 February 1970; APN, Notice de renseignements sur Njonteu Jean, alias Dieu de la Paix, Département du Mungo, 29 September 1971.

92. The French government in Algeria also used the *balançoire* for the interrogation of suspects.

93. For written accounts by BMM prisoners at Tcholliré, a grueling BMM work camp in the north of Cameroon, see "Emmanuel Bityeki, ancien détenu politique," *La nouvelle expression*, édition spéciale, 26 December 2001; Albert

Mukong, *Prisoner without a Crime: Disciplining Dissent in Ahidjo's Cameroon*, 2nd ed. (Paris: NUBIA Press, 1989).

94. Michel Kamwa, intrvw., Banka, Baham, 2 September 2002.

95. "Bityeki," *La nouvelle expression*.

96. The repression of the "rebellion" in the Bamileke came just after the ZOPAC operation in the Sanaga-Maritime, and administrators and some Bamileke elite drew parallels between the two regions. See CAOM, Affaires politiques 3301, Rapport de Sûreté, 15–25 December 1958.

97. APN, Procès verbal de la réunion des chefs de service chargés de la sécurité dans le département du Mungo, 20 May 1961. See also M. le Premier Ministre à M. le Préfet du Mungo, 2 October 1959, which stresses the importance of the "population's participation," in facilitating the maintenance of order and security.

98. APN, Rapport annuel d'activités, 1 January–31 December 1972: M. le Directeur général de la DIRDOC et de la sécurité à la Présidence de la République Unie du Cameroun, Nkongsamba, 5 January 1973. Immediately after independence, psychological campaigns of this sort were conceived and executed primarily by Sadou Daoudou, the minister of armed forces, who declared that the "maquis would be liquidated" through a combination of military action, the psychological evolution of the population, and the tapering off of international support for the UPC. CHAN, Foccart papers, Fonds publics 466, AFP 106, Yaoundé, 1962, Cameroun, Affaires intérieures 1962.

99. APN, Passation de commandement entre Mm. Stanislas Joë Bias, Préfet sortant et Luc Loë, Préfet entrant, Nkongsamba, 17 avril 1972.

100. APN, Rapport annuel d'activités, 1 January–31 December 1972: M. le Directeur général de la DIRDOC et de la sécurité à la Présidence de la République unie du Cameroun, Nkongsamba, 5 January 1973.

101. CAOM, Affaires politiques 3327/2, Note sur la situation politique au Cameroun, 1–28 February 1959, which reported that after the attack on the Bandjoun chefferie, "most of the population is remaining silent and they refuse to divulge information, as they are fearful of repercussions from the terrorists."

102. APN, Procès verbal d'un CCO restreint tenu à Dibombari, 16 October 1970, Département du Mungo, refers to the "*mutisme douteux dans la plupart des milieux Bamileke.*" See also the report that Bamileke planters' failure to report maquisards' passage through their fields and a corpse lying on the road demonstrated that "the majority of these Bamileke subjects encourage the guerilla war." APN, Bulletin de renseignements, "Assassinat et activités rebelles," Gendarmerie Loum, 19 September 1964.

103. In his article based largely on personal observation and interviews conducted during the early postcolonial period, Jean-François Bayart describes the atmosphere of fear. Bayart, "One-Party Government and Political Development in Cameroon," *African Affairs*, 72, no. 287 (1973): 125–44, 137.

104. Ibid., 132.

105. Awasom, "Politics and Constitution-Making," 9–21.

106. NYPL, ILRM, box 14, file: General Correspondence: Cameroons, Marcel Bebey-Eyidi to Roger Baldwin, 24 October 1961.

107. NYPL, ILRM, box 14, file: General Correspondence: Cameroons, Marcel Bebey-Eyidi to Roger Baldwin, 3 July 1959.

108. The authors of the open letter were Bebey-Eyidi, Charles Okala, André-Marie Mbida, and Theodore Mayi Matip.

109. NYPL, ILRM, box 14, file: General Correspondence: Cameroons, Emmanuel Ngalle to Roger Baldwin, 12 November 1962.

110. NYPL, ILRM, box 14, file: General Correspondence: Cameroons, press release, 1 December 1962.

111. NYPL, ILRM, box 14, file: General Correspondence: Cameroons, Bebey-Eyidi (Maison d'Arrêt à Yoko) to Roger Baldwin, 6 June 1963.

112. CAOM, Affaires politiques 3348/1, Directeur de la Sûreté, J. Cardin à M. le Ministre de la France d'outre-mer, Rapport de Sûreté, 26 September 1958, "Circonstances dans lesquelles Ruben Um Nyobé a trouvé la mort."

113. CAOM, Affaires politiques 3301, Note sur la situation politique au Cameroun, 1–30 September 1958.

114. "Paix à Ruben Um Nyobé," *L'effort camerounais*, no. 155 (21 September 1958).

115. The newspapers "seized" by decree: *L'humanité*, no. 1362 (12 September 1958); *Le patriote*, no. 54–56 (19, 20, 23 September 1958); *La tribune du pays*, no. 4 (15–21 September 1958); *France-observateur*, no. 437 (18 September 1958); *Ami du peuple*, no. 14 (18, 21 September 1958); *Tribune du peuple*, no. 20 (September 1958).

116. "Paix à Ruben Um Nyobé," *L'effort camerounais*, no. 155 (21 September 1958).

117. See chapter 5.

118. CAOM, Affaires politiques 3301, Rapport de Sûreté, 25 October–15 November 1958.

119. CAOM, Affaires politiques 3327/2, Note sur la situation politique au Cameroun, 1–31 May 1959.

120. Although the Foccart papers related to the Moumié assassination have not yet been declassified and the French presidency denied my request to see them, an account of the event has been pieced together, mostly through memoirs and personal accounts, over the years. For an overview of existing accounts and the literature pertaining to Moumié's death, see Deltombe, Domergue, and Tatsitsa, *Kamerun!* 473–78.

121. See, for example, "Seven Condemned to Death in Criminal Court in Douala," in CAOM, AGEFOM 1007/3570, AFP spécial outre-mer, no. 3919, 2–3 August 1959.

122. APN, J. B. Ndoumou, Chef de la BMM, Nkongsamba, a/s Le terrorisme et la lutte antiterroriste dans le Mungo à M. le Directeur général de la DIRDOC et de la sécurité à la présidence de la république fédérale à Yaoundé, 4 August 1970.

123. On the constitutional referendum, see Jean-François Bayart, *L'état au Cameroun*, 2nd ed. (Paris: Presses de la fondation nationale des sciences politiques, 1985), 70, 73–82.

124. CAOM, Affaires politiques 3281/1, AFP no. 17, 23–30 May 1960. On Momo, see chapter 5.

125. Ignace Néguin Djoko, intrvw., Baham center, August 2002.

126. *La presse du Cameroun*, no. 4008 (3 September 1963).

127. *La presse du Cameroun*, no. 4012 (7–8 September 1963).

128. *La presse du Cameroun*, no. 4046 (19–20 October 1963).

129. The Law on Repression of Subversion stipulated, "En temps de guerre ou si l'état d'exception ou d'urgence a été proclamé par décret, des tribunaux militaires peuvent être crées par décret. Les jugements rendus par les tribunaux militaires permanents ou temporaires ne sont pas susceptibles d'appel. En outre, les tribunaux militaires prononcent obligatoirement la confiscation au profit de la nation des biens du condamné de quelque nature qu'ils soient, Divis ou Indivis, dont le condamné ne peut établir l'origine légitime. Les procédures de subversion en cours ou en instance de jugement ou d'appel lors de la promulgation de la loi qui vient d'être publiée, sont déférés de plein droit et en l'état aux tribunaux militaires." *La presse du Cameroun*, no. 4052 (26–27 October 1963).

130. CHAN, Foccart papers, Fonds publics, Saint Mleux à affaires étrangères, 7 January 1964.

131. *La presse du Cameroun*, no. 4056, 31 October–1 November 1963.

132. This account is from AFP, 3 January 1964, and is included in the Foccart papers.

133. CHAN, Foccart papers, Fonds publics, Saint Mleux à Affaires étrangères, 7 January 1964. On the same day, at the same time, Noé Tankeu, commanding officer of the ALNK based in the Wouri; Théodore Kilama Mpouma (aka Makanda Pouth), commanding officer of the ALNK military district in the Sanaga-Maritime and the Nkam; and two other "outlaws" were publicly executed in Douala.

134. Ignace Néguin Djoko, intrvw., Baham center, 26 August 2002. In this section, I cite only the oral informants that specifically agreed to being named as narrators of these events. Other Bahams spoke of the events on condition of anonymity.

135. Ignace Néguin Djoko, Baham centre, 26 August 2002.

136. Ibid.

137. Ibid.

138. François Tchuenkam, intrvw., La'agweu, Baham, September 2002.

139. Compare to the description of Mpodol Um Nyobé's death in the Sanaga-Maritime in Achille Mbembe, "Pouvoir des morts, language des vivants: Les errances de la mémoire nationaliste au Cameroun," in Bayart, Mbembe, and Toulabor, *Politique par le bas*, 183–229.

140. François Tchuenkam, intrvw., La'agweu, Baham, September 2002.

141. See conclusion.

142. François Tchuenkam intrvw.

143. I draw this account from CHAN, Foccart papers, Fonds publics 466, Jean-Pierre Bénard, Ambassadeur de France au Cameroun à M. le Secrétaire d'état aux affaires étrangères, au sujet du conflit entre le governement et la hierarchie catholique, Yaoundé, 2 March 1962. See also references to the incident made by Bishop Zoa in Yaoundé in *L'effort camerounais*, 11, 18, 25 February, 1962.

144. Among the surviving political prisoners was Jean-Paul Sende, a well-known UPC leader and activist throughout the nationalist period.

145. The Ndongmo affair, which coincided with the arrest of his alleged co-conspirator, Ernest Ouandié, culminated in two trials in December 1970: the first, of twenty-eight people accused of conspiring against the state from 1961 to 1970, the second, of seventy-six people for an attempted coup d'état. See Paul-Valentin Emog, *Le porteur de cornes: Monseigneur Albert Ndongmo (1925–1992)* (Yaoundé: Les Éditions Terre Africaine, 2005); Deltombe, Domergue, and Tatsitsa, *Kamerun!* chap. 33. For a complete list of the names of those tried and their sentences, see François Fotso, *La lutte nationaliste au Cameroun, 1940–1971* (Paris: L'Harmattan, 2010), 330–55.

146. See Srila Roy, "The Grey Zone: The 'Ordinary' Violence of Extraordinary Times," *Journal of the Royal Anthropological Institute* 14, no. 2 (2008); Javier Auyero, *Routine Politics and Violence in Argentina: The Gray Zone of State Power* (Cambridge: Cambridge University Press, 2007).

147. APN, Bulletin de renseignements, "Attaque rebelle de la clinique du Docteur Happi," 13 July 1970, Armée de Terre, Secteur militaire du Littoral, 3e bureau.

148. Ibid.

149. APN, Fiche d'interrogatoire, Gendarmerie, Région du Littoral, Compagnie de Nkongsamba, Brigade de Manjo, Manjo, 30 July 1970.

150. APN, Renseignements judiciaires, Procès verbal, no. 1144, Brigade de Manjo, 7 December 1970.

151. This account comes from two oral informants. The first, Joseph Fokou, lived in the neighborhood near the bar and was an eyewitness to the fight between the soldiers. He provided the names of the bars, the woman, and the corporal-chief. Fabien Kange Ewane, who later forsook the priesthood to become a historian after the Ndongmo affair and due to the racism he faced in the Vatican, was an eyewitness to the priests' intervention and follow-up care of the victims. Joseph Fokou, intrvw., Nkongsamba, March 2003; Professor Kangue Ewane, intrvw., Yaoundé, June 2002.

152. The details of this story are taken from "Peine de mort à Th. Nya Nana et à ses 3 principaux complices." *L'effort camerounais*, no. 513 (7 November 1965). See also APN, Rapport hébdomadaire, August 1965.

153. "Peine de mort à Th. Nya Nana et à ses 3 principaux complices." *L'effort camerounais*, no. 513 (7 November 1965).

154. Deltombe, Domergue, and Tatsitsa, *Kamerun!* 569–70.

155. For reports of the Loum clinic attack, see APN, Synthèse mensuelle de renseignements, 27 June–31 July 1970, Forces armées nationales, Secteur militaire du Littoral, Quartier de Nkongsamba, 1 August 1970; APN, Rapport de Sûreté, 9 July 1970, "Incursion rebelle à Loum"; APN, Bulletin de renseignements, "Attaque rebelle de la clinique du Docteur Happi," Armée de Terre, Secteur militaire du Littoral, 2e bureau, 13 July 1970; APN, Rapport de Sûreté, "Attentats terroristes du 9 Juillet 1970," 14 July 1970; APN, Note de renseignements, "Attentats terroristes du 9 juillet 1970 contre le clinique Happi à Loum," 15 July 1970; APN, Note de renseignements, "A/S attentats terroristes du 9 juillet 1970 à Loum," 15 July 1970; APN, Message porté, Autorité origine: Co-brigade Manjo, Destinataires: Préfet du Mungo, Sous-Préfet de Manjo, Co-compagnie gendarmerie Nkongsamba, 29

July 1970; APN, Rapport de Gustave Kouambo, Officier de police, Chargé du commissariat de sécurité publique de la ville de Loum, Incrimination: Attentats rebelles, 19 July 1970; APN, Informateur du service, "Commentaire sur l'attaque de la clinique du Docteur Happi à Loum," 23 July 1970; APN, Note de renseignements, "Situation à Loum après le raid terroriste du 9 juillet 1970," 23 July 1970; APN, Bulletin de renseignements spécial, "Attaque terroriste du 9 juillet à Loum," Ministère des forces armées, Secteur militaire du Littoral, Quartier de Nkongsamba, 13 July 1970.

156. APN, Informateur du service, "Commentaire sur l'attaque de la clinique du Docteur Happi à Loum," 23 July 1970; APN, Note de renseignements, "Situation à Loum après le raid terroriste du 9 juillet 1970," 23 July 1970.

157. APN, Rapport politique trimestriel, no. 63/RPT/CF/DMG/SP, January–March 1975.

158. Bayart, "One-Party Government."

159. See for example, APN, Mbende Martin, Maître d'école officielle de Manjo à M. le Préfet du Mungo s/c M. le Commissaire de la Brigade Mixte, Nkongsamba, 23 June 1970; APN, Bulletin de renseignements, "Les activités des Témoins de Jehovah," 5 June 1971, Brigade de gendarmerie de Melong; APN, Bulletin de renseignements, Brigade routière de Nkongsamba, au sujet des activités des Témoins de Jehovah, 21 May 1970.

160. And no less than six official reports, addressed to everyone from the Loum gendarmerie to the Mungo prefect, to the minister of armed forces: APN, Eloumou Victor, Maréchal des Logis-Chefs, Commandant de la brigade de gendarmerie de Loum (Moungo) à M. le Préfet, Moungo, 26 December 1975; "Examen de Situation—Kamgue Barthélemy," Rapport du SEDOC, BMM du Moungo à Nkongsamba, Alexandre Mbody, Officier de police de la Sûreté nationale du Cameroun; SEDOC, BMM Nkongsamba à M. le Préfet, 3 February 1976; "Demande de renseignement sur la procédure établie contre Kamgue pour subversion," Ministre des Forces armées à M. le Préfet du Moungo, 25 February 1976; Luc Loé, Préfet du Moungo à M. le Ministre des Forces armées, 26 April 1976.

161. On this point see Mark Neocleous, "The Problem with Normality: Taking Exception to 'Permanent Emergency,'" *Alternatives: Global, Local, Political* 31, no. 2 (2006): 191–213.

162. Ibid., 208.

163. Ibid.

164. See Jacques Rancière, "Who Is the Subject of the Rights of Man?" *South Atlantic Quarterly* 103, nos. 2–3 (2004): 297–310; Neocleous, "Problem with Normality," 208.

CONCLUSION: "AFTER THE WAR, WE STOP COUNTING THE DEAD"

1. As quoted in *La presse du Cameroun*, 14 January 1959.

2. Jean-François Bayart, "One-Party Government and Political Development in Cameroun," *African Affairs* 72, no. 287 (1973): 125–44, 128.

3. Jean-François Bayart, *L'état au Cameroun* (Paris: Presses de la fondation nationale des sciences politiques, 1979), 163.

4. Sindjoun-Pokam, *La philosophie politique trahie: Le monofascisme* (Paris: Atelier Silex, 1987), 65.

5. As quoted in Bayart, "One-Party Government," 128.

6. See also chapter 4.

7. The history of the UPC's Second Front, established in the northern regions of the Republic of Congo, has yet to be researched. No published scholarly accounts exist, although Jean-François Bayart makes brief reference to it, as does Victor Le Vine. See Bayart, *État au Cameroun*, 119–20; Le Vine, *The Cameroon Federal Republic* (Ithaca: Cornell University Press, 1971), 128. See also Daniel Abwa, *Ngouo Woungly-Massaga alias Commandant Kissamba: "Cameroun, ma part de vérité"* (Paris: Éditions Minsi, 2005), 129, 165, 172, 187, 199. While some scholars ascribe the factionalization of UPC exiles to the Sino-Soviet split, in the mid-1960s, Massaga's testimony suggests that there may be more to the story.

8. But for a measured, historical discussion of the relationship between Pan-Africanism and African nationalisms during the twentieth century, see Toyin Falola, *Nationalism and African Intellectuals* (Rochester: University of Rochester Press, 2001): 97–142.

9. Jan Eckel, "Human Rights and Decolonization: New Perspectives and Open Questions," *Humanity: An International Journal of Human Rights, Humanitarianism, and Development* 1, no. 1 (2010): 111–35.

10. See Jane Burbank and Frederick Cooper, *Empires in World History: Power and the Politics of Difference* (Princeton: Princeton University Press, 2010), 425; Cooper, "Possibility and Constraint: African Independence in Historical Perspective," *Journal of African History* 49, no. 2 (2008): 167–96.

11. Gary Wilder, "Untimely Vision: Aimé Césaire, Decolonization, Utopia," *Public Culture* 21, no. 1 (2009): 101–40, 108.

12. Richard Joseph, *Radical Nationalism in Cameroun: The Social Origins of the UPC Rebellion* (Oxford: Oxford University Press, 1977); Elizabeth Schmidt, "Anticolonial Nationalism in French West Africa: What Made Guinea Unique?" *African Studies Review* 52, no. 2 (2009): 1–34; Klaas van Walraven, "Decolonization by Referendum: The Anomaly of Niger and the Fall of Sawaba, 1958–1959," *Journal of African History* 50, no. 2 (2009): 269–92.

13. Patrick Williams, "'Faire peau neuve': Césaire, Fanon, Memmi, Sartre and Senghor," in *Francophone Postcolonial Studies: A Critical Introduction*, ed., Charles Forsdick and David Murphy (New York: Oxford University Press, 2003), 181.

14. Christopher J. Lee, "Between a Moment and an Era: The Origins and Afterlives of Bandung," introduction to Lee, *Making a World after Empire: The Bandung Moment and Its Political Afterlives* (Athens: Ohio University Press, 2010), 22–23. Lee maintains that an outdated scholarly focus on political units—"in particular, the nation-state and empire"—has proven insufficient to keep pace with postcolonial political conditions and has occluded the history of connections within and across the Afro-Asian divide.

15. See, for example, Vijay Prashad, *The Darker Nations: A People's History of the Third World* (New York: New Press, 2007); Lee, *Making a World after Empire*; Jean Allman, "Nuclear Imperialism and the Pan-African Struggle for Peace and Freedom, Ghana, 1959–1962," *Souls: A Critical Journal of Black Politics, Culture, and Society* 10, no. 2 (2008): 83–102.

16. Prashad, *Darker Nations*, 45–46. See also Lee, "Asian-African Conference," 87.

17. Curiously, although the case of the UPC demonstrates that, even in this "first phase" of Africa's decolonization, exiled nationalists played a crucial role in the struggle for nation, the literature does not reflect this. To my knowledge, there is only one historical study devoted to the UPC's external activity. See Dieudonné Pouhe Pouhe, "Les liaisons extérieures de l'UPC, 1948–1960" (master's thesis, University of Yaoundé I, 1999). In contrast, the role of exile and transregional organization in later liberation movements in eastern and southern Africa is well documented. See, for example, Liisa H. Malkki, *Purity and Exile: Violence, Memory, and National Cosmology among Hutu Refugees in Tanzania* (Chicago: University of Chicago Press, 1995); Norma Kriger, *Zimbabwe's Guerilla War: Peasant Voices* (Cambridge University Press, 1992), esp. chap. 3; James D. Sidaway and David Simon, "Geopolitical Transition and State Formation: The Changing Political Geographies of Angola, Mozambique, and Namibia," *Journal of Southern African Studies* 19, no. 1 (1993): 6–28; Stephen Ellis, "The Historical Significance of South Africa's Third Force," *Journal of Southern African Studies* 24, no. 2 (1998): 261–99; Raymond Suttner, "Cultures of the African National Congress of South Africa: Imprint of Exile Experiences," *Journal of Contemporary African Studies* 21, no. 2 (2003): 303–20; Nadia Manghezi, *The Maputo Connection: The ANC in the World of Frelimo* (Johannesburg: Jacana, 2009); Michael G. Panzer, "The Pedagogy of Revolution: Youth, Generational Conflict, and Education in Mozambican Nationalism and the State, 1962–1970," *Journal of Southern African Studies* 35, no. 4 (2009): 803–20. One of the sole studies to acknowledge the influence of earlier anticolonial liberation struggles, specifically the decision to adopt violence as a strategy and China's, as well as Ghana's, support for this initiative, on the later such movements in southern Africa, albeit somewhat superficially, is, for the ANC, Stephen Ellis, "The Genesis of the ANC's Armed Struggle in South Africa, 1948–1961," *Journal of Southern African History* 37, no. 4 (2011): 657–76.

18. Matthew Connelly, "Rethinking the Cold War and Decolonization: The Grand Strategy of the Algerian War for Independence," *International Journal of Middle East Studies* 33, no. 2 (2001): 221–45; Meredith Terretta, "Cameroonian Nationalists Go Global: From Forest *Maquis* to a Pan-African Accra," *Journal of African History* 51, no. 2 (2010): 189–212; Jeffrey S. Ahlman, "The Algerian Question in Nkrumah's Ghana, 1958–1960: Debating 'Violence' and 'Nonviolence' in African Decolonization," *Africa Today* 57, no. 2 (2010): 66–84. For British assessment of the Algeria-Ghana-Guinea-UPC alliance, see, for example, NA, FO 371/147056, Mr. Watson, Dakar, to Foreign Office, 9 January 1960.

19. "Rapport d'Aït Ahmed," December 1948, quoted in Connelly, "Rethinking the Cold War," 223.

20. Terretta, "Cameroonian Nationalists," 197.

21. Connelly, "Rethinking the Cold War," 223.
22. Ibid., 224.
23. Ibid., 224.
24. See chapter 3 of this volume.
25. Connelly, "Rethinking the Cold War," 232.
26. Lee, *World after Empire*.
27. On the various groups, see Kwesi Armah, *Peace without Power: Ghana's Foreign Policy, 1957–1966* (Accra: Ghana University Press, 2004), 96–104.
28. See Frantz Fanon, *The Wretched of the Earth*, trans. Richard Philcox (1963; repr., New York: Grove Press, 2004); Emmanuel Hansen, "Frantz Fanon: Portrait of a Revolutionary Intellectual," *Transition* 46 (1974): 25–36. There is extensive scholarship and commentary on the prevalence of France's postcolonial control and exploitation of its formal colonial territories. To start, see François-Xavier Verschave, *La Françafrique: Le plus long scandale de la République* (Paris: Stock, 1998). See also the memoirs of Jacques Foccart, the author and orchestrator of French policy toward the former colonial territories in Africa from 1960 to 1974: Jacques Foccart and Philippe Gaillard, *Foccart parle: Entretiens avec Philippe Gaillard*, 2 vols. (Paris: Fayard/Jeune Afrique, 1995–97). For a Fanonian retrospective on postcolonial Africa, see Achille Mbembe, *Sortir de la grande nuit* (Paris: La Découverte, 2010). On the precise nature of the bilateral agreements drawn up between France and the Ahdijo regime, beginning in December 1958, while French Cameroon was still under trusteeship, see Thomas Deltombe, Manuel Domergue, and Jacob Tatsitsa, *Kamerun! Une guerre cachée aux origines de la Françafrique (1948–1971)* (Paris: La Découverte, 2011), 456–64.
29. On this point, see Antoinette Burton, "The Sodalities of Bandung: Toward a Critical 21st Century History," epilogue to Lee, *World after Empire*, 353.
30. William Appleman Williams, *The Tragedy of American Diplomacy: United States Foreign Policy 1945–1980* (1959; New York: Norton, 1988); Gabriel Kolko, *Confronting the Third World: United States Foreign Policy, 1945–1980* (New York: Pantheon, 1988); H. W. Brands, *The Specter of Neutralism: The United States and the Emergence of the Third World, 1947–1960* (New York: Columbia University Press, 1989); Peter Hahn, *The United States, Great Britain, and Egypt, 1945–1956: Strategy and Diplomacy in the Early Cold War* (Chapel Hill: University of North Carolina Press, 1991); Vladislav Zubok and Constantine Pleshakov, *Inside the Kremlin's Cold War: From Stalin to Khrushchev* (Cambridge, MA: Harvard University Press, 1996).
31. Connelly, "Rethinking the Cold War," 221–22; Zachary Karabell, *Architects of Intervention: The United States, the Third World, and the Cold War, 1946–1962* (Baton Rouge: Louisiana State University Press, 1999); Fawaz Gerges, *The Superpowers and the Middle East: Regional and International Politics, 1955–1967* (Boulder: Westview, 1994); Elizabeth Schmidt, *Cold War and Decolonization in Guinea, 1946–1958* (Athens: Ohio University Press, 2007). For a comprehensive overview of the Cold War in Africa see Schmidt, *Foreign Intervention in Africa: From the Cold War to the War on Terror* (Cambridge: Cambridge University Press, 2013).
32. Mary L. Dudziak, *Cold War Civil Rights: Race and the Image of American Democracy* (Princeton: Princeton University Press, 2000); Thomas Borstelmann,

The Cold War and the Color Line: American Race Relations in the Global Arena (Cambridge, MA: Harvard University Press, 2001).

33. Connelly's article offers a minute, chronological account of just how adept FLN leaders were at navigating and diplomatically manipulating superpower rivalries. Connelly, "Rethinking the Cold War."

34. Jean-Martin Tchaptchet, *Quand les jeunes Africains créaient l'histoire*, vol. 2 of *Récit autobiographique* (Paris: L'Harmattan, 2006).

35. This was, of course, a strategy that UPC leaders had in common with a number of other anticolonialist leaders at the time. On this point, see Connelly, "Rethinking the Cold War," 221–22.

36. Meredith Terretta, "'We Had Been Fooled into Thinking that the UN Watches over the Entire World': Human Rights, UN Trust Territories, and Africa's Decolonization," *Human Rights Quarterly* 34, no. 2 (2012): 329–60. On Scott, see also Carol Anderson, "International Conscience, the Cold War, and Apartheid: The NAACP's Alliance with the Reverend Michael Scott for South West Africa's Liberation, 1946–1951," *Journal of World History* 19, no. 3 (2008): 297–325; Anne Yates and Lewis Chester, *The Troublemaker: Michael Scott and His Lonely Struggle against Injustice* (London: Aurum Press, 2006).

37. Lucien Lazare, *L'abbé Glasberg* (Paris: Cerf, 1990); COSE, *À la recherche d'une patrie: la France devant l'immigration* (Montrouge: Éditions Réalités, 1946); COSE, *La leçon sociale de l'affaire "Exodus"* (Montrouge: Éditions Réalités, 1947). Glasberg's activism on behalf of exiles and asylum seekers would later influence the founding, in 1971, of the NGO France, Terre d'Asile. For Glasberg's personal connections with upécistes, initiated via student groups of Cameroonian nationalists in France in the 1950s and lasting into the 1970s (when the priest became a key player in an international initiative to stay the execution of the commander in chief of the UPC army, Ernest Ouandié, in 1970), see the files contained in the collection Comité international de la défense d'Ernest Ouandié, at the Institute of International Social History, Amsterdam.

38. See, for example, United Press, "France Sends Troops to Crush Red-Led Uprising in Cameroons: Acts to Prevent New 'Algeria' in African Territory Where Rebels Burned 60 Villages," *New York Times*, 6 January 1958, which describes a "Communist-led uprising" in Cameroon but adds that most of Communist leader Ruben Um Nyobé's followers "are not concerned with politics. They regard him as a prophet with magic powers and swear death to anyone who betrays him." Later in the same article, Um Nyobé is portrayed as "a member of the ... Bassa tribe ... his followers offer sacrifices to him during night feasts in the deep jungles."

39. Connelly, "Rethinking the Cold War," 232.

40. Ibid., 232.

41. Terretta, "Cameroonian Nationalists," offers an explanation of why the UPC's African support dwindled steadily throughout the early 1960s.

42. On the nature of these bilateral agreements, which began to be put in place in December 1958, see Deltombe, Domergue, and Tatsitsa, *Kamerun!* 456–64. According to this account, the bilateral agreements reached between France and the Ahidjo administration of French Cameroon served as a model for those drawn up for other former French territories after independence. Ibid., 464–66.

Glossary

chuep'si. Sacred site of protection, justice, reconciliation, and community or lineage identity; material symbol of the connection between the living and the unseen inhabitants of *gung*.

chuep'si mbem. A sacred site within a family compound; site of the residence of the compound's guardian spirits.

djem djem. Pods filled with seeds associated with twins in the Grassfields region.

djie dandan. A straight path or road.

feuveuck. The chieftaincy's sacred site in Baham.

fo (pl., *mfo*). A ruler of a Grassfields polity; usually glossed as chief.

fonte (pl., *mfonte*). A *fo* who has pledged loyalty to another *fo*, thus becoming a "lesser" *fo*.

ghèkè. A ritual specialist who knew how to manipulate *kè* (s.v.).

gung. A polity comprising land, people, and governance; a nation.

indique. A spy or informer.

kamsi (pl., *mkamsi*). A titled diviner or healer (or both); lit., God's notable.

kamveu. A council to the *fo*, made up of the descendants of the nine cofounders of the chieftaincy.

ké. Mystical energy; often glossed as magic or power.

keu-keu. Meaning politics, this term literally refers to massive entanglement of wire or string with no beginning or end.

kolo. A term that *upécistes* used to refer to a *colon*, or white settler.

kungang. A secret association of diviners, healers, and guardians of chieftaincy protocol that serves as council to the *fo*.

kwè. An alliance.

kwepe. A copper bracelet worn by a chief or notable.

la'a. A home, compound, district, or village.

lepue. The state of sovereignty, autonomy, or independence.

loi-cadre. The establishment of parliamentary assemblies to govern internal affairs in France's colonies, overseas territories, and, contrary to UN statutes, UN trust territories

Kamerun. Spelling of *Cameroon* denoting a desire for reunification and distance from British and French administration; adopted by *upécistes* after the British proscription of the party in 1957.

kamveu. The governing council of the *fo*.

kolo. A *colon*, or colonialist; beginning in 1957, spelled with a *k* in reference to the nationalist spelling of *Cameroon* (*Kamerun*).

kungang. A secret association that regulates the mystical sphere of power in the chieftaincy.

la'akam. The site of a *fo*'s initiation upon succession to power.

lamidats. A traditional form of government in Islamized northern Cameroon.

maquis. Underground resistance.

maquisard. A freedom fighter, usually (but not always) a member of or recruited by members of the nationalist party (the UPC or the JDC); the term took on a pejorative meaning in the early postcolonial years due to anti-UPC propaganda campaigns waged by the Ahidjo regime.

mbem. Spirit protectors.

mfingung. Traitors; lit., sellers of the country.

mfo. See *fo*.

mkamsi. See *kamsi*.

mpouogung. Patriots; lit., children of the country.

mwabo. See *wabo*.

mwala (pl., *wala*). Notables who made up the cabinet of the *fo*; often glossed as ministers, in contemporary Bamileke parlance.

mwala djyeh. The *mwala* of fertility, fecundity, and rain.

pfeukang. A tree (*Dracaena deistelina*) used in a variety of ways in the Grassfields region to request peace, reconciliation, or protection, or to show good will; lit., tree of peace.

Si. God or land.

ta djie. A *mwala* (minister), making up the *fo*'s cabinet and assisting in chieftaincy governance; lit., Father of the road.

Tâ Ntomdjap. A name for Fo Kamdem II of Baham; lit., Father of the Seed Grain of *Njap* (a green, leafy vegetable).

tchinda. Armed guards of the *fo*.

tsa. The chief's compound.

tseu. A dance traditionally performed by the *fo* and notables of *gung* on rare occasions of celebration.

upéciste. A nationalist; member or supporter of the UPC.

wabo (pl., *mwabo*). A nobility title granted by the *fo* affording the right to govern a district within the chieftaincy.

wala. See *mwala*.

woumbe. See *wabo*.

yam. A tree (*Ficus aganophila* Hutch.) used to delineate boundaries of a plot of land, and planted in the compound's *chuep'si mbem*.

Bibliography

ARCHIVES

Affaires politiques (Fonds ministériels). Centre des archives d'outre-mer.
Agence économique. Centre des archives d'outre-mer.
Archives nationales Yaoundé, Cameroon.
Archives préfectorales de Dschang, Cameroon.
Archives préfectorales de Nkongsamba, Cameroon.
British National Archives, Kew, United Kingdom.
Centre des archives d'outre-mer, Aix-en-Provence, France.
Centre d'histoire et d'études des troupes d'outre-mer, Fréjus, France.
Centre historique des Archives nationales, section du 20ᵉ siècle, Paris, France.
Comité international de la défense d'Ernest Ouandié, Amsterdam, the Netherlands.
Foccart papers (public and private collections). Centre historique des Archives nationales, section du 20ᵉ siècle, Paris, France.
Ghana National Archives, Accra.
Institute of International Social History, Amsterdam, the Netherlands.
International League of the Rights of Man, New York, United States.
League of Nations Annual Reports.
New York Public Library, Rare Books and Manuscripts Division.
United Nations General Assembly, New York, United States.
United Nations Microprint Series, 1946–60.
United Nations Trusteeship Council, New York, United States.

PERIODICALS

Africasia. No. 25 (October 26, 1970).
Afrique nouvelle.
Le Bamiléké: Organe mensuel de liaison des chefferies de la région Bamiléké et des Bamilékés de l'extérieur. 1955–59.
Drum Call. Vols. 34–42 (1955–63).
L'effort camerounais. 1959–72.
Le monde non chrétien. 1947–69.
La nouvelle expression. 2001–3.
L'opinion au Cameroun: Organe progressiste d'expression, d'information et d'éducation des camerounais. 1955–72.

La presse du Cameroun. 1955–60.
Récits missionnaires illustrés. Paris, Société des missions évangéliques, 1921–35.
Sunday Telegraph. 1961.
La voix du Cameroun. Vol. 302 (February–March 2002).

POLITICAL PARTY TRACTS AND PAMPHLETS

Union camerounaise (UC). *Cinquième congrès de l'UC.* Bafoussam, 20 November–4 December 1965.
———. *Deuxième séminaire de l'UC.* Yaoundé, 15–23 June 1964.
———. *Première conseil national de l'UC.* Yaoundé, 14–20 April 1963.
———. *Quatrième congrès du parti politique de l'UC.* Ebolowa, 4–8 July 1962.
Union des populations du Cameroun (UPC). *From Algeria to the Kamerun.* Cairo: Foreign Delegation of the Union of the Populations of the Cameroons, [1958?].
———. *Les grandes lignes de la situations au Cameroun.* N.p., 196?.
———. *The Kamerun.* Cairo, 1957.
———. "Memorandum Submitted to the Conference of Independent African States Held at Addis Ababa, 14th–18th June, 1960." London, 1960.
———. *La tutelle internationale à l'épreuve.* Cairo: Le service de l'information de l'UPC à l'étranger, [1959?].
———. *The UPC Denounces the Planned Systematic Tortures in the Kamerun.* Cairo: Bureau of Leading Committee of the Union of the Populations of the Cameroons, 1958.
———. *L'UPC parle . . .* Paris, 1971.
———. *La vérité sur le "Comité révolutionnaire": Communiqué du Bureau du comité directeur de l'UPC.* Bureau du comité directeur de l'UPC/One Kamerun Movement. Accra: UPC, 1963.

INTERVIEWS

Achu, Thaddeus. Mankon, 18 December 2001.
Balogog, Emmanuel. Nkongsamba, 11 March 2002.
Bomda, Daniel. Nkongsamba, 29 March 2003.
Djimi, Victor. Demgo, Baham, March 2003.
Djoko, Ignace Néguin, *dit* Souop Cuichoue, Baham, 2 March, 22 March 2002.
Djonteu, Jean. Demgo, Baham, 4 September 2002.
Djuidje. Sou'o, Baham, 29 August 2002.
Fokou, Joseph. Nkongsamba, 14 March 2002.
Kamgaing, Joseph. Demgo, Baham, 31 August 2002.
Kamguia, Michel Débonaire. Chiala, Baham, 23 August 2002.
Kamto, Bernard. Banka, Baham, 22 November 2002.
Kamwa, Michel, *dit* Sop Kamogne Mecha'ac. Banka, Baham, 2 September 2002.
Kange Ewane, Fabien. Yaoundé, 20 June 2002.
Kengne, Joseph *dit* Woumbe Sop Kamga. Bamendjou, 2 September 2002.
Kepya Tchiwo, Romeo Charley, Nkongsamba, 11 March 2002.
Mewa, Thérèse, Baham, 6 September 2002.

Mkam, Jean Joseph. Nkongsamba, 14 March 2002.
Mwafo Kouomou. Batousouo'o, Baham, 14 April 2003.
Ngakou, Joseph. Bamendjou, 16 November 2002.
Ngande-Sanga, Léon. Nkongsamba, 13 March 2002.
Ngoundjou, Lucienne. Nkongsamba, 4 March 2002.
Nguemegne, Jacques Philbert. Dschang, 21 March 2002.
Nguetchouang, Rebecca. Bamendjou, 1 September 2002.
Njapa, Job. Nkongsamba, 7 November 2002.
Noubi, Jeanette. Yaoundé, 16 February 2002.
Noubi, Pierre. Yaoundé, 16 February 2002.
Nyamnjoh, Francis. Mankon, 18 December 2001.
Sighoko. Bafoussam, 14 November 2002.
Sop, Jean. Baham, 30 August 2002.
Tagne, Joseph-René. Nkongsamba, 27 February 2002.
Takam, Elie. Bamendjou, 2 September 2002.
Tamko Max, Victor. Dschang, 21 March 2002.
Tamwa, Etienne. Baham, 1 September 2002.
Tchedim, Paul. Baham, 3 September 2002.
Tchienmou, Isaac. Baham, 2 September 2002.
Tchuenden, Mekeu. Baham, 12 November 2002.
Tchuenkam, André. Baham, 12 November 2002.
Teguia, Eric. Nkongsamba, 28 April 2002.
Teguia, Gabriel. Baham, 14 November 2002.
Tetzusunke. Baham, 14 November 2002.
Tocpa Taakou'o. Baham, 1 September 2002.

BOOKS AND ARTICLES

Abwa, Daniel. *Ngouo Woungly-Massaga alias Commandant Kissamba: "Cameroun, ma part de vérité."* Paris: Éditions Minsi, 2005.

Ahlman, Jeffrey S. "The Algerian Question in Nkrumah's Ghana, 1958–1960: Debating 'Violence' and 'Nonviolence' in African Decolonization." *Africa Today* 57, no. 2 (2010): 66–84.

Albert, André, SCJ. *Au Cameroun français: Bandjoun.* Montreal: Les éditions de l'arbre, 1943.

Allman, Jean. "Nuclear Imperialism and the Pan-African Struggle for Peace and Freedom, Ghana, 1959–1962." *Souls: A Critical Journal of Black Politics, Culture, and Society* 10, no. 2 (2008): 83–102.

———. *The Quills of the Porcupine: Asante Nationalism in an Emergent Ghana.* Madison: University of Wisconsin Press, 1993.

Anderson, Benedict. *Imagined Communities: Reflections on the Origins and Spread of Nationalism.* 1983. London: Verso, 2001.

Anderson, Carol. *Eyes Off the Prize: The United Nations and the African American Struggle for Human Rights, 1944–1955.* Cambridge: Cambridge University Press, 2003.

———."International Conscience, the Cold War, and Apartheid: The NAACP's Alliance with the Reverend Michael Scott for South West Africa's Liberation, 1946–1951." *Journal of World History* 19, no. 3 (2008): 297–325.

Appiah, Kwame. "Cosmopolitan Patriots." *Critical Inquiry* 23, no. 3 (1997): 617–39.

Apter, David E. "Ghana's Independence: Triumph and Paradox." *Transition* 98 (2008): 6–23.

Argenti, Nicolas. *The Intestines of the State: Youth, Violence, and Belated Histories in the Cameroon Grassfields.* Chicago: University of Chicago Press, 2007.

Armah, Kwesi. *Peace without Power: Ghana's Foreign Policy, 1957–1966.* Accra: Ghana University Press, 2004.

Austen, Ralph. "The Metamorphoses of Middlemen: The Duala, Europeans, and the Cameroon Hinterland, ca. 1800–ca. 1960." *International Journal of African Historical Studies* 16, no. 1 (1983): 1–24.

Austen, Ralph, and Jonathan Derrick. *Middlemen of the Cameroons Rivers: The Duala and Their Hinterland, c. 1600–c. 1960.* Cambridge: Cambridge University Press, 1999.

Auyero, Javier. *Routine Politics and Violence in Argentina: The Gray Zone of State Power.* Cambridge: Cambridge University Press, 2007.

Awasom, Nicodemus F. "Politics and Constitution-Making in Francophone Cameroon, 1959–1960." *Africa Today* 49, no. 4 (2002): 3–30.

Bakhtin, Mikhaïl. *Speech Genres and Other Late Essays.* Translated by Vern McGee. Austin: University of Texas Press, 1986.

Baldwin, Roger. "Report from the UN." *Africa Today* 3, no. 3 (1956): 10.

Barbier, Jean-Claude, Jacques Champaud, and Francis Gendreau. *Migrations et développement: La région du Moungo au Cameroun.* Paris: ORSTOM, 1983.

Bayart, Jean-François. *L'état au Cameroun.* Paris: Presses de la fondation nationale des sciences politiques, 1979. Reprinted and expanded, 1985, 2nd ed. Page references are to the 1985 edition.

———. *L'état en Afrique: La politique du ventre.* Paris: Fayard, 1989.

———. *The Illusion of Cultural Identity.* Translated by Steven Rendall et al. Chicago: University of Chicago Press, 2005.

———. "One-Party Government and Political Development in Cameroon." *African Affairs* 72, no. 287 (1973): 125–44.

Bayart, Jean-François, Achille Mbembe, and Comi Toulabor. *Le politique par le bas en Afrique noire: Contributions à une problématique de la démocratie.* Paris: Karthala, 1992. Reprinted with preface and notes by Jean-François Bayart, 2008.

Bayémi, Jean-Paul. *L'effort camerounais, ou, la tentation d'une presse libre.* Paris: L'Harmattan, 1989.

Berry, Sara. *Fathers Work for Their Sons: Accumulation, Mobility, and Class Formation in an Extended Yorùbá Community.* Berkeley: University of California Press, 1985.

Berman, Bruce, and John Lonsdale. *Unhappy Valley: Conflict in Kenya and Africa.* 2 vols. Athens: Ohio University Press, 1992.

Bernault, Florence. "Body, Power and Sacrifice in Equatorial Africa." *Journal of African History* 47, no. 2 (2006): 207–39.

———. *Démocraties ambigües en Afrique centrale: Congo-Brazzaville, Gabon, 1940–1965.* Paris: Karthala, 1996.
Binet, Jacques. "Droit foncier coutumier au Cameroun." *Monde non-chrétien*, no. 18 (1951).
Bjornson, Richard. *The African Quest for Freedom and Identity: Cameroonian Writing and the National Experience.* Bloomington: Indiana University Press, 1991.
Borstelmann, Thomas. *The Cold War and the Color Line: American Race Relations in the Global Arena.* Cambridge, MA: Harvard University Press, 2001.
Boutchoueng, Mélanie. "Ernest Ouandié (1924–1971): L'homme et son action politique." Master's thesis, University of Yaoundé I, 1994.
Branch, Daniel. *Defeating Mau Mau, Creating Kenya: Counterinsurgency, Civil War, and Decolonisation.* Cambridge: Cambridge University Press, 2009.
———. "Loyalists, Mau Mau and Elections in Kenya: The First Triumph of the System, 1957–1958." *Africa Today* 53, no. 2 (2006): 27–50.
Brands, H. W. *The Specter of Neutralism: The United States and the Emergence of the Third World, 1947–1960.* New York: Columbia University Press, 1989.
Burbank, Jane, and Frederick Cooper. *Empires in World History: Power and Politics of Difference.* Princeton: Princeton University Press, 2010.
Burke, Roland. *Decolonization and the Evolution of International Human Rights.* Philadelphia: University of Pennsylvania Press, 2010.
Burton, Antoinette. "The Sodalities of Bandung: Toward a Critical 21st Century History." Epilogue to Lee, *Making a World*, 351–61.
Burton, Antoinette, Augusto Espiritu, and Fanon Che Wilkins. "The Fate of Nationalisms in the Age of Bandung." *Radical History Review*, no. 95 (2006): 145–48.
Callahan, Michael D. *Mandates and Empire: The League of Nations and Africa, 1914–1931.* Brighton, UK: Sussex Academic Press, 1998.
———. *A Sacred Trust: The League of Nations and Africa, 1929–1946.* Brighton, UK: Sussex Academic Press, 2004.
COSE (Centre d'orientation sociale des étrangers). *A la recherche d'une patrie: La France devant l'immigration.* Montrouge: Éditions réalités, 1946.
———. *La leçon sociale de l'affaire "Exodus."* Montrouge: Éditions réalités, 1947.
Chafer, Tony. "Education and Political Socialisation of a National-Colonial Political Elite in French West Africa, 1936–1947." *Journal of Imperial and Commonwealth History* 35, no. 3 (2007): 437–58.
———. *The End of Empire in French West Africa: France's Successful Decolonization?* Oxford: Berg, 2002.
———. "Teaching Africans to Be French? France's 'Civilising Mission' and the Establishment of a Public Education System in French West Africa, 1903–30." *Africa* 56, no. 2 (2001): 190–209.
Chatap-Ekindi, Odile. "Changements et ruptures dans le Mungo de 1911 à 1950." Doctoral thesis, University of Provence, 1992.
Chem-Langhëë, Bongfen. "Slavery and Slave-Marketing in Nso' in the Nineteenth Century." *Paideuma* 41 (1995): 177–90.

Chendjou, Jean-Joseph. "Les Bamilékés de l'ouest Cameroun: Pouvoirs, économie et société: 1850–1916: La situation avant et après l'accentuation des influences européenes." Doctoral thesis, University of Paris I, 1986.

Chilver, Elizabeth M. "Nineteenth-Century Trade in the Bamenda Grassfields, Southern Cameroons." *Afrika und Übersee* 45, no. 4 (1961): 233–58.

———. "Paramountcy and Protection in the Cameroons: The Bali and the Germans, 1889–1913." In *Britain and Germany in Africa: Imperial Rivalry and Colonial Rule*, edited by Prosser Gifford and Wm. Roger Louis, 479–511. New Haven: Yale University Press, 1967.

Chindji-Kouleu, Ferdinand. *Histoire cachée du Cameroun*. Yaoundé: Editions Saagraph, 2006.

Clark, Roger S. "The International League for Human Rights and South West Africa, 1947–1957: The Human Rights NGO as Catalyst in the International Legal Process." *Human Rights Quarterly* 3, no. 4 (1981): 101–36.

Conklin, Alice. *A Mission to Civilize: The Republican Idea of Empire in France and West Africa, 1895–1930*. Stanford: Stanford University Press, 1997.

Conklin, Alice, Sarah Fishman, and Robert Zaretsky. *France and Its Empire since 1870*. Oxford: Oxford University Press, 2011.

Connelly, Matthew. *A Diplomatic Revolution: Algeria's Fight for Independence and the Origins of the Post–Cold War Era*. Oxford: Oxford University Press, 2002.

———. "Rethinking the Cold War and Decolonization: The Grand Strategy of the Algerian War for Independence." *International Journal of Middle East Studies* 33, no. 2 (2001): 221–45.

Cooper, Frederick. *Africa since 1940: The Past of the Present*. Cambridge: Cambridge University Press, 2002.

———. *Decolonization and African Society: The Labor Question in French and British Africa*. Cambridge: Cambridge University Press, 1996.

———. "Possibility and Constraint: African Independence in Historical Perspective." *Journal of African History* 49, no. 2 (2008): 167–96.

Coquery-Vidrovitch, Cathérine. "Nationalité et citoyenneté en Afrique occidentale française: Originaires et citoyens dans le Sénégal colonial." *Journal of African History* 42, no. 2 (2001): 285–305.

Débarge, Josette. *La mission médicale au Cameroun*. Récits missionnaires illustrés, no. 35. Paris: Société des missions évangéliques, 1934.

Defresnes, Roland. "Voyage au pays de la peur: Dans les maquis Bamiléké." *Afrique nouvelle*, no. 659 (30 March 1960).

Deltombe, Thomas, Manuel Domergue, and Jacob Tatsitsa. *Kamerun! Une guerre cachée aux origines de la Françafrique, 1948–1971*. Paris: La Découverte, 2011.

Dongmo, J.-L. *La maîtrise de l'espace agraire*. Vol. 1 of *Le dynamisme Bamiléké (Cameroun)*. Yaoundé: Centre d'édition et de production pour l'enseignement et la recherche, 1981.

Djiomo, Gabriel. "L'église catholique et l'Union des populations du cameroun (UPC) à l'ouest: 1948–1970." Master's thesis, University of Yaoundé I, 1999.

Donnat, Gaston. *Afin que nul n'oublie: L'itinéraire d'un anti-colonialiste: Algérie, Cameroun, Afrique*. Paris: L'Harmattan, 1986.

Duara, Prasenjit. *Rescuing History from the Nation: Questioning Narratives of Modern China*. Chicago: University of Chicago Press, 1995.
Dudziak, Mary L. *Cold War Civil Rights: Race and the Image of American Democracy*. Princeton: Princeton University Press, 2000.
Duncan, Patrick. "Non-Violence at Accra." *Africa Today* 6, no. 1 (1959): 30–32.
Echenberg, Myron. *Colonial Conscripts: The* Tirailleurs Sénégalais *in French West Africa, 1857–1960*. Portsmouth, NH: Heinemann, 1991.
Eckel, Jan. "Human Rights and Decolonization: New Perspectives and Open Questions." *Humanity: An International Journal of Human Rights, Humanitarianism, and Development* 1, no. 1 (2010): 111–35.
Eckert, Andreas. "African Rural Entrepreneurs and Labor in the Cameroon Littoral." *Journal of African History* 40, no. 1 (1999): 109–26.
Edwards, Brent Hayes. *The Practice of Diaspora: Literature, Translation, and the Rise of Black Internationalism*. Cambridge, MA: Harvard University Press, 2003.
Elkins, Caroline. "The Struggle for Mau Mau Rehabilitation in Late Colonial Kenya." *International Journal of African Historical Studies* 33, no. 1 (2000): 25–57.
Ellis, Stephen. "The Genesis of the ANC's Armed Struggle in South Africa, 1948–1961." *Journal of Southern African History* 37, no. 4 (2011): 657–76.
———. "The Historical Significance of South Africa's Third Force." *Journal of Southern African Studies* 24, no. 2 (1998): 261–99.
Emog, Paul-Valentin. *Le porteur de cornes: Monseigneur Albert Ndongmo (1925–1992)*. Yaoundé: Les éditions terre africaine, 2005.
Essome, Hermine Nicole Jombe. "Le Mungo et l'agitation syndicalo-politique, 1944–1958." Master's thesis, École normale supérieure de Yaoundé, 1989.
Eyinga, Abel. *L'UPC: Une révolution manquée?* Paris: Éditions Chaka, 1991.
Falola, Toyin. *Nationalism and African Intellectuals*. Rochester: University of Rochester Press, 2001.
Fanon, Frantz. *Toward the African Revolution: Political Essays*. Translated by Haakon Chevalier. 1967. Reprint, New York: Grove Press, 1988.
———. *The Wretched of the Earth*. Translated by Richard Philcox. 1963. Reprinted with a forward by Homi K. Bhabha. New York: Grove Press, 2004.
Feierman, Steven. "Africa in History: The End of Universal Narratives." In *After Colonialism: Imperial Histories and Postcolonial Displacements*, edited by Gyan Prakash, 40–65. Princeton: Princeton University Press, 1995.
———. "Colonizers, Scholars, and the Creation of Invisible Histories." In *Beyond the Cultural Turn: New Directions in the Study of Society and Culture*, edited by Victoria B. Bonnell and Lynn Hunt, 182–215. Berkeley: University of California Press, 1999.
———. *Peasant Intellectuals: Anthropology and History in Tanzania*. Madison: University of Wisconsin Press, 1990.
Feitlowitz, Marguerite. *A Lexicon of Terror: Argentina and the Legacies of Torture*. New York: Oxford University Press, 1998.
Feldman-Savelsberg, Pamela. "Cooking Inside: Kinship and Gender in Bangangté Idioms of Marriage and Procreation." *American Ethnologist* 22, no. 3 (1995): 483–501.

———. *Plundered Kitchens, Empty Wombs: Threatened Reproduction and Identity in the Cameroon Grassfields*. Ann Arbor: University of Michigan Press, 1999.

Feldman-Savelsberg, Pamela, Flavien T. Ndonko, and Song Yang. "Remembering 'The Troubles': Reproductive Insecurity and the Management of Memory in Cameroon." *Africa* 75, no. 1 (2005): 10–29.

Ferme, Mariane C. *The Underneath of Things: Violence, History, and the Everyday in Sierra Leone*. Berkeley: University of California Press, 2001.

Ferme, Mariane C., and Danny Hoffman. "Hunter Militias and the International Human Rights Discourse in Sierra Leone and Beyond." *Africa Today* 50, no. 4 (2004): 73–95.

Fields, Karen. *Revival and Rebellion in Colonial Central Africa*. Princeton: Princeton University Press, 1985.

Foccart, Jacques, and Philippe Gaillard. *Foccart parle: Entretiens avec Philippe Gaillard*. 2 vols. Paris: Fayard/Jeune Afrique, 1995–97.

Fohom, Fabien. "L'usine à café dans le Moungo de 1935 à 1986: Une analyse historique." Master's thesis, University of Yaoundé I, 1988, 16–17.

Fotso, François. *La lutte nationaliste au Cameroun, 1940–1971*. Paris: L'Harmattan, 2010.

Fowler, Ian, and David Zeitlyn, eds. *African Crossroads: Intersections between History and Anthropology in Cameroon*, vol. 2 of *Cameroon Studies*, edited by Shirley Ardener, E. M. Chilver, and Ian Fowler. Providence, RI: Berghahn Books, 1996.

Frankel, Philip. "The Politics of Passes: Control and Change in South Africa." *Journal of Modern African Studies* 17, no. 2 (1979): 199–217.

Gaines, Kevin K. *American Africans in Ghana: Black Expatriates and the Civil Rights Era*. Chapel Hill: University of North Carolina Press, 2006.

Gardinier, David. *Cameroon: United Nations Challenge to French Policy*. Oxford: Oxford University Press, 1963.

Gausset, Quentin. "Historical Account or Discourse on Identity? A Reexamination of Fulbe Hegemony and Autochthonous Submission in Banyo." *History in Africa* 25 (1998): 93–110.

Geiger, Susan. *TANU Women: Gender and Culture in the Making of Tanganyikan Nationalism, 1955–1965*. Portsmouth, NH: Heinemann, 1997.

Gerges, Fawaz. *The Superpowers and the Middle East: Regional and International Politics, 1955–1967*. Boulder: Westview, 1994.

Geschiere, Peter. "Chiefs and Colonial Rule in Cameroon: Inventing Chieftaincy, French and British Style." *Africa: Journal of the International African Institute* 63, no. 2 (1993): 151–75.

———. "Hegemonic Regimes and Popular Protest: Bayart, Gramsci, and the State in Cameroon." In *State and Local Community in Africa*, edited by Wim van Binsbergen and G. Hesseling. Brussels: Centre d'études et de documentation africaine, 1986.

———. *The Modernity of Witchcraft: Politics and the Occult in Postcolonial Africa*. Charlottesville: University Press of Virginia, 1997.

———. *The Perils of Belonging: Autochthony, Citizenship, and Exclusion in Africa and Europe.* Chicago: University of Chicago Press, 2009.

Greene, Sandra E. *Sacred Sites and the Colonial Encounter: A History of Meaning and Memory in Ghana.* Bloomington: Indiana University Press, 2002.

Guiffo, Jean-Philippe. *Nkongsamba: Mon beau village.* Yaoundé: Éditions de l'Essoah, 2001.

Guyer, Jane. *Family and Farm in Southern Cameroon.* Boston: Boston University Press, 1984.

———. "Traditions of Invention in Equatorial Africa," *African Studies Review* 39, no. 3 (1996): 1–28.

Hahn, Peter. *The United States, Great Britain, and Egypt, 1945–1956: Strategy and Diplomacy in the Early Cold War.* Chapel Hill: University of North Carolina Press, 1991.

Hansen, Emmanuel. "Frantz Fanon: Portrait of a Revolutionary Intellectual." *Transition* 46 (1974): 25–36.

Heinzen, Barbara J. "The United Fruit Company in the 1950s: Trusteeships of the Cameroons." *African Economic History* 12 (1983): 141–56.

Homberger, Lorenz, ed. *Cameroon: Art and Kings.* Zurich: Museum Rietberg, 2008.

Hurault, Jean. *La structure sociale des Bamiléké.* Paris: Mouton, 1962.

Hussain, Nasser. *The Jurisprudence of Emergency: Colonialism and the Rule of Law.* Ann Arbor: University of Michigan Press, 2003.

Joseph, Richard, ed. *Gaullist Africa: Cameroon under Ahmadu Ahidjo.* 1978. Reprint, Enugu, Nigeria: Fourth Dimension, 2002.

———. "National Politics in Postwar Cameroon: The Difficult Birth of the UPC." *Journal of African Studies* 2, no. 2 (1975): 201–29.

———. *Radical Nationalism in Cameroun: Social Origins of the UPC Rebellion.* Oxford: Oxford University Press, 1977.

———. "Settlers, Strikers, and *Sans-Travail*: The Douala Riots of September 1945." *Journal of African History* 15, no. 4 (1974): 669–87.

Kago Lele, Jacques. *Tribalisme et exclusions au Cameroun: Le cas de Bamiléké.* Yaoundé: Éditions du Crac, 1995.

Kamé, Bouopda Pierre. *De la rébellion dans le Bamiléké.* Paris: L'Harmattan, 2008.

Kaptue, Léon. *Travail et main-d'oeuvre au Cameroun sous régime français, 1916–1952.* Paris: L'Harmattan, 1986.

Karabell, Zachary. *Architects of Intervention: The United States, the Third World, and the Cold War, 1946–1962.* Baton Rouge: Louisiana State University Press, 1999.

Kiegaing, Joseph Kamdem. "Les sites sacrés chez les Baham (Ouest-Cameroun)." Master's thesis, University of Yaoundé I, 2002.

Kirk-Greene, A. H. M. "The Thin White Line: The Size of the British Colonial Service in Africa." *African Affairs* 79, no. 314 (1990): 25–44.

Klose, Fabian. *Menschenrechte im Schatten kolonialer Gewalt: Die Dekolonisierungskriege in Kenia und Algerien, 1945–1962.* Munich: R. Oldenbourg Verlag, 2009.

———. "'Source of Embarrassment': Human Rights, State of Emergency, and the Wars of Decolonization." In *Human Rights in the Twentieth Century*, edited by Stefan-Ludwig Hoffman, 237–57. Cambridge: Cambridge University Press, 2011.

Kolko, Gabriel. *Confronting the Third World: United States Foreign Policy, 1945–1980*. New York: Pantheon, 1988.

Kriger, Norma J. *Guerilla Veterans in Post-War Zimbabwe: Symbolic and Violent Politics, 1980–1987*. Cambridge: Cambridge University Press, 2003.

———. *Zimbabwe's Guerilla War: Peasant Voices*. Cambridge: Cambridge University Press, 1992.

Kwayeb, Enock Katté. *Les institutions de droit public du pays Bamiléké, Cameroun: Évolution et régime actuel*. Paris: Libraire générale de droit et de jurisprudence, 1960.

Laburthe-Tolra, Philippe. *Initiations et sociétés secrètes au Cameroun. Essai sur la religion Béti*. Paris, Karthala, 1985.

———. *Les seigneurs de la forêt: Essai sur le passé historique, l'organisation sociale et les normes éthiques des anciens Béti du Cameroun*. Paris: Publications de la Sorbonne, 1981.

Lam, André. "Plaidoyer pour une culture en déclin: Le cas du peuple Ngoh/Ngoe dans la région des monts Manengouba, Koupé et Nlonako, Cameroun." Unpublished manuscript, Yaoundé, 1995.

Lan, David. *Guns and Rain: Guerrillas and Spirit Mediums in Zimbabwe*. Berkeley: University of California Press, 1985.

Larson, Pier. "'Capacities and Modes of Thinking': Intellectual Engagements and Subaltern Hegemony in the Early History of Malagasy Christianity." *American Historical Review* 102, no. 4 (1997): 969–1002.

Laurent, Marc-Olivier. "Pouvoir et société dans le pays Bamiléké: La chefferie traditionnelle face au changement social dans la région de Banka-Bafang. Doctoral thesis, University of Paris V, René Descartes, 1981.

Lazare, Lucien. *L'abbé Glasberg*. Paris: Cerf, 1990.

Le Bayon, Goustan. *Les prêtres du Sacré-Coeur et la naissance de l'église au Cameroun*. Paris: Procure des missions SCJ, 1986.

Lecoq, Raymond. *Les Bamilékés*. Paris, 1953.

Lee, Christopher J. "At the Rendezvous of Decolonization: The Final Communiqué of the Asian-African Conference, Bandung, Indonesia, 18–24 April 1955." *Interventions* 11, no. 1 (2009): 81–93.

———, ed. *Making a World after Empire: The Bandung Moment and Its Political Afterlives*. Athens: Ohio University Press, 2010.

Le Vine, Victor. *The Cameroon Federal Republic*. Ithaca: Cornell University Press, 1971.

———. *The Cameroons from Mandate to Independence*. Berkeley: University of California Press, 1964.

Lindsay, Lisa A. *Working with Gender: Wage Labor and Social Change in Southwestern Nigeria*. Portsmouth, NH: Heinemann, 2003.

Lohrmann, Ullrich. *Voices from Tanganyika: Great Britain, the United Nations and the Decolonization of a Trust Territory, 1946–1961*. Berlin: Lit Verlag, 2007.

Lombard, Jacques. *Autorités traditionnelles et pouvoirs européens en Afrique noire: Le déclin d'une aristocratie sous le régime colonial.* Paris: Librairie Armand Colin, 1967.

Lugard, Frederick D. *The Dual Mandate in British Tropical Africa.* Edinburgh: W. Blackwood and Sons, 1922.

Makonnen, Ras T. *Pan-Africanism from Within.* Edited by Kenneth King. Nairobi: Oxford University Press, 1973.

Malaquais, Dominique. *Architecture, pouvoir et dissidence au Cameroun.* Paris: Karthala, 2002.

———. "Building in the Name of God: Architecture, Resistance and the Christian Faith in the Bamileke Highlands of Western Cameroon." *African Studies Review* 42, no. 1 (1999): 48–78.

Malkki, Liisa H. *Purity and Exile: Violence, Memory, and National Cosmology among Hutu Refugees in Tanzania.* Chicago: University of Chicago Press, 1995.

Mamdani, Mahmood. *Citizen and Subject: Contemporary Africa and the Legacy of Late Colonialism.* Princeton: Princeton University Press, 1996.

Manghezi, Nadia. *The Maputo Connection: The ANC in the World of Frelimo.* Johannesburg: Jacana, 2009.

Mann, Gregory, and Baz Lecocq. "Between Empire, *Umma*, and the Muslim Third World: The French Union and African Pilgrims to Mecca, 1946–1958." *Comparative Studies of South Asia, Africa and the Middle East* 27, no. 2 (2007): 361–83.

Manning, Patrick. *Francophone Sub-Saharan Africa, 1880–1995.* 2nd ed. Cambridge: Cambridge University Press, 1998.

Martin, Phyllis. *Leisure and Society in Colonial Brazzaville.* Cambridge: Cambridge University Press, 1995.

Mbatchou, Stella. "Contribution à la connaissance de l'histoire de l'armée de libération nationale kamerunaise (ALNK), 1959–1971." Master's thesis, University of Yaoundé I, 2003.

Mbembe, Achille. "Domaines de la nuit et autorité onirique dans les maquis du Sud-Cameroun, 1955–1958." *Journal of African History* 31, no. 1 (1991): 89–121.

———. "Écrire l'Afrique à partir d'une faille." *Politique africaine* no. 51 (1993): 69–97.

———. Introduction to *Le problème national kamerunais*, by Ruben Um Nyobé. Paris: L'Harmattan, 1984.

———. *La naissance du maquis dans le Sud-Cameroun (1920–1960)* Paris: Karthala, 1996.

———. "Pouvoir des morts, language des vivants: Les errances de la mémoire nationaliste au Cameroun." In Bayart, Mbembe, and Toulabor, *Politique par le bas*, 183–229.

———. *Sortir de la grande nuit: Essai sur l'Afrique décolonisée.* Paris: La Découverte, 2010.

Mbock, Pierre. "La vie d'une église au Cameroun." Translated by P. Galland. *Récits missionnaires illustrés*, no. 31. Paris: Société des missions évangéliques, 1931.

Mepin, Daniel. "Je mourrai face au soleil: Epopée tragique en 15 tableaux." Unpublished manuscript, 1983.
Michel, Marc. "Une décolonisation confisquée? Perspectives sur la décolonisation du Cameroun sous tutelle de la France, 1955–1960." *Revue française d'histoire d'outre-mer* 86 (1999): 229–57.
———. "Les plantations allemandes du Mont Cameroun, 1885–1914." *Revue française d'histoire d'outre-mer* 57 (1970): 183–213.
Miller, Daniel, ed. *Worlds Apart: Modernity through the Prism of the Local*. London: Routledge, 1995.
Momo, Grégoire. *Informations sur le terrorisme en pays Bamiléké: Ses causes et effets*, unpublished manuscript, 1986.
Morgenthau, Ruth Schachter. *Political Parties in French-Speaking West Africa*. Oxford: Clarendon Press, 1967.
Mortimer, Edward. *France and the Africans, 1944–1960: A Political History*. London: Faber and Faber, 1969.
Moyn, Samuel. *The Last Utopia: Human Rights in History*. Cambridge, MA: Harvard University Press, 2010.
Mukong, Albert. *Prisoner without a Crime: Disciplining Dissent in Ahidjo's Cameroon*. 2nd ed. Paris: NUBIA Press, 1989.
Ndefo Noubissi, Thomas A. "La police et la question nationale au Cameroun sous administration française (1945–1960)." Master's thesis, École normale supérieure de Yaoundé, 2001.
Neocleous, Mark. "The Problem with Normality: Taking Exception to 'Permanent Emergency.'" *Alternatives: Global, Local, Political* 31, no. 2 (2006): 191–213.
Ngapeth-Biyong, Marie-Irène. *Cameroun: Combats pour l'indépendance*. Paris: L'Harmattan, 2010.
Nguiffo, Louis Tissot [Wafeu Kam Tameu]. *Contributions à l'histoire du royaume Baham*. Yaoundé: Éditions Traditions Vivantes, 1995.
Nhongo-Simbanegavi, Josephine. *For Better or for Worse? Women and ZANLA in Zimbabwe's Liberation Struggle*. Harare: Weaver Press, 2000.
Nkuissi, B. "Nkongsamba: Les années obscures de la fondation de 1898 à 1923: Essai de monographie urbaine." DES memoir, University of Lille, 1967.
Nicod, Henri. "Une école de catéchistes au Cameroun." *Récits missionnaires illustrés*, no. 28. Paris: Société des missions évangéliques, 1930.
Njiké-Bergeret, Claude. *Ma passion africaine*. Paris: Éditions Jean-Claude Lattès, 1997.
Nken, Simon. *L'UPC: De la solidarité idéologique à la division stratégique, 1948–1962*. Paris: Éditions Anibwé, 2010.
———. "Louis-Paul Aujoulat: Figure controversée de la vie politique camerounaise, 1935–1956." *Canadian Journal of African Studies* 44, no. 2 (2010): 256–82.
Nkwi, Paul, and Jean-Paul Warnier. *Elements for a History of the Western Grassfields*. Yaoundé: Department of Sociology, University of Yaoundé, 1982.
Nugent, Paul. *Africa since Independence*. New York: Palgrave MacMillan, 2004.

Olaniyan, Tejumola. "Cartooning Nigerian Anticolonial Nationalism." In *Images and Empires: Visuality in Colonial and Postcolonial Africa*, edited by Paul Landau and Deborah D. Kaspin. Berkeley: University of California Press, 2002.

Onana, Janvier. *Le sacre des indigènes évolués: Essai sur la professionalisation politique (l'exemple du Cameroun)*. Paris: Dianoïa, 2004.

Oppen, Achim von. "The Village as Territory: Enclosing Locality in Northwest Zambia, 1950s to 1990s." *Journal of African History* 47, no. 1 (2006): 57–75.

Ouden, Jan H. B. den. "In Search of Personal Mobility: Changing Interpersonal Relations in Two Bamiléké Chiefdoms." *Africa: Journal of the International African Institute* 57, no. 1 (1987): 3–27.

Panzer, Michael G. "The Pedagogy of Revolution: Youth, Generational Conflict, and Education in Mozambican Nationalism and the State, 1962–1970." *Journal of Southern African Studies* 35, no. 4 (2009): 803–20.

Pasha, Mustapha K., and John D. Rusk. "Africa Rights Monitor: South Africa: Terror and Resistance." *Africa Today* 33, no. 1 (1986): 69–79.

Perrois, Louis, and Jean-Paul Notué. *Rois et sculpteurs de l'ouest Cameroun: La panthère et la mygale*. Paris: Karthala, 1997.

Peterson, Derek. *Creative Writing: Translation, Bookkeeping, and the Work of Imagination in Colonial Kenya*. Portsmouth, NH: Heinemann, 2004.

Plummer, Brenda Gayle. *Rising Wind: Black Americans and U.S. Foreign Affairs, 1935–1960*. Chapel Hill: University of North Carolina Press, 1996.

Pommerolle, Marie-Émmanuelle. "A quoi servent les droits de l'homme? Action collective et changement politique au Cameroun et au Kenya." Doctoral thesis, University of Montesquieu-Bordeaux IV, 2005.

Pouamoun, Youba. "Félix-Roland Moumié, 1925–1960: L'intinéraire d'un nationaliste intransigeant." Master's thesis, École normale supérieure de Yaoundé, 1997.

Pouhe Pouhe, Dieudonné. "Les liaisons extérieures de l'UPC, 1948–1960." Master's thesis, University of Yaoundé, 1999.

Power, Joey. *Political Culture and Nationalism in Malawi: Building Kwacha*. Rochester: University of Rochester Press, 2010.

Prashad, Vijay. *The Darker Nations: A People's History of the Third World*. New York: New Press, 2007.

Rancière, Jacques. "Who Is the Subject of the Rights of Man?" *South Atlantic Quarterly* 103, nos. 2–3 (2004): 297–310.

Ranger, Terence. "Nationalist Historiography, Patriotic History, and the History of Nation: The Struggle over the Past in Zimbabwe." *Journal of Southern African Studies* 30, no. 2 (2004): 215–34.

Robertson, Roland. "Glocalization: Time-Space and Homogeneity-Heterogeneity." In *Global Modernities*, edited by Mike Featherstone, Scott Lash, and Roland Robertson, 25–44. Thousand Oaks, CA: Sage, 1995.

Rohde, E. "Inconsistent Temporalities in a Nation-State." In Miller, *Worlds Apart: Modernity through the Prism of the Local*, edited by Daniel Miller, 23–42. London: Routledge, 1995.

———. "'Projet Rive Gauche du Noun': The Miscarriage of Bamiléké Settlement Projects under French Administration in Bamoun (Cameroon)." In *Land Law and Land Ownership in Africa: Case Studies from Colonial and Contemporary Cameroon and Tanzania*, edited by Robert Debusmann and Stefan Arnold, 203–21. Bayreuth: Bayreuth African Studies, 1996.

Rowlands, Michael. "Inconsistent Temporalities in a Nation-Space." In *Worlds Apart: Modernity through the Prism of the Local*, edited by Daniel Miller, 23-42. New York: Routledge, 1995.

Rowlands, Michael, and Jean-Pierre Warnier. "Magical Iron Technology in the Cameroon Grassfields." In *African Material Culture*, edited by Mary Jo Arnoldi, Christraud Geary, and Kris Hardin, 51–72. Bloomington: Indiana University Press, 1996.

Roy, Srila. "The Grey Zone: The 'Ordinary' Violence of Extraordinary Times." *Journal of the Royal Anthropological Institute* 14, no. 2 (2008): 316–33.

Sanneh, Lamin. *Translating the Message: The Missionary Impact on Culture*. Maryknoll, NY: Orbis, 1989.

Sarraut, Albert. *Mise en valeur des colonies françaises*. Paris: Payot, 1923.

Savage, Michael. "The Imposition of Pass Laws on the African Population in South Africa, 1916–1984." *African Affairs* 85, no. 339 (1986): 181–205.

Schatzberg, Michael G. "The Metaphors of Father and Family." In *The Political Economy of Cameroon*, edited by Schatzberg and I. William Zartmann. New York: Praeger, 1986.

———. *Political Legitimacy in Middle Africa: Father, Family, Food*. Bloomington: Indiana University Press, 2001.

———. "Seeing the Invisible, Hearing Silence, Thinking the Unthinkable: The Advantages of Ethnographic Immersion." Paper presented at the 104th annual meeting of the American Political Science Association, Boston, 28–31 August 2008.

Schler, Lynn. "Ambiguous Spaces: The Struggle over African Identities and Urban Communities in Colonial Douala, 1914–45." *Journal of African History* 44, no. 1 (2003): 51–72.

———. *The Strangers of New Bell: Immigration, Public Space and Community in Colonial Douala, Cameroon, 1914–1960*. Pretoria: University of South Africa Press, 2008.

Schmidt, Elizabeth. "Anticolonial Nationalism in French West Africa: What Made Guniea Unique?" *African Studies Review* 52, no. 2 (2009): 1–34.

———. *Cold War and Decolonization in Guinea, 1946–1958*. Athens: Ohio University Press, 2007.

———. "Cold War in Guinea: The Rassemblement Démocratique Africain and the Struggle over Communism, 1950–1958." *Journal of African History* 48, no. 1 (2007): 95–121.

———. *Foreign Intervention in Africa: From the Cold War to the War on Terror*. Cambridge: Cambridge University Press, 2013.

———. *Mobilizing the Masses: Gender, Ethnicity, and Class in the Nationalist Movement in Guinea, 1939–1958*. Portsmouth, NH: Heinemann, 2005.

———. "Top Down or Bottom Up? Nationalist Mobilization Reconsidered, with Special Reference to Guinea (French West Africa)." *American Historical Review* 110, no. 4 (2005): 975–1014.
Scott, James C. *Domination and the Arts of Resistance: Hidden Transcripts*. New Haven: Yale University Press, 1990.
Sharp, Thomas. "Binaries of Nations: The 'Anglophone Problem' in Cameroon and the Presentation of Historical Narratives on the Internet." Master's thesis, University of Manchester, 2008.
Sidaway, James D., and David Simon. "Geopolitical Transition and State Formation: The Changing Political Geographies of Angola, Mozambique, and Namibia." *Journal of Southern African Studies* 19, no. 1 (1993): 6–28.
Sighoko Fossi, Abraham. *Discours politiques*. Paris: L'Harmattan, 2007.
———. *Papa s'appelait Fossi Jacob: Itinéraire d'un martyr de l'indépendance du Cameroun*. Paris: L'Harmattan, 2011.
Sindjoun, Luc. *L'état ailleurs: Entre noyau dur et case vide*. Paris: Economica, 2002.
———. "L'opposition au Cameroun, un nouveau jeu politique parlementaire." Introduction to *Comment peut-on être opposant au Cameroun? Politique parlementaire et politique autoritaire*, edited by Sindjoun. Dakar: Codesria, 2004.
Sindjoun-Pokam. *La philosophie politique trahie: Le monofascisme*. Paris: Atelier Silex, 1987.
Slageren, Jaap van. *Les origines de l'église évangélique du Cameroun: Missions européennes et christianisme autochtone*. Leiden: Brill, 1972.
Sonke, Alex Bertrand. "La chefferie Baham de 1945 à 1960: Ses rapports avec la puissance coloniale et les nationalistes." Master's thesis, University of Yaoundé I, 1993–95.
Spear, Thomas. "Neo-Traditionalism and the Limits of Invention in British Colonial Africa." *Journal of African History* 44, no. 1 (2003): 3–27.
Stephens, Michelle Ann. *Black Empire: The Masculine Global Imaginary of Caribbean Intellectuals in the United States, 1914–1962*. Durham: Duke University Press, 2005.
Stoler, Ann Laura. *Along the Archival Grain: Epistemic Anxieties and Colonial Common Sense*. Princeton: Princeton University Press, 2009.
Straker, Jay. *Youth, Nationalism, and the Guinean Revolution*. Bloomington: Indiana University Press, 2009.
Suttner, Raymond. "Cultures of the African National Congress of South Africa: Imprint of Exile Experiences." *Journal of Contemporary African Studies* 21, no. 2 (2003): 303–20.
Takougang, Joseph. "The *Union des Populations du Cameroun* and Its Southern Cameroons Connection." *Revue française d'histoire d'outre-mer* 83, no. 319 (1996): 8–24.
Takougang, Joseph, and Milton Krieger. *African State and Society in the 1990s: Cameroon's Political Crossroads*. Boulder: Westview, 1998.
Tatsimo, Jean. *La place du "la'kem" chez les Bamiléké: Le cas des Nda'a*. Douala: Éditions Saint-François, 1993.

Tavernier, Olivier. "Histoire de la chefferie Baham de ses origines à nos jours." Master's thesis, University of Aix-en-Provence, 1995.

Tchaptchet, Jean-Martin. *Quand les jeunes Africains créaient l'histoire*. Vol. 2 of *Récit autobiographique*. Paris: L'Harmattan, 2006.

Tchegho, Jean-Marie. *L'enracinement culturel en Afrique: Une nécessité pour un développement durable: Le cas des Bamiléké du Cameroun*. Yaoundé: Éditions CLÉ, 2001.

Terretta, Meredith. "Cameroonian Nationalists Go Global: From Forest *Maquis* to a Pan-African Accra," *Journal of African History* 51, no. 2 (2010): 189–212.

———. "Chiefs, Traitors, and Representatives: The Construction of a Political Repertoire in Independence-Era Cameroun," *International Journal of African Historical Studies* 43, no. 2 (2010): 227–58.

———. "'God of Peace, God of Independence': Village Nationalism in the *Maquis* of Cameroun, 1957–1971." *Journal of African History* 46, no. 1 (2005): 75–101.

———. "A Miscarriage of Revolution: Cameroonian Women and Nationalism." *Stichproben: Wiener Zeitschrift für kritische Afrikastudien* 12 (2007): 61–90.

———. *Petitioning for Our Rights, Fighting for Our Nation: The History of the Democratic Union of Cameroonian Women, 1949–1960*. Buea: Langaa, RPCIG, 2013.

———. "'We Had Been Fooled into Thinking That the UN Watches over the Entire World': Human Rights, UN Trust Territories, and Africa's Decolonization." *Human Rights Quarterly* 34, no. 2 (2012): 329–60.

Thomas, Lynn M. *Politics of the Womb: Women, Reproduction, and the State in Kenya*. Berkeley: University of California Press, 2003.

Todorov, Tzvetan. *Mikhaïl Bakhtine: Le principe dialogique: Suivi de Écrits du cercle de Bakhtine*. Paris: Seuil, 1981.

Um Nyobé, Ruben. *Écrits sous maquis*. Edited by J.-A. Mbembe. Paris: L'Harmattan, 1989.

———. *Le problème national kamerunais*. Edited by J.-A. Mbembe. Paris: L'Harmattan, 1984.

Vansina, Jan. *Oral Tradition as History*. Madison: University of Wisconsin Press, 1985.

———. *Paths in the Rainforests: Toward a History of Political Tradition in Equatorial Africa*. Madison: University of Wisconsin Press, 1990.

Vaughan, Olufemi. *Nigerian Chiefs: Traditional Power in Modern Politics, 1890s–1990s*. Rochester: University of Rochester Press, 2006.

Verschave, François-Xavier. *La Françafrique: Le plus long scandale de la république*. Paris: Stock, 1998.

Von Eschen, Penny. *Race against Empire: Black Americans and Anticolonialism, 1937–1957*. Ithaca: Cornell University Press, 1997.

Wagoue, Esaïe. "L'impact du mouvement nationliste UPC à Banyangam: 1955–1965." Master's thesis, École normale supérieure de Yaoundé, 1993.

Walraven, Klaas van. "Decolonization by Referendum: The Anomaly of Niger and the Fall of Sawaba, 1958–1959." *Journal of African History* 50, no. 2 (2009): 269–92.

———. "From Tamanrasset: The Struggle of Sawaba and the Algerian Connection, 1957–1966." *Journal of North African Studies* 10, nos. 3–4 (2005): 507–27.

Warnier, Jean-Pierre. "Chefs de l'ouest et formation de l'état au Cameroun." In *Le retour des rois: Les autorités traditionnelles et l'état en Afrique contemporaine*, edited by Claude-Hélène Perrot and François-Xavier Fauvelle-Aymar, 315–22. Paris: Karthala, 1999.

———. *Échanges, développement, et hiérarchies dans le Bamenda pré-colonial (Cameroun)*. Stuttgart: Franz Steiner Verlag, 1985.

———. *L'esprit d'entreprise au Cameroun*. Paris: Karthala, 1993.

———. "The Grassfields of Cameroon: Ancient Center or Recent Periphery?" *Africa Today* 58, no. 3 (2012): 58–72.

———. "Histoire du peuplement et genèse des paysages dans l'ouest camerounais." *Journal of African History* 25, no. 4 (1984): 395–410.

———. "Métallurgie ancienne, identifications et domestication de la violence au Cameroun." In *Matière à politique: Le pouvoir, les corps et les choses*, edited by Jean-François Bayart and Warnier, 181–93. Paris: Karthala, 2004.

———. "Rebellion, Defection and the Position of Male Cadets: A Neglected Category." In Fowler and Zeitlyn, *African Crossroads*, 115–24.

———. "Slave-Trading without Slave-Raiding in Cameroon." In "Slavery and Slave Dealing in Cameroon in the Nineteenth and Twentieth Centuries," edited by Bongfen Chem-Langhéé, special issue, *Paideuma* 41 (1995): 251–72.

White, Luise. *The Assassination of Herbert Chitepo: Texts and Politics in Zimbabwe*. Bloomington: Indianan University Press, 2003.

———. *Speaking with Vampires: Rumor and History in Colonial Africa*. Berkeley: University of California Press, 2000.

———. "Telling More: Lies, Secrets, and History." *History and Theory: Studies in the Philosophy of History* 39, no. 4 (2000): 11–2

Wilder, Gary. "Colonial Ethnology and Political Rationality in French West Africa." In *Ordering Africa: Anthropology, European Imperialism, and the Politics of Knowledge*, edited by Helen Tilley and Robert J. Gordon, 336–75. Manchester: Manchester University Press, 2007.

———. "Untimely Vision: Aimé Césaire, Decolonization, Utopia." *Public Culture* 21, no. 1 (2009): 101–40.

Williams, Patrick. "'Faire peau neuve': Césaire, Fanon, Memmi, Sartre and Senghor." In *Francophone Postcolonial Studies: A Critical Introduction*, edited by Charles Forsdick and David Murphy, 181–90. New York: Oxford University Press, 2003.

Williams, William Appleman. *The Tragedy of American Diplomacy: United States Foreign Policy 1945–1980*. 1959. New York: Norton, 1988.

Yates, Anne, and Lewis Chester. *The Troublemaker: Michael Scott and His Lonely Struggle against Injustice*. London: Aurum Press, 2006.

Yearwood, Peter J. "'In a Casual Way with a Blue Pencil': British Policy and the Partition of Kamerun, 1914–1919." *Canadian Journal of African Studies* 27, no. 2 (1993): 218–44.

Young, Crawford. "Nation, Ethnicity, and Citizenship: Dilemmas of Democracy and Civil Order in Africa." In *Making Nations, Creating Strangers: States* and Citizenship in Africa, edited by Sara Dorman, Daniel Hammett, and Paul Nugent, 241–64. Boston: Brill, 2007.

Zeitlyn, David. "Spiders in and out of Court, or, 'The Long Legs of the Law: Styles of Spider Divination in their Sociological Contexts." *Africa: Journal of the International African Institute* 63, no. 2 (1993): 219-40.

Zintgraff, Eugen. *Nord-Kamerun: Schilderung der im Auftrage des Auswärtigen Amtes zur Erschliessung des nördlichen Hinterlandes von Kamerun während der Jahre 1886–1892 unternommenen Reisen.* Berlin: Gebrüder Paetel, 1895.

Zubok, Vladislav, and Constantine Pleshakov. *Inside the Kremlin's Cold War: From Stalin to Khrushchev.* Cambridge, MA: Harvard University Press, 1996.

Index

Accra, Ghana, 11, 16, 199–200, 215; patterns of political liberation and, 259
Africa Bureau (AB), 261
African Affairs Centre, 17, 198–99, 200, 202, 317n125. *See also* Nkrumah, Kwame
Afro-Asian Solidarity Organization (AASO), 199–200; directors' committee of, 316n98
Ahidjo, Ahmadou, 4, 177, 201, 224, 242; bilateral agreements with France and, 262, 336n41; emergency decrees and, 219, 228, 248; "ethic of unity" and, 252; government of, 19, 21–22, 248; one-party state and, 221, 235–37, 249; plenary powers laws of 1959 and, 218–19
Ahmed, Aït, 257
Albert, R. P., 56
Algeria, 17, 257, 322n15, 327n92
All-African Peoples' Conference (AAPC), 17, 200; UPC and, 201–2; use of violence and, 202–3
American Committee on Africa, 103
Anderson, Benedict, 102
Anderson, Carol, 11
Appiah, Kwame, 105
Arab, Adam, 76, 122
Argenti, Nicolas, 79–80, 309n144
Armée de libération nationale (ALN), 180
Armée de libération nationale du Kamerun (ALNK), 18, 25, 180, 186, 189, 192, 197; African Affairs Centre and, 205; arms procurement and, 209–11, 319n171; attack targets of, 211–12; Catholic clergy and, 213–14; centralization of command and, 204; civilian coercion and, 215; civilian populations and, 208–9, 319n152; composition of, 205; difficulties of, 216; dissenting bands and, 207; European settlers and, 211–12; funding sources and, 208–9; maquis and, 207; revolutionary tax and, 208; spiritual realm and, 214; training and, 206; tribunals of, 214–15; women and, 214; zones and, 207–8
Assemblée législative du Cameroun (ALCAM). *See* Legislative Assembly of Cameroon

Assemblée territoriale du Cameroun (ATCAM). *See* Territorial Assembly of Cameroon
Associated Union of Functionaries and Agents of Cameroon, 88
Aujoulat, Louis-Paul, 123, 302n25

Baham, 11, 134–35, 141; commemoration of May 1955, 148; dispute with Bandjoun and, 48–49; district chiefs and, 306n87; feuveuck and, 40–41; German colonization and, 33–34; Mantem assassinations and, 193–95; myths of origin and, 32, 305n76; political songs and, 165; postcolonial state and, 254; reconciliation ceremony of 1967 in, 241, 250; tax boycott in, 145, 160; tseu dance and, 168–69; violence in, 180
Baham II, 54; emigration and, 54; Noun River resettlement project and, 53–54, 278n99
Baldwin, Roger, 171, 203, 236, 261. *See also* International League of the Rights of Man (ILRM)
Bali, 33, 277n76
Bamiléké, Le, 144
Bamileke Region, 1, 9, 10, 11, 12, 118; casualties in, 179; chieftaincy of origin and, 12–13, 15, 78–79, 79–81, 84, 171–72; chieftaincy politics and, 92, 120, 155–56, 172, 297n115; definition of, 12, 263n1, 273n13; depositions of mfo and notables and, 156, 163, 173–74; discipline and, 191–92; French administration and, 54, 279n100; identity, independence and, 171–72; identity, Mungo Region and, 61, 78–79; identity, narratives of the past and, 13–14, 172–73, 270n55; independence and, 223; iron technology and, 190–91; land distribution in, 125, 299nn140–41; legitimacy of political representatives and, 138; loi-cadre and, 138; military forces in, 222–23, 323n19, 323n20; militia violence in, 187; nationalism and, 307n109; nationalists *versus* "collaborationists" in, 162; oaths of loyalty and, 188–89; protected

359

Bamileke Region (*cont.*)
resettlements and, 225–27; "rebellion" in, 328n96, 328n102; "red zones" of, 217; *Song of the Night Fight Fighters* and, 164–65; spirituality in, 13, 188–92; time of troubles in, 1; titled immigrants and, 91; UPC, chiefs (mfo) and, 118, 120–23; uprisings in (May, 1955), 126–28, 299n142, 299n150; vaccination and, 189; violence and, 16, 173; war of independence and, 188; women and, 188; young chiefs (mfo) and, 15, 120, 121; ZOPAC and, 328n96. *See also* Kemajou, "Prince" Daniel

bananas, 89, 124, 287n126; Bamileke immigrants and, 72; as cash crop, 61, 72, 211; European planters and, 65

Bandjoun, 58, 59; French administration of, 58–59; German rule and, 34; "native command" and, 53; tax collection in, 53. *See also* Kamga, Joseph

Bandung Conference, 198–99, 256, 258, 315n95

Bardet, Max, 178

Basso, Jean Albert, 237

Battalion of the Tirailleurs of Cameroon (BTC), 221, 223, 323n19

Bayangam, 118

Bayart, Jean-François, 109, 116, 293n56, 297n109, 302n22, 328n103

Bebey-Eyidi, Marcel, 153, 203, 234, 236–37

Bénard, Jean-Pierre, 226

Biya, Paul, 19, 322n13

Blanchet, André, 178

Bloc démocratique camerounais (BDC), 9–10, 124

Boisson, Pierre, 63

Bondja, Isaac, 71, 83–84, 283n58

Bonnecarrère, Paul, 70–71

book overview, 14–19; documentation and, 3, 272n81; Grassfields political culture and, 30; post-independence and, 3–4; sources and methodology of, 22, 272n79; structure of, 11; subaltern actors and, 3; vernacularization and, 20–21

Bopda, 58

Borne, René, 121–22

Botsio, Kojo, 201

Boumendjel, Ahmed, 201

Brévié, Jules, 50–51

Briand, Max, 178, 179, 223–24

Brigade mixte mobile de recherche et d'exploitation opérationnelles (BMM), 219, 233–35

British Cameroon, xvi, 6, 150; casualty numbers and, 178; elections and, 9; German colony and, 9; sources and, 26; UPC and, 6–7, 25, 120, 148, 197, 199

Brockway, Fenner, 261

Burbank, Jane, 316n105, 333n10

Bureau of African Affairs, 11, 17, 76, 198, 200, 202

Bussu, 32

cacao, 65, 69, 71; coffee and, 75, 122; economic crisis of 1929–34 and, 71

Cameroon, definition of, 264n2

Catholic Church: Ahidjo government and, 242–43; BDC and, 124; black-dog oathing ceremony and, 252; Federal Republic of Cameroon and, 242–43; French social Catholicism and, 299n135; missions, attacks on, 177, 211, 213; primary school in Baham, 142

Centre des archives d'outre-mer (CAOM), Aix-en-Provence, 24

Centre d'histoire et d'études des troupes d'outre-mer (CHETOM), Fréjus, 24

Centre historique des archives nationales (CHAN), Paris, 24

chieftaincies, 31, 269n46; administration of justice and, 41–42; Ahidjo regime and, 252; balance of power and, 35–36; colonial administration and, 136; concept of "nation" and, 138; conventional scholarship and, 31; decolonization, lepue and, 174; districts and, 37, 42–43, 273n2; ethnic identity and, 32, 269n48; family conflicts and, 43–44; the fo and, 35–36; foreign rule and, 163; French "civilization" of, 48; French legal codes and, 56–57; French perceptions of chiefs as feudal lords and, 46–48; French policies and, 57–60; German colonization and, 33–34; justice, administration of, 41–42; kamveu and, 35, 36, 38; ké and, 38–39; kungang and, 36, 38–39; lineages and, 43–44; magic, mysticism and, 38–39, 50; malefic associations and, 50; mfonte and, 37; mwala and, 35, 37; myths of origin and, 30–32, 65, 270n55, 271n63, 282n26; nationalist politics of the late 1950s and, 159–62; "native command" and, 50–51; notables and, 36–37, 38, 80, 82–83; politics and, 135; regional differences and, 137; ruse, magic, oratory skills, wealth and, 32–33; sacred sites (chuep'si) and, 40–41, 44–46; social mobility and, 57–58, 60, 80–82; spatial delineation of, 37; spiritual technologies and, 38–39, 66, 282n30; tax collection and, 52, 53, 77, 101, 146, 278n90; tortoises and, 42, 188, 189, 275n46; truth telling, oathing and, 42–43, 44, 312n50; United Nations and, 55–56; wabo and, 37. *See also* Grassfields region

Chindji-Kouleu, Ferdinand, 178–79, 310n9

Christianity, 57–58, 84, 270n53, 279n111, 280n113. *See also* Catholic Church

coffee, 124, 125; Bamileke immigration and,

360 ← Index

61; Bamileke Region and, 75, 284n75; cacao and, 75, 122; French policies and, 75; French regulation of, 75
Cognet, M., 144–45
Cold War, 25; African nationalists and, 104, 255; Nkrumah and, 198; postcolonial viewpoint and, 259–62
Communism, 88. *See also under* Union des populations du Cameroun (UPC)
Company of Plantations, 63, 89
Conakry, Guinea, 5, 17; ALNK training in, 206; congress at, 99; UPC headquarters in, 202. *See also* Guinea
Confédération générale du travail (CGT), 88
Conference of Brazzaville, 88
Conference of Independent African States, 200
Connelly, Matthew, 7
Cooper, Frederick, 3, 132, 255, 293n59, 316n105
Coordination des indépendants camerounais (INDECAM), 98

Daoudou, Sadou, 224, 328n98
Débarge, Josette, 49
Delangue, Charles, 182
Delauney, Maurice, 128–29
Deltombe, Thomas, 289n12
Demgang, Abraham, 195
Djileu, Joseph, 196–97
Djimi, Victor, 149–50
Djoko, Ignace Néguin, 119, 232–33; on Kamden Ninyim's execution, 240
Djonteu, Jean, 193, 204, 207, 216, 246
Djoumessi, Mathias, 121, 154, 298n123; RDA and, 288n8
Djuatio, Etienne, 154
Domergue, Manuel, 289n12
Domtchueng, Benoît, 142, 194, 302n28
Donnat, Gaston, 88
Dopo, Lydia, 6
Douala, 64, 65; ALNK and, 213; lineages and, 137; politicization of, 92; railroad and, 14, 68; UPC and, 97, 107–8; white settler population and, 14. *See also* Mungo Region
Duara, Prasenjit, 309n145
Dzukam, Chrétien, 108, 149, 151, 303n47; arrest of, 185; background of, 148

Eboué, Félix, 55, 279n103
Eckel, Jan, 255
Eckert, Andreas, 80
École nationale de la France d'outre-mer, 144
economic crisis of 1929–34; Bamileke planters and, 72; cacao and, 71–72
effort camerounais, l', 242
Ekwabi, Jean, 150, 151
Elong, Alfred, 117

Emachoua, Chrestine, 6, 147
Emock, Thomas, 204–5
étoile, L', 111
Évolution sociale camerounaise (ESOCAM), 9, 98, 123, 290n18, 298n129
Ewane, Essoa, 70

Fankem, Emmanuel (Fermeté), 18
Fanon, Frantz, 17, 202, 259
Federal Republic of Cameroon, 230; amnesty issue and, 323n17; BMM and, 230, 233–35; Catholic Church and, 242–43; civic guard and, 224–25; concealment, coded language in, 231–32; conventional scholarship and, 322n14; culture of violence in, 232, 243; expulsions and, 228; grid strategy and, 227, 325n56; Law on Repression of Subversion of 1962, 240, 330n129; Mungo and Bamileke Regions and, 229; Ndongmo affair and, 242–43, 331n145; neighborhood and block chiefs and, 227–28; police checkpoints in, 230; police raids in, 229–30; population movements and, 228–29; press in, 237–38, 329n115; protected resettlements and, 225–26; public executions and, 237–38; reorganization of, 1962, 221; as single-party state, 221; state of emergency and, 228, 326n62; use of informants and, 229; use of spies and, 230–31. *See also* Ahidjo, Ahmadou
Feierman, Steven, 11
Feze, Marcel Ngandjong, 39, 121, 135, 140, 144, 148; exile of, 156
FIDES, 303n41
Fines, Ernest, 88, 90
Foccart, Jacques, 24, 226, 324n44
Fochivé, Jean, 224
Fongang, Henri, 145, 303n36
Fosso, François, 116
Fotso, François, 312n42
Fouman-Nti, André, 240
Foyer de progrès de la jeunesse de Bayangam (FOPROJEUBA), 118, 119
French Cameroon, 50, 99–100; administrators' perceptions and, 47–48, 51; administrative objectives in, 52; anti-UPC strategies and, 123–26; Bamileke Region and, 46–60; "customary law" and, 72–73; deposition of mfo and, 49–50; "direct administration" and, 46–47; Ecole des cadres and, 107–8, 292n50; ethnic prejudices, racism and, 86, 126, 136–37; évolués and, 101, 290n17; functions of chiefs in, 47–48; greater France concept and, 10–11, 99–100, 116, 131–32, 133, 138; loi-cadre legislation and, 100, 137; May, 1955 and, 126–29; Mbo-Bamileke tensions and, 125; mise en valeur

French Cameroon (cont.)
policies in the 1920s and, 69–70, 73–74, 283n50; mystical secret associations and, 50–51; Noun River resettlement project and, 53–54; parochialism and, 136; perception of Bamileke chiefs and, 120–21; politicospiritual realm in, 59–60; spiritual landscape in, 54–55; taxation in, 52; traditional authorities and, 58–59; troops in Cameroon and, 178; as United Nations trust territory, 55–56; zoning and classification in Mungo Region, 68–69. *See also specific names, topics, and regions*
French Communist Party (PCF): RDA and, 288–89n10
French Togo, 289n16
Front de libération nationale (FLN), 8, 17, 257; ALN and, 180; GPRA files and, 26; strategy and, 261; UPC and, 257–58

Gabiapsi, André, 23
General Conference on International Labor Organization, 89
Gentil, Robert, 52–53, 278n96; settlement projects and, 54–55
German Cameroon, 33–34, 46. *See also* Kamerun
Ghana: African Affairs Centre and, 17, 198–99, 200, 202, 317n125; independence of, 198; Nkrumah regime and, 254
Glasberg, Alexandre, 261, 336n37
glocal, 4, 266n14
Grassfields region, 1, 8–9; Christian missionization in, 279n111; colonial rule and, 45–46; conventional scholarship and, 31; definition of, 263n1; eighteenth century and, 31–32; ethnic identity and, 32; external challenges and, 34; French policies and, 57–60; German rule and, 33–34, 46; nationalism and, 307n109; political and spiritual practices and, 12, 37, 66, 270n52, 273n4, 274n21, 275n29, 286n100; sacred sites (chuep'si) and, 13, 40, 44–46, 143, 276n62; Si and, 13, 40, 44; slavery and, 31, 273n7. *See also* chieftaincies
Guemdjo, Kamdem, 45
Guinea, 132, 308n125. *See also* Conakry, Guinea
gung: definitions of, 2, 13, 29–30, 156, 166, 314n77; la'a and, 29; as nation of people, 91; nationalism and, 34. *See also* lepue; mfingung; mpouogung

Hadj, Messali, 257
human rights, 3, 5–8, 11, 89, 102, 104, 129–31, 260, 261, 264n6. *See also* Baldwin, Roger; International League of the Rights of Man (ILRM); Universal Declaration of Human Rights (UDHR)

independence, war of. *See* lepue; war of independence
Institut d'études politiques de Paris, 144
International League of the Rights of Man (ILRM), 7, 103, 139, 171, 261. *See also* Baldwin, Roger
Islam, 9, 32, 58, 98
Issoufou, Mama, 76

Jeunesse camerounaise française (JEUCAFRA), 139
Jeunesse démocratique camerounaise (JDC), 7, 25, 97, 183; Joint Proclamation and, 114–15
Joseph, Richard, 62, 283n146, 284n68

Kamdem II, 48, 168
Kamdem III, 33–34
Kamdjom, Lucas, 118–19
Kamé, Pierre Bouopda, 183
Kamé, Samuel, 141, 157, 165, 182, 224, 226, 252, 306n84, 324n32; background of, 144; Ninyim and, 241, 324n32
Kamen, Sakéo, 117
Kamerun, 2, 8, 46, 166–67, 182, 309n129
Kamga, Joseph, 53, 58, 59, 122, 129, 149, 181, 224–25
Kamgaing, Mathias Kom, 118, 189
Kamgue, Barthélemy, 247–48, 332n160
Kamguia, Michel Debonnaire, 142
Kamguie, Joseph, 241
Kamogne, Souop, 234
Kamtche, Sadrack, 72–73
Kamto, Bernard, 194, 232
Kamwa, Max, 49, 54, 134, 277n75; as administrative auxiliary, 142; funeral celebrations for, 168; succession of, 302n26
Kanga, Victor, 151
Kemajou, Paul, 156
Kemajou, "Prince" Daniel, 121, 124–25, 154, 155, 173–74
Kenya, 312n50, 322n15
keu-keu, 253
Kiegaing, Joseph, 22
Kingué, Abel, 4–5, 103, 111, 117, 127; Bamileke region and, 123–24
Klose, Fabian, 321n4
Kouam, Maurice, 194
Kouam, Romain, 229, 326n74
Kwakep, Jean-Marie, 243
Kwamm, Maurice, 160, 306n98, 307n101; on Teguia and, 160

labor: Bamileke immigration and, 61, 74–76, 86–87; bananas and, 61; coffee and, 61, 75; mandate system and, 65; Mungo Region and, 63; organizations and, 88–89; shortage of, 68; strikes and, 89–90; unions in French territories and, 88; use of force and, 63, 85, 281n13

Lagarde, Marcel, 154
Lakondji, Nkiké, 77–78
Lamberton, Jean, 222
Law on Repression of Subversion of 1962, 219–20, 240
Layou, Philippe, 230
League of Nations, 9, 46; annual reports to, 73; Permanent Mandates Commission (PMC) of, 67–68
Lee, Christopher J., 256, 333n14
Legislative Assembly of Cameroon (ALCAM), 134, 218, 300n1; Ahidjo regime and, 236–37; Group of Eight and, 159–61; 1956 election and, 138, 152–54; Statute of Cameroon and, 170–71
Lele, Jacques Kago, 178–79
lepue, 13, 33, 84; chieftaincy politics and, 34–35, 37, 132; decolonization of chieftaincy and, 174; definitions of, 16, 29–30, 33, 155, 162–63; as "independence from European rule," 138; nationalism and, 34–35; nationalist fighters and, 188; taxation and, 146–47; violence and, 155. *See also* gung
Levy, Primo, 216
Little Red Book (Mao), 8
loi-cadre, 100; chieftaincies and, 137; elections and, 9, 10; French Togo and, 289n16. *See also under* France
Loum, 77–78, 245–47
Lumière, 111
Lumumba, Patrice, 17, 201

Magwa, Emilienne, 165
Maka, 137–38
Makonnen, Ras T., 17
Malaquais, Dominique, 298n123, 312n42
Mao Tse-tung: ALNK and, 180, 206–7, 216; *Little Red Book*, 8
Mapondjou, Elisabeth, 150
maquis, 7–8, 129; Bamileke chieftaincies and, 180–83; casualties and, 179–80; Catholic clergy and, 213–14; cha-cha-cha and, 191–92, 314n71; civil self-defense units and, 218, 225, 243; connection with UPC armies and, 185–87; court of, 214–15; culture of violence and, 244–46; establishment of camps and, 184–85, 186; Grassfields spiritual technology and, 188–92; international and local warfare methods and, 207–10; Kamdem Ninyim supporters and, 157–58; Mungo Region and, 192–98; needs of, 17; organization of, 18–19, 208, 311n26; popular support and, 235; pueh kè and, 189, 313n63; punishments and, 191–92, 314n72; singing and, 187–88; Um Nyobé, French administrators and, 151–52; women and, 321n194. *See also under* Union des populations du Cameroun (UPC)

Marchand, Théodore, 67–68, 69, 74, 87
Markoff murder, 244–45, 247
Massing, Joseph, 151, 304n58
Massudom, Fotso, 58
Matene, Agathé, 5–6
Mayounga, Pauline, 230–31, 232
Mballa, Joseph, 129
Mbembe, Achille, 20, 117, 137, 296n99
Mbida, André-Marie, 171, 177, 236, 323n17
Mboutchak, Cathérine (aka Fidelité), 214
Mboya, Tom, 17, 201
Mekou, Samuel, 105–6, 205
Menon, Lakshmi, 113–14
Messali Hadj, Ahmed Ben, 103
Messmer, Pierre, 152, 171
mfingung: definitions of, 13, 16, 34, 125, 158, 168; punishment of, 173, 177, 182; revenge and, 170; UPC and, 192–93; violence and, 187
Ministry of the Armed Forces, 224
mise en valeur, 69–71, 283n50
Momo, Grégoire, 187
Momo, Paul, 165, 181, 184, 186, 198, 204, 239, 312n44
monde, Le, 178
Mopen, Noé, 239, 241
Mougnol, Ismanou, 231
Moulendé, Martin, 71, 283n58, 320n187
Moumbain, Esaïe, 106
Moumié, Félix, 17, 24, 99, 102, 110–11, 148, 152, 205, 262; AAPC and, 201; assassination of, 238, 262, 329n120; background of, 105–6; in Sudan and Cairo, 199; support of Kamden Ninyim and, 159
Moumié, Marthe, 108
Mourning after the Deposition of Fo Ninyim (song), 166–68
Mouthemy, André, 123, 124
Mouvement d'action national (MACNA), 98
Movement for Colonial Freedom, 261
mpouogung, 13, 16, 182
Mugabe, Robert, 19
Mungo Region, 67; autochthonous land ownership in, 72, 85–86, 283n63; Bamileke competitiveness and, 82, 286n104; Bamileke immigrants, territorial elections and, 90–91; Bamileke organizational skills and, 87–88; Bamileke political representation in, 79, 286n94; Bamileke work ethic in, 72, 283n61; cooperatives and trade unions in, 89; Council of Notables and, 76–77, 285n85; economic crisis of 1929–34, 71–72; economic stratification in, 71; as economic unit, 76; ethnicization of land ownership in, 73–75; European plantations in, 62, 67, 68, 74–75, 283n57; French Communist organizers and, 14; French land administration and, 65, 74–75, 281n20, 284n73; French zoning

Index ⟿ 363

Mungo Region (cont.)
and classification systems, 68–69;
geography, agriculture of, 64–65, 66, 68, 71, 81, 286n102; immigrants as "strangers" in, 72–73, 76, 284n65, 284n67, 284n68, 285n80; indigenous population of, 62, 280n4; labor shortage in, 68, 72, 283n41, 283n60; land ownership and, 14, 62–63; land-use contracts and, 65–66; lawlessness in, 247; maquis and, 192–98; Mbo population and, 70; mfingung and, 192–93; militia violence in, 187; mystical technologies in, 192, 274n14; "native command" in, 76–77, 285n87, 285n91; Ngol-Manjo case and, 125; political influence of, 93; post–World War II in, 85; settlement and transformation of, 61–62, 66, 282n30; spiritual realm in, 66; UPC and, 101–2; UPC nationalism and, 14–15; UPC regional section, formation of, 119–20; UPC violence and, 195–98; violence and, 16; wartime importance of, 192
mystical technologies, 274n14

Nana, Jean, 49–50
Nana, Thadée Nya, 245
Naoussi, Anatole, 145
National (Sacred) Union, 152
National (Sacred) Union (MACNA), 140–41, 302n22
National Archives, The, 25
National Archives, Yaoundé, 24
nationalism. See Union des populations du Cameroun (UPC)
Ndami, Chantal, 24
Nde, Joseph, 145
Ndengoue, Daniel, 195, 196, 197
Ndenmen, Agar, 83–84
Ndongmo, Albert, 24, 243, 246, 247, 250
Ndoumou, J. B., 238
Nganjong, 52–53
Ngapeth, Job, 106
Ngapeth-Biyong, Marie-Irène, 106
Ngayewang, Pierre, 153
Ngolle, Jean-Jacques, 251
Nguembou, David, 196
Nguemdjo, Kamdem, 167–68
Nguengang, 196
Nguiffo, Laurent, 194
Niabang Company, 70, 84
Nintcheu, Raphaël, 213
Ninyim, Pierre Kamdem, 15, 119, 121, 134–35, 140, 141, 155, 302n29; background of, 141–44; birth of, 305n68; deposition of, 135–36; Domtchueng and, 302n28; execution of, 168, 238, 240; impact of the deposition of, 170, 184, 192, 233; imprisonment of, 156, 159, 304n50; 1956 election and, 152–53; Priso and, 150; trial of, 135, 180–81, 239;

UPC local committees and, 147–49; as UPC spokesman, 144. See also Teguia, Jean-Marie
Ninyim, Pierre Kamdem versus Teguia, Jean-Marie, 135–36, 157–58, 192, 239; in Baham, 181; popular narratives and, 163–69, 302n26; reconciliation and, 241; rules of succession and, 160–61; songs and, 163–65, 187–88; traditional governance, colonial systems and, 161–63; violence and, 193, 195
Njine, Michel, 154
Njoya, Arouna, 76
Nkette, "Feinboy," 78
Nkongsamba, 11, 14, 76; Bamileke immigrants in, 87; Council of Notables and, 76–77, 91; importance of, 67, 101; nationalization of politics in, 101; public executions in, 247; as research base, 22; UPC and, 117–20; as UPC center for Bamileke Region, 149; as urban center, 69
Nkongsamba Diocese archives, 24
Nkrumah, Kwame, 16–17, 200–201; government of, 11, 254, 257; Pan-Africanism and, 10, 17, 198–99. See also African Affairs Centre; Bureau of African Affairs
Nkwemo, 321n199
Nkwemo, Michel (aka Nkrumah), 214
Noubi, Jeanette, 226
Nouvelle, 214, 321n198
Nyah, Magdalene, 246
Nzezip, Ouambo (Mwabo), 52

Okala, Charles, 153
Olaniyan, Tejumola, 296n96
Olympio, Sylvanus, 103, 112
Omog, Gertrude, 205
Onana, Janvier, 269n39, 294n77
One Kamerun, 26
Orabona, François, 122
Organization of African Unity, 259
Ouandié, Ernest, 18, 24, 103–4, 150, 205, 245–46; in Accra, 202; background of, 106; execution of, 215, 247
Ouandié, Marthe, 108
overview of book. See book overview
Owona, Professor, 24

Padmore, George, 17
Pan-Africanism, 4, 103–4, 291n29; Brazzaville group and, 258; Casablanca group and, 258; federation and, 258; historians and, 255; Spirit of Bandung and, 198. See also Accra, Ghana; Nkrumah, Kwame; specific organizations
Pandong, Fritz, 70–71, 90
Pastoral Company, 70
Penda, Marthe, 10
Penlap, Edouard, 184

petitioning, 114, 267n24, 269n39, 294n77, 295n83; Tanganyika and, 295n84. *See also under* Union des populations du Cameroun (UPC); *under* United Nations
pidgin English, 1, 8, 62, 196, 232
Pierre, Simo, 182, 184, 198, 204
Pleven, René, 97
Pogo, Jean-Bernard (Defotimsa), 22, 253
Pokam Kamwa, Joseph Bu, 170
Potasse d'Alsace, 84
Poukam I, 48–49
Poukam II, 253
Pouth, Théodore Makanda, 239
Power, Joey, 11
Prashad, Vijay, 256
Pré, Roland, 98, 106, 109, 112, 115, 129, 130, 171, 293n58
presse du Cameroun, La, 159, 160, 239
Priso, Paul Soppo, 139, 141, 150–51, 152, 159, 236, 301n17, 301n20; amnesty issue and, 323n17; loi-cadre and, 140
Progressive Party of Kamerun, 159
Puloch, Louis Le, 219

Ranger, Terence, 19–20
Rassemblement démocratique africain (RDA), 99, 288n8, 288–9n10; PCF and, 288–89n10
Rassemblement du peuple camerounais (RPC), 123–24
Raynaud, Mr., 77
reconciliation ceremonies, 251–52; feuveuck and, 241, 250–51; oath of the black dog and, 251–52; state administrators and, 251
Republic of Congo, 333n7
Ritz, M., 143
Roberts, Holden, 17
Ryckmans, Pierre, 113

Saah, Jean, 76, 79
Sanaga-Maritime Region, xv, 237; assassination of Um Nyobé and Basso in, 237, 330n139; CNO in, 158, 183, 185, 312n37; ESOCAM and, 123; French troops in, 223; maquis in, 7, 198; mission schools in, 280n113; nationalists in, 133; political parties in, 98, 117; spiritual technologies and, 188; UPC and, 235; violence in, 177; voting in, 152, 304n64; ZOPAC and, 328n96
Sango, Kamdeu, 106
Sanneh, Lamin, 270n53
Schatzberg, Michael, 30, 272n79, 273n3, 275n32
Schler, Lynn, 285n87, 285n91
Schmidt, Elizabeth, 11, 262, 288–89n10
Scott, James C., 292n46
Scott, Michael, 112–13
Sende, Jean-Paul, 330n144

Sepo, Jean, 185
Service des études de la documentation (SEDOC), 219
Simo, Pierre, 238
Singap, Martin, 150, 183–84, 185, 204, 215, 217, 312n39; death of, 207
Sinistre de la défense nationale du Kamerun (SDNK), 150, 184, 313n57
slavery, 31
Sokodjou, Jean-Phillipe Rameau, 121, 135, 140, 156
Song of the Night Fighters, The, 164–65
Soulier, Maurice, 88
Souopdounze, 160–61
South Africa, 326n65
Statute of Cameroon, 170–71
Stoler, Ann Laura, 296n98
suicide, 169–70
Syndicat de défense des interêts bananiers africains (SDIBA), 89
Syndicat de défense des interêts bananiers du Cameroun (SDIBC), 89
Syndicat des planteurs autochthones de la région du Mungo (SPARM), 90

Tagatsing, Sop Alexandre, 204; pregnant women and, 204, 317n22
Tagny, Mathieu, 106, 151, 158, 161–62; Bamileke region and, 123–24; on Kamden Ninyim, 161–62; UPC use of violence and, 158–59
Takala, Celestin, 288n8
Takounga, Henri, 196
Tamo, Henri (aka Leconstant Pengoye), 205
Tatsitsa, Jacob, 289n112
Tavernier, Olivier, 277n75
taxation: Baham and, 145; Bamougoum and, 145; Iepue and, 146–47; UPC Kumba Resolution and, 144–45
Tchaffi, Passa, 5–6
Tchatchueng, Marcus, 118
Tchembiap, Abraham, 128
Tchi-Tchi, André, 193, 194, 314n79
Tchomte, André, 126
Tchoua, Isaac, 71, 283n58
Tchoupe, François, 231–32
Tchoupo, David, 127
Tchoutouo, Nono, 49
Tchuenkam, Emil, 79
Tchuenkam, Ta Gue, 165–66, 308n128
Tchuente, Elias, 108, 118
Teguia, Jean-Marie, 135, 157, 165, 181; Baham communities and, 193; death of, 253; flight to Bamun and, 181; legitimacy of the rule of, 157, 160; mother's name and, 165, 308n121. *See also* Kamé, Samuel; *under* Ninyim, Pierre Kamden *versus* Teguia, Jean-Marie
Teitgen, Pierre-Henri, 109, 115–16

Index ⟿ 365

Territorial Assembly of Cameroon (ATCAM), 139, 150, 300n11; Djoumessi and, 154; Ekwabi and, 150; Independent Peasants coalition in, 150; loi-cadre and, 182; Priso and, 139–40. *See also* Kemajou, "Prince" Daniel
"time of troubles," 1, 23, 179, 193, 227, 250, 251, 254
Torre, Xavier, 201
tortoises, 42, 188, 189, 275n46
Touré, Ahmed Sékou, 17, 199
Tubman, William, 242
Tuekam, Didier, 156

Um Nyobé, Ruben, 3, 7, 97, 99, 100, 102–3, 106, 151–52, 257, 330n139; background of, 105; Bamileke region and, 123–24; death of, 198, 237; France and, 289n12; New Year's memorandum of 1956 and, 139; petitioning and, 112; RDA and, 288n8; UDEFEC and, 114; United Nations and, 110, 113; on UPC leadership, 118
Union camerounaise (UC), 220. *See also* Union nationale camerounaise (UNC)
Union démocratique des femmes camerounaises (UDEFEC), 5, 25, 97, 103, 149; Joint Proclamation and, 114–15; petitioning and, 113–14
Union des populations du Cameroun (UPC), 2, 4–8; AAPC and, 201–2; additional studies on, 25–26; anticolonialism and, 104; autonomous social sites and, 107, 292n46; boycott of 1956 election and, 151–53; Cold War and, 260; Comité national d'organisation (CNO) and, 158, 183, 312n37; Communism and, 88, 99–100, 105, 117, 260, 261, 293n57, 336n38; directors' bureau, 197, 315n92; discursive genre and, 109, 116–17, 295n124, 296n98; disintegration and weakening of, 18–19; exile and, 199–200, 334n17; as extrametropolitan movement, 2–3, 8–9, 11, 104, 264n4; FLN and, 257; Fongang's death and, 146; formation of, 97; French colonial administrators and, 106–7, 109–10, 115, 123–26, 292n45; geographical focal points and, 11; greater France concept and, 289n10; history of, 20, 98–99; indigenous languages and, 10; internal documents of, 25; international organizations and, 103–4; international politics of decolonization and human rights and, 6–7, 103–4; iron technology and, 190–91; Joint Proclamation and, 114–15, 130; Kumba Resolution and, 144; leadership of, 10, 105–7; leadership training and, 107–8, 110; leadership travel and, 4–8, 107, 109; letter k and, 8; local and global politics and, 4–8, 102, 272n76; loi-cadre and, 100; Mantem assassinations and, 193–95; maquis and, 7, 18, 129, 157, 185, 268n31, 311n26; May, 1955 violence and, 126–29, 131; mfingung and, 13, 34, 125, 145, 158, 168, 170, 173, 177; multidimensional perspective and, 2; Mungo Region and, 90, 117–20; new chronology and, 21; NGOs and, 260–61; objectives of, 2, 98; oral voices and, 111; organization of, 104–5; Pan-Africanism and, 17, 198, 256–57; petitioning and, 5–6, 112–13, 294n77, 295n83; political repertoire of, 116–17, 267n115; politics of chieftaincy and, 121–23; politics of land distribution and, 125–26; print culture of, 110–11; Program in Six Points and, 139, 145–46; proscriptions of, 7, 10, 15, 98, 125, 126–30, 133; RDA and, 99; regional sections of, 119; Second Front of, 333n7; spiritual technologies and, 188; spread of anticolonial sentiment and, 97; supporters of, 101, 115, 289n17, 290n18, 290n19; Third World politics and, 8; "traitors (mfingung) to the nation" and, 156, 158; traitors and patriots and, 15–16; transregional assistance and, 257, 259; underground militias of, 7; United Nations and, 102–3, 110, 112–13, 130–32; vernacularization and, 20, 114, 267n26, 307n113; violence and, 17–18, 193–95; war veterans and, 115–16
Union des syndicats confédérés du Cameroun (USCC), 88, 89, 90, 97; Joint Proclamation and, 114–15
Union nationale camerounaise (UNC), 21, 150, 221; military presence and, 222–23; tribalism and, 252. *See also* Union camerounaise (UC)
United Nations, 297n115; consistency and, 130–32; Fourth Committee of, 112–13, 130; petitioning of, 5–6, 112–13, 163–64, 303n42; resolution on Cameroon independence, 1959, 203, 236; trust territories of, 1, 4, 9; Trusteeship Council and, 22, 113
United Republic of Cameroon. *See* Federal Republic of Cameroon
United States of Africa, 10, 17, 198, 256, 259
United States of America, 203, 260
Universal Declaration of Human Rights (UDHR), 4, 103. *See also* Baldwin, Roger
upécistes. *See* Union des populations du Cameroun (UPC)

Vallée, Michel, 127, 128
Van Vollenhoven, Joost, 46, 47
Versailles, Treaty of, 47
violence, 65; AAPC and, 202–3; Baham and, 135; depositions of mfo and notables and, 158, 170; independence era and, 179; lepue and, 155; May 1955 and, 126–29; mfingung and, 187; as mode of life, 216; 1956

elections and, 182; political ideology and, 247–48; state security forces and, 220–21; tax boycott and, 145–46; UPC and, 185
Viossat, A., 86
voix du Cameroun, La, 111

Wambo, Isaac, 193, 195
Wanko, Samuel, 182–83, 323n17; amnesty issue and, 323n17; assassination of, 221–22
war of independence: casualties in, 178–79; dialects and, 187; Grassfields spiritual technology and, 188–92; local nature of, 185–86; songs and, 187–88. *See also specific regions, people, and events*
Warnier, Jean-Pierre, 31, 79–80, 84, 286n104
Wedji, Pierre, 246

White, Luise, 327n79
Wilder, Gary, 255
Williams, Patrick, 255–56
women, 188, 214, 308n125; maquis and, 321n194; petitioning and, 113–14

yam trees, 43, 276n51
Yankam, Jean, 319n153
Yitna, François, 245
Youmbi, Abel, 246

Zimbabwe, 19
Zoa, Monsignor, 242
Zone de Pacification (ZOPAC), 312n37, 328n96
Zuguiebou, 32

www.ingramcontent.com/pod-product-compliance
Lightning Source LLC
Chambersburg PA
CBHW031230290426
44109CB00012B/233